Psychology Revivals

Human Suggestibility

Originally published in 1991, *Human Suggestibility* is a collection of papers that reflected recent advances in the study of human suggestibility at the time, including not only the topic of hypnosis, but also suggestibility as related to advertising, mental illness, forensics, political persuasion and the biological aspects of the suggestion process.

The book is divided into four parts: 'The Nature of Suggestibility', which provides a history of thinking on this subject. 'Theoretical Perspectives', intended to give a cross-section of theoretical viewpoints on suggestibility in its various forms. 'Researching Suggestibility' that deals with quantitative studies relating to suggestion and suggestibility. Finally, 'Applications and Implications' looks at ways in which our knowledge of suggestibility has found useful application in such diverse fields as education, advertising, forensics and clinical psychology.

Today it can be read in its historical context.

Human Suggestibility

Advances in Theory, Research, and Application

Edited by
John F. Schumaker

Routledge
Taylor & Francis Group
LONDON AND NEW YORK

First published in 1991
by Routledge

This edition first published in 2026 by Routledge
4 Park Square, Milton Park, Abingdon, Oxon, OX14 4RN

and by Routledge
605 Third Avenue, New York, NY 10158

Routledge is an imprint of the Taylor & Francis Group, an informa business

A Library of Congress record exists under ISBN: 9780415902151

ISBN: 978-1-041-27180-2 (hbk)
ISBN: 978-1-003-75311-7 (ebk)
ISBN: 978-1-041-27181-9 (pbk)

Book DOI 10.4324/9781003753117

HUMAN SUGGESTIBILITY

ADVANCES IN THEORY, RESEARCH, AND APPLICATION

EDITED BY JOHN F. SCHUMAKER

ROUTLEDGE NEW YORK AND LONDON

Published in 1991 by

Routledge
An imprint of Routledge, Chapman and Hall, Inc.
29 West 35 Street
New York, NY 10001

Published in Great Britain by

Routledge
11 New Fetter Lane
London EC4P 4EE

Printed in the United States of America

Library of Congress Cataloging in Publication Data
Human suggestibility : advances in theory, research, and application /
edited by John F. Schumaker.
p. cm.
Includes bibliographical references and index.
ISBN 0-415-90215-0 (cloth)
1. Mental suggestion. I. Schumaker, John F., 1949–
BF1156.S8H85 1991
153.8'5—dc20 90-42174

TABLE OF CONTENTS

Part Three: Researching Suggestibility

Part Four: Applications and Implications

INTRODUCTION

Suggestibility is one of the most intriguing dimensions of human behavior. We stand out very conspicuously from the rest of creation in relation to this puzzling aspect of ourselves. Boris Sidis (1898) saw suggestibility as such a dominant feature of our species that he referred to the human being as "a suggestible animal." Suggestibility does, in fact, seem to be an ever-present determining factor in our behavior. One might even question whether anything we do, feel, or believe is *not* somehow linked to suggestion. Our struggle to understand the process of suggestion may actually be hampered by its ubiquitous and all-pervasive nature. In a sense, we might have too many clues.

There is little question that a grasp of the workings of the suggestibility process can offer us new and improved ways in which to understand ourselves. Beyond that, I believe that many applications would derive from such an understanding, ones that could benefit us in countless ways. In fact, one principal goal of this volume is to examine some of the ways that we can make beneficial application of our knowledge of suggestion. As will be seen, progress has already been made in this regard.

The advances we have made are even more remarkable because suggestibility is a sorely neglected area of study. Part of the problem could be that, historically, suggestibility has been viewed as a less than noble human characteristic. Someone who is "suggestible" might be seen as gullible, naive, easily influenced, lacking in self-determination, unable to think critically, and so forth. Very few people would feel flattered if told that they were very suggestible. Even the scientific study of suggestibility has been viewed with a certain degree of skepticism. For example, there is but a single entry for suggestibility in *Psychological Abstracts*. Also, as Wagstaff (chapter 6, this volume) observes, the term does not even appear in the popular *Oxford Companion to the Mind*. These are poor reflections on the merits attached to this potentially fruitful area of study.

While this particular field might not enjoy the same status as more fashionable scientific pursuits, there has been some fine suggestibility research to emerge over the years. Some recent work is highly innovative and we have seen the emergence of new ways to conceptualize and study suggestibility. Still, it is true that the amount of research is still quite small in relation to the great importance of this topic of study. In light of this, it is not surprising that a great deal remains to be learned about all facets of the suggestibility process. It is also to be expected that the relatively small number of scholars working on this subject are not in full agreement about the general or specific workings of suggestibility. For this reason, I will approach this introduction in terms of the *questions* that are currently being asked and debated.

This introduction will not constitute an in-depth analysis of all aspects of suggestibility. More detailed accounts of specific topics will be found in the various chapters of this book. However, this introduction will offer a brief overview of some commonly discussed issues related to suggestibility. It should also serve to acquaint the uninitiated reader with some of the terminology and concepts used by people involved in the investigation of suggestibility.

How does one define suggestion and suggestibility?

The terms "suggestion" and "suggestibility" are global ones that have carried many meanings over the past century. Some of these meanings have differed considerably from one another. Despite their common usage in psychology, psychiatry, and medicine, these terms have not exported themselves well to other disciplines. One would think, for example, that anthropologists would find these concepts very useful, yet these terms are rarely if ever used in that field. Sociologists and social psychologists study phenomena such as mass hysteria, riots, fanatical cult consumption, political brainwashing, usually without mention of any of the above terms or concepts.

There are those, including myself, who would support efforts to find an entirely new method for describing the class of behavior which is the subject of this volume. This would provide a fresh conceptual start and relieve us from the weight of all the contradictory and partially overlapping meanings inherent in our present nosology. If this was ever done, I hope it would be in conjunction with investigators from a wide range of disciplines. Suggestibility, or whatever one eventually calls it, has a rightful place in many diverse fields. Our chances to advance our understanding of this remarkable aspect of our behavior would be increased greatly if common conceptual and terminological ground could be found. Since such a development is not on the immediate horizon, we might turn to a discussion of current terminology.

The actual word "suggestion" can be employed in a number of ways, a fact that contributes to the confusion surrounding the term. The word "suggestion" can refer to a *specific* influential message or communication (e.g., "the Holy Ghost is entering your body," or "the room is becoming very hot"). Or, the same word can refer to parts of the larger process, or the entire process by which suggestions are delivered and received. For instance, someone could refer to the "suggestion situation," or the "suggestion procedure," or the "suggestion process." A person might also state that an act or belief was the result of suggestion, which implies the *method* as well as the message.

The term "suggestibility" is often used to indicate a person's *propensity* to respond to suggested communications. This can be seen in Sidis's (1898) definition of suggestibility as "a peculiar state of mind which is favorable to suggestion" (p. 15). Similarly, Eysenck, Arnold, and Meili (1975) refer to suggestibility as "the individual *degree* of susceptibility to influence by suggestion and hypnosis" (p. 1076). In this regard, a great deal of energy has gone into a determination of the individual differences that exist in terms of *degree* of suggestibility. This is the case with suggestibility both within, and outside of, the context of hypnosis. It should be added, however, that some thinkers reject the notion of suggestibility as either a "state" or an enduring "trait," claiming instead that the suggestion process is largely a function of situational demand characteristics, social role-playing, and so forth (e.g., Sarbin & Coe, 1972; Spanos, 1982). In fact, they might be more inclined to study *situational* differences, rather than individual differences (see chapter 6 in this book by Graham Wagstaff).

Eysenck, Arnold, and Meili (1975) define the suggestion process as "a process of communication during which one or more persons cause one or more individuals to change (without critical response) their judgments, opinions, attitudes, etc., or patterns of behaviour" (p. 1077). McDougall's (1908) definition, while one of the earliest, is still widely accepted. He writes that suggestion is a method of communication "resulting in the acceptance with conviction of the communicated proposition in the absence of logically adequate grounds for its acceptance" (p. 100). Such a definition implies that suggestive behavior is not entirely rational in nature, a point of view that is shared by some, but not all. The same is true of the defintion by Eysenck, Arnold, and Meili since it describes a wide variety of changes that a person makes *without critical response*.

Gheorghiu (1989b) shares the sentiment that suggestion must be understood, at least partially, in terms of nonrational forms of cognition. This is apparent in his description of suggestion as a demand situation that can induce "conscious uncontrolled responses" in which the individual has somehow eliminated the possibility of responding in an alternative fashion. On the other hand, the social psychological explanation views suggestion as a form of strategic enactment which involves rational thought and conscious planning (Barber, 1969; Spanos, 1986; Wagstaff, 1981). Disagreements about the fundamental nature of suggestibility tend to reflect the differing assumptions that people hold about the human being generally. This is certainly true concerning the debate over the extent to which suggestive responding is rational or irrational.

What are the components of suggestion?

The concept of suggestion can be approached from several angles. For instance, one can speak of the different methods, or communication channels, by which suggestions are conveyed. The most common of these are heterosuggestion (or interpersonal suggestion) and autosuggestion (or intrapersonal suggestion). In chapter 1 of this volume, Ernest Hilgard compares these two methods of suggestion in a discussion of self-hypnosis. Specifically, he refers to certain advantages offered by heterosuggestion.

It is also possible to study suggestion in terms of situational or contextual variables. The actual setting, for example, may partially determine the likelihood that a person will respond to a suggestion. Clinical or laboratory settings might prove intimidating and anxiety-arousing for some people, and this could determine the degree of response or nonresponse to a suggestion. Highly contrived and artificial settings have the potential to elicit a different set of responses than more naturalistic settings. Certain room arrangements or objects within the room may arouse suspicion and impede the suggestion process.

One can also examine suggestibility with reference to the private or public nature of the source of suggestion. We typically think that suggestions of the "hypnotic" variety are relatively private means of suggestion. That may be true in some cases, but it could be argued that "hypnotic" suggestion can take place at the collective level. For example, see chapter 18 by Stephen Jay Gould for a discussion of the potentially "hypnotic" effects of mass communications. Michael J. Apter, in chapter 7 of this volume, makes reference to "mass suggestibility" that can characterize large gatherings of people.

Some investigators have chosen to study suggestion in terms of *how* the suggestive communication is made. The degree to which the message is clear to the receiver will have an influence on the effectiveness of the suggestive message. Likewise, suggestions might be verbal or nonverbal in nature. Nonverbal suggestions require that certain additional cognitive functions (most notably, sight) play a role when a person receives, and makes a response (or nonresponse) to, a suggestion. Vision is not a requisite of other types of suggestion (e.g., "hypnotic" suggestion). Some might also claim that nonverbal suggestions, by their very nature, are more ambiguous than verbal suggestions.

The *force* of a suggestion can have an effect on the receiver. Suggestions that are presented gently will be perceived differently than those delivered with emotive and shock value. Responses can also be expected to vary in terms of the amount of "request" or "command" inherent to the suggestion. Hilgard makes the point in his chapter that suggestive responding is subjectively different from a deliberate compliant response to a request. He cites the example of a suggestion such as "Raise your arm" and notes how differently it would be understood by changing it to "Please raise your arm." A response to the latter phrase would be as much an appropriate social response as it would be a form of suggestive behavior. In fact, some would maintain that it can no longer be labeled a suggestion under those conditions. A factor related to force of suggestion would be *duration* of suggestion. In the same way that degree of force can influence the receiver, one would expect that long-lasting or repetitious suggestions would vary in effectiveness from suggestive communications which have very brief periods of exposure.

A study of suggestion can also be framed in terms of the personal characteristics of the communicator. There are many stories about people who "fall" into a "hypnotic" trance simply as a result of meeting a famous hypnotist. The communicator's reputation, looks, level of confidence, degree of concern, choice of communication style (authoritarian, yielding, etc.)—all these could be expected to influence the receiver and therefore the nature and extent of suggestive response.

Suggestion can also be studied in relation to a person's motivation or willingness to respond to suggestions. This can be done by searching for personality variables that are associated with increased compliance to suggestive communications. Or, alternatively, some researchers have focused on people's inclination to *resist* suggestions. Since suggestion situations are commonly thought to have an element of persuasion, a number of investigators have also attempted to isolate certain personal and situational factors that determine influenceability, or vulnerability to persuasion. For example, there seems to be a relationship, albeit a confusing one, between self-esteem and susceptibility to social influence (e.g., Janis & Field, 1959; Zellner, 1970). Also, very low and very high levels of anxiety appear to reduce vulnerability to social influence, while moderate levels of anxiety seem to increase social influenceability (e.g., Lazarus, 1981; McGuire, 1989). Lehmann (1970) looked separately at acute and chronic anxiety as they have a differential impact on social influence, while also examining the interaction of anxiety and self-esteem in the context of influenceability. McGuire (1989) refers to other variables that could have an effect on social influence, and consequently the likelihood that a person will act in compliance with suggestions. Among these are the timing, and the type, of influential message, as well as certain ability factors (e.g., attention, comprehension) and sex differences.

Finally, one may concentrate on the actual content of the suggestions themselves. Some suggestions are designed to influence sensory processes, and to bring about sensory distortions (e.g., De Pascalis & Caddia, 1985; Gheorghiu & Reyher, 1982) while others are designed to target motor or sensory-motor processes (e.g., Gheorghiu & Walter, 1989). Still other suggestions aim at memory processes (e.g., Gudjonsson, 1983; Loftus, 1979). Chapter 12 of this book (by Kelly Toland, Hunter Hoffman, and Elizabeth Loftus) deals specifically with the distortive effects of suggestion on memory.

How has suggestion and suggestibility been circumscribed and subclassified?

The study of any form of behavior depends on the ability to somehow circumscribe, or set limits on, the concepts involved. Unfortunately, the concepts of suggestion and suggestibility have been so loosely circumscribed that consensus meanings have not been reached. Most people in this area would agree that there are different *magnitudes* of suggestive responding. For instance, let us take the extreme example of a woman who responds positively to the suggestion that she will feel no pain during a Caesarean birth operation. That would usually be seen as a greater *degree* of suggestive response than if someone looked skywards because he/she wandered upon a gathering of people whose faces were turned skywards. All but a few theoretical troublemakers would agree that the former example constitutes a situation wherein there is both a suggestion (i.e., "you will feel no pain") and suggestibility (as indicated by response in the form of analgesia).

The second example is more difficult. It illustrates how suggestion and suggestibility can become blurred with other factors and processes. These include influence (and influenceability), group pressure, social contagion, situational demand characteristics, conformity, obedience, and even simple learned associations. From experience, most people have learned that groups of people look upwards when something is happening up there. To confuse matters further, one could introduce a personality trait, such as "curiosity," into the equation. In the above example, it might make as much sense to speak of degree of curiosity as it would degree of "suggestibility." Even so, some people would assert that the group's skyward look was an indirect nonverbal suggestion, and that the extent to which a person responded was a reflection of degree of suggestibility. Such people might refer to the commonly accepted distinction between direct and indirect suggestion provided by Sidis (1898). For Sidis, an indirect suggestion was one whereby the person received a communication in the form of a movement, a gesture, or an object which "in silent fashion tells the subject what to do" (p. 90). Young's (1931) definition of indirect suggestion is equally vague and all-encompassing. He describes this type of suggestion as "a method of indirect appeal to the person to be influenced" (p. 89). Such definitions would lead us to the dubious conclusion that most of our external world is a suggestion in one form or another, and that almost all of our behavior is a manifestation of suggestibility.

A growing number of investigators feel that suggestibility cannot be regarded as a single one-dimensional construct. In the above two examples, a good case could be made that "looking upwards" should not be placed on the same continuum as the woman who responded to the suggestion to feel no pain during major surgery. That is, we may be speaking of different *kinds* of responses, rather than different degrees of suggestive responding. One obvious solution to this problem would be to set guidelines that would restrict the use of terms such as "suggestion" and "suggestibility." In chapter 5 of this book, I spell out the advantages of more tightly defined definitions of these terms. But this has not happened. Instead of developing a nosological system that separates suggestion and suggestibility from largely unrelated methods of influence, there has been a tendency to create a rather large menagerie of suggestibility subtypes. While some of these may be useful, we retain a general predicament wherein we have allowed a number of disparate phenomena to be grouped according to the same label. The extent to which this is a problem can be seen when we look at some of the ways that suggestion and suggestibility have been categorized.

The term "suggestion" is often subdivided in order to reflect the *procedure* or method by which the suggestions are delivered. A rough distinction has been made in this regard between "hypnotic" and "nonhypnotic" suggestion. A hypnotic suggestion, as defined by Wagstaff (1981), is one that is "delivered during or after the initial part of the (hypnotic) induction procedure and involves instructions to the subject suggesting to him that he will respond in a certain way. . ." (p. 14–15). Wagstaff adds that these always occur while the person is said to be under the influence of induction, and before the individual is told to "wake up." Nonhypnotic (or "waking") suggestions, on the other hand, are quite simply those which are administered without formal hypnotic induction procedures. As benign as it might seem, even this basic hypnotic/nonhypnotic distinction is fraught with problems. For one, hypnotic procedures and the "state" (or pretense, as some would say) of hypnosis remains a mystery at all levels. Also, very difficult questions concerning the fundamental workings of human consciousness come into play as well. For example, Tart (1986) takes the position that "hypnosis, in various forms, is a major part of everyday life for almost all people" (p. 71). He maintains that the normal "waking" state is simply a less obvious form of "trance." Such a thesis dates back to Sandor Ferenczi (1952/1916) who tried to destroy the myth of hypnosis while referring to the suggestive and hypnotic mechanisms that are *normally* in place.

The terms "direct" and "indirect" are commonly used to distinguish between different types of suggestion. Stone and Lundy (1985) recently made a differentiation between passive and authoritarian modes of suggestion, with these representing indirect and direct suggestion, respectively. The well-known distinction between "primary" and "secondary" suggestibility reflects both the mode of suggestion and the nature of the response (Eysenck, 1943; Eysenck & Furneaux, 1945). Primary suggestibility is thought to be the result of direct suggestions that yield ideo-motor responses. The Body Sway Test and the Chevreul's Pendulum Test are thought to be effective measures of this type of suggestive response. Significant correlations have been reported between primary suggestibility and hypnotizability. On the other hand, secondary suggestibility, which reportedly does not correlate with hypnotizability, involves indirect suggestion wherein the communicator does not make explicit the desired behavior. The Progressive Lines and the Ink Blot tests are commonly regarded as measures of this latter type of suggestibility. Eysenck and Furneaux (1945) also posited the existence of "tertiary" suggestibility in which attitudes are influenced by interpersonal factors such as the prestige or status of the suggester. Likewise, Aveling and Hargreaves (1921) understood suggestive responding along a prestige/nonprestige continuum, leading some to make reference to "prestige" and "nonprestige" suggestibility.

These subtypes are described at several points in this volume. The development of all these subtypes have proceeded on the grounds that suggestibility cannot be understood as a single unitary construct. In chapter 3, H. J. Eysenck gives his rationale for creating the primary, secondary, and tertiary subdivisions. The reader will see that Eysenck takes the position that there are *many* types of suggestibility, so many in fact that he questions the usefulness of the term "suggestibility." In chapter 14, Gisli Gudjonsson describes his recent concept of "interrogative" suggestibility. That refers to "the extent to which, within a closed social interaction, people come to accept messages communicated during formal questioning, as the result of which their subsequent behavioural response is affected" (Gudjonsson & Clark, 1986). Stephen Jay Gould, in chapter 18 of this book, introduces "advertising suggestibility."

Not surprisingly, the various attempts to subclassify suggestibility are an ongoing source of debate. Some argue for the merits and potential applications for these subclassifications, while others insist that these will not be meaningful until we have a better understanding of the *general* principles involved in the suggestion process. In some ways, it does seem that we have raced ahead of ourselves in this respect, given that we are still battling to coordinate ourselves with regard to the more basic concepts and terminology in this area of study.

Some critics also claim that our current distinctions are misleading in that they foster an "either/or" type of mentality regarding the nature of suggestion. For example, it might be more accurate to view suggestion along a direct/indirect continuum. In the same way, one might be overly simplistic in regarding suggestions as *either* primary *or* secondary. In actual fact, many suggestions do not fall clearly into either category and many are sure to contain elements of both. One could also argue that it would be more advantageous to speak of a continuum of suggestion in terms of "hypnotic" and "nonhypnotic" responding, rather than take an either/or view. This would even allow for the possibility that the "waking" state is subject to certain degrees of "trance," or "hypnosis," as Tart (1986) would describe it. Still another criticism of our current system of subcategorization is that conclusions about specific suggestibility subtypes do not allow one to make meaningful statements about larger factors or processes that might be operating as common denominators.

How do hypnosis and dissociation relate to the suggestion process?

The term "hypnosis" conjures up an endless array of images in people's minds. Likewise, many people over the years have conjured up theories that attempt to explain this seemingly unusual phenomenon. But, as mentioned earlier, there is not even a consensus opinion that hypnosis is, in fact, unusual. The fundamental workings of hypnosis remain a mystery, which accounts for the lack of agreement concerning a useful definition for hypnosis. In fact, at one point the Hypnosis Division of the American Psychological Association resorted to a *vote* for an acceptable definition.

Theoretical formulations of hypnosis have depicted this type of behavior in diverse ways. Some accounts emphasize that hypnosis is a unique "state," and in particular an *altered* state. Orne (1959), for instance, described the essential features of hypnosis as an altered state of consciousness in which a person can bypass objective reality. This, according to Orne, enables a person to tolerate inconsistencies in logic and to experience as real what are, in fact, distortions of perception and memory. To this, he added that the "hypnotic" subject feels a *compulsion* to follow cues (i.e., suggestions) from outside sources. Of course, such a model would again stand in stark contrast to the previously mentioned theorists who would place hypnosis in a social psychological framework.

The many differences of opinion on the subject of hypnosis will become apparent to the reader of this book. What is certain is that the concept of suggestion has remained a major feature of almost all theoretical conceptions of hypnosis. During "hypnosis," or "hypnotic" procedures, people are given suggestions. The extent to which they comply is the usual touchstone by which to decide whether or not they were actually "hypnotized." The same guideline is used to indicate "depth" of "hypnosis." Our supposed tests of hypnotic susceptibility are essentially devices which quantify a person's yield to a set of standardized suggestions.

The close association between suggestion and "hypnosis" can be traced to the work of Bernheim (1964/1888). He was one of the first investigators to offer an in-depth formulation for the workings of suggestion in the context of hypnosis. In so doing, he drew a very close parallel between these two. In fact, Bernheim's essential view of hypnosis was as a state of enhanced suggestibility.

Currently, the tendency to *equate* "hypnosis" with suggestibility is seen by many as over-simplistic (e.g., Bowers, 1976; Hilgard, 1973; Sheehan & Perry, 1976). However, the majority of people in this field would probably concede that enhanced suggestibility seems to be a major feature of hypnosis. Weitzenhoffer (1980) reviewed some research dealing with the effects of hypnotic induction on level of suggestibility. He adamantly concluded that hypnotic procedures did, in fact, serve to amplify the level of direct suggestibility. In chapter 4 of this book, Etzel Cardeña and David Spiegel cite a number of studies which support the view that nonvoluntary compliance with suggestion is increased following hypnotic induction procedures.

If one cannot equate suggestion and hypnosis despite the fact that elevated suggestibility is a dominant feature of hypnosis, one is inclined to search for a larger context within which to make sense of hypnosis and suggestion generally. That is not an unreasonable course of action when one keeps in mind that the procedure known as "hypnosis" is, to a large extent, a culture-bound phenomenon. There are, in fact, many types or variations of "hypnosis" throughout the world, even though their outward manifestations are quite different. Some of these might carry labels such as trance, possession, witchcraft, visionary experience, ecstasy, and shamanism. The reader can refer to chapter 8 in this book, by Colleen Ward and Simon Kemp, for a discussion of the distinctions between different types of "altered states" of consciousness.

With specific reference to "trance," Bourguignon and Evascu (1977) observed that the vast majority of cultures in the world have some form of institutionalized "trance." One would not say that hypnosis is institutionalized in any real way in Western culture. Yet many have made reference to "hypnotic trance." Trance, however, has not proved a popular framework within which to conceptualize hypnosis. Anthropologists use the term quite freely, but they have rarely ventured into the arena of hypnosis with that term. It is, again, very unfortunate that psychology, psychiatry, and anthropology have not had a closer alliance. I have no doubt that we would be closer to an accurate appreciation of what it is we are calling hypnosis.

In all probability, "trance" will not be seen as the common denominator in hypnosis and related forms of behavior. Since trance is subject to so much variation, we might feel more inclined to continue our search for a process that is still more fundamental. In psychology, but not anthropology, there have been periodic efforts to understand hypnosis in the broader context of dissociated consciousness. Dissociation is a concept that dates back to the pioneering work of Pierre Janet (1889), with a recent revival of that concept owed to Hilgard's (1986/1977) neo-dissociation theory. At one point, Hilgard (1965) made the very clear statement that "dissociation is the secret of hypnosis" (p. 71).

The concept of dissociation is inconsistent with the notion that consciousness is singular and continuous in nature. Instead, consciousness is seen as a hierarchical system of cognitive control whereby information can be processed along multiple independent, or largely independent, pathways. Volition, self-initiative, and critical awareness are the higher levels of control from which a person can become disengaged if the need or demand situation is encountered.

Hilgard (1986/1977) explains a wide range of phenomena, in addition to hypnotic responding, on the basis of dissociated consciousness. These include multiple personality disorder, fugue, psychogenic amnesia, and other dissociative and "hysterical" disorders. The list also includes nonclinical manifestations such as possession, shamanistic practices, age regression, automatic handwriting, and so forth. In a dissociated state, the person is thought to become removed from his/her higher-order, or "executive" control, functions. Hilgard (1965) also felt that dissociation was characterized by a subsidence of the person's "planning function." One could say that such an individual has been able to override what Gheorghiu (1989a) refers to as our "conscious monitoring authority" (p. 42).

In their chapter, Cardeña and Spiegel argue that a suppression of these executive functions, via the mechanism of dissociation, is a prerequisite to suggestibility as it is revealed through hypnotic procedures. In other words, dissociation prepares a person to respond to communications that might otherwise be rejected if executive control was operative. So, while all have not embraced the concept, dissociation has emerged as a potential common denominator for suggestive responding and a wide variety of related behavior. Dissociation might also form the basis for a distinction between suggestive responding and other types of persuasion which seem to involve greater degrees of "executive" processing.

Another construct that has been used to account for hypnotic suggestibility is "absorption" (Tellegen & Atkinson, 1974). This refers to a person's inclination to focus complete and undivided attention onto specific external or internal stimuli. This form of cognition, according to Tellegen and Atkinson, has the effect of "absorbing" or binding, all of a person's perceptual, ideational, and imaginative resources. Most people who are familiar with hypnosis would agree that "absorption" seems to be a common feature of hypnotic induction procedures. Cardeña and Spiegel make the case in their chapter that "absorption" works in conjunction with the dissociation process in bringing about the type of suggestive responding that occurs during hypnosis. The reader is referred to their chapter for a detailed account of their integrative model of hypnosis. One might also find it interesting to read about Mordecai Kaffman's formulation of "monoideistic" disorders (chapter 15) in the context of "absorption." As one can see, that class of psychopathology is characterized by highly focused (or "absorbing") ideation that serves to construct and maintain specific symptom patterns.

Those people supporting a strict social psychological view of suggestion and hypnosis would find very little utility in constructs of dissociation or absorption. If they do have a broad "umbrella" concept by which to understand hypnosis and related phenomena, it might be the *social situation*. According to the social psychological model, hypnosis is a social invention. It is only one type of social situation, with specific role demands to which people will accommodate themselves. In this formulation, the hypnotic "subject" is an active part of that specific role-enactment procedure, with the "hypnotist" playing an equal part in the overall performance. And "hypnotic" and other types of suggestive responding would be seen as just that—performances.

How does one measure suggestibility?

The close association between the suggestion process and hypnosis has led to a preponderance of tests that specifically measure hypnotic susceptibility. One example is the Stanford Scale of Hypnotic Susceptibility (SHSS) (Weitzenhoffer & Hilgard, 1959, 1962), which comes in three forms, namely A, B, and C. The induction procedure of forms A and B include specific instructions for relaxation with the person receiving the suggestion that he/she is lapsing into a sleep-like state of hypnosis. Following this, a series of suggestions or "items" are administered, most of which are motor suggestion (e.g., "your hand is too heavy to lift"). The SHSS also contains the verbal inhibition item "you cannot say your name" and a hallucinatory one suggesting "there is a fly buzzing round your head." Form C of the SHSS was designed to reduce the number of motor suggestions and to increase the number of items that entail distortions of cognition.

Other tests include the Revised Stanford Profile Scale of Hypnotic Susceptibility (SPSHS), Forms I and II (Weitzenhoffer and Hilgard, 1967), and the Barber Suggestibility Scale (Barber, 1969). The SPSHS bears some resemblance to certain multi-scale intelligence and personality tests (e.g., WAIS, MMPI) and thus allows one to assess individual strengths and weaknesses regarding responsiveness to hypnotic suggestion. In partial contrast to more traditional methods, Shor (1979) prescribes a phenomenological approach to the assessment of hypnotic susceptibility, one that takes into account objective as well as subjective measures. The Harvard Group Scale of Hypnotic Susceptibility (Shor & Orne, 1962) is a translated version of the SHSS:A specifically intended for group administration. Some of the above tests can take up to three hours to administer, a problem which led Morgan and Hilgard (1979a, 1979b) to develop the Stanford Hypnotic Clinical Scale (SHCS). This included separate versions for adults and children. The SHCS correlates quite highly with the SHSS and has the distinct clinical and experimental advantage of a relatively brief, twenty-minute administration.

Gheorghiu (1989a) notes that our tests of suggestibility are sometimes understood in the context of the distinction between "primary" and "secondary" (Eysenck & Furneaux, 1945), as well as the distinction between "direct" and "indirect" suggestion. For instance, tests of "primary" suggestibility usually involve *motor* suggestions of a *direct* nature (e.g., the Body Sway Test). On the other hand, tests of "secondary" suggestibility tend to engage the *sensory* processes through *indirect* suggestion (e.g., the heat illusion test). Gheorghiu criticizes this longstanding tradition of associating direct (and "primary") suggestibility to the motor processes, and indirect (and "secondary") suggestibility to the sensory processes. In so doing, he makes it clear that *both* motor and sensory processes are subject to influence by *both* direct and indirect suggestion.

A number of other criticisms have surfaced regarding the nature of our currently available tests of suggestibility. Some of these concern the fact that most of them are, in fact, tests of hypnotic susceptibility. With few exceptions (e.g., the Hypnotic Induction Profile; Spiegel, 1978), most tests involve the provision of suggestions, not unlike those typically used during actual hypnotic induction procedures. This is seen as problematic by some people who are interested in studying suggestibility in a broader context than hypnosis. Tests of hypnotizability are also given in a benevolent authoritarian format, one to which certain people might not be responsive. The more "permissive" suggestions that have emerged from the Milton Erickson school of thought on hypnosis are sometimes seen as an alternative method of assessment and induction. Another criticism is that, despite the fact that concepts such as "nonhypnotic" and "waking" suggestibility have been discussed for some time, we have not seen the development of tests that will adequately assess suggestibility independent of the hypnotic context. Of course, from a research perspective this situation leads to serious methodological and theoretical difficulties. In fact, a review of suggestibility research will reveal that many investigators have attempted to measure nonhypnotic forms of suggestibility (e.g., placebo responsiveness, social suggestibility, etc.) using tests of hypnotic susceptibility. Such a practice is made even more worrisome given the evidence that hypnotic and nonhypnotic forms of suggestibility may be largely independent of one another (Evans, 1967; McGlashan, Evans, & Orne, 1969; Moore, 1964).

Weitzenhoffer (1980, 1989) has recently criticized the widely used tests of suggestibility, some of which he himself was co-developer (with Ernest Hilgard). Certain of these relate to the unclear criteria for hypnosis, and also the inability of these tests to distinguish between voluntary and involuntary responses to suggestion. Hilgard responds to these and other such criticisms in a detailed way in his chapter in this volume. He also provides a history of their development and a rationale for their present form and content.

Gheorghiu (1989a) refers to other criticisms that can be made about the status of suggestibility tests and their applications. For example, he observes that some of our most commonly used tests (e.g., the Body Sway Test, the Pendulum Test) lack sufficiently standardized guidelines for administration and interpretation. A great deal of variation can be seen with regard to the time allowed for completion of the tests, the conditions under which they are given, the sequencing of test items, the initial instructions given to test subjects, and so forth. According to Gheorghiu, these factors make it nearly impossible to compare research results, even when the same tests were used in the different studies.

Hilgard is probably correct when he writes in his chapter that our measurement devices have served us in many ways. As he notes, they have provided the basis for a large body of empirical research that has advanced our knowledge of this subject area. In many ways, however, our "knowledge" of the suggestibility process is shaped by the structure and content of our measurement devices. Researchers tend to draw conclusions from within the theoretical and practical confines of the methods for quantifying suggestive behavior. Gheorghiu (1989a) comments that even the questions we ask about the suggestibility process tend to be those that will be convenient for study by our available measurement tools. In a very real way, this may limit our horizons and prevent us from asking large new questions that could take us toward a better general understanding of suggestibility.

A comprehensive discussion of the many issues, problems, and prospects related to the assessment of suggestibility is well beyond the scope of this introduction. However, the testing of individual differences is a crucial matter for most people involved in the study of suggestibility. The different chapters of this book will offer a variety of perspectives on this subject, and the reader should gain an appreciation for the theoretical and logistical challenges that we face in this regard.

What additional factors influence and correlate with suggestibility?

A considerable amount of research has aimed at the delineation of specific variables that relate to suggestibility. The variables include age, sex, intellectual capacity, personality characteristics, mental health status, and so forth. Since most suggestibility tests are, in effect, measures of hypnotizability, most of these variables have been studied in the context of hypnotic responsiveness.

A notable exception would be the body of research looking at factors that correlate with interrogative suggestibility. As noted previously, this subtype of suggestibility is based upon leading questions and does not resemble other classifications of suggestibility that are more aligned to "hypnotic" suggestion. Gudjonsson and Lister (1984), for instance, discovered that interrogative suggestibility was inversely correlated with self-esteem, while Gudjonsson (1987) found that this form of suggestibility was more apparent in those people with higher levels of anxiety. Interrogative suggestibility has also been found to be positively related to neuroticism (Gudjonsson, 1983). Such a finding is similar to the studies that show a positive correlation between "primary" suggestibility and neuroticism. However, it should be remembered that interrogative suggestibility has not been found to correlate significantly with primary suggestibility (see chapter 14 by Gudjonsson in this book).

Recent evidence suggests that suggestibility plays a role with regard to symptom formation and maintenance in certain "monoideistic" disorders (e.g., anorexia nervosa, paranoia, certain types of phobia) as well as multiple personality disorder, bulimia, and post-traumatic stress disorder. In this regard, some investigators have found it useful to discuss changes in suggestibility that occur from pre-onset to post-onset phases of certain forms of psychopathology. See chapter 11 in this book by Gary Groth-Marnat for a detailed discussion on this subject. The reader is also referred to chapter 15 by Mordecai Kaffman, who looks closely at "monoideistic" disorders in relation to the suggestion process. Also, Judith Rhue and Steven Jay Lynn (chapter 10 in this volume) examine multiple personality disorder in the context of suggestibility and dissociation.

Hilgard's chapter in this book includes a section dealing with correlates of hypnotizability. He pays particular attention to the variables of absorption and imaginative involvement as factors that correlate positively with hypnotic responsiveness. Hilgard speculates about another variable that could relate to hypnotizability, namely the capacity to make one's mind blank. This "trait," he says, could play a role in the posthypnotic amnesia that is often observed following hypnotic procedures. Hilgard also discusses the controversies surrounding recent efforts to modify people's degree of hypnotizability.

One of the more consistent findings concerning suggestibility is that it appears to decrease with age (London & Cooper, 1969; Stukat, 1958).

Morgan and Hilgard (1973) tested a large number of subjects ranging in age from five upwards. They found that subjects in the nine-to-twelve age range were the most suggestible, while those least responsive to suggestions were those forty years of age and over. Barber (1969) used the Barber Suggestibility Scale in measuring responsiveness to waking suggestions. He found that suggestibility peaked between nine and ten years of age, after which it decreased until age fourteen. Barber reported that level of suggestibility was relatively unchanged from fourteen to twenty-two years of age. Wagstaff (1981) discusses these findings in relation to conformity which has been shown to vary with age in a somewhat similar way to suggestibility. Bowers (1976) attributes the overall inverse relationship between age and hypnotic suggestibility to a decrease in interpersonal trust that might occur as people get older.

It should be mentioned that some of the interesting work in the area of children's eyewitness testimony has led some to question the *extent* to which suggestibility declines with age (see Ceci, Toglia, & Ross, 1987). Furthermore, there are a few studies which have not actually found the characteristic decline in suggestibility with age (e.g., Marin, Holmes, Guth, & Kovac, 1979). While it is true that the bulk of evidence shows that young people are more responsive to their adult counterparts, this seems to depend on such variables related to comprehension and attention (Loftus & Davies, 1984). Also, as Kelly Toland, Hunter Hoffman, and Elizabeth Loftus mention in chapter 12 of this book, suggestibility in children is influenced by the authority of the source of the suggestion. They refer to research which shows that children are more suggestible to memory-distorting suggestions when the source of misinformation is an adult rather than a child.

Intelligence does not seem to be a good indicator of suggestibility. Most studies find little or no correlation between these two variables. Eysenck (1947) did report lower suggestibility by subjects of either very low or very high intelligence, but his general conclusion was that intelligence was not an important determinant of responsiveness to suggestion. Sex, as a variable, also does not seem to interact consistently with measures of suggestibility. The research findings in this regard are very mixed, so much so that general conclusions are difficult to make. An overriding variable seems to be the sex of the person delivering the suggestions. For instance, greater responsiveness to sensory suggestion was shown to result when a person received suggestions from someone of the same sex (Gheorghiu & Kiel, 1976; Netter, 1989).

In chapter 10 in this book, Judith Rhue and Steven Jay Lynn discuss the curious relationship that has been reported between fantasy proneness and hypnotic responsiveness. It was initially thought that fantasy proneness was highly correlated with hypnotizability (Wilson & Barber, 1981, 1983). But as Rhue and Lynn point out, our understanding of the nature and degree of that relationship needs considerable revision. Some studies have shown sociability to be a dimension of personality that has some bearing on suggestive behavior (Barber, 1956). That is similar to the findings of Gibson and Corcoran (1975) that "stable extroverts" were highly responsive to hypnotic suggestion. Wagstaff (1981) adds support to this with his observations that certain nonsuggestible people are slightly inclined to be unsociable and suspicious. He weaves that into his argument for a social psychological explanation of the suggestion process.

The search for differences in suggestibility in terms of introversion and extroversion has not been fruitful. An exception is again interrogative suggestibility, which has been shown to correlate with external locus of control (Gudjonsson, 1987). Taken as a whole, available research does not offer compelling evidence that personality variables play a major role with regard to individual differences in responsiveness to suggestion.

Most correlates of suggestibility (or, in most cases, hypnotic responsiveness) have derived from questionnaires of various sorts. However, some efforts have been made to circumvent the inevitable shortcomings and limitations of questionnaire studies in seeking to uncover nonquestionnaire correlates of suggestive responding. For example, Evans, Gustafson, O'Connell, Orne, and Shor (1969) and Evans (1977) discovered that they could administer suggestions to sleeping subjects without arousing some of them. One such suggestion was "whenever I say the word 'itch' your nose will feel itchy until you scratch it." They controlled for voluntary responding by using only those subjects who showed no EEG signs of arousal during the administering of suggestions. These researchers found that some subjects responded so well that even the cue word "itch" would cause them to scratch their nose. An additional finding was that these sleeping responses to suggestion did relate to a person's degree of hypnotic responsiveness. However, Evans, et al. (1969) found that sleep responding correlated better with items measuring dissociative control, rather than the motor and imagery items. Evans (1989) draws on factor analytic studies in making the case that response to suggestion during hypnosis differs significantly from nonhypnotic suggestive behavior. He argues that the former is best understood in the context of dissociation, while the latter should be understood in the domain of social influence. Therefore, Evans views the processes of hypnosis and general suggestibility as largely independent ones. The same is true of placebo responding, which he sees as independent again from both hypnotic and nonhypnotic categories of suggestion.

Are we progressing toward a biology of suggestion?

While acknowleding that we are still in the early stages of a physiological understanding of the suggestion process, there is a growing body of research to indicate that such a basis does exist. This is a controversial subject, since some theoretical stances hinge largely on the social and/or psychological workings of suggestion. Of course, distinct biological changes which accompany suggestive behavior do not, by themselves, allow one to discount social psychological formulations. But they do lend some credence to a "state" model of suggestion in that one could argue for biological "states" that are requisite to (or at least concomitant with) positive responses to suggestion.

A biological framework for suggestion is given some shape by research showing that genetics may partially determine degree of responsiveness to suggestion (e.g., Morgan, 1973). This is consistent with the findings that response to suggestion (or at least hypnotic suggestion) is relatively stable over time (see Hilgard's chapter in this book). This line of evidence is not without its critics, who point to the usual potential pitfalls of twin studies and genetics research generally. Even so, several other attempts to ascertain the psychophysiological basis of the suggestion process are showing a great deal of promise.

In a study by Morgan, MacDonald, and Hilgard (1974), highly hypnotizable people were found to have more alpha brain wave activity in the "waking" state. Other studies have been unable to find a similar relationship (e.g., Edmonston & Grotevant, 1975) and some researchers question the usefulness of alpha EEG recordings in relation to the suggestion process.

More enthusiasm has come in this regard from brain asymmetry studies. Shifts of cortical activity to the right hemisphere have been noted following hypnotic induction (Crawford & Allen, 1983; Frumkin, Ripley, & Cox, 1978; Gruzelier, 1987), while EEG shifts to the right hemisphere have been observed under similar conditions (Bányai, Mészáros, & Csokay, 1985; MacLeod-Morgan, 1979). Spiegel, Cutcomb, Ren, and Pribram (1985) measured amplitude of cortical event-related potentials (ERPs) and found greater right-hemisphere involvement following hypnotic induction, while decreases in left-hemisphere involvement during hypnosis have been found in relation to measured electrodermal responses (e.g., Gruzelier, 1987; Gruzelier,

Brow, Perry, Rhonder, & Thomas, 1984). Mészáros, Crawford, Szabó, Nagy-Kovács, and Révész (1989) point out the rather crude nature of the left/right-hemisphere distinction. Their research shows that, with specific reference to degree of responsiveness to hypnotic suggestions, it is also possible to speak more specifically about asymmetry between various anterior and posterior portions of the brain. See chapter 13 in this book by John Shea for a more thorough summary of this work in this intriguing area, and also for a discussion of some criticisms of these and other psychophysiological studies. Shea's chapter also deals with the intriguing effects of suggestion on the immune system.

Of what value is suggestibility?

Very few investigators have asked this question. Some seem to think that the human being is suggestible for no apparent reason, in which case this becomes a nonquestion. Others, if pushed on the subject, might concede the possibility that it could be of some significance, or value. However, the question is a very difficult one and most have stayed well clear of it. It forces one to conceptualize suggestibility in terms of complex adaptive processes occurring at the individual and collective level. One is required to take the study of suggestion into largely uncharted territories, such as the nature of consciousness and reality, the structure of identity, the interface of the individual and culture, and the extent to which bias is necessarily built into human cognition. Another problem is that an answer often leads one into the realm of physical and/or cultural evolution and sociobiology. These theoretical perspectives are not entirely in vogue in the social sciences at present. Also, an answer sometimes carries the implicit assumption that suggestibility is a universal characteristic of our species. While one would be hard pressed to argue against the universality of suggestibility, the acceptance of this proposition again paves the way for a biologically based understanding of the suggestion process. That runs counter to the arguments set out by people who are inclined toward social psychological explanations of suggestibility.

A small number of thinkers have started to look at the potential merits of suggest-*ability*. Gheorghiu (1982, 1989a), for example, makes the claim that suggestibility is a useful coping mechanism that might be understood in a similar way to Lazarus's (1979) conception of defense mechanisms. His concept of "substitution" as the essence of the suggestion process involves the overriding premise that suggestion can benefit us in important ways. One aspect of the "substitution" or suggestion mechanism is our ability to bypass our higher-order "conscious monitoring authority" (Gheorghiu, 1989a, p. 42). Suggestibility then becomes an adaptive device that affords the individual the capacity for denial, illusion, and false or overly optimistic beliefs. These could be helpful in coping with stress and situational conflicts, and in the maintenance of the overall psychological and biological homeostasis of the individual. In chapter 9 of this book, Frederick Gibbons looks specifically at suggestibility in relation to self-illusions that act in the service of mental health. My own chapter deals with the adaptive value of suggestibility, as well as the capacity for dissociation. I argue that these vital faculties make possible a wide range of uniquely human behavior, all of which carry crucial survival advantages.

The above questions are but a small sample of those that are being asked with relation to the topic of suggestibility. The chapters that follow in the volume will ask, and attempt to answer, many more.

Organization and content of this volume

This volume is divided into four sections. The first is titled "The Nature of Suggestibility." As that title suggests, this section includes chapters which offer perspectives on the essential or fundamental nature of the suggestion process. These are intended to provide the reader with a history of thinking on this subject. It is also hoped that the reader will come away with a knowledge base that will give additional perspective to chapters that appear later in the book.

Chapter 1. In the first chapter of this book, Ernest Hilgard discusses suggestion and suggestibility within the context of hypnosis. In setting the boundaries for "the domain of hypnosis," he clarifies some matters of terminology and addresses some of the major issues and debates that have arisen over the years. Hilgard looks specifically at some of Weitzenhoffer's criticisms of tests of hypnotic susceptibility, some of which were developed conjointly by Hilgard and Weitzenhoffer. Hilgard also gives a brief overview of recent developments and debates related to self-hypnosis, the modification of hypnotic susceptibility, and the correlates of hypnotizability. One of the general conclusions of his chapter is that the topics of suggestion and suggestibility generate more controversy than is justified in light of our present state of knowledge.

Chapter 2. Vladimir Gheorghiu and Peter Kruse present an integrative model of suggestion. In so doing, they point out that, in recent decades, psychology has suffered from an unfortunate trend away from integrative models of human behavior. Gheorghiu and Kruse also argue that suggestive phenomena should form the basis of a legitimate paradigmatical field of study. Within a constructivistic theoretical framework, these authors maintain that suggestion is a general cognitive strategy that is useful in reducing ambiguity and instability. This is based on the assumption that our world is basically ambiguous and unstable, and also that "order formation" is an important ongoing feature of cognition. Gheorghiu and Kruse account for individual differences in suggestibility in terms of nervous system strength and sensitivity, as well as their construct of "hysteresis," which refers to the tendency to persist in a single stable state. They cite some of their research which supports their hypotheses. Gheorghiu and Kruse also refer to the influence of belief systems and the importance of reality criteria as they play a role in the cognitive construction of personal reality.

Chapter 3. Hans J. Eysenck gives his chapter the provocative title "Is Suggestibility?" He argues that there is no single unitary trait of suggestibility, and also that there is no uniformity of response to the various kinds of suggestion. Eysenck refers to the "will-o'-the-wisp" nature of suggestibility and takes the position that we are dealing with many different types of suggestibility that bear very little relation to each other. He defends the distinction that he (and Furneaux) made between primary and secondary suggestibility. Eysenck also recommends that future research should be devoted to a further delineation of the various types of suggestibility, and also to the ways in which these relate to other variables (e.g., personality, intelligence, hypnotic susceptibility, etc.).

The second section of this book is titled "Theoretical Perspectives." These chapters are intended to give a cross-section of theoretical viewpoints on suggestibility in its various forms.

Chapter 4. Etzel Cardeña and David Spiegel present an integrative model of hypnosis, one that views hypnotic occurrences as the result of suggestibility, dissociation, and absorption. These are seen as the processes which are responsible for the changes in attentional continuity and focus which characterize hypnotic cognition. These authors maintain that ordinary conscious experience has much less thematic continuity than is typically thought to be the case. In fact, ordinary consciousness involves a continual shifting of psychological content. In contrast, Cardeña and Spiegel claim that hypnotic cognition is associated with greater continuity of conscious experience as well as decreased critical and self-reflective processes. Enhanced suggestibility is thus seen as a natural outcome of the cognitive changes that take place in the hypnotic context. Cardeña and Spiegel conclude that hypnotic cognition, while unique in certain ways, can nonetheless be understood as a variation of the workings of ordinary forms of cognition.

Chapter 5. My own chapter considers our suggestive and dissociative capacities in a psychobiological framework and speculates about the possible adaptive value of these features of cognition. I propose that we evolved into a "suggestible animal" for a number of reasons, all of which relate to survival at some level. In developing my argument, I claim that suggestive responding, if strictly defined, must be seen as operating in conjunction with dissociation. While dissociation is viewed as a necessary precursor of suggestibility, it is possible for dissociation to be utilized without suggestion. This happens on an everyday basis when "absorption" is used to facilitate mild dissociation for the purpose of neurological conservation and economy of effort. At other times, it is clear that dissociation and suggestion are conjoint operations. The benefits provided by the workings of these cognitive abilities are, a) reality transcendence; b) social cohesion and social control; c) emotional discharge; d) flight from self; and e) escape from trauma and irreconcilable conflict. Certain examples of religious belief and psychopathology (most notably anorexia nervosa) are used to illustrate the operations of suggestion and dissociation as they are carried out in the larger context of culture.

Chapter 6. Graham Wagstaff's chapter presents a social psychological model of suggestibility. He questions past categorizations of suggestion and suggestibility, as well as the "classic suggestion tests." In line with a social psychological approach to this subject, Wagstaff argues that an understanding of the suggestion process should revolve around the "social situation." He adds that we must view people as active, rather than passive, participants in the suggestion situation. He rejects the view that suggestion is a passive and automatic process. Instead he sees people as active participants whose behavior is deliberate, strategic, and meaningful. Part of Wagstaff's argument is that suggestion is a manifestation of compliance, and social demand characteristic. His social psychological formulation is used to explain responsiveness to suggestion both within and outside the context of hypnosis. Wagstaff concludes by saying that, if we can finally get suggestion in accurate perspective, the task of researching this process has yet to begin.

Chapter 7. Michael J. Apter explains suggestibility in terms of his "Reversal Theory," a "structural-phenomenological" approach which views conscious experience as the pivotal starting point by which to understand behavior. He delineates three types of suggestibility in terms of the different "metamotivational modes," or states of mind, which are part of Reversal Theory. The first, rather weak "background" type of suggestibility is seen as a form of conformity which is a common experience for most people. A second, and stronger, type of suggestibility is a combination of the "alloic" and "mastery" metamotivational modes. This second type is sometimes experienced as a willingness to be dominated by, and to submit to others. Alternatively, the person might feel as if he/she is no longer interacting with a specific other, but rather that he/she is part of a larger third force (as in the case of "mass suggestibility"). Apter views hypnosis as an enigmatic third type of suggestibility and details its workings in terms of the different metamotivational modes. He does not regard his conception of hypnosis as incompatible with either neo-dissociation theory or the view that hypnosis is largely imaginative involvement and role-playing.

Chapter 8. Colleen Ward and Simon Kemp present a cross-cultural and historical account of suggestibility in relation to religious experiences and altered states of consciousness (ASCs). They point out that suggestibility is a factor in determining the nature of the experience of an ASC, and that it also affects when and how often ASCs occur. They focus on spirit possession and visionary experiences, and compare these to "hypnotic" types of responses. Special consideration is given to Thaipusam, the Malaysian religious practice in which devotees allow their bodies to be pierced with hooks, needles, and skewers. While emphasizing the social and cultural underpinnings of this remarkable form of behavior, Ward and Kemp do not feel that these states can be understood as mere role enactment (as proposed by Spanos). Suggestibility and trance, as these are determined by social forces at the micro and macro levels, are also discussed in terms of visions and possessions that occurred in Medieval and Early Modern Europe. It is argued that some of these experiences served to contribute to personal psychological well-being and identity, and also to cohesion and unity at the cultural level.

In the third section of this book, "Researching Suggestibility," the chapters deal with quantitative studies that relate to suggestion and suggestibility. Most of these make reference to certain theoretical implications that derive from the research under consideration.

Chapter 9. The chapter by Frederick Gibbons and Sue Boney McCoy concerns itself with the role of attention in the suggestibility process, with special reference to self-perception and self-deception. This discussion gives an overview of self-awareness theory before discussing suggestibility in relation to focus of attention. In this regard, they make mention of self-focus and placebo response, the "veracity hypothesis," self-focus and self-presentation, and the potential limits of self-knowledge. The workings of the suggestion process are described in relation to self-illusion, which seems to be an important factor in psychological well-being. Gibbons and McCoy cite research which supports their thesis that suggestibility, as well as the ability to self-delude, is dependent upon an external focus. Similarly, they state that the self-serving cognitive biases offered by suggestibility are inhibited under conditions of internal focus. These authors describe certain ways in which reduced suggestibility and accurate self-perceptions are not necessarily "depressogenic." But they still conclude that suggestibility, as it operates in the service of self-illusion, relieves people from the "burden" of accurate self-focus. Gibbons and McCoy take this discussion into a societal context and discuss such issues as deindividuation, contagion, and inhibition. They also speak of suggestibility with reference to the "remote control" form of regulation that society exerts over its members.

Chapter 10. Judith Rhue and Steven Jay Lynn explore the relationships between fantasy proneness, hypnotizability, and multiple personality. They provide a critical overview of earlier research which showed an exceptionally close link between fantasy proneness and hypnotic susceptibility. Rhue and Lynn summarize a number of their own studies which, while still supporting a connection between fantasy proneness and hypnotizability, indicate that the relationship is not as simple or as close as previously thought. Space is devoted to research into the developmental pathways to fantasy proneness. These include parental encouragement of fantasy, and also physical punishment. The authors point out that some developmental factors that increase fantasy proneness have also been found to increase hypnotic susceptibility. The defensive nature of fantasy is discussed in relation to certain types of psychopathology, with special consideration given to multiple personality disorder. Dissociation, imagination, and fantasy are seen as adaptive, goal-directed processes that interact with each other in the formation and maintenance of multiple personality disorder. Rhue and Lynn also outline some of the similarities between fantasizers and people with multiple personality disorder. These include the fluid nature of their boundaries between reality and fantasy, their use of fantasy for adaptive and defensive purposes, and also their responsiveness to hypnotic and suggestive procedures.

Chapter 11. Gary Groth-Marnat provides a comprehensive overview of research on the relationship between suggestibility and psychopathology. He points out that most studies in this area have concerned themselves with hypnotic susceptibility. This is due, he says, to the lack of an acceptable composite test of nonhypnotic suggestibility. He reveals that the few existing studies of nonhypnotic suggestibility and psychopathology show contradictory results. Groth-Marnat's review indicates that people with different types of psychopathology do, in fact, vary considerably in degree of hypnotic susceptibility. In general, low levels of hypnotic responsiveness are associated with certain psychotic, affective, and general anxiety disorders. Groth-Marnat finds that higher levels of hypnotizability are associated with multiple personality disorder, post-traumatic stress disorder, phobias, bulimia, and anorexia nervosa. He cautions that it is too early to draw conclusions about the cause-effect nature of these relationships. As an interesting sidelight, he gives evidence that hypnotizability is related to positive mental health in nonpatient populations.

Chapter 12. The next chapter by Kelly Toland, Hunter Hoffman, and Elizabeth Loftus is concerned with research on the distortive effects of suggestion on memory. They describe studies showing that postevent suggestions can alter not only memory of specific objects, but also subjective recollections such as the entire emotional context of an event. These authors use the term "misinformation effect" to describe postevent suggestions that serve to impair memory performance. They cite a series of studies dealing with factors that influence suggestibility and therefore the likelihood that suggestions will result in memory impairment. These factors include, a) the strength of the original memory for the event; b) whether or not the person is warned about potentially misleading information; c) the amount of time that elapsed since the person witnessed an event; d) the blatancy of the misleading information; e) the person's prior commitment to an inaccurate memory; and f) the perceived expertise of the source of the misleading information. This chapter includes a discussion of two theories of the "misinformation effect," namely the alteration hypothesis and the coexistence hypothesis. The authors also describe research showing that certain techniques make it possible to recover information that would otherwise be lost as the result of misleading suggestions. These findings are seen as support for the coexistence of two memories. Toland, Hoffman, and Loftus also discuss the crucial question of whether or not subjects actually believe in memories that are distorted through suggestion. They refer to a body of research which suggests that misled people are, in fact, convinced of their distorted memories. These and other issues are treated in light of the Chinese government's apparent attempts to alter people's recollections of the 1989 Tiananmen Square massacre.

Chapter 13. John Shea examines the role of a specific area of suggestion, usually described as "placebo effects," in creating bodily change, including changes in immune responses. He considers common definitions of placebo effects, the relationship of placebos to other areas of suggestion, and the power of expectancies to create bodily changes.

He goes on to consider the place of hypnotic strategies, and other related techniques in creating organismic conditions, such as hemispheric asymmetries, which may facilitate the use of symbolic suggestions (images) in self-healing. Finally, he draws attention to studies linking individual differences, such as hypnotizability and "absorption," to the capacity to utilize placebos in the health and immune context. In particular, he describes a specific group of people, high in both overall stress and "absorption," who show apparently low immune responsiveness. He concludes that placebo effects remain poorly understood. However, he notes that, since they are potentially very powerful, further study should be an important objective of psychologists.

The fourth section, "Applications and Implications," contains five chapters looking at ways in which our knowledge of suggestibility has found useful application in such diverse fields as education, advertising, forensics, and clinical psychology.

Chapter 14. Gisli Gudjonsson introduces the theoretical model of interrogative suggestibility as set out by Gudjonsson and Clark (1986) and discusses applications and implications for police interviewing. Mention is given to five interrelated components of interrogative suggestibility, and these are distinguished from other types of suggestibility. Gudjonsson also describes the manner in which leading questions, negative feedback, uncertainty, interpersonal trust, and expectation of success are aspects of the interrogative suggestibility process. He discusses certain predictions which are possible in terms of these variables. The author describes the Gudjonsson Suggestibility Scales which were developed specifically for forensic applications. These measure the extent to which criminal suspects and witnesses are able to cope with certain aspects of police interrogation. Gudjonsson addresses such issues as retracted confessions, false confessions, and erroneous testimony in light of his research on various aspects of interrogative suggestibility. He concludes that interrogative suggestibility is a reliable indicator that has an important place in both the process and outcome of police interviewing.

Chapter 15. Mordecai Kaffman outlines the role of the suggestion process in the formation of "monoideistic" forms of psychopathology, using anorexia nervosa as a paradigm. He writes that, in this class of disturbance (which includes paranoia, obsessions, dysmorphophobia, and some types of depression), one can observe highly constricted cognition at the core of the disorder. That is, there seems to be a "monoideistic" nucleus which often takes the form of a rigid and narrow idea that commands the person's complete attention. Kaffman points out the many parallels between hypnotic procedures and those employed by the person in the construction of monoideistic disorders. He argues that the closed one-way inner dialogue that sustains these "auto-hypnotic" disorders can often be traced to two-way communications that were characteristic of family interactions. This is illustrated quite clearly in his description of communications that take place in the families of potential anorexics. Kaffman also compares people with monoideistic disturbances to fanatical, "brain-washed" disciples of extreme religious cults and draws our attention to the inadequacy of our current psychotherapy approaches. Kaffman describes new directions for the treatment of this form of psychopathology, while referring to his psychotherapy outcome research at his Kibbutz Clinic in Israel.

Chapter 16. Albert Ellis takes the position that a great portion of emotional disturbance is the direct result of suggestions that people absorb. These can be suggestions from an external source which we simply accept, or they can be internally generated suggestions. He argues that depression, anxiety, low self-regard and even problems of addiction can be traced to these types of suggestion. In making his case, Ellis postulates that the human being is, by nature, a "self-suggester." We appear to be biologically inclined to be "gullible" and to absorb the preconceived values, goals, standards as set out by culture, family, peer groups, and so forth. But Ellis maintains that many "self-suggestions" are irrational inventions that lead to faulty conclusions, illogical and anti-scientific thought, inflexibility, and dogmatism. He makes reference to internal and external suggestions in the context of rational-emotive therapy (RET) and cognitive-behavior therapy (CBT). Ellis acknowledges that people will probably not completely curb their natural appetite for external suggestion, or their tendency to engage in self-defeating autosuggestion. However, he does feel that RET and CBT are useful methods for gaining at least partial control over these potentially damaging processes.

Chapter 17. Annette Shuck describes how suggestion is formally and informally employed in educational settings. She gives a historical overview of research relating to the utilization of suggestion for educational purposes. In so doing, Shuck points out that, unlike Western European and North American pedagogy, the use of suggestion has a long and rich history in Soviet-Bloc countries. She discusses "suggestopedia," which involves the effective use of suggestion within the context of educational pedagogy. As she states, these suggestions can be conscious or unconscious, and verbal or nonverbal. An in-depth description is provided of some formal suggestopedia techniques (e.g., the Lozanov method). These generally aim to improve learning, as well as self-image and confidence, through the use of strategically employed suggestion in the classroom. Shuck describes a number of factors related to the style and setting of teaching which influence suggestibility (i.e., student's responsiveness to suggestions). She concludes her chapter with a discussion of the future of suggestion in education. Shuck counters some of the criticisms that have been made of suggestopedic educational approaches and concludes that, given the potential benefits, suggestion is vastly underutilized in current educational strategies.

Chapter 18. Stephen Jay Gould argues for a relationship between the advertising and hypnotic processes to the extent that both employ persuasive communications that lead to behaviors that are not normally part of a person's behavioral repertoire. Also, he shows that both are characterized by "absorbing" states in which the person's attention is focused in such a way that he/she becomes susceptible to suggestion. Gould writes about advertising suggestion in relation to automatic behavior and subliminal stimulation. He also introduces the construct of "advertising suggestibility" and discusses some of the basic elements of this type of responsiveness to suggestion. These include the advertising stimulus which serves as the intended suggestion, the consumer state (analagous to the hypnotic state), and the consumer response to the ad suggestion (similar to a post-hypnotic response). Gould advocates the development of assessment devices to measure advertising suggestibility in relation to all of the above components of this process. He also supports research that would endeavor to establish the correlates of advertising suggestibility in terms of personality and psychophysiological variables, and also the characteristics of advertising stimuli and responses.

References

Aveling, F., & Hargreaves, H.L. (1921). Suggestibility with and without prestige in children. *British Journal of Psychology, 12,* 53–75.

Bányai, E.I., Mészáros, I., & Csokay, L. (1985). Interaction between hypnotist and subject: A social psychological approach. In D. Waxman, P.C. Misra, & M.A. Basker (eds.), *Modern trends in hypnosis.* New York: Plenum.

Barber, T.X. (1956). A note on hypnotizability and personality traits. *International Journal of Clinical and Experimental Hypnosis, 4,* 109–14.

Barber, T.X. (1969). *Hypnosis: A scientific approach.* New York: Van Nostrand Reinhold.

Bernheim, H. (1964). *Hypnosis and suggestion in psychotherapy.* New York: University Books. (Originally published in 1888.)

Bourguignon, E., & Evascu, T. (1977). Altered states of consciousness within a general evolutionary perspective: A holocultural analysis. *Behavioral Science Research, 12,* 197–216.

Bowers, K.S. (1976). *Hypnosis for the seriously curious.* Monterey, CA: Brooks/Cole.

Ceci, S.J., & Toglia, M.P., & Ross, D.F. (eds.) (1987). *Children's eyewitness memory.* New York: Springer

Crawford, H.J., & Allen, S.N. (1983). Enhanced visual memory during hypnosis as mediated by hypnotic responsiveness and cognitive strategies. *Journal of Experimental Psychology: General, 112,* 662–85.

De Pascalis, V., & Caddia, F. (1985). Effect of suggestion on perception: Replication of Gheorghiu and Reyher's study. *Perceptual and Motor Skills, 61,* 123–30.

Edmonston, W.E., & Grotevant, W.R. (1975). Hypnosis and alpha density. *American Journal of Clinical Hypnosis, 30,* 69–75.

Evans, F.J. (1967). Suggestibility in the normal waking state. *Psychological Bulletin, 67,* 114–29.

Evans, F.J. (1977). Hypnosis and sleep: The control of altered states of awareness. In W.E. Edmonston (ed.), *Conceptual and investigative approaches to hypnosis and hypnotic phenomena. Annals of the New York Academy of Science, 296,* 162–75.

Evans, F.J. (1989). The independence of suggestibility, placebo response, and hypnotizability. In V.A. Gheorghiu, P. Netter, H.J. Eysenck, & R. Rosenthal (eds.), *Suggestion and suggestibility: Theory and research.* Berlin: Springer-Verlag.

Evans, F.J., Gustafson, L.A., O'Connell, D.N., Orne, M.T., & Shor, R.E. (1969). Sleep induced behavioral response: Relationship to susceptibility to hypnosis and laboratory sleep patterns. *Journal of Nervous and Mental Disease, 148,* 467–76.

Eysenck, H.J. (1943). Suggestibility and hysteria. *Journal of Neurology and Psychiatry, 36,* 349–54.

Eysenck, H.J. (1947). *Dimensions of personality.* London: Routledge and Kegan Paul.

Eysenck, H.J., Arnold, W.J., & Meili, R. (1975). *Encyclopedia of psychology: Volume two L to Z.* Bungay, Suffolk: Fontana.

Eysenck, H.J., & Furneaux, W.D. (1945). Primary and secondary suggestibility: An experimental and statistical study. *Journal of Experimental Psychology, 35,* 485–503.

Ferenczi, S. (1952). *First contributions to psychoanalysis.* Translated by E. Jones. London: The Hogarth Press (originally published in 1916).

Frumkin, L.R., Ripley, H.S., & Cox, G.B. (1978). Changes in cerebral hemispheric lateralization with hypnosis. *Biological Psychiatry, 13,* 741–50.

Gheorghiu, V.A. (1982). Aspecte psihologice ale sugestiei si sugestibilitatii. In V.A. Gheorghiu & I. Ciofu, *Sugestie si sugestibilitate: Aspecte psihologice si psihofiziologice* (pp. 11–148). Bucharest: Editura Academiei.

Gheorghiu, V.A. (1989a). The development of research on suggestibility: Critical considerations. In V.A. Gheorghiu, P. Netter, H.J. Eysenck, & R. Rosenthal (eds.), *Suggestion and suggestibility: Theory and research.* Berlin: Springer-Verlag.

Gheorghiu, V.A. (1989b). The difficulty in explaining suggestion. In V.A. Gheorghiu, P. Netter, H.J. Eysenck, & R. Rosenthal (eds.), *Suggestion and suggestibility: Theory and research.* Berlin: Springer-Verlag.

Gheorghiu, V.A., & Kiel, M. (1976). Indirekte und indirekt-direkte Form einer sensorischen suggestibilitätsskala. *Revue Roumaine des Sciences Sociales, 20,* 29–46.

Gheorghiu, V.A., & Reyher, J. (1982). The effect of different types of influence on an indirect form of a scale of sensory suggestibility. *American Journal of Clinical Hypnosis, 24*, 191–99.

Gheorghiu, V.A., & Walter, B. (1989). The effect of suggestion and countersuggestion on motor processes. *Personality and Individual Differences, 10*, 239–46.

Gibson, H.B., & Corcoran, M.E. (1975). Personality and differential susceptibility to hypnosis: Further replication and sex differences. *British Journal of Psychology, 66*, 513–20.

Gruzelier, J. (1987). The neuropsychology of hypnosis. In M. Heap (ed.), *Hypnosis: Current clinical, experimental and forensic practices.* London: Croom Helm.

Gruzelier, J., Brow, T., Perry, A., Rhonder, J., & Thomas, M. (1984). Hypnotic susceptibility: A lateral predisposition and altered cerebral asymmetry under hypnosis. *International Journal of Psychophysiology, 2*, 131–39.

Gudjonsson, G.H. (1983). Suggestibility, intelligence, memory recall and personality: An experimental study. *British Journal of Psychiatry, 142*, 35–37.

Gudjonsson, G.H. (1987). Historical background to suggestibility: How interrogative suggestibility differs from other types of suggestibility. *Personality and Individual Differences, 3*, 347–55.

Gudjonsson, G.H., & Clark, N. (1986). Suggestibility in police interrogation: A social psychological model. *Social Behaviour, 1*, 83–104.

Gudjonsson, G.H., & Lister, S. (1984). Interrogative suggestibility and its relationship with self-esteem and control. *Journal of the Forensic Science Society, 24*, 99–110.

Hilgard, E.R. (1965). *Hypnotic susceptibility*. New York: Harcourt, Brace and World.

Hilgard, E.R. (1973). The domain of hypnosis: With comments on alternative paradigms. *American Psychologist, 23*, 972–82.

Hilgard, E.R. (1986/1977). *Divided consciousness: Multiple controls in human thought and action*. New York: Wiley.

Janet, P. (1889). *L'automatisme psychologique*. Paris: Felix Alcan.

Janis, I.L., & Field, P.B. (1959). Sex differences and personality factors related to persuasibility. In C. I. Hovland & I. L. Janis (eds.), *Personality and persuasibility* (pp. 55–68). New Haven, CT: Yale University.

Lazarus, R.S. (1979, June). The cost and benefits of denial. Paper presented at the conference "The effectiveness and cost of denial," University of Haifa, Israel.

Lazarus, R.S. (1981). The stress and coping paradigm. In C. Eisdorfer, D. Cohen, A. Kleinman, & P. Maxim (eds.), *Models for clinical psychopathology*. New York: Spectrum.

Lehmann, S. (1970). Personality and compliance: A study of anxiety and self-esteem in opinion and behavior change. *Journal of Personality and Social Psychology, 15*, 76–86.

Loftus, E.F. (1979). *Eyewitness testimony*. Cambridge, MA: Harvard University Press.

Loftus, E.F., & Davies, G.M. (1984). Distortions in the memory of children. *Journal of Social Issues, 40*, 51–67.

London, P., & Cooper, L.M. (1969). Norms of hypnotic susceptibility in children. *Developmental Psychology, 1*, 113–24.

MacLeod-Morgan, C. (1979). Hypnotic susceptibility, EEG theta alpha waves, and hemispheric specificity. In G. D. Burrows, D. R. Collison, & L. Dennerstein (eds.), *Hypnosis 1979*. Amsterdam: Elsevier/North Holland Biomedical.

Marin, B.V., Holmes, D.L., Guth, M., & Kovac, P. (1979). The potential of children as eyewitnesses. *Law and Human Behavior, 3*, 295–305.

McDougall, W. (1908). *An introduction to social psychology*. London: Methuen.

McGlashan, T.H., Evans, F.J., & Orne, M.T. (1969). The nature of hypnotic analgesia and placebo response to experimental pain. *Psychosomatic Medicine, 31*, 227–46.

McGuire, W.J. (1989). A mediational theory of susceptibility to social influence. In V. A. Gheorghiu, P. Netter, H.J. Eysenck, & R. Rosenthal (eds.), *Suggestion and suggestibility: Theory and research* (pp. 305–22). Berlin: Springer-Verlag.

Mészáros, I., Crawford, H.J., Szabó, C., Nagy-Kovács, A., & Révész, Z. (1989). Hypnotic susceptibility and cerebral hemisphere preponderance: Verbal-imaginal discrimination task. In V.A. Gheorghiu, P. Netter, H.J. Eysenck, & R. Rosenthal (eds.), *Suggestion and suggestibility: Theory and research* (pp. 191–203). Berlin: Springer-Verlag.

Moore, R.K. (1964). Susceptibility to hypnosis and susceptibility to social influence. *Journal of Abnormal and Social Psychology, 68*, 282–94.

Morgan, A.H. (1973). The heritability of hypnotic susceptibility in twins. *Journal of Abnormal Psychology, 82*, 55–61.

Morgan, A.H., & Hilgard, E.R. (1973). Age differences in susceptibility to hypnosis. *International Journal of Clinical and Experimental Hypnosis, 21*, 78–85.

Morgan, A.H., & Hilgard, J.R. (1979a). The Stanford Hypnotic Clinical Scale for Adults. *American Journal of Clinical Hypnosis, 21*, 134–47.

Morgan, A.H., & Hilgard. J.R. (1979b). The Stanford Hypnotic Clinical Scale for Children. *American Journal of Clinical Hypnosis, 21*, 148–69.

Morgan, A.H., MacDonald, H., & Hilgard, E.R. (1974). EEG alpha: Lateral asymmetry related to task and hypnotizability. *Psychophysiology, 11*, 275–82.

Netter, P. (1989). Sensory suggestibility: Measurement, individual differences and relation to placebo and drug effects. In V.A. Gheorghiu, P. Netter, H.J. Eysenck, & R. Rosenthal (eds.), *Suggestion and suggestibility: Theory and research*. Berlin: Springer-Verlag.

Orne, M.T. (1959). The nature of hypnosis: Artifact and essence. *Journal of Abnormal and Social Psychology, 58*, 277–99.

Sarbin, T.R., & Coe, W.C. (1972). *Hypnosis: A social psychological analysis of influence communication*. New York: Holt, Rinehart and Winston.

Sheehan, P.W., & Perry, C.W. (1976). *Methodologies of hypnosis: A critical appraisal of contemporary paradigms of hypnosis*. Hillsdale, NJ: Laurence Erlbaum.

Shor, R.E. (1979). The fundamental problem in hypnosis research as viewed from historic perspectives. In E. Fromm & R.E. Shor (eds.), *Hypnosis: Developments in research and new perspectives* (pp. 15–44). New York: Aldine.

Shor, R.E., & Orne, E.C. (1962). *Harvard Group Scale of Hypnotic Susceptibility, Form A*. Palo Alto, CA: Consulting Psychologists.

Sidis, B. (1898). *The psychology of suggestion*. New York: Appleton.

Spanos, N.P. (1982). Hypnotic behavior: A cognitive, social psychological perspective. *Research Communications in Psychology, Psychiatry, and Behavior, 7*, 199–213.

Spanos, N.T. (1986). Hypnosis and the modification of hypnotic susceptibility: A social psychological perspective. In P. Naish (ed.), *What is hypnosis?: Current theories and research* (pp. 85–120). Milton Keynes, UK: Open University Press.

Spiegel, H. (1978). *Manual for the hypnotic induction profile.* New York: Basic.

Spiegel, D., Cutcomb, S., Ren, C., & Pribram, K. (1985). Hypnotic hallucination alters evoked potentials. *Journal of Abnormal Psychology, 94,* 249–55.

Stone, J.A., & Lundy, R.M. (1985). Behavioral compliance with direct and indirect body movement. *Journal of Abnormal Psychology, 94,* 256–63.

Stukat, K.G. (1958). *Suggestibility: A factorial and experimental analysis.* Stockholm: Almqvist and Wiksell.

Tart, C.T. (1986). *Waking up: Overcoming the obstacles to human potential.* Boston: Shambhala.

Tellegen, A., & Atkinson, G. (1974). Openness to absorbing and self-altering experiences ("absorption"), a trait related to hypnotic susceptibility. *Journal of Abnormal Psychology, 83,* 268–77.

Wagstaff, G.F. (1981). *Hypnosis, compliance, and belief.* New York: St. Martin's Press.

Weitzenhoffer, A.M. (1980). Hypnotic susceptibility revisited. *American Journal of Clinical Hypnosis, 22,* 130–46.

Weitzenhoffer, A.M. (1989). *The practice of hypnosis.* (2 vols.) New York: Wiley.

Weitzenhoffer, A.M., & Hilgard, E.R. (1959). *Stanford Hypnotic Susceptibility Scale, Forms A and B.* Palo Alto, CA: Consulting Psychologists.

Weitzenhoffer, A.M., & Hilgard, E.R. (1962). *Stanford Hypnotic Susceptibility Scale, Form C.* Palo Alto, CA: Consulting Psychologists.

Weitzenhoffer, A.M., & Hilgard, E.R. (1967). *Revised Stanford Profile Scales of Hypnotic Susceptibility, Forms I & II.* Palo Alto, CA: Consulting Psychologists.

Wilson, S.C., & Barber, T.X. (1981). Vivid fantasy and hallucinatory abilities in the life histories of excellent hypnotic subjects ("somnambules"): Preliminary report with female subjects. In E. Klinger (ed.), *Imagery, Volume 2: Concepts, results, and applications* (pp. 158–72). New York: Plenum.

Wilson, S.C., & Barber, T.X. (1983). The fantasy-prone personality: Implications for understanding imagery, hypnosis, and parapsychological phenomena. In A.A. Sheikh (ed.), *Imagery: Current theory, research, and application* (pp. 340–87). New York: Wiley.

Young, P.C. (1931). Suggestion as indirection. *Journal of Abnormal and Social Psychology, 26,* 69–90.

Zellner, M. (1970). Self-esteem, reception, and influenceability. *Journal of Personality and Social Psychology, 15,* 87–93.

PART ONE

THE NATURE OF SUGGESTIBILITY

1

SUGGESTIBILITY AND SUGGESTIONS AS RELATED TO HYPNOSIS

Ernest R. Hilgard

Although many of those who write about suggestion relate suggestibility and hypnosis, the concept of suggestion had a history in sociology and psychology before it became tied to hypnosis by Bernheim (1963/1888, 1910), who was founder of the Nancy school of hypnosis in France. Both books mention hypnotism and suggestion in their titles, although one was written much earlier in his career than the other. The tie between hypnosis and suggestion was continued in the later books of others, such as those of Hull (1933) and Weitzenhoffer (1953). However, Hull's title refers to hypnosis and suggestibility, while Weitzenhoffer uses the terms "hypnotism" and "suggestibility." There may be noted this difference in the use of words in the titles of the three authors, although this is not troublesome unless one wishes to make an issue of it.

Some matters of terminology

Weitzenhoffer (1989) is adamant that a distinction should be made, at least between hypnotism and hypnosis. For him, a hypnotist is one who practices hypnotism, while hypnosis refers to the condition which the hypnotist hopes that he will produce (or that will appear) in the person hypnotized. I have tended to use hypnosis and hypnotism as synonyms, following the practice of Hull, who was doing his work in this area at Yale University when we were colleagues there.

The terms "suggestion" and "suggestibility" are also used without always calling attention to their conceptual differences. Note that, of the authors above, in the titles of their books, Bernheim paired hypnotism with suggestion, Weitzenhoffer paired hypnotism with suggestibility, and Hull paired hypnosis with suggestibility. There is a commonly agreed upon difference that "suggestion" refers to a type of influential communication, while "suggestibility" refers to the individual differences between those responding to suggestion under comparable circumstances. The conceptual boundaries implied by these familiar terms are a source of some confusion, although in a more general sense they are distinguishable.

The editors and authors of a recent book on suggestion and suggestibility concern themselves with some of the confusion that results from the way these terms are used (Gheorghiu, Netter, Eysenck, & Rosenthal, eds., 1989). The book, a veritable gold mine of information about suggestion and suggestibility, records the proceedings of the First International Symposium on Suggestion and Suggestibility, held at the University of Giessen in the Federal Republic of Germany in 1987.

A preliminary characterization of suggestion

Suggestion is a form of communication that produces a compliant response that differs in its subjective aspects from a deliberate response to a request. The difference is expressed linguistically as that between, "Please, now raise your arm," and, "Raise your arm!" The word "please" invites an appropriate social response which need not be made if you refuse to accept the invitation (i.e., if you indicate, "I do not wish to follow your request"). The shade of difference between the refusal of such an invitation and the failure to accept the direct suggestion is the difference between refusing an invitation and defying a command.

In a military situation the refusal to obey a command might have serious consequences, but the refusal of an invitation might be less serious. This would be clear if the invitation came in the form: "Who wants to be first to try this out?" Not everyone would have to volunteer in order to comply.

The above defining illustrations have been based on verbal forms of direct requests or commands. Yet it is well known that there are many other forms of communication that can be interpreted as suggestions, including "leading questions," now categorized as *interrogative* suggestibility (Gudjonsson, 1989). Then there is the overlap between imitation and suggestion, and other forms of nonverbal suggestion. More remains to be said.

Suggestibility characterized

Suggestibility can be differentiated from suggestion because, as noted above, it refers to individual differences among persons who receive suggestions under essentially similar conditions. As a matter of definition, it need not imply a general trait of suggestibility, for a general definition does not have to specify all the conditions, some of which may or may not be effective for the same individual. The nub of the definition is that "suggestibility" refers to the *effectiveness* of a given kind of suggestion under carefully stated conditions for a given individual. Included here is the context in which the suggestion is given and the demand characteristics that are inherent in the suggestion.

Hypnotic response to suggestions

Hypnosis adds complications of its own. While I find it possible to make the same distinction between a request and a command within testing for hypnotic responsiveness, Weitzenhoffer (1974) objects on the grounds that a highly hypnotizable person will no longer make the distinction. That is, such a person will interpret a simple request as a direct suggestion because of the demand characteristics implied in such a request. Weitzenhoffer misunderstands my point that, even within attempted hypnosis, the response to a request in the form of "please close your eyes" does not distinguish between a hypnotizable and a nonhypnotizable person. The subjective interpretation of a hypnotically more responsive person already hypnotized may differ from that of a less hypnotizable person. The reason is that the highly suggestible hypnotized person, especially if experiencing hypnosis, may interpret a simple suggestion as though it were a command. However, the highly responsive subject when *not* hypnotized would *also* respond like the nonhypnotizable to an invitation to cooperate by accepting an invitation.

There is a complication here because both the less and the more hypnotizable subject will respond to some hypnotic-like suggestions *prior to* an attempted hypnotic induction. In fact, it is of the very nature of a hypnotic induction for the hypnotist to offer suggestions that are responded to in the nonhypnotic condition before the hypnotic condition develops. Also, there is no detectable sharp dividing line to indicate when the response is a nonhypnotic one and when it becomes a hypnotic one. It would be more comfortable for the investigator if there were some precise indicator of the establishment of a hypnotic condition, but so far that has eluded investigators.

A familiar issue concerns the increase in suggestibility as a consequence of an attempted hypnotic induction. It is generally thought that such an increase occurs when the subject is sufficiently capable of becoming hypnotized. Some experiments in the Stanford laboratory indicated that this is the case (Weitzenhoffer & Sjoberg, 1961; Hilgard & Tart, 1966). To continue with the issue of conceptual clarity we must consider what is meant by the suggestibility of the hypnotized person, a point that revolves about individual differences under highly similar conditions of suggestion.

The domain of hypnosis

The best evidence for individual differences comes from the results obtained with scales that yield quantitative measures of hypnotic responsiveness, following standardized induction procedures. Again, considering that we are looking for a definition of individual differences in hypnotic suggestibility, the results of such measurements assist in specifying what I have called *the domain of hypnosis* (Hilgard, 1973).

The kinds of behaviors shown and experiences reported by a hypnotized subject, after an appropriate induction, have been well known for a century at least, some for much longer. Recognizing them as indicative of hypnosis provides an ostensive definition of hypnosis: in general terms, what it is that we are called upon to explain.

Included are the loss of voluntary control and the involuntary production of contractures and anesthesias, the creation of hallucinations, age regression, posthypnotic amnesia, and the posthypnotic performance of acts suggested during hypnosis (but with amnesia for the suggestions). Anyone who has seen a valid demonstration of hypnosis knows something about its domain. This serves as a preliminary form of definition and it does not bias the theoretical interpretation to be given. It is particularly impressive that a great variety of behaviors and experiences can be demonstrated in a single session of hypnosis. This leads to the possibility that they have something in common in the way of an aptitude, acquired skill, or trait of suggestibility.

Because some of these responses to suggestion are given by individuals who do not become hypnotized, a criterion is needed to determine at what level we should speak of reaching the hypnotic condition, or state of hypnosis or trance (or whatever term is favored on the basis of some selected orientation toward hypnosis).

Something further needs to be said about the position taken by Weitzenhoffer in the two-volume work recently published as a capstone to his earlier books and articles on hypnosis, the publication referred to above (Weitzenhoffer, 1989). He has had a long familiarity with the lore of hypnosis, and is widely experienced in it, both in the laboratory and in clinical practice. I owe a great deal to him, because when he joined me I had had scarcely any direct experience with hypnosis. I had only published one article on heterosuggestion and autosuggestion without a prior induction of hypnosis (Berreman & Hilgard, 1936). However, I had long been interested in, and had conducted several seminars on hypnosis at the graduate level. When we constructed the Stanford Hypnotic Susceptibility Scales, I relied heavily upon his experience in designing and writing the items of the scales, just as both of us relied on the earlier scale by Friedlander and Sarbin (1938). I have never belittled his important role, and even though I was director of the laboratory and deeply involved in the writing and testing of the items selected for inclusion in the scales, I insisted that he should be the senior author of the scales (Weitzenhoffer & Hilgard, 1959, 1962, 1967/1963). More hands assisted in the ultimate scale construction and standardization. For example, the *Manual* for the Stanford Profile Scales of Hypnotic Susceptibility was prepared by and published under the authorship of Hilgard, Lauer & Morgan (1963).

Weitzenhoffer in later years (e.g., Weitzenhoffer, 1980), and now in his recent book, launched an attack on the scales that he had such a large part in constructing. Because these scales have been widely used in both English and translated forms, and have served their purposes well, a little digression is needed to clarify the basis of his attack, and to offer some words in defense of the scales.

The major issue is the criterion of hypnosis. Those who have used the scales for their purposes usually adopt the position that there are degrees of hypnotic responsiveness. Furthermore, in order to select subjects for experiments that require that they show a satisfactory amount of responsiveness, some lower limits are commonly set, such as a score of 8 out of 12 items on SHSS:C. Weitzenhoffer finds no fault with this, except that he would prefer the terms "common hypnosis" or "conventional hypnosis" to describe the kind of hypnosis involved. In our work we have often found that an arbitrary range of scores on the simpler scales is not a severe enough requirement. Also, when hypnotic tasks too difficult for subjects arbitrarily classified as highly responsive on the simpler scales are studied, we have turned to high scores on the profile scales that test hypnotic responsiveness well above that of high scores on the simple scales.

Weitzenhoffer has shown the validity of the items that are employed in conventional hypnosis, such as posthypnotically induced behavior, positive hallucinations, suggested anesthesias (negative hallucinations), analgesias, age regression, hypnotically induced amnesia, and other alterations (Weitzenhoffer, 1989, I.251–78).

He is less sanguine about suggested secondary personalities, the hidden observer, and related effects. These include the effects of hypnotic suggestions on learning processes and performance, the transcendence of voluntary acts under hypnosis, and the power of hypnosis to permit the carrying out of antisocial acts (Weitzenhoffer, 1989, I.278–83). It should be noted that the scales include none of these controversial items. About the hidden observer, upon which I have published (e.g., Hilgard, 1986/1977), he takes the dogmatic position that it is all a matter of suggestion, without having taken seriously the studies that have shown that this explanation is inappropriate (e.g., Nogrady, McConkey, Laurence, & Perry, 1983).

Why, then, does he characterize the scales as studies of suggestibility rather than of hypnosis? This is owing to his return to the earlier definition of "artificial somnambulism" of the nineteenth-century hypnotists, for whom the truly hypnotized person invariably showed spontaneous posthypnotic amnesia. In laboratory studies such spontaneous amnesia is very rare (Hilgard & Cooper, 1965). By this criterion, research studies have been dealing only with conventional hypnosis, not "true" hypnosis, even though conventional hypnosis does very well in psychotherapy or other applications of hypnosis.

If one were to insist on limiting hypnosis to those with spontaneous amnesia, the general study or practice of hypnosis would have to be given another name, even though it went on as usual. Weitzenhoffer knows this, of course, and offers such names as *somnambulic hypnosis* for true hypnosis and *conventional* or *nonsomnambulic* hypnosis for the rest. I agree with him that the term "somnambulist" for the high-scoring subject on the hypnotic scales is a misnomer according to the history of the term. To have a term to designate the very high subjects, I have used the term "virtuoso" because those subjects who score very high on the profile scales are about as rare as those who achieve concert-performance level in musical performance skills.

Weitzenhoffer bases his emphasis on somnambulism on the practices of those such as Bertrand (1823), who listed several characteristics of artificial somnambulism, translated as follows by Weitzenhoffer (1989, I.208):

1. Spontaneous post-somnambulic amnesia
2. Spontaneous analgesia
3. Acute sense of timing
4. Hallucinatory activity
5. Improved ability to recall
6. Thought transmission
7. Sight without eyes
8. Control of own physiological processes

9. Ability to prescribe remedies for various illnesses
10. Prophesy with regard to the future course of illnesses
11. Mental inertia (hypersuggestibility, compliance, and inability to initiate acts)
12. Ability to take on the illness of another person, thereby curing the latter

This list may indeed represent some of the beliefs at the time. But in view of the generally gullible beliefs, which oppose our more current critical knowledge, there appears little justification for feeling any assurance that even those items that we generally favor as representative of hypnosis today actually appeared in the pure forms proposed by Bertrand. These include items such as spontaneous postsomnambulic amnesia, spontaneous analgesia, and control over one's own physiological processes. Over-beliefs were characteristic of even such ordinarily good investigators as Binet and Féré (1888), whose published account led Hull to state, after extolling Binet's other contributions: "Even so, the fact remains that there has rarely been written a book containing a greater aggregation of results from wretched experiments, all put forward with loud protestations of impeccable scientific procedure and buttressed by the most transparent sophistries, than this book by Binet and Féré" (Hull, 1933).

I believe it important to be familiar with the ideas of the early investigators, but we can scarcely be guided by their beliefs unless we can substantiate them. Bernheim is a somewhat better model than Bertrand, but it must be remembered that he became increasingly interested in waking hypnosis and psychotherapy. Hypnosis, by its definition including spontaneous amnesia, played little part in either of these. It is doubtful if Liébault, to whom Bernheim deferred, would have been interested in such a definition. He "hypnotized" all of his rural patients as they came to him, many at once, and I doubt if he gave weight to any criteria other than that many of them got well.

This digression has been intended to clarify some differences between my conception of the domain of hypnosis and Weitzenhoffer's preferred definition as somnambulism, a term that I have avoided using in my work. I wish now to return to my effort to delineate the domain of hypnosis or, in agreement with Weitzenhoffer, conventional hypnosis as we know it in the laboratory and clinic.

Unless we narrow the boundaries of what we conceive as belonging to hypnosis by defining it as somnambulistic hypnosis, we face the problem of placing other limits on what belongs within conventional hypnosis. We know that there are many candidates such as highway hypnosis, being hypnotized by political oratory, and self-hypnosis. All of these have to be confronted, as well as some practices that are used in conventional hypnosis if they do not appear to belong.

In order to be more specific about what belongs to hypnosis and what kinds of so-called hypnotic experiences lie outside, we can turn to the information that has come to us from measurements.

The intercorrelations between the responses to the suggestions included in the scales are all positive and, with substantial samples, significant. In the SHSS: Form A, they range from a low of .21 between postural sway (an easily passed waking suggestion measured prior to attempted hypnotic induction) and arm immobilization (the most difficult of the challenge items as measured following attempted induction), to a high of .84 between finger lock and arm rigidity. The latter two are challenge items of moderate and approximately equal difficulty. Also, each of the items correlates with the sum of the items passed, minus the score on the item being studied. These correlations (biserial) ranged from a low of .38 for postural sway to a high of .83 for arm rigidity, with a median value of .66 (Hilgard, 1965). With this much internal consistency the items must be measuring something in common that reflects individual differences in suggestibility following an attempted hypnotic induction. (The fact that an induction has been *attempted* does not mean that the person has become *hypnotized*. That depends on other criteria, and is not the proper interpretation of all positive responses to suggestion that occur during testing, merely because an induction has been attempted.) It has long been my practice to refer to *attempted* induction whenever the hypnotizability of the subject is unknown before the attempt. In repeated inductions, one may indeed refer to the induction as designed to reinstate the hypnotic experience if prior inductions have indicated that the subject meets the criteria of hypnotic responsiveness used for the purpose at hand. The measure is not one of hypnotic depth, but of hypnotic responsiveness under stated conditions. Depth is based on the analogy with sleep (even though hypnosis is no longer conceived as sleep). That is, a person, whether or not suffering from insomnia, might be assigned some measure of sleep proneness without *at any one time* being more or less deeply asleep. Likewise, a highly responsive hypnotic subject does not *at all times* go around at the level of hypnosis which he or she is capable of achieving.

The items in Form A are a limited selection of the possible items, many others of which were added in the later scales—SHSS: Form C and the Stanford Profile Scales of Hypnotic Susceptibility (SPSHS, Forms I and II). All the retained items had similar properties of positive intercorrelations with other items in the various scales, and also significant correlations with the total scores (minus that item) in the scales in which they were embedded.

The face validity of the performances and self-reports of the high subjects has indicated that the common success in becoming hypnotized could be characterized as hypnotic responsiveness or, as named in the Stanford scales, relative susceptibility.

Validation of the effectiveness of suggestion for those selected as highly hypnotizable on measurement scales has been advanced by psychophysiological studies. There is no longer a search for a single sign that will tell us that a person is hypnotized. Too many things happen within hypnosis for this to be a profitable search, at least by presently available methods. However, differences between the high hypnotizables and the low, as they respond to specific suggestions, are proving more rewarding. For example, Crawford (1989) reports a study on regional blood flow as measured by the 133-xenon inhalation method. She and her collaborators found that highly responsive hypnotic subjects demonstrated greater ability than the lows to turn off all cognitive awareness of pain, whether cold pressor or ischemic (tourniquet) pain. In a study of the cortical event-related potentionals (ERPs), Spiegel (1989) found a reduction in P300 when highly hypnotizables experienced "blocking" hallucinations, whether visual or somatosensory. Mészáros, Crawford, Szabó, Nagy-Kovács, and Révész (1989) used a combination of EEG and reaction time measures and asked subjects to state their preferences for imaginal versus verbal stimuli. The highs expressed a preference for imaginal stimuli, while lows expressed a preference for verbal stimuli. The highs also yielded shorter reaction times to imaginal than to verbal stimuli. The predominant preference for imaginal stimuli and the reaction times, as well as the EEG evidence, supported the hypothesis of right-hemisphere involvement.

These and other studies in other chapters indicate that we are much closer to understanding the physiological correlates of high hypnotizability and of the nature of hypnotic involvement in cognitive tasks while hypnotized.

Delimiting the domain of hypnosis

It is possible to move from a general familiarity with hypnotic phenomena to a more precise delimitation of the field.

1. The first point is that hypnotic behavior cannot be defined simply as a response to suggestion. I have already referred to the tie between hypnosis and suggestion made earlier by the Nancy school, and in the

titles of books in this century. A hypnotic scale developed later by Barber (1969) than the Stanford scales was called by him the Barber Suggestibility Scale or BSS. His inclination at the time was to believe that the induction of 'hypnosis' (in quotation marks) did essentially nothing but provide suggestions that could be acted upon equally well without induction. Would it not then follow that all we referred to as hypnosis was encompassed by suggestion and suggestibility? The answer to this question is in the negative. Although hypnotic-like behaviors are commonly responses to suggestion, the domain of suggestion includes responses that do not belong within hypnosis, and the phenomena of hypnosis cover more than specific responses to suggestion.

There are three lines of evidence for excluding some kinds of responses to suggestion from the domain of hypnosis.

First is the distinction made by Hull (1933) between *personal* and *impersonal* heterosuggestion, and clarified by Eysenck and Furneaux (1945) as *primary* and *secondary* suggestibility. These distinctions persisted in Eysenck's recent chapter presented at the above-mentioned symposium on suggestion and suggestibility (Eysenck, 1989). Primary suggestibility is defined by responses in waking suggestion, such as postural sway, that predict the usual phenomena of hypnosis. Secondary suggestibility is defined by such tests as Binet's progressive weights, a form of test that Hull called impersonal heterosuggestion. Later investigators confirmed the distinction through correlation and factor-analytic studies (e.g., Stukat, 1958). This distinction points to one difference between suggestions that bear upon hypnosis and some other kinds of effective suggestions that do not belong.

Second, forms of social suggestibility described by such names as conformity and gullibility are not correlated with hypnotic-like behaviors (Burns & Hammer, 1970; Moore, 1964).

Third, studies of the effectiveness of placebos have shown that whatever makes one person more vulnerable to the indirect suggestions involved in a placebo is not the same as hypnotic responsiveness (McGlashan, Evans, & Orne, 1969; Evans, 1989). A valuable aid to later studies has been Gheorghiu's concept of sensory suggestion as measured according to his experimentally devised scale (e.g., Gheorghiu, Hodapp, & Ludwig, 1975), also offered in both a direct and indirect form (Gheorghiu & Kiel, 1976). Netter has carried out a number of experiments that show that Evans's findings may have been overgeneralized. When care is taken to do placebo studies in which the placebo effect is studied with careful reference to the modality of the sensory experiences involved, there may indeed be a relation to the response to sensory suggestion (e.g., Netter, 1986, 1989).

By accepting that the various manifestations of primary suggestibility lie within the hypnotic domain, we may assert that the other responses to suggestion, as described above, lie *outside* the domain. This supports the position that it is not enough to define hypnosis as a response to suggestion, without being more specific.

2. A second point in defining the domain of hypnosis is the persistence of individual differences in whatever underlies primary suggestibility. The most pertinent evidence comes from a longitudinal study in which the same fifty subjects were tested on SHSS:A, first while they were undergraduate students, a second time after a period of 10 years, and a third time after a lapse of another 15 years. This represents a comparison of repetition of the testing over a 25-year period, with all the life changes to be expected between college years and middle life (Piccione, Hilgard, & Zimbardo, 1989). The resulting correlations were positive and high enough to resemble results in longitudinal studies of measured intelligence, and higher than those in studies of repeated personality measures. The actual scores at the end in most cases fell within 1 or 2 points on the 12-item SHSS:A scale.

Another line of evidence comes from a twin study from the Stanford laboratory in which there is a strong indication of a hereditary component to individual differences in hypnotizability. This is indicated by the substantial correlation of the scores of monozygotic (identical) twins as compared with dizygotic twins or ordinary siblings, yielding a heritability index (h^2) of .62, highly significant (Morgan, 1973). A corresponding study in Australia led to similar conclusions (Rawlings, 1972). Such a finding does not mean that hypnotizability is immutable, any more than the studies on the hereditary nature of intelligence mean that there is no environmental effect. (For a recent discussion of hereditary and environmental effects in intelligence and personality, see Loehlin, 1989.)

3. A third point relating to the domain of hypnosis concerns the subjective reports of the reality of the experiences that take place during measurement. They tend to give phenomenological support to the objective scores, even if some of the objective reports require correction on the basis of the subjective reports. Numerous studies have indicated that the obtained 'objective' reports correlate highly with scores 'corrected' by the subjective reports. When subjective reports were included in a testing with SHSS:A, the correlation with the more advanced Profile Scale scores rose only from .73 to .76 (Ruch, Morgan, & Hilgard, 1974).

Thus we can find a coherent way to define the domain of hypnosis with the assistance of standardized scales. Individual differences, as so measured, are remarkably stable amid the life changes in the normal environment. This is especially true when no special methods are used to alter them. The findings leave two major questions unanswered:

A. What are the correlates of hypnotizability that help to explain the individual differences?

B. Under what circumstances can significant changes in hypnotizability come about?

A complete answer to these questions, acceptable to all, has not yet been achieved. But there are signs of progress that are being followed with interest.

The correlates of hypnotizability

In answer to the first question, the best evidence that we have arose in connection with a careful interview program by Josephine Hilgard and her associates conducted by them on the basis of before-and-after attempted hypnotic induction (Hilgard, 1979/1970). She showed statistically significant relationships between a number of kinds of imaginative involvement, often starting in childhood, that were mildly predictive of hypnotic responsiveness in the early adult years. These included such types of involvement as the reading of fiction, drama (whether in acting or watching of plays), affective arousal through sensory stimulation (as in music), religious commitments, imagery, imagination and creative experiences, reported imaginary companions, and adventuresomeness in some forms.

Based in part on interview findings, Tellegen and Atkinson (1974) developed a pencil-and-paper inventory with questions similar in format to those on the Minnesota Multiphasic Personality Inventory (MMPI). However, they stressed what they called absorption, defined as "total" attention that fully engaged the individual's representational resources. The result is a heightened sense of the attentional object, imperviousness to distracting events, and an altered sense of reality in general. This expresses very well what Josephine Hilgard had called imaginative involvement. They tested their scale against a modified form of the Harvard Group Scale of Hypnotic Susceptibilty (HGSHS:A; Shor & Orne, 1962), a scale based originally on the items of SHSS:A, and also against shortened forms of the MMPI that were based on the two factors of the MMPI, namely Stability-Instability, and Introversion-Extroversion. The results, cross-validated by using regression weights from a subsample, showed a moderate but significant positive correlation of .43 between absorption and the hypnotizability scores. But nothing of significance was found between hypnotizability and the two subscales of the MMPI (correlations of −.02 and −.18). Because of these findings, Tellegen and Atkinson concluded that "continued study of this trait should prove useful for the study of both personality and hypnosis." Another way of reading their findings is that they show why previous efforts to find correlations between familiar personality measures and hypnosis had failed. It was because those constructing personality inventories had not thought to devise questions bearing on the trait of absorption, so central to hypnotizability.

The prominence of posthypnotic amnesia suggests another possible "trait" important in hypnosis (in a sense the opposite of absorption), and that is the capacity to make the mind blank. This was studied in some unpublished but provocative work of Charles Tart while in the Stanford laboratory. A later, factor analytic investigation hinted that amnesia had a special role, possibly related to this ability (Hilgard, Sheehan, Monteiro, & Macdonald, 1981). The experimental evidence is not strong, but there appears to be an opportunity for research. Something other than imaginative involvement or absorption is needed to increase the correlations between related personal characteristics and hypnotic responsiveness.

How modifiable is hypnotizability?

The second question raised earlier had to do with the modification of hypnotizability when special efforts were made to alter hypnotic potential. There have been many attempts to study this, and some controversies have resulted, as in the case of intelligence measurement. Most of the earlier reviews of the evidence showed that slight modifications were possible. But even after careful attempts, with moderate success, it usually turned out that there was a high correlation between early measurements and those after efforts to modify (Perry, 1977). More recently, dramatic improvements have been reported by Spanos and his associates. However, before their results can be widely accepted, they require careful study by others. There must be adequate controls for the demand characteristics in their cognitive skill training procedures. These appear to encourage the subject to substitute voluntary action for the automatisms conventionally associated with hypnosis. Any prominence to be given to the role of compliance is, of course, denied by him (Spanos, 1989).

The domain of hypnosis has been specified by showing (a) that it commonly involves suggestion, but not all kinds of suggestion; (b) that the behaviors and experiences studied reflect individual differences that we are just beginning to understand; and (c) that the subjective reports, correlating significantly with objective behavior, can at the same time produce correctives to measures based on objective performance alone, and enrich our knowledge of the hypnotic experience.

Self-Hypnosis

While conventional hypnosis usually implies a hypnotist who gives the suggestions and a subject or patient who receives and acts upon them, strange as it may seem at first, a person can hypnotize herself or himself. It is not actually so strange if one considers the mental processes that go on when making up one's mind in different circumstances. After retiring, thoughts of the day sometimes seem to postpone going to sleep until you tell yourself it is now time to forget these thoughts and go to sleep. Even the old device of counting sheep is a self-imposed instruction to do something to inhibit other thoughts and to allow sleep to overtake you. In ordinary wakeful existence there are choices to make, often resolved by talking to oneself about what the alternatives might lead to. In other words, a pseudo-dyadic relation of speaker and listener is not so foreign to ordinary experience.

Self-hypnosis usually is more successful after some experience of heterohypnosis, because such experience helps to indicate what you might expect in the way of your own experiences in hypnosis, however induced. Also, the experience provides a model induction procedure that was successful for you when someone else used it with you. Now you can recall what was said, or even imagine the original hypnotist's voice while you repeat the suggestions for yourself. The division of control systems continues within hypnosis so that, whenever you wish, you can arouse yourself from hypnosis by using the same ceremony that was used by your hypnotist. I have found it wise, in assisting a subject to learn self-hypnosis, to have a practice session in my presence, with the instruction: "Just hypnotize yourself by taking the role of hypnotist toward yourself. Then, when you feel that you are in the hypnotic condition, give yourself some suggestions, whatever you wish, similar to those that I gave you. Then cancel the specific suggestions and test yourself to see that each is no longer operative, and your controls of movement and perception are normal. When you feel that you have satisfied your curiosity about hypnotizing yourself, return to your normal state of awareness arousing yourself from hypnosis in the manner that you experienced it with me. Let me know when your self-hypnosis practice is over."

My reasoning is fairly obvious. In most cases, I will have been the previous hypnotist. If some other person did the prior hypnotizing, I adjust the instructions accordingly, so that the self-hypnosis will reflect the previous experience. Note that self-hypnosis is very seldom more successful than heterohypnosis. By getting practice in a short session of entering hypnosis by oneself, and then terminating it, the subject's fears of not being able to terminate are overcome. The subsequent discussion can clear up any questions. Detailed discussion of techniques of self-hypnosis can be found in Weitzenhoffer (1957, 1989).

On the experimental side, to determine how self-hypnosis fits into the general domain of hypnosis, two investigations may be mentioned. The first of these was performed in the Stanford laboratory and reported by Ruch (1975). He showed, for example, that a subject never exposed to heterohypnosis, but given the barest of instructions on how to proceed, may yield the usual responses to suggestion. This is provided that subsequent testing confirms that he or she responds to heterohypnosis. Such a result brings self-hypnosis within the domain of hypnosis as I have defined it. A larger series of experiments by Fromm, et al. (1981) examine how successful self-hypnosis can be after considerable practice, following an introduction to heterohypnosis through testing on the Stanford scales.

Suggestibility independent of hypnotic context

The kinds of suggestions used in hypnosis ("Your arm is rising", "You can't open your eyes") may be effective in producing the enactment of the suggestions even though there has been no prior attempt to induce hypnosis. The result is not surprising because, as noted earlier, similar suggestions are used in the effort to induce hypnosis, as in the arm-levitation and eye-closure types of induction. A suggestion without a deliberate attempt to induce hypnosis cannot necessarily be a suggestion *without* hypnosis. In other words, the hypnotic induction ceremony itself has very uncertain boundaries.

It is possible, however, to obtain positive responses to suggestion even when the subject is instructed to *resist* becoming hypnotized. (This is the other side of self-hypnosis. Instead of seeking to assist in producing hypnosis, the subject gives himself or herself self-suggestions to resist becoming hypnotized, while the heterosuggestions are permitted to remain effective at a nonhypnotic level.) There are interesting questions here concerning the degree of automaticity to be expected by contrast to voluntary acquiescence. But the answers are not easy, and I will not go into them at this point.

A continuing program in the study of the nature of suggestion and suggestibility, often independent of hypnosis, was undertaken by Vladimir Gheorghiu while still in Romania, with publications as early as 1966 in both his native language and in English (Gheorghiu, 1966; Gheorghiu, Meiu, Onofrei, & Timofte, 1966). He continued, despite the necessity of overcoming many political difficulties at home, with a move to West Germany, where he was welcomed on his record as a research scholar, aided also since he had taken his Ph.D. there. He has continued the program that he initiated and has had a number of associates join him in his work at the University of Giessen. We also owe to Gheorghiu and his associates the most careful and extensive studies of suggestibility independent of the hypnotic context. He has recently provided a major review of the history of research on suggestibility (Gheorghiu, 1989a). He calls our attention to the serious work of some American psychologists in the 1890s, three at Yale University (Gilbert, 1894; Scripture, 1893; Seashore, 1895), and one Harvard-trained (Sidis, 1898). He gives credit to Binet in France, who first took seriously the question of several kinds of suggestibility (Binet, 1900). Gheorghiu of course brought his historical references up to date.

Gheorghiu (1989b) comments critically that there have been many inadequate test procedures. He also regards the distinction between direct and indirect suggestion, and the further distinction between primary and secondary suggestion, as too sweeping. He states that insufficient attention is given to the specific features of the procedures employed. Gheorghiu also observes, for example, that *direct* suggestibility tends to be largely verbal and to be used in connection with motor tests (body sway, Chevreul pendulum), while *indirect* suggestion is assigned to sensory and perceptual procedures (inkblots, the heat illusion). In fact, both sensory and motor tests can be influenced by direct and indirect suggestions.

Furthermore, there has been too little attention to contextual features. Subjects serving in an experiment are exposed to strange tasks. They face a problem-solving situation in which they typically try to find out what is actually being investigated, and any attempts at deception may have other consequences than those intended. The coping function is one of the topics that Gheorghiu has studied extensively (Gheorghiu, 1982), along with other motivational implications of responses to suggestion.

Gheorghiu (1989b) also faces the conceptual problems of defining and explaining suggestion. He lays out a program that would ultimately clarify these problems, continuing the efforts that he has made in research studies and his book-length treatments (e.g., Gheorghiu & Coifu, 1982; Gheorghiu, 1987).

He points out that suggestion always makes demands on the subject by guiding the behavior in a specific direction, but there is no guarantee that the subject will comply, since alternatives are always open. It would no longer be a suggestion situation if constraints were imposed so that there was no freedom of action. This appears to be somewhat paradoxical, for when the suggestion prevails the person may not realize while responding that other possible actions had been eliminated.

Because of the compulsive quality of some reactions to suggestion, it is sometimes said that the response is, by definition, irrational because it is made involuntarily and uncritically. Gheorghiu points out that rational mechanisms are not the basis of suggestion processes, but they definitely can be one basis for their influence, as in persuasive communications by a clever salesman.

Gheorghiu's (1989a, b) efforts to keep in focus the versatility and complexity of suggestion processes leads him to present a schema, which I present, if incompletely, in an outline along the following lines.

I. *The Content of Suggestion: Effects Which Can be Caused*
   A. Psychic events which are:
      (a) Evoked or annulled
      (b) Accentuated or diminished
      (c) Conserved or distorted
   B. Specific substitutional processes in (a), (b), and (c)

II. *The Form of Suggestion: Carrying the Content*
   A. Sources of the Demand Situation
      (a) Intraindividual (Self-suggestion)
      (b) Interindividual (Heterosuggestion)
      (c) Extraindividual (Influence of physical or social environment)
   B. Contexts in which Suggestive Directedness Occurs
      (a) Contexts of analogy
      (b) Contexts of cues
      (c) Model contexts
      (d) Involvement contexts
      (e) Challenge contexts
      (f) Other contexts?

III. *The Mode of Suggestion: The Concrete Means by Which Suggestive Contents are Conveyed*
   A. Aspects of mode
      (a) Spontaneously or deliberately produced

(b) Verbal or nonverbal
(c) Gentle or shock-like
(d) Exerts momentary or long-lasting effects
(e) Effects in peripheral or central mechanisms

IV. *The Need for Integrative Theories*

While this outline is necessarily sketchy as a portrayal of Gheorghiu's efforts at a tighter conceptualization, he has certainly made a good start in the direction that he sees is much needed.

Concluding remarks

Suggestion generates more controversy than the verified knowledge about the forms of suggestion and its effects justify. The controversies often exist in the relation between suggestion and hypnotic phenomena. It has been necessary, therefore, to clarify the rather obvious distinction between *suggestion* as a form of communication designed to elicit a compliant response, and *suggestibility* as implying that there are more or less persistent individual differences in the degree to which suggestions will be responded to under similar circumstances by the persons receiving the suggestions. There are different varieties of suggestion, so that any generalization from one test of suggestion may be misleading. Still, such matters are of the kind that a scientific psychology should settle by investigation.

Similarly, for hypnosis, there are many kinds of attempted induction. Their results also differ within a population of those exposed to hypnotic interactions. Hence hypnotizability becomes a controversial term similar, in that respect, to suggestion and suggestibility.

There are various sources of controversy. Some are merely a matter of what words to use, and, if the choice is merely a matter of preference, they can be used interchangeably. Such is the case between "hypnosis" and "hypnotism". Then there are problems with the criteria to be used to set the boundaries between hypnotic and nonhypnotic effects when precision is desired. I have favored an empirical approach to the problem of the domain of hypnosis. The intention is to set criteria for behavior and experiences that belong to this domain, and also to determine the boundaries for exclusion. It should be possible to achieve agreement on these matters, but it has not been attained. The only advice is to be as sensible as possible under the circumstances while being tolerant of those who disagree.

References

Barber, T.X. (1969). *Hypnosis: A scientific approach.* New York: Van Nostrand Reinhold.

Bernheim, H. (1910). *Hypnotisme et suggestion.* Paris: Doin & Fils.

Bernheim, H. (1963). *Hypnosis and suggestion in psychotherapy.* Reprinted, New Hyde Park, NY: University Books. (English translation published 1888.)

Berreman, J., & Hilgard, E.R. (1936). The effects of personal heterosuggestion upon postural movement. *Journal of Social Psychology, 7,* 289–300.

Bertrand, A. (1823). *Traité du somnambulisme.* Paris: Dentu.

Binet, A. (1900). *La suggestibilité.* Paris: Schleicher Frères.

Binet, A., & Féré, D. (1888). *Animal magnetism.* (Original in French, 1886.)

Burns, A., & Hammer, G. (1970). Hypnotizability and amenability to social influence. Paper presented at the meeting of the Society for Clinical and Experimental Hypnosis. Philadelphia, October–November.

Evans, F.J. (1989). The independence of suggestibility, placebo response, and hypnotizability. In V.A. Gheorghiu, P. Netter, H.J. Eysenck, & R. Rosenthal (eds.), *Suggestion and suggestibility: Theory and research* (pp. 145–54). Berlin Heidelberg: Springer-Verlag.

Eysenck, H.J. (1989). Personality, primary and secondary suggestibility, and hypnosis. In V.A. Gheorghiu, P. Netter, H.J. Eysenck, & R. Rosenthal (eds.), *Suggestion and suggestibility: Theory and research* (pp. 57–67). Berlin Heidelberg: Springer-Verlag.

Eysenck, H.J., & Furneaux, W.D. (1945). Primary and secondary suggestibility: An experimental and statistical study. *Journal of Experimental Psychology, 35,* 485–503.

Friedlander, J.W., & Sarbin, T.R. (1938). The depth of hypnosis. *Journal of Abnormal and Social Psychology, 33,* 453–75.

Fromm, E., Brown, D.P., Hurt, S.W., Oberlander, J.Z., Boxer, A.M., & Pfeifer, G. (1981). The phenomena and characteristics of self-hypnosis. *International Journal of Clinical and Experimental Hypnosis, 29,* 189–245.

Gheorghiu, V.A. (1966). Probleme metodologice ale cercetarii sugestici si sugestibilitatii. *Revista de psihologie, 12,* 377–83.

Gheorghiu, V.A. (1982). Aspecte psihologie ale sugestici si sugestibilitatii. In V.A. Gheorghiu & I. Ciofu. *Sugesti si sugestibilitate: Aspecte psihologice si psiofiziologice.* Bucharest: Editura Academiei, 11–148.

Gheorghiu, V.A. (1987). *Sugestia.* Warzawa: Wiedza Powszechna.

Gheorghiu, V.A. (1989a). The development of research on suggestibility: Critical considerations. In V.A. Gheorghiu, P. Netter, H.J. Eysenck, & R. Rosenthal (eds.), *Suggestion and suggestibility: Theory and research* (pp. 3–55). Berlin Heidelberg: Springer-Verlag.

Gheorghiu, V.A. (1989b). The difficulty of explaining suggestion: Some conceivable solutions. In V.A. Gheorghiu, P. Netter, H.J. Eysenck, & R. Rosenthal (eds.), *Suggestion and suggestibility: Theory and research* (pp. 99–112). Berlin Heidelberg: Springer-Verlag.

Gheorghiu, V.A., & Ciofu, I. (1982). *Sugesti si sugestibilitate: Aspecti psihologice si psihofiziologice.* Bucharest: Editura Academiei.

Gheorghiu, V.A., Hodapp., V., & Ludwig, C.M. (1975). Attempts to construct a scale for the measurement of the effect of suggestion on perception. *Educational and Psychological Measurement, 35,* 341–52.

Gheorghiu, V.A., & Kiel, M. (1976). Indirekte und indirekt-direkte Form einer sensorischen Suggestibilitätsskala. *Revue Roumaine des Sciences Sociales* (Série de Psychologie), *20,* 29–46.

Gheorghiu, V.A., Meiu, G., Onofrei, A., & Timofte, G. (1966). Experimental investigation on suggestibility: Effects of direct and indirect suggestions. *Revue Roumaine des Sciences Sociales* (Série de Psychologie), *10,* 163–74.

Gheorghiu, V.A., Netter, P., Eysenck, H.J., & Rosenthal, R., eds. (1989). *Suggestion and suggestibility: Theory and research.* Berlin Heidelberg: Springer-Verlag.

Gilbert, J.A. (1894). Research on the mental and physical development of school children. *Studies from the Yale Psychological Laboratory, 2,* 40–100.

Gudjonsson, G.H. (1989). Theoretical and empirical aspects of interrogative suggestibility. In V.A. Gheorghiu, P. Netter, H.J. Eysenck, & R. Rosenthal (eds.), *Suggestion and suggestibility: Theory and research* (pp. 135–43). Berlin Heidelberg: Springer-Verlag.

Hilgard, E.R. (1965). *Hypnotic susceptibility.* New York: Harcourt, Brace and World.

Hilgard, E. R. (1973). The domain of hypnosis, with some comments on alternative paradigms. *American Psychologist, 28,* 972–82.

Hilgard, E.R. (1986/1977). *Divided consciousness: Multiple controls in human thought and action.* New York: Wiley.

Hilgard, E.R., & Cooper, L.M. (1965). Spontaneous and suggested posthypnotic amnesia. *International Journal of Clinical and Experimental Hypnosis, 13,* 261–73.

Hilgard, E.R., Lauer, L.W., & Morgan, A.H. (1963). *Manual for the Profile Scales of Susceptibility.* Palo Alto, CA: Consulting Psychologists Press.

Hilgard, E.R., Sheehan, P.W., Monteiro, K.P., & Macdonald, H. (1981). Factorial structure of the Creative Imagination Scale as a measure of hypnotic responsiveness: An international comparative study. *International Journal of Clinical and Experimental Hypnosis, 29,* 66–76.

Hilgard, E.R., & Tart, C. (1966). Responsiveness to suggestions following waking and imagination instructions and following induction of hypnosis. *Journal of Abnormal Psychology, 71,* 196–208.

Hilgard, J.R. (1979/1970). *Personality and hypnosis: A study of imaginative involvement.* Chicago: University of Chicago Press.

Hull, C.L. (1933). *Hypnosis and suggestibility.* New York: Appleton-Century. (Paper edition, with Foreword by E.R. Hilgard. New York: Appleton-Century-Crofts, 1968.)

Loehlin, J.C. (1989). Partitioning environmental and genetic contributions to behavioral development. *American Psychologist, 44,* 1285–92.

McGlashan, T.H., Evans, F.J., & Orne, M.T. (1969). The nature of hypnotic analgesia and placebo response to experimental pain. *Psychosomatic Medicine, 31,* 227–46.

Mészáros, I., Crawford, H.J., Szabó, C., Nagy-Kovács, A., & Révész, Z. (1989). Hypnotic susceptibility and cerebral hemisphere preponderance: Verbal-imaginal discrimination task. In V.A. Gheorghiu, P. Netter, H.J. Eysenck, & R. Rosenthal (eds.), *Suggestion and suggestibility: Theory and research* (pp. 191–203). Berlin: Springer-Verlag.

Moore, R.K. (1964). Susceptibility to hypnosis and susceptibility to social influence. *Journal of Abnormal and Social Psychology, 68,* 282–94.

Morgan, A.H. (1973). The heritability of hypnotic susceptibility in twins. *Journal of Abnormal Psychology, 82,* 55–61.

Netter, P. (1986). Systematik der am Placeboeffect beteiligten Faktoren und Beispiele für ihre statisteschen Wirkungen und Wechselwirkungen. In H. Hippius (ed.), *Das Placebo-Problem* (pp. 61–75). Stuttgart: Fischer.

Netter, P. (1989). Sensory suggestibilty: Measurement, individual differences, and relation to placebo and drug effects. In V.A. Gheorghiu, P. Netter, H.J. Eysenck, & R. Rosenthal (eds.), *Suggestion and suggestibility: Theory and research* (pp. 123–33). Berlin Heidelberg: Springer-Verlag.

Nogrady, H., McConkey, K.M., Laurence, J.R., & Perry, C. (1983). Dissociation, duality, and demand characteristics in hypnosis. *Journal of Abnormal Psychology, 92,* 223–35.

Perry, C. (1977). Is hypnotizability modifiable? *International Journal of Clinical and Experimental Hypnosis, 25,* 125–46.

Piccione, C., Hilgard, E.R., & Zimbardo, P.G. (1989). On the degree of stability of measured hypnotizability over a 25-year period. *Journal of Personality and Social Psychology, 56,* 289–95.

Rawlings, R.M. (1972). The inheritance of hypnotic amnesia. Paper presented at the 44th Congress of the Australian and New Zealand Society for the Advancement of Science, Sydney, Australia.

Ruch, J.C. (1975). Self-hypnosis: The result of heterohypnosis or vice versa? *International Journal of Clinical and Experimental Hypnosis, 23,* 282–304.

Ruch, J.C., Morgan, A.H., & Hilgard, E.R. (1974). Measuring hypnotic responsiveness: A comparison of the Barber Suggestibility Scale and the Stanford Hypnotic Susceptibility Scale, Form A. *International Journal of Clinical and Experimental Hypnosis, 22,* 365–76.

Scripture, E.W. (1893). Tests on school children. *Educational Review, 5,* 52–61.

Seashore, C.E. (1895). Measurement of illusions and hallucinations in normal life. *Studies from the Yale Psychological Laboratory, 2,* 1–67.

Shor, R.E., & Orne, E.C. (1962). *Harvard Group Scale of Hypnotic Susceptibility.* Palo Alto, CA: Consulting Psychologists Press.

Sidis, B. (1898). *The psychology of suggestion.* New York: Appleton.

Spanos, N.P. (1989). Interpretational sets, hypnotic responding, and the modification of hypnotizability. In V.A. Gheorghiu, P. Netter, H.J. Eysenck, & R. Rosenthal (eds.), *Suggestion and suggestibility: Theory and research* (pp. 169–75). Berlin Heidelberg: Springer-Verlag.

Stukat, K.G. (1958). *Suggestibility: A factorial and experimental analysis.* Stockholm: Almqvist and Wiksell.

Tellegen, A., & Atkinson, G. (1974). Openness to absorbing and self-altering experiences ("absorption"), a trait related to hypnotic susceptibility. *Journal of Abnormal Psychology, 82,* 268–77.

Weitzenhoffer, A.M. (1953). *Hypnotism: An objective study of suggestibility.* New York: Wiley.

Weitzenhoffer, A.M. (1957). *General techniques of hypnotism.* New York: Grune and Stratton.

Weitzenhoffer, A.M. (1974). When is an "instruction" an "instruction?" *International Journal of Clinical and Experimental Hypnosis, 22,* 258–69.

Weitzenhoffer, A.M. (1980). Hypnotic susceptibility revisited. *American Journal of Clinical Hypnosis, 22,* 130–46.

Weitzenhoffer, A.M. (1989). *The practice of hypnotism.* (2 vols). New York: Wiley.

Weitzenhoffer, A.M., & Hilgard, E.R. (1959). *Stanford Hypnotic Susceptibility Scale, Forms A and B.* Palo Alto, CA: Consulting Psychologists Press.

Weitzenhoffer, A.M., & Hilgard, E.R. (1962). *Stanford Hypnotic Susceptibility Scale, Form C.* Palo Alto, CA: Consulting Psychologists Press.

Weitzenhoffer, A.M., & Hilgard, E.R. (1967/1963). *Revised Stanford Profile Scales of Hypnotic Susceptibility, Forms I and II* (with revised standardization data). Palo Alto, CA: Consulting Psychologists Press.

Weitzenhoffer, A.M., & Sjoberg, B.M. (1961). Suggestibility with and without "induction of hypnosis." *Journal of Nervous and Mental Disease, 132,* 204–20.

2

THE PSYCHOLOGY OF SUGGESTION: An Integrative Perspective

Vladimir Gheorghiu and Peter Kruse

Suggestion research is a typical example of the way integrative approaches have been abandoned in modern psychology. The investigation of suggestive influences was a central topic when scientific psychology was young and when integrative thinking was common. Nearly every important psychologist in those earlier days dealt with this subject and made useful contributions to our understanding of the suggestion process (Binet, 1900; Bernheim, 1888; Freud, 1963/1940; James, 1896; Janet, 1889, 1919; McDougall, 1908; Pavlov, 1953; Sidis, 1898; Wundt, 1892). But in the climate of increasing specialization since that time, the topic has taken a backseat to other emerging subdivisions of psychology. In fact, the study of suggestion has been limited largely to the field of learning (Hull, 1933), differential psychology (Allport, 1961; Eysenck, 1947; Stukat, 1958), social psychology (Asch, 1952; Coffin, 1941; Katz, 1951; McGuire, 1968, 1985; Newcomb, 1950; Sherif, 1935), and clinical psychology (Kretschmer 1963; Stokvis & Pflanz, 1961). If we exclude the field of hypnosis, suggestion has not yet become a truly independent domain of psychological research. With few exceptions, psychological studies make no reference to the important theoretical and empirical advances in this area.

Nevertheless, it is not difficult to find numerous psychological phenomena that could be discussed in close connection with suggestion and suggestibility. But they are usually analyzed using different terminology and different frames of reference. Some of these are: imitative behavior and social contagion, conformity and compliance, changes of attitude, phenomena of bias, processes of expectancy formation, defense mechanisms, and so forth. In addition to the fact that suggestion has been widely neglected by research, the concept of suggestion has also been systematically misused by pseudoscientists. It has therefore gained a reputation that has been detrimental to the promotion of scientific efforts in this area. As a consequence, problems and phenomena related to suggestion and suggestibility have been greatly underrepresented in the last several decades. In fact, suggestion has often been evaluated as marginal or even bizarre.

But, fortunately, times are changing. Increasingly, discussion is turning to the effects of suggestion, and to practical applications in clinical work, forensic psychology, education, and sports. There is much talk about the influence of suggestion in advertising and politics, suggestion and suggestibility in a hypnotic and a normal waking state, suggestion and the placebo effect, suggestion as a research method, suggestion as an explanation for various processes of "substitution," suggestion as self-fulfilling prophecy, and so forth. In recent years, national and international congresses and symposia have seen lively discussions on all aspects of suggestion. This book, as well as the congress volume of the First International Symposium of Suggestion and Suggestibility in Giessen (Gheorghiu, Netter, Eysenck, & Rosenthal, 1989), give some representative examples of this encouraging development.

The multitude of individual empirical results and controversial theoretical explanations is in contrast to the growing conviction that suggestive phenomena are by no means mere curiosities, but rather the basis for a paradigmatical field of psychological research. But our current need for integrative approaches concerning the understanding of cognitive processes leads psychology back to the topics of its beginnings.

Suggestion as a general cognitive strategy

To use a more general perspective seems to be the only way to evaluate the real psychological relevance of suggestion phenomena. The starting point of the following argument will be the assumption that the world we live in is basically ambiguous, and also that the process of individual experience and action is a continuous one of conscious or subconscious disambiguation. One of the main cognitive strategies we use to perform this disambiguation is suggestion.

Ambiguity and instability

In perception everything seems to be unambiguous and stable. Our world is usually experienced as being the trivial consequence of an unambiguous and stable reality we simply copy by the help of our sense organs. But, as demonstrated by research in Gestalt-psychology, our perceptual world is largely a product of a process of autonomous order formation, rather than a mere representation. What we see, hear, or feel depends on the activity of cognitive principles of order formation which themselves are usually not experienced. For example, in the case of visual perception, any stimulus situation except a completely homogeneous field can be regarded as ambiguous. The discrimination of figure and ground, as well as the boundary function of discontinuity or contour, is always a performance of the perceiver, and not an inherent property of the stimulus. Gestalt principles, like the law of proximity, the law of good continuation, or simply the dominance of symmetry, decide what is seen. The basic process of actual genetic object constitution is far too quick to be consciously realized.

In multistable patterns like the Necker cube, Rubin's "vase/faces" figure, or Boring's "young wife/mother-in-law" figure, different stable percepts coexist on the basis of one unchanged stimulus situation. The different percepts change continuously during prolonged observation. At any one time, only one version is experienced and the alternation process itself cannot be consciously analyzed because of its speed. Change comes about voluntarily (e.g., by the help of eye movements, or refocusing of attention), or spontaneously as the result of an underlying physiological adaptation. The active disambiguation which can be demonstrated by multistable patterns is not an exception constructed by some sophisticated psychologists or by artists like M.C. Escher or Salvador Dali; instead, it is a basic characteristic of perception in general. One can claim that, in a way, any stimulus situation is multistable and that, therefore, any perception is a process of disambiguation (see Kruse, 1988).

What holds true for perception has to be suggested even more for cognitive functions which are less determined by the given situation. In most situations in everyday life we must decide what to do, how to make sense of what we experience, or how to attach value to what we are confronted with on the basis of inadequate or ambiguous information. And even when situations seem to be clear, ambiguity may be inside of us. This is the case, for example, in conflicts where we are confronted with alternatives which are equally attractive or unattractive.

The principal relevance of situational ambiguity and personal instability is also a central starting point of the integrative stress-theory developed by Lazarus and Folkman (1984). The authors hint that, in most situations, the information given is not sufficient to allow definite appraisals or to make clear behavioral decisions. Novelty, event uncertainty, and the question of "whether" (imminence), "when" (temporal uncertainty), and "how long" (duration) an event will occur are necessarily attributed to nearly any situation (see also Kahneman, Slovic, & Tversky, 1982). Lazarus and Folkman differentiate between ambiguity and resulting uncertainty, and also between lack of situational clarity and a person's confusion about the meaning of the environmental configuration. They postulate a close connection between this uncertainty or individual instability and stress, and conclude that the anxiety caused by individual instability elicits a basic coping strategy of cognitive stabilization.

There is a striking discrepancy between the suggested generality of situational ambiguity and the fact that individual instability is seldom experienced. In a manner parallel to the process of perception, the ambiguity of everyday situations is not accompanied by a corresponding amount of realized instability. Concerning individual experience, instability is and—in view of the affordances of survival—has to be an exceptional case. In perception, stimulus ambiguity is solved by a very efficient process of autonomous order formation of which we are not necessarily aware. Consequently, one can assume that, in complex situations of everyday life, cognitive strategies operate to achieve disambiguation.

It is one of the main tasks of the individual to reduce the situational or psychic degrees of freedom (i.e., to solve the contradiction between the multitude of possibilities and the necessity to permit only one alternative). Otherwise, the individual would not be able to act. One can assume that at least three different strategies are used to solve that problem:

1. *reflex mechanisms,* such as rule-driven behavioral patterns in which alternative solutions are nearly quite excluded: on the basis of this strategy, the behavioral decision seems to be exclusive and conclusive;
2. *suggestive mechanisms,* which attribute the existence of unambiguity in the presence of possible (but most of the time not consciously realized) alternatives: the behavioral decision gains the character of an "as if" exclusiveness; and
3. *rational mechanisms,* with which a clear decision comes about by turning the alternatives over in one's mind: in this context, the behavioral decision can be regarded as a situation of more or less conscious problem-solving.

Naturally the three basic strategies are not as clearly separable as suggested by this categorization. Combinations or intermediate forms of these strategies are usually used to clear up the situational ambiguity or to solve the individual instability. Behavioral decisions which lie under some prejudices seem to belong to the strategy of suggestion, but such decisions tend to act more like a reflex mechanism. Prejudices usually allow only a limited latitude for alternative behaviors.

Sometimes suggestive influences are part of rational decisions (e.g., what is plausible seems to be right).

If one looks closely at the special conditions of human life, the outstanding significance of the strategy of suggestion becomes evident. We have nearly no rigid rule-driven behavioral patterns, and we usually live in environments of tremendous social and material complexity. Rational strategies are typically not fast enough to compensate for a lack of reflex mechanisms and to guarantee an adequate disambiguation and stabilization. Sometimes rational strategies produce a sort of "blocking up" of behavior. Suggestive mechanisms seem to fill the gap. In ambiguous situations and in the case of individual instability, suggestion leads to a direct reduction of degrees of freedom without wasting conscious intellectual capacity in the disambiguation process. In this view, suggestion is a ubiquitous but—because of its nature—seldom realized part of human behavior. Furthermore, it is by no means a marginal aspect of cognitive activity. Suggestion is normal and necessary (see Gheorghiu, 1982, 1989a, b; Kruse, 1989; Kruse & Gheorghiu, 1989).

But suggestion, like the other mechanisms mentioned above, is not only a strategy to make unambiguous and stable order available as an indispensable basis of action: suggestion can also be used in an attempt to produce psychic instability. This may be the case in situations where a suboptimal and fixated level of learning has to be passed (see Gibbons & Wright, 1981; Lazarus & Folkman, 1984) or in situations where it makes sense to maintain situational ambiguity or the individual instability as, for example, in the maintenance of hope (see Lazarus & Folkman, 1984).

Ambiguity, instability, and suggestion/suggestibility

Since the early days of scientific analysis of suggestion phenomena, the relation between situational ambiguity, individual instability, and suggestion/suggestibility has been of key importance. Explicitly or implicitly, this can be traced back through all facets of research on suggestion. As far back as Binet (1900), mention is made that the degree of vagueness of a situation is a central aspect of suggestion. The more ill-defined or ambiguous a stimulus, the more it may be subject to reinterpretation. A person's suggestibility is inversely related to the certainty of the person's behavioral decisions or subjective valuations (see Binet, 1900).

These ideas were elaborated in more detail by Sherif (1935) and Coffin (1941). Sherif pointed out that, in a vague or ambiguous situation, there is no "perception of chaos." Instead, there is still the experience of order, and this process of order formation is dominated by internal functions like attitude, set, drive, and emotional state. Sherif postulated a general psychic tendency towards unambiguous order formation. Considering the possibilities and limits of suggestive influences, he arrived at two main conclusions. On the one hand, he attributed to suggestion the capacity to reduce ambiguity or to control instability. On the other hand, he concluded that, in well-defined situations, the readiness to respond to suggestions is relatively small (see also Coffin, 1941; Luchins, 1945, Newcomb, 1950). However, this latter conclusion must be viewed cautiously since Asch (1956) demonstrated that even clearly structured stimulus situations can be reinterpreted by group pressure.

Sherif used the highly ambiguous perceptual phenomenon of the autokinetic effect to investigate suggestive processes. Somehow, stimulus ambiguity plays an important role in nearly every experiment on suggestion. In the phase of instability which is prompted by the presentation of ill-defined or ambiguous stimuli, little causes may have great effect. Following its inherent tendency towards stable order, the cognitive system brings into play every subtle influence in order to come to a clear decision. Suggestion is one of these subtle influences. In line with the present argument, a hypothetical explanation for individual differences in the readiness to respond to suggestions can be proposed.

Suggestibility as a personal trait may be due to habitual interpersonal variations of cognitive instability. Individual cognitive systems differ with regard to the amount of instability they tolerate and also the speed and power of their inherent tendency toward stable order. This is strongly reminiscent of Pavlov's theory of types of higher nervous activity (Pavlov, 1955). In his typology, individual nervous systems are mainly classified according to nervous system strength and mobility of the nervous processes. Strength and sensitivity are in an inverse relationship to each other. The strongest system is the most stable and at the same time the least sensitive. The weakest system is the least stable and the most sensitive (see also Nebelytsyn, 1964). A stable system is very reliable concerning its inner states but not very adaptive, while a system which is more often in an unstable state is less reliable but highly adaptive. In this view, a strong nervous system (i.e., a system with a clear tendency toward stable order) is only to a small extent sensitive to subtle influences, and therefore low in suggestibility. A weak nervous system is highly suggestible. Theoretically this classification of individual nervous systems is substantiated by modern trends in self-organization theory (see Kruse & Stadler, 1989).

On the psychological level, these ideas suggest a strong relationship between habitual differences in innersystemic instability, and adaptive mental functions like cognitive flexibility and suggestibility. The main empirical problem is to find an adequate way of measuring the degree of innersystemic instability which characterizes a person.

In our own experiments we tried to solve this problem by using multistable patterns. As explained above, different percepts change continuously during prolonged observation of such ambiguous stimuli. The rate of this apparent change varies from person to person. Some are very low concerning this parameter and some are quite high. Depending on the special stimulus situation, the ratio may be, for example, from around one to twenty. As proven by many independent investigations, the rate of apparent change typical for a person is very reliable (Bergum & Bergum, 1980). Another possible parameter is the stability of one perceptual alternative when the multistable pattern is biased more and more in favor of one of the other alternatives. This tendency to persist in one stable state is called hysteresis. People who have a high rate of apparent change tend to be low in hysteresis because they change easily between different stable states. It is theoretically meaningful to take the rate of apparent change and the amount of hysteresis as indicators of the habitual innersystemic instability (see Kruse & Stadler, 1989).

The reliable interpersonal differences in rate of apparent change and the amount of hysteresis can be seen as an effect of habitual individual differences in innersystemic instability. This results in the following concrete empirical hypotheses: 1) the rate of apparent change while observing multistable patterns correlates positively with suggestibility (also, for adaptive cognitive functions, positive correlations are to be expected for rate of apparent change and for suggestibility); and 2) the amount of hysteresis while observing gradually biased multistable patterns correlates negatively with suggestibility.

Our research provided evidence for these hypotheses. In these studies, suggestibility was measured using the Sensory Suggestibility Test (SST) constructed by Gheorghiu (see Gheorghiu & Reyher, 1982). During administration of the SST, subjects are confronted with a number of situations which seem to allow measurement of threshold perception. In tactile, auditory, and visual items, real stimulation alternates with situations where stimulation is only simulated. To enhance the plausibility of the procedure, the subjects are warned of the possibility that sometimes no objective stimulation is applied. The test score depends on how often a subject reports a perception in the absence of objective stimulation. The individual rate of apparent change was measured by presenting the multistable display of a stroboscopic alternative movement and by using the phenomenon of binocular rivalry. The amount of hysteresis was measured on the basis of the stroboscopic alternative movement (for details of the procedure see Kruse & Stadler, 1989; Kruse, Gheorghiu, & Stadler, 1990).

The results confirm the hypotheses. There is a significant positive correlation between the rate of apparent change measured with the stroboscopic alternative movement and the score of the SST ($n=85$, $r=.25$, $p<.05$). The same holds true for binocular rivalry ($n=45$, $r=.34$, $p<.05$). The amount of hysteresis measured with the stroboscopic alternative movement shows a significant negative correlation to the score of the SST ($n=45$, $r=-.42$, $p<.01$). Taking only subjects with a high rate of apparent change and those with a low rate of apparent change, and also subjects low in amount of hysteresis and those high in amount of hysteresis, a highly significant difference between the scores of the selected extreme groups was found (t-test, $p<.005$). People who are high in rate of apparent change and low in amount of hysteresis (i.e., people who have a high degree of habitual innersystemic instability) are highly suggestible. People who are low in rate of change and high in hysteresis (i.e., people who have a low degree of innersystemic instability) are low in their readiness to respond to suggestive influences.

The results are further supported by existing empirical findings. A positive relationship was shown between cognitive flexibility, creative potential, originality in thinking, and rate of apparent change (Gräser, 1977; Klintman, 1984). Comparable correlations were also found for these adaptive cognitive functions and suggestibility (Crawford, 1989). Suggestibility and rate of apparent change are reduced with age (Feingold, 1982; Heath & Orbach, 1963; Stukat, 1958). Obviously, individual cognitive systems differ in the basic cognitive strategy they prefer. Some systems tend to lean strongly towards stability and are very reliable concerning their inner states, but less sensitive and less able to adapt. Also, some systems are more frequently, and for longer periods of time, in unstable states. They are therefore less reliable, but more sensitive and more able to adapt. One very interesting approach to the understanding of suggestibility is to search for psychological and physiological functions which are responsible for, or which correlate with, these individual differences. The idea that stimulus ambiguity and cognitive instability are central aspects of the process of suggestion is a viewpoint which seems to be very promising and deserving of further attention.

Suggestion and reality criteria

In view of the idea that our perceptual world is the result of a continuous disambiguation, cognitive processes have to be regarded as an active construction. Cognitive states govern the conscious or subconscious reduction of possible alternatives or perceptual and behavioral order formation, the attribution of meaning, and the valuation of experiences. The given situation gains the character of a more or less unspecific boundary condition which only constrains the internal processes. For the phenomena of suggestion, the active attribution of meaning is of special interest. The close connection between the aspect of interpretation and the basic ambiguity of situations is nicely illustrated by the German word *Mehrdeutigkeit,* which is used as a synonym for ambiguity. Ambiguity is defined as the possibility of multiple interpretations.

Suggestive influences can be understood as a process of putting a special interpretation "under" (i.e., "substitution," see Gheorghiu, 1989b) in a situation which is basically ambiguous. Stated another way, this is a process of creating individual instability in a situation where a person had already made a clear decision. Here the question arises whether, or to what extent, the attribution of meaning and the mechanisms of decision are controlled by the person in case of suggestion. In recent literature, an understanding of suggestion is advocated in which individual mechanisms of control take part, whether or not the process itself is consciously realized (Bowers, 1984; Gheorghiu, 1989a, b; Hilgard, 1977, 1979; Kihlstrom, 1984; Kruse & Gheorghiu, 1989). If the presence of such mechanisms of control is accepted, it follows that there should be special cognitive criteria which are responsible for the acceptance or rejection of a suggested solution. As described for general disambiguation, which is an essential part of the cognitive construction, the activity of such internal criteria cannot be limited to suggestion. Any situation we experience and any decision we make has to satisfy these criteria in order to be accepted as real, right, or relevant. Again, suggestion is no exceptional case, but rather a paradigmatical field for understanding cognition in general.

In relation to suggestion, the already mentioned "as if" character is stressed. Any suggestion has to be accepted *as if* there is no other possible way of interpretation, valuation, or behavior. By means of suggestive influences (e.g., mere assumptions attributed an evidential weight as if they were checked by systematic investigations), an ambiguous situation is interpreted as if there is only one way of understanding. That is, one of many possible forms of behavior is chosen as if it is the only adequate alternative. All these internal decisions are guided by cognitive criteria which allow the necessary discrimination between "true" and "false," "real" and "imagined," "adequate" and "inadequate," and "possible" and "impossible." Additionally, any suggestion has to meet or satisfy these criteria to be effective (see Gheorghiu, 1989b).

It seems meaningful to assume that a hierarchy of individual criteria of acceptance is part of any individual cognitive system, and also that a central aspect of suggestion is the tendency to make decisions in accordance with these criteria. In terms of the research summarized below, these criteria are subsumed under the wider concept of "reality criteria" (for details see Kruse, 1989). The individual reality criteria make it possible for a person to act in a "real" world regardless of whether or not this world is real in an objective sense. It is only the momentary or persistent belief of the person that he or she has acted adequately that is of interest. Heckhausen (1980) came to the same conclusion concerning attributional processes. In our view, reality criteria are not—as it should be in the framework of Hilgard's "neodissociation theory" (Hilgard, 1977)—internal states which guide the activity of cybernetic mechanisms of control. Instead, the reality criteria are the control mechanisms themselves.

Some research already exists on the problem of cognitive determination of apparent reality of an experienced or remembered event. Using the category of "reality testing" or "reality decision" (Segal, 1971), this was investigated in the context of our ability to discriminate between a perception and an imagination, a dream or a hallucination. In some early research on this subject, Külpe (1902) and Perky (1910) were able to demonstrate that this discrimination is by no means trivial. Under special conditions, a perception is regarded to be an imagination or a hallucination, and vice versa. Michotte (1948, 1957) and Phémister (1951) found that the impression of reality (réalité apparente) is not a discrimination between real and unreal, but rather a continuous dimension which is governed by a multitude of different criteria (for a list of possible reality criteria, see Kruse & Stadler, 1990). Johnson and Raye (1981) and Lindsay and Johnson (1987) produced similar findings concerning the matter of when it is that a remembrance is accepted as the result of a "real" event, and also when it is valued as imaginary. Additionally, the investigations of the relevance of intersubjective experiences in situations of uncertainty have to be mentioned here (see Kahneman, et al., 1982).

Except for the work of Lindsay and Johnson, the relation between cognitive reality criteria and suggestion has only been an implicit topic of most investigations. Recently, Lundy (1989) attempted to analyze the connection between suggestion and the cognitive construction of individual reality in more detail. On the basis of G.A. Kelly's (1955) "theory of personal constructs," Lundy stressed the fundamental importance of individual conceptions of reality for understanding the process of suggestion (see also Sheehan, 1989). Using the theoretical concept of radical constructivism, Kruse (1989) explicitly discussed the relevance of reality criteria in this context.

Empirical methods are clearly relevant to an analysis of the general or individual criteria (or hierarchy of criteria) which are involved in the process of suggestion. The same is true of the criteria which a concrete suggestion has to meet or pass in order to be accepted and transformed in cognitive reality. Therefore, we will not simply list or theoretically substantiate possible reality criteria. Instead, we will outline some of our research which was designed to examine the postulated connection between the internal attribution of reality and the well-known effects of suggestion/suggestibility.

In the following experiments, we investigated three different reality criteria which are theoretically significant for the suggestion process: the criterion of plausibility, the criterion of intersubjective confirmation, and the criterion of correspondence with an existing anticipation.

We all have a strong tendency to act in accordance with our beliefs and our knowledge. Most of the time, we insinuate that we have plausible arguments for what we are doing. But usually we do not really test these arguments. What we have is more like an intuitive feeling that things are right. Together with the individual and social need to be able to explain our behavior, this intuition plays a part in suggestive processes. In research on suggestion, there has been a tendency to understand the suggestive influence as a stimulation of irrational behaviors. Therefore, the seemingly rational category of plausibility has been of only marginal interest. In the first experiment to be outlined, we tried to demonstrate that there is a correlation between plausibility and the effectiveness of a suggestive influence.

In the process of deception, as Irle (1979) points out, we are always concerned with a minimization of the veridicality of a situation and with a maximization of the subjective certainty. The objective of an experiment on deception is therefore to maximize the certainty of the subject. Most studies conducted in the field of sensory suggestibility show a lack of plausibility when the subject is critical and not deceived by the procedure employed (Evans, 1967; Gheorghiu, 1989a). In order to maintain the credibility of the experimental situation and the experimenter, it is necessary to inform the subjects of the fact that sometimes no objective stimulation is given. One way to give this information without making the experimenter responsible for the decision (whether a stimulus is given or not) is to let the subject choose a "program" which seemingly determines the procedure. Investigations conducted on the basis of this indirect-direct version of the Sensory Suggestibility Test (Gheorghiu & Kiel, 1976) show that the mean score is significantly reduced when subjects are informed of the possibility of deception ($x=11.62$ to $x=6.15$), but that subjects seldom get to the bottom of the procedure (Feingold, 1982). To enhance the plausibility of the indirect-direct version, the Sensory Suggestibility Test (SST) was embedded into a series of other tests of perception, such as the measurement of critical flicker fusion and the Stroop-Test. This procedure (see Gheorghiu, et al., 1989) significantly increased the mean score ($x=6.0$ to $x=8.9$).

The plausibility of the test procedure is an even greater problem with motor suggestibility. In motor suggestibility, different procedures are utilized to elicit spontaneous movements. Subjects are confronted with the contradiction that they are asked to move without being active, or that they are asked to stop moving without deliberate suppression. The effectiveness of a given suggestion depends on how much the text or the vehicle used is able to give a plausible explanation of this inherent contradiction. When reactions seem to be a plausible consequence of a given situation, or when their occurrence seems to have a satisfactory explanation, they are elicited more often. Using classical tests of motor suggestibility, Gheorghiu and Hübner (1990) were able to demonstrate that suggestibility is significantly enhanced by making the spontaneous change in motor behavior more plausible.

Possibly the most powerful criterion for the evaluation of the reality content of an event or an idea is the criterion of intersubjective confirmation. In fact, from the beginning, this criterion has played a major part in research on suggestion (Asch, 1956; Binet, 1900; Coffin, 1941; Crutchfield, 1955; Hood & Sherif, 1962; Stukat, 1958). In the context of ill-defined situations, there is an increased tendency to adopt the behavior of others uncritically. Individual instability is reduced by social adaptation. As a rule, the suggestive effects of model situations refer to imitative tendencies under the influence of a "co-judge," (i.e., a confidant to the experimenter). In classical experiments, the co-judges were usually different from the subjects with respect to one or more aspects (age, competence, etc.). In situations in which the status of both were nearly equal, discretion was hardly ensured until the end of the experiment. To solve this problem, one can design experiments where the role of the co-judge is taken over by a subject without being informed of the role.

In corresponding investigations—performed again on the basis of the SST—two subjects were confronted with the same perceptual tasks (Gheorghiu & Feingold, 1981). Real stimulation was only given to one subject (co-judge). The other subject was told to share the same conditions and to have the same task, but no real stimulation was given. The score of the SST was significantly increased when the uninformed co-judge was present (x=8 to x=10.3). In another study (Chemnitz, Feingold, & Gheorghiu, 1981), we were able to show that the influence of the co-judge is even stronger when there is a sympathetic relationship between the two subjects (x=10.91 to x=13.81).

Correspondence with an existing anticipation is another criterion which is of importance in the suggestion process. Somehow, in every suggestive process there is a self-fulfilling mechanism that is either implicitly or explicitly based on expectancy formation. Therefore, the significance of expectancies for the behavioral consequences of a suggestive influence was also one of the early topics of research on suggestion (Binet, 1900; Coffin, 1941; Scripture, 1893; Seashore, 1895; Sherif, 1935; Stukat, 1958). The research on self-fulfilling prophecies can be seen in close connection to this (Rosenthal & Jacobson, 1968; Rosenthal & Rubin, 1978). The suggestive impact that an expectancy has on behavior is obvious, and to induce an expectancy is comparable to inducing a behavior by more direct suggestive influences. If, by means of adequate treatment, the belief of being a highly suggestible person is induced in a subject, the score of the SST is increased (Gheorghiu & Sander, 1973).

But what happens if the experimenter is convinced that the subject is highly suggestible? Even in this very indirect form, the expectancy has an effect on the suggestion process. In an investigation designed to answer the question, we examined the experimenter effect on suggestibility. By means of a plausible pre-test, subjects were introduced to the experimenter as being a high or low suggestible. The two groups were formed randomly. Suggestibility was then measured using the indirect-direct form of the SST described above. On the basis of this procedure, subjects said to be low in suggestibility had a relatively low score, and subjects said to be high had a relatively high score in the SST (x=6.6 to x=11.4). The difference is significant (Kruse, et al., 1990).

Conclusions and perspectives

Suggestion is by no means a marginal aspect of cognitive activity. Suggestion phenomena are subsumed under various psychological categories and are part of many cognitive and social processes. When psychology again attempts to develop integrative theories of cognition, suggestion may regain its status as a paradigmatical field of research. In view of suggestive phenomena, the information-processing approach to cognition loses credence, while a constructivistic understanding proves more useful. The world of phenomena is more the product of an innercognitive process of construction than a representation of an external reality. The stable order that we experience and that we need to be able to act is the result of an autonomous order formation which can be seen as a continuous disambiguation. Suggestion is one main cognitive mechanism we use to perform this disambiguation and to gain stability. It is a mechanism of disambiguation and stabilization, and differences in suggestibility are an effect of habitual differences in innersystemic instability. Such a view offers us a promising approach for a deeper understanding of all processes involved. In addition, the impact of belief-systems and the importance of reality criteria are a necessary part of the cognitive construction of individual reality. These are also empirical consequences which warrant further investigation.

References

Allport, G.W. (1961). *Pattern and growth in personality.* New York: Holt, Rinehart and Winston.

Asch, S.E. (1952). *Social psychology.* Englewood Cliffs, NJ: Prentice-Hall.

Asch, S.E. (1956). Studies of independence and conformity: A minority of one against a unanimous majority. *Psychological Monographs, 70*(9, Whole No. 416), 1–12.

Bergum, J.E., & Bergum, B.O. (1980). Reliability of reversal rates as a measure of perceptual stability. *Perceptual and Motor Skills, 50,* 1038.

Bernheim, H. (1888). *Hypnosis and suggestion in psychotherapy.* (Reprinted New York: University Books, 1964.)

Binet, A. (1900). *La suggestibilité.* Paris: Schleicher Frères.

Bowers, K.S. (1984). On being unconsciously influenced and informed. In K.S. Bowers & D. Meichenbaum (eds.), *The unconscious reconsidered.* New York: Wiley.

Chemnitz, G., Feingold, E., & Gheorghiu, V.A. (1981). Beeinflussung kognitiver prozesse von schülern verschiedenen alters und geschlechts durch ihre mitschüler. *Psychologie in Erziehung und Unterricht, 28,* 7–12.

Coffin, T.E. (1941). Some conditions of suggestion and suggestibility: A study of certain attitudinal and situational factors influencing the process of suggestion. *Psychological Monographs, 4,* 53.

Crawford, H.J. (1989). Cognitive and physiological flexibility: Multiple pathways to hypnotic responsiveness. In V.A. Gheorghiu, P. Netter, H.J. Eysenck, & R. Rosenthal (eds.), *Suggestion and suggestibility: Theory and research* (pp. 155–67). Berlin: Springer.

Crutchfield, R.S. (1955). Conformity and character. *American Psychologist, 10*, 191–99.

Evans, F.J. (1967). Suggestibility in the normal waking state. *Psychological Bulletin, 67*, 114–29.

Eysenck, H.J. (1947). Dimensions of personality. Routledge and Kegan Paul.

Feingold, E. (1982). *Untersuchungen zur sensorischen suggestibilität sowie zum zusammenhang zwischen sensorischer suggestibilität und der placebo-ansprechbarkeit im schmerzbereich.* Doctoral dissertation, Mainz.

Freud, S. (1963). Massenpsychologie und ich-analyse. In *Gesammelte Werke* (Vol. 13). Frankfurt: Fischer. (Originally published in 1940.)

Gheorghiu, V.A. (1982). Aspecte psihologice ale sugestiei si sugestibilitatii. In V.A. Gheorghiu, & I. Coifu, *Sugestie si sugestibilitate: Aspecte psihologice si psihofiziologice* (pp. 11–148). Bucharest: Editura Academiei.

Gheorghiu, V.A. (1989a). The development of research on suggestibility: Critical considerations. In V.A. Gheorghiu, P. Netter, H.J. Eysenck, & R. Rosenthal (eds.), *Suggestion and suggestibility: Theory and research* (pp. 3–55). Berlin: Springer.

Gheorghiu, V.A. (1989b). The difficulty in explaining suggestion: Some conceivable solutions. In V.A. Gheorghiu, P. Netter, H.J. Eysenck, & R. Rosenthal (eds.), *Suggestion and suggestibility: Theory and research* (pp. 99–112) Berlin: Springer.

Gheorghiu, V.A., & Feingold, E. (1981). The effect of a "co-judge"-influence on sensory suggestibility. *Revue Romaine des Sciences Sociales, Serié de Psychologie, 25*, 159–67.

Gheorghiu, V.A., & Hübner, M. (1990). "Argumente" als suggestive vehikel der beeinflussung motorischer verhaltensweisen (in Vorber).

Gheorghiu, V.A., & Kiel, H. (1976). Indirekte und indirekt-direkte form einer sensorischen suggestibilitätsskala. Vergleichende untersuchung. *Revue Romaine des Sciences Sociales, Serié de Psychologie, 20*, 29–46.

Gheorghiu, V.A., Netter, P., Eysenck, H.J., & Rosenthal, R. (eds.). (1989). *Suggestion and suggestibility: Theory and research.* Berlin: Springer.

Gheorghiu, V.A., & Reyher, J. (1982). The effect of different types of influence of an "indirect-direct" form of a scale of sensory suggestibility. *American Journal of Clinical Hypnosis, 24*, 191–99.

Gheorghiu, V.A., & Sander, D. (1973). Untersuchungen zur änderung der suggestibilität unter bestimmten einstellungen. In G. Reinert (ed.), *Bericht über den 27. Kongress der Deutschen Gesellschaft für Psychologie.* Göttingen: Hogrefe.

Gibbons, F.X., & Wright, R.A. (1981). Motivational biases in causal attributions of arousal. *Journal of Personality and Social Psychology, 40*, 588–600.

Gräser, H. (1977). *Spontane reversionsprozesse in der figural-wahrnehmung.* Doctoral dissertation, Trier.

Heath, H.A., & Orbach, J. (1963). Reversibility of the Necker cube: IV. Responses of elderly people. *Perceptual and Motor Skills, 17*, 625–26.

Heckhausen, H. (1980). *Motivation und handeln.* Berlin: Springer.

Hilgard, E.R. (1977). *Divided consciousness: Multiple controls in human thought and action.* New York: Wiley.

Hilgard, E.R. (1979). Divided consciousness in hypnosis: The implications of the hidden observer. In E. Fromm & R.E. Shor (eds.), *Hypnosis: Developments in research and new perspectives* (pp. 45–80). New York: Aldine.

Hood, W.R., & Sherif, M. (1962). Verbal report and judgement of an unstructured stimulus. *Journal of Psychology, 54,* 121–30.

Hull, C.L. (1933). Hypnosis and suggestibility: An experimental approach. New York: Appleton-Century-Crofts.

Irle, M. (1979). Das instrument der "täuschung" in der verhaltens—und sozialwissenschaftlichen forschung. *Zeitschrift für Sozialpsychologie, 10,* 305–30.

James, W. (1896). *The principles of psychology.* New York: Holt.

Janet, P. (1889). *L'automatisme psychologiques.* Paris: Alcan.

Janet, P. (1919). *Les médications psychologiques.* Paris: Alcan.

Johnson, M.K., & Raye, C.L. (1981). Reality monitoring. *Psychological Review, 88,* 67–85.

Kahneman, D., Slovic, B., & Tversky, A. (1982). *Judgement under uncertainty: Heuristics and biases.* Cambridge: Cambridge University Press.

Katz, D. (1951). *Handbuch der psychologie.* Basel: Schwalbe.

Kelly, G.A. (1955). *The psychology of personal constructs.* New York: Norton.

Kihlstrom, J.F. (1984). Conscious, subconscious, unconscious: A cognitive perspective. In K.S. Bowers & D. Meichenbaum (eds.), *The unconscious reconsidered* (pp. 149–211). New York: Wiley.

Klintman, H. (1984). Original thinking and ambiguous figure reversal rates. *Bulletin of the Psychonomic Society, 22,* 129–31.

Kretschmer, E. (1963). *Medizinische psychologie.* Stuttgart: Thieme.

Kruse, P. (1988). Stabilität, instabilität, multistabilität: Selbstorganisation und selbstreferentialität in kognitiven systemen. *Delfin, 11,* 35–57.

Kruse, P. (1989). Some suggestions about suggestion and hypnosis: A radical constructivist view. In V.A. Gheorghiu, P. Netter, H.J. Eysenck, & R. Rosenthal (eds.), *Suggestion and suggestibility: Theory and research* (pp. 91–98). Berlin: Springer-Verlag.

Kruse, P., & Gheorghiu, V.A. (1989). Suggestion, hypnose, die kategorie des unbewussten und das phänomen der dissoziation: Ordnungsbildung in kognitiven systemen. *Hypnose und Kognition, 6,* 49–61.

Kruse, P. Gheorghiu, V.A., & Stadler, M. (1990). Cognitive multistability and suggestion (in preparation).

Kruse, P., & Stadler, M. (1989). Stability and instability in cognitive systems: Multistability, suggestion, and psychosomatic interaction. In H. Haken & M. Stadler (eds.), *Synergetics of cognition* (pp. 201–15). Berlin: Springer.

Kruse, P., & Stadler, M. (1990). Über wirklichkeitskriterien. In V. Riegas & C. Vetter (eds.), *Die konstruierte wirklichkeit.* Frankfurt: Suhrkamp.

Külpe, O. (1902). Ueber die objektivirung und subjectivirung von sinneseindrücken. *Philosophische Studien, 19,* 508–56.

Lazarus, R.S., & Folkman, S. (1984). *Stress, appraisal and coping.* New York: Springer.

Lindsay, D.S., & Johnson, M.K. (1987). Reality monitoring and suggestibility: Children's ability to discriminate among memories from different sources. In S.J. Ceci, M.P. Toglia, & F. Ross (eds.), *Children's eyewitness memory* (pp. 92–121). New York: Springer.

Luchins, A.S. (1945). Social influences on perception of complex drawings. *Journal of Social Psychology, 21,* 257–73.

Lundy, R.M. (1989). The internal confirmation of personal constructs: Why suggestions are not accepted. In V.A. Gheorghiu, P. Netter, H.J. Eysenck, & R. Rosenthal (eds.), *Suggestion and suggestibility: Theory and research* (pp. 79–90). Berlin: Springer-Verlag.

McDougall, W. (1908). *Introduction to social psychology.* London: Methuen.

McGuire, W.J. (1968). Personality and susceptibility to social influence. In E.F. Borgatta & W.W. Lambert (eds.), *Handbook of personality theory and research* (pp. 1130–87). Chicago: Rand-McNally.

McGuire, W.J. (1985). Attitudes and attitude change. In G. Lindzay & E. Aronson (eds.), *Handbook of social psychology* (3rd edition, Vol. 2, pp. 233–346). New York: Random House.

Michotte, A. (1948). L'énigme psychologique de la perspective dans le dessin linéaire. *Bulletin de l'Académie Royale de Belgique, 5,* 268–88.

Michotte, A. (1957). Les variations de réalité apparente de la troisième dimension dans les perceptions visuelles. *Archivo di Psychologia, Neurologia e Psichatrica, 18,* 203–13.

Nebelytsyn, V.D. (1964). An investigation of the connection between sensitivity and strength of the nervous system. In J.A. Gray (ed.), *Pavlov's typology* (pp. 402–45). Oxford: Pergamon Press.

Newcomb, t.M. (1950). *Social psychology.* New York: Dryden.

Pavlov, I.P. (1953). *Sämtliche Werke.* Berlin: Akademie. (Originally published in 1924–1927.)

Pavlov, I.P. (1955). *Selected works.* Moscow: Foreign Language Publishing House.

Perky, C.W. (1910). An experimental study of imagination. *American Journal of Psychology, 21,* 422–52.

Phémister, M. R. (1951). An experimental contribution to the problem of apparent reality. *The Quarterly Journal of Experimental Psychology, 3,* 1–18.

Rosenthal, R., & Jacobson, L. (1968). *Pygmalion in the classroom: Teacher expectation and student intellectual development.* New York: Holt, Rinehart and Winston.

Rosenthal, R., & Rubin, D.P. (1978). Interpersonal expectancy effects: The first 345 studies. *Behavioral and Brain Sciences, 3,* 377–415.

Scripture, E.W. (1893). Test of school children. *Educational Review, 5,* 52–61.

Seashore, C.E. (1895). Measurement of illusions and hallucinations in normal life. *Studies from the Yale Psychological Laboratory, 2,* 1–67.

Segal, S.J. (1971). Processing of the stimulus in imagery and perception. In S. J. Segal (ed.), *Imagery: Current cognitive approaches.* New York: Academic.

Sheehan, P.W. (1989). Commentary on "Theoretical and historical perspectives." In V.A. Gheorghiu, P. Netter, H.J. Eysenck, & R. Rosenthal (eds.), *Suggestion and suggestibility: Theory and research* (pp. 113–20).

Sherif, M. (1935). A study of some social factors in perception. *Archives of Psychology, 187,* 60.

Sidis, B. (1898). *The psychology of suggestion.* New York: Appleton.

Stokvis, B., & Pflanz, M. (1961). *Suggestion.* Stuttgart: Hippokrates.

Stukat, K.G. (1958). *Suggestibility: A factorial and experimental analysis.* Stockholm: Almqvist and Wiksell.

Wundt, W.M. (1892). *Hypnotismus und Suggestion.* Leipzig: Engelmann.

3

IS SUGGESTIBILITY?

H. J. Eysenck

There can be no doubt about the importance of the concept of suggestibility in the popular mind, or in the writings of psychologists. It is usually believed that some people are more suggestible than others, and suggestibility is used as a term to denote this dispositional trait, which is assumed to underlie the individual acts of acceding to suggestions of one kind or another. In this chapter an attempt is made to look at the evidence for or against this notion of a unitary trait of suggestibility. In other words, we are asking the question of whether suggestibility does or does not exist as a unitary trait. There is now much evidence to suggest that the answer is decisively in the negative, and that there are at least two, and probably many more types of "suggestibility" which are quite independent of each other. These correlate quite differently with such variables as intelligence, hypnotizability, etc.

There has been a comparative lack of interest in work on suggestibility in the past fifty years or so, due perhaps to widespread acceptance of Mischel's (1968) suggestion that personality traits were much less important in determining behaviour than were situations; this belief has been strongly criticized by Eysenck and Eysenck (1980), and has now been largely abandoned. The publication of the present volume, and the book on *Suggestion and Suggestibility* by Gheorghiu, Netter, Eysenck, and Rosenthal (1989) suggests a renewed interest in the topic.

The broad generality of the notion of suggestion and suggestibility is illustrated by the fact that Thomas Brown (1960/1820) proposed to account for human behaviour in terms of "Laws of Suggestion" instead of "Laws of Association," believing that, in the association of ideas, one mental item "suggests" another. His treatment emphasizes not only the primary laws of similarity, contrast, and contiguity, but also secondary laws, such as what would now be considered "moderating variables." These secondary laws reappear in William James's (1890) *Principles of Psychology* under the guise of habit, recency, vividness, and emotional congruity. An excellent historical account of the concept, both in its pre-experimental and its more recent development, has been given by Gheorghiu (1989).

The concept of suggestibility is intimately related to very important psychological concepts. I have already referred to Brown's view that suggestion should take the place of association in the list of the most important laws of mental determinants. In modern times of course we do not talk about laws of association any more, but consider rather the principles of conditioning. These principles, as Weitzenhoffer (1957) has pointed out, are prominent candidates for explaining the phenomena of hypnosis and suggestibility. There are obvious similarities between conditioning and suggestion. Take the example of Pavlov's dog, conditioned to salivate at the sound of a bell by associating the sound of a bell with the presentation of food. A layman might easily say that the bell "suggested" food, and thus produced the conditioned response. This would be an S-S explanation, which has now superseded the more usual S-R type of explanation. Obviously such a suggestion needs empirical confirmation, which in turn requires the independent measurement of suggestibility (are some dogs more suggestible than others?), and a correlation with conditionability (there is no doubt that some dogs are more conditionable than others). This problem brings us back to our original question: is there a general factor of suggestibility, or are there many different types of suggestibility?

Another correlate of suggestibility is the placebo response (Beecher, 1959; White, Tursky, & Schwartz, 1985). As is well known, substances and procedures known to have no biological effects on pain, fever, or other symptoms or behaviours can mimic such effects to a very marked degree. Thus, pain killers usually affect subjective pain to an extent which, while it is larger than the effect of placebos, may not be very much larger, depending on the degree of pain, experience, presentation of the placebo, and other factors. Placebo treatment in psychiatry is just about as effective as psychotherapeutic techniques (Prioleau, Murdoch, & Brody, 1983; Rachman & Wilson, 1980; Smith, Glass, & Miller, 1980). Psychotherapists do not usually like to be reminded of this fact, but it is important because it illustrates that power of suggestibility, which is usually regarded as the underlying reason for the effectiveness of placebo treatments.

Suggestion has often been linked with hypnosis, and suggestibility with hypnotizability. There is no doubt that some tests of suggestibility, particularly those of what Eysenck and Furneaux (1945) have called "primary suggestibility," correlate with hypnotizability (Eysenck, 1989). But it would be wrong to *identify* primary suggestibility and hypnosis (Gheorghiu, 1989). The relationship is rather like that between *neuroticism* and *neurosis* (Eysenck, 1947). The former is a dispositional characteristic of personality, the latter a specific state, correlated with the former, but not identical with it. This is an important distinction which should always be borne in mind.

With or without inducing hypnosis, suggestion can have very powerful and amazing effects. Some of these have been well documented and replicated, and indicate how important the scientific study of suggestion and suggestibility may be. Thus Bruno Bloch (1927), the famous "wart doctor" of Zurich, used an impressive "wart-killing machine," with flashing lights, a noisy motor, and "powerful X-rays." Patients placed their affected body parts in the machine, and when told that the warts were dead had them painted with a brightly colored harmless dye. Patients were then told that the warts must not be washed or touched until they had disappeared. In 30% of his cases, Dr. Bloch reported a complete disappearance of all warts after one treatment—a very much higher rate of success than that occasionally reported for spontaneous cures. Similarly, claims are made that female breasts can be enlarged. R.D. Willard (1977) performed a controlled study of 32 women between the ages of 19 and 54. Women were treated for 12 weeks, given suggestions of deep relaxation and told to imagine warming of the breasts, and to feel them pulsating. Nearly 85% of the women were reported as having some breast enlargement, with 46% requiring a larger bra size. These findings are consistent with those of four other published reports of breast enlargement elicited by suggestion (Haniotes, 1977; LeCron, 1969; Staib & Logan, 1977; Williams, 1974).

Again, allergic reactions of the skin can be provoked by suggestion alone. Two Japanese researchers (Ikemi and Nakagawa, 1962) performed a series of experiments on 13 high-school boys who were known to be highly allergic to a certain plant. Five of the boys were given an hypnotic induction with repeated suggestions of relaxation and drowsiness. The other eight were not given a formal hypnotic induction, but were merely given strong suggestions. With their eyes closed, all the boys were then told that they were being touched on the arm with the leaves of a "poison ivy-type" plant. In fact, they were being touched by the leaves of a harmless plant, yet all 13 boys demonstrated some degree of dermatitis, including itching, redness, papules, swelling, and blisters, in response to their belief that they were being touched by the poisonous leaves. In the next stage of the experiment, the experimenters reversed the procedure, telling each boy that he was being touched by the leaves of the harmless plant. In actuality, the boys were being stroked on the arm with the poison ivy-type leaves. In this situation, when led to believe that the leaves were harmless, 11 of the 13 did not react to the poisonous leaves with their usual skin eruption.

These and many more examples of the powerful effects of suggestion and hypnosis have been well documented (e.g., Barber, 1984). Amputation of limbs under hypnosis, with the suggestion that no pain was being felt, has been reliably reported many times. Furthermore, had it not been for the discovery of anaesthetics, hypnosis would undoubtedly have become much more popular in medical circles. These facts raise serious theoretical questions, and also suggest many practical applications of suggestion and hypnosis.

In some of these studies it is difficult to know to what extent hypnosis is involved, and whether straightforward suggestion or hypnotic suggestion is active. Barber (1984) appears to discount hypnosis as a state, possibly enhancing the effects of suggestion, but this view is not held very widely among experts on hypnotism.

In view of the importance of the concept of suggestibility, it seems odd that there has been so very little empirical and experimental work in connection with it. Stress, anxiety, and depression are traits which have been investigated much more thoroughly in the last fifty years than has suggestibility (in the sense that some people are more prone to react with strain to stressful events, while others react with anxiety, anxiety-proneness, or depression). It is interesting to ask why there should be such a disproportion: looking at the entries under these terms in the *Psychological Abstracts*, one will find that there are hundreds of entries under the headings of anxiety and depression, as opposed to one for suggestibility!

The first, and perhaps the most obvious reason is that research in psychology has tended to concentrate on states of mental illness, perhaps because there is a hope that psychological treatment may cure or ameliorate these illnesses. Thus anxiety and depression are major causes of discomfort and distress for millions of people. Research into their effects, their causation, and their treatment is therefore of considerable social importance. Suggestibility is not a "disease" in this sense, and hence attracts much less attention. If people are suggestible to claims made for religious beliefs, political ideologies, or nationalistic identifications, it is doubtful whether they would consider these as the results of suggestibility, or would want to be "cured."

The second reason is probably the "will-o'-the-wisp" character of suggestibility, as compared with the much more clear-cut nature of anxiety and depression. To be suggestible, according to the dictionary, is to be "easily influenced by ideas provided by other persons" (Collins,

1987). But what *kind* of ideas, and provided by whom? There is a whole range of ideas and persons constituting complex continua. If I suggest to you that the earth is round, or that the speed of light is an absolute value, this surely differs considerably from suggesting that you will be reunited after death with your loved ones who preceded you, or that your country is the best in the world. Similarly, the acceptance of these suggestions will depend very much on whether they are made by a professor of physics, a priest, or someone having no such qualifications whatsoever.

Anxiety and depression, on the other hand, are characterized very clearly by orderly reactions which can be directly related to stressful incidents of one kind or another. These orderly reactions can be measured psychophysiologically, or we can look at hormone secretion or even such things as the size of the adrenals. Thus it is easier to conceive of people as prone to anxiety, or to depression, by observing their reactions to empirical manipulations of certain stressors. While even this type of research presents great difficulties (Eysenck & Eysenck, 1985), at least in principle such research approaches the normal type of scientific work carried out in psychology. Suggestibility, as I will point out presently, presents peculiar difficulties for this kind of approach.

There is another way in which anxiety and depression are clearly much easier to investigate. A person is normally well aware of his state of anxiety, or his degree of depression. Fear thermometers have been used in research and have shown a high degree of reliability and validity when results are compared with the outcome of psychophysiological investigations (Rachman & Hodgson, 1980). The very definition of suggestibility precludes such a recourse to introspection. A person who is easily influenced by suggestions would strenuously deny that he has been so influenced, and will quite honestly declare that his reactions are due to perfectly rational motives. Suggestions often work through a pretence. If the victim is aware of the pretence, he is no longer suggestible. Thus clearly we cannot use self-knowledge and self-awareness in the way that we can use it for the determination of anxiety and depression; this is the major drawback for an investigation of suggestibility.

Sometimes, of course, we are well aware of cause and effect in the case of suggestion. We may see a woman behaving in a "suggestive" manner, and we are perfectly aware of both the intent and the effect. Would we consider this a case of suggestibility? There are many such problems which are partly semantic, but mainly due to the lack of proper definition or analysis of the very concept of "suggestibility." Such analysis should precede the empirical investigation of the concept, but as Gheorghiu, et al. (1989) make clear, there has been little such preliminary discussion of the many uses of the term. If we follow Brown (1960/1820) in identifying "suggestion" with "association," an identification which seems perfectly justifiable semantically, then it would be very difficult to adopt the notion of a *trait* of suggestibility—everybody would be suggestible, and probably to the same extent, because everyone forms associations, and no one has suggested that the tendency to form associations can be regarded as the basis for a trait! Clearly, this would be an extreme degree of generalization of a concept, but not one which would contradict common semantic uses.

The more restricted use of the term "suggestibility," which is quite widely adopted, would reduce its applicability to cases where we have two persons, namely Person A, the suggestor, and Person B, the suggestee. A attempts to influence B to believe something, to act in a certain way, or to perceive something along lines which are not congruent with reality. This influence has to be asserted indirectly, i.e., not through bribing or punishing B, or attempting to influence him overtly. Thus to say, "Raise your arm, or I'll hit you over the head with my stick!" would not be a case of suggestion. But to get B to stand up, with his arm stretched out in front of him, and then to say to him, "Just hold out your arm as you're holding it now and listen to what I am saying. Your arm is beginning to feel lighter and lighter, it is beginning to rise, your arm is going up and up. . .," would be a case of suggestion. It may or may not be followed by an actual raising of the arm or, in the case of people who are negatively suggestible, by a lowering of the arm!

Such a suggestion may be conveyed either verbally, as in the above case, or indirectly, as in the case of the Binet Weight Illusion. The second of these involves a series of weights which are arranged in front of B, the first weighing 20 grams, the next 40 grams, the next 60 grams, the next 80 grams, and the next 100 grams, with all the following weights being exactly 100 grams. The first few weights give the suggestion that later weights will increase in weight, and this suggestion may be accepted or rejected depending on the subject's "suggestibility." Procedures such as these may give rise to tests of suggestibility, but these suffer from obvious defects which are often neglected in scientific discussion.

Consider the arm-raising test, or the even more widely used Body-Sway ("falling forward") test, in which the suggestion is made to the subject that he or she is falling forward, and the actual maximum displacement forward and backward is measured. There are great individual differences in response to this test, and these are certainly related to important external variables, such as degree of neurotic

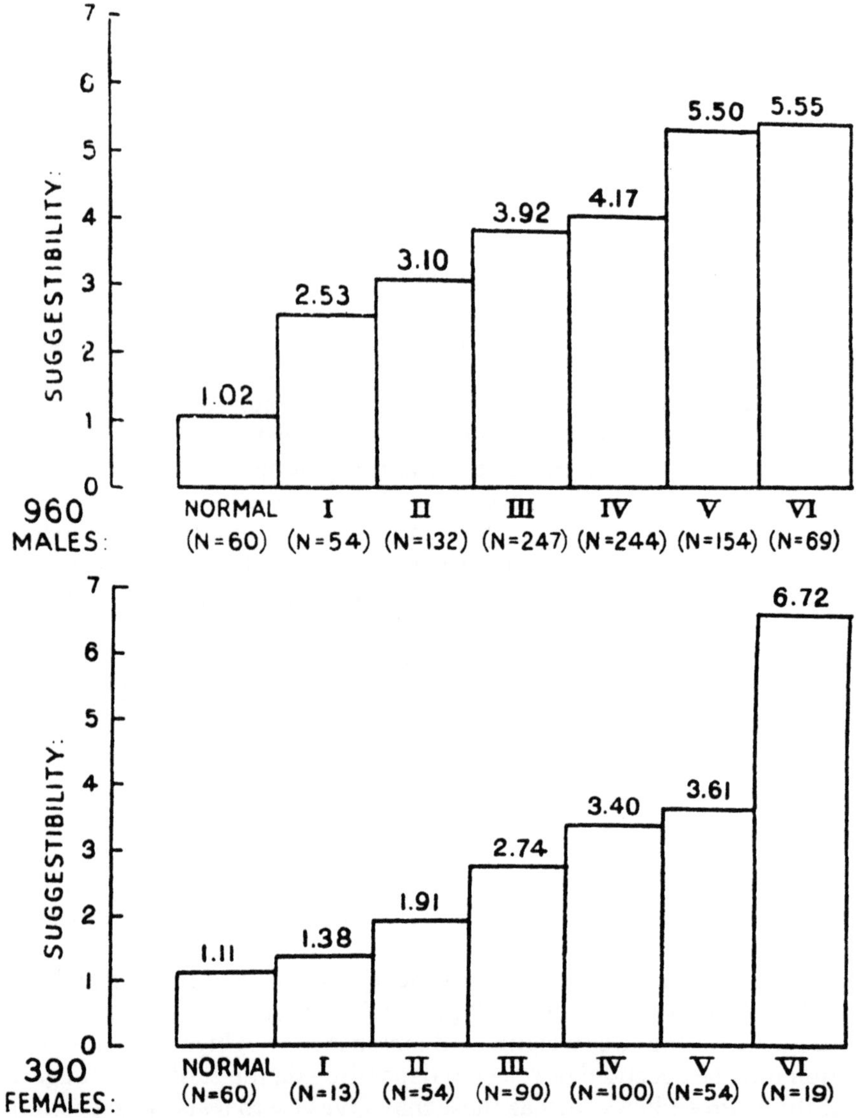

Figure 3.1. Body-sway suggestibility as a function of degree of neuroticism in males and females. (Eysenck, 1947.)

involvement (Eysenck, 1947). Figure 3.1 shows the degree of suggestibility, as so measured, for a group of normal (non-neurotic) subjects, and six groups increasing in degree of neurotic involvement as rated by the psychiatrists in charge of them.

What can be said about this measure of suggestibility? The first question of course is whether suggestibility, so measured, is identical with suggestibility measured along different lines. We will take up this point very shortly, but as shown by Eysenck and Furneaux (1945), the Body-Sway test does not correlate at all with tests like the Binet Weight Illusion test! Similarly, we did not find that the Weight Illusion test correlated with degree of neuroticism, so that obviously we are dealing here with two quite different types of suggestibility, and the use of the very term thus becomes highly questionable.

The test at least appears to be objective, but this too may be an illusion. In some of my early experiments I had two assistants who administered the tests to large random samples of the population. One was a tall, good-looking, very self-possessed woman who spoke firmly and inspired confidence. The other was a rather smaller, 'mousy' individual who appeared somewhat afraid of being in the same room with the subject. When I compared the mean amount of sway produced by the subjects tested by my assistants, the subjects tested by the former swayed almost twice as much as those tested by the latter! In other words, the results of any test depend to a very large extent on the tester, and are thus not a pure measure of the suggestibility of the subject, even if we were willing to grant that we were measuring suggestibility.

The next step in my procedure was to use a gramophone record, with the instructions spoken by myself. This seemed to be a much more objective method, but I soon noted that there was a curious interaction effect between the message recorded and the behavior of the subject. The instructions read: "You are falling, you're falling forward, you're falling forward *now,* you're falling, you're falling forward, you're falling forward *now.* . . ." The subjects of course, standing there with their eyes closed, are swaying forward and backward to some extent in any case, regardless of instructions (static ataxia). I found that if a forward sway coincided with the statement, "you're falling forward *now,*" the person became more suggestible. However, people swaying backwards at the time became less suggestible. In other words, quite accidental features of the procedure might influence the degree of suggestibility! Other factors which seemed to influence the degree of suggestibility were expectations, what subjects might have heard about the test previously, their reactions to the reception they received in the laboratory, etc. Thus even apparently very objective tests may be subject to external influences which in part at least destroy its objectivity. Nevertheless, and in spite of these complications, we found the test to have a reasonable reliability, and to show quite considerable correlations with external measures, such as that of neuroticism.

There is, however, another complication involved in this type of test, a complication which the simple score does not recognize. We found it necessary to discriminate between *attitude* and *aptitude,* and we believe that this distinction is a fundamental factor for many other types of psychological measure, as well as for the Body-Sway and other tests of suggestibility. We assume that people have aptitudes, probably determined to some degree by genetic causes, and in part by antecedent life experiences which determine the extent to which suggestion may be effective. This is the notion underlying our thinking about suggestibility. However, in addition to this aptitude, we must consider also the attitude of the person to the general testing situation. If the subject is hostile, does not wish to co-operate, disregards instructions, etc., the reaction to suggestion would be much less positive than if that person is in a friendly, co-operative mood, with a positive attitude towards the experiment and the test in general. Similarly, attitudes may be a powerful component of an individual's response to hypnotic suggestion. It is probably the person's attitude which is partially affected by the various external influences mentioned above, such as those disturbing the measurement of suggestibility in the Body-Sway test.

Eysenck and Rees (1945) carried out an investigation designed to look at this particular problem. Our subjects were screened by the Body-Sway test to form contrasting groups of high and low susceptibility. Subjects were tested in the normal state, and then in a narcotic state induced by the injection of sodium amital. (Similar results were also obtained by using inhalation of nitrous oxide in place of the injected drug.) We thought that these drugs would alter the subject's *attitude,* and decrease the ability for conscious resistance to suggestion. In order to test subjects in the drugged condition, their reactions to suggestion were tested by a task they could perform easily in a totally relaxed condition (i.e., the Press-Release test, in which the subject lies on a couch holding a soft rubber bulb in his hand). The experimenter suggests that the subject is squeezing the bulb tighter and tighter, and the actual pressure on the bulb is recorded on a pneumatically controlled recording device. It was found that in response to suggestion the pressure on the bulb was increased by narcosis for the group which was originally of *high* suggestibility when screened. However, narcosis did not alter significantly the response of those originally of *low* suggestibility. The subjects had been instructed to try to resist the effects of the suggestion and to keep their hand pressure constant. We therefore reasoned that the drug was *decreasing* conscious control in both groups, so that what was manifested in the drugged state was a differential degree of *aptitude* between the two groups. The group with high aptitude showed a greatly increased response. But the other group, having little natural aptitude, showed little change in response, even when conscious control was decreased by the drug, i.e., when their attitudes were manipulated. The inability to replicate many experiments on suggestibility and hypnosis may be due to a neglect of this factor of attitude. It is an important one in all psychological experiments, and should always be investigated experimentally.

Considerations of this kind are thus particularly important when we consider the problem of replicability. Consider as a model case that of eye-blink conditioning, which I have discussed in some detail elsewhere (Eysenck, 1981). On the basis of my theory of personality, I had predicted that eye-blink conditioning would be positively correlated with introversion, but not at all with neuroticism. Kenneth Spence, on the basis of his theory, predicted that eye-blink conditioning would be positively correlated with neuroticism (anxiety), but not at all with introversion. We both published the outcomes of the studies, verifying our own hypotheses, and disproving those of the other! Clearly here was a case of "failure to replicate" of considerable interest and importance. How is this possible? There were slight differences in our methods of measurement, but there is no way in which these could account for the differences in our findings.

Gregory Kimble, who had noted that Spence's results could only be replicated north of the Mason-Dixon line, but never south, finally visited Spence's laboratory, and suggested an explanation. Our practice had always been to reduce anxiety as far as possible in our subjects. This was done by removing all the apparatus from the testing room, by reassuring subjects that there would be no electric shocks and no pain of any kind, and quite generally treating them in a kindly and considerate manner. Spence, on the other hand, arranged things in such a way that their anxiety would be maximised by having all the apparatus in full view, issuing no reassurance about electric shocks (of which subjects in a psychology laboratory are rightly afraid), and doing nothing to allay their anxiety. Hence, differences in anxiety had maximum scope in Spence's laboratory, and they drowned any possible differences in arousal level between extroverts and introverts. In our own laboratory, differences in anxiety had little or no chance to emerge, and hence differences in arousal level between extroverts and introverts had maximum scope. Thus anxiety-produced differences in *attitude* determined the differential outcome of the experiments, leading to an apparent lack of confirmation. If we agree that there are important similarities and possible causal relations between conditioning and suggestibility, then the example may serve to explain some of the failures to replicate in suggestibility experiments to be mentioned presently.

These considerations are particularly appropriate for looking at answers to the question of whether suggestibility is indeed a single trait, extending over many different methods of measurement, or whether it is merely a common term for a number of quite separate and different types of "suggestibility." Binet (1900) raised the problem in his original contribution: "Since there is certainly not one unique and absolute aptitude for suggestion, and since people are prone to suggestion from all possible sources, and through every avenue by which one perceives and reasons, whether one is conscious of this or whether one merely desires it, there are grounds for wondering whether a person's suggestibility, when measured by process 'a' is the same as when measured as the result of process 'b,' 'c' . . ., 'd' . . . and so on" (p. 309).

Binet himself observed that unconscious motor reactions induced by means of suggestion seemed to take place independently of other forms of responsiveness to suggestion. Pearce (1902) seemed to favour a general factor, but he only worked with tests of motor suggestibility. Later workers, such as Scott (1910), Town (1916), Aveling and Hargreaves (1921), Otis (1924), and Estabrooks (1929) found rather weak, or nonexistent relationships between the different suggestion procedures. Eysenck (1943) and Eysenck and Furneaux (1945) used a number of tests and correlated them. They discovered *two* major factors, one loading on the direct motor procedures of ideomotor activity (primary suggestibility), and another composed rather of indirect sensory test procedures (secondary suggestibility). Correlations producing the factor of primary suggestibility were considerably larger than those responsible for secondary suggestibility, but that might in part be due to greater reliability of the measures. Primary suggestibility very significantly predicted hypnotizability, but was not correlated with intelligence. Secondary suggestibility was correlated with intelligence, but did not predict hypnotizability. There was no correlation between primary and secondary suggestibility.

Many replications have been reported since that day, such as those of Benton and Bandura (1953), or Stukat (1958). Others, like Hammer, Evans, and Bartlett (1963) looked at other possible factors of suggestibility, and more recently so-called interrogative suggestibility has been looked at and found uncorrelated with other types of suggestibility (Gheorghiu, Grimm, & Hodapp, 1978; Gudjonsson, 1987; Young, Bentall, Slade, & Dewey, 1987).

Replications of the Eysenck and Furneaux (1945) results have only been partial, and occasionally completely missing, as in the Benton and Bandura (1953) study. However, this failure to replicate has to be looked at in the context of differential attitudes. The work of Eysenck and Furneaux was done on random samples of neurotic soldiers of average intelligence; that of Benton and Bandura on students of quite high intelligence. There are many relevant differences between these two samples. The mean sway of the group tested by Eysenck and Furneaux was 6.5 inches, that of the group tested by Benton and Bandura was 1.7 inches! These results suggest that there was a very negative attitude among the students, compared with the rather positive attitude among the patients. Traditionally, American students are rather suspicious of being tested in psychological laboratories, and react negatively to this. It would seem that many of the students showed no suggestibility at all, whereas this was quite rare among the patients. This difference in population parameters by itself might account for the rather low correlations of those among the primary suggestibility tests (Benton and Bandura, 1953). It is a pervading weakness of much American research that it is carried out on college sophomores, who by no stretch of the imagination can be regarded as a random sample of the population. Neither, of course, can the neurotic patients from the Eysenck and Furneaux study; the Stukat study is perhaps closer to such a desirable state.

The complete absence of secondary suggestibility in the Benton and Bandura study may be due in part to differences in IQ, which are commented on in fact by Benton and Bandura. If these suggestibility tests are correlated with intelligence, as Binet, Eysenck, and Furneaux had found, then increasing the mean IQ in the samples, and reducing the variance, would inevitably reduce the applicability of the tests.

On the whole, it seems likely that the distinction between primary and secondary suggestibility is a reasonable one which can be replicated when appropriate samples are chosen, and appropriate tests administered under conditions where attitudes are relatively favourable. Nevertheless, the answer to Binet's question must inevitably be that there is no general factor of suggestibility, but that there are at least two, and probably many others, including that of "interrogative suggestibility." Evaluative conditioning, although labelled "conditioning," appears to be another sort of suggestibility, and one might continue to suggest several others (Hammer, Evans, & Bartlett, 1963).

We can see that the question raised at the beginning of this chapter, "Is Suggestibility?" must be answered in the negative. There is no single, unitary trait of suggestibility, no one, uniform type of reaction to different kinds of suggestion in human subjects. There are several, or possibly many different suggestibilities which bear no relation to each other. These are uncorrelated and, in turn, correlate differentially with other cognitive and emotional variables. This finding is of considerable interest and importance, although of course it does make books containing in their title the word "suggestibility" of rather doubtful value! Suggestibility in this respect contrasts very markedly with anxiety, which does seem to possess a very definite central core. Possibly it is because of this, as well as the other reasons already mentioned, that there has been so much more investigation of anxiety than of suggestibility. However, in science, negative conclusions can be as important as positive ones. Future work should certainly be oriented to the discovery of the different suggestibilities that may exist, to more accurate and reliable measurement, and to discovery of their relations to such variables as personality, hypnotizability, intelligence, etc. As the rest of this book will show, much already has been accomplished along these lines.

References

Aveling, F., & Hargreaves, H.C. (1921). Suggestibility with and without prestige in children. *British Journal of Psychology, 12,* 53–75.

Barber, T.X. (1984). Changing "unchangeable" bodily processes by (hypnotic) suggestions: A new look at hypnosis, cognitions, imagining, and the mind-body problem. In A.A. Sheikh (ed.), *Imagination and healing* (pp. 69–127). Farmingdale, NY: Baywood.

Beecher, H.K. (1959). *Measurement of subjective responses.* New York: Oxford University Press.

Benton, A.L., & Bandura, A. (1953). "Primary" and "secondary" suggestibility. *Journal of Abnormal and Social Psychology, 48,* 336–40.

Binet, A. (1900). *La suggestibilité.* Paris: Schleicher Frères.

Bloch, B. (1927). Über die heilung der warzen durch suggestion. *Klinische Wochenschrift, 6,* 2271–79; 2320–25.

Brown, T. (1960). *Lectures on the philosophy of the human mind.* London: Tegg. (Memoir by D. Welsh, 20th ed: Original published in 1820.)

Collins. (1987). *The Collins dictionary and thesaurus* (p. 1004). London: Collins.

Estabrooks, G.H. (1929). Experimental studies in suggestion. *Journal of Genetic Psychology, 36,* 120–39.

Evans, F.J. (1967). Suggestibility in the normal waking state. *Psychological Bulletin, 67,* 114–29.

Eysenck, H.J. (1943). Susceptibility to a visual illusion, as related to primary and secondary suggestibility, and other functions. *British Journal of Psychology, 34,* 32–36.

Eysenck, H.J. (1947). *Dimensions of personality.* London: Routledge and Kegan Paul.

Eysenck, H.J. (1981). *A model for personality.* New York: Springer.

Eysenck, H.J. (1989). Personality, primary and secondary suggestibility, and hypnosis. In V.A . Gheorghiu, P. Netter, H.J. Eysenck, & R. Rosenthal (eds.), *Suggestion and suggestibility: Theory and Research* (pp. 57–67). New York: Springer-Verlag.

Eysenck, H.J., & Eysenck, M.W. (1985). *Personality and individual differences: A natural science approach.* New York: Plenum.

Eysenck, H.J., & Furneaux, W.D. (1945). Primary and secondary suggestibility: An experimental and statistical study. *Journal of Experimental Psychology, 35,* 485–503.

Eysenck, H.J., & Rees, W.L. (1945). States of heightened suggestibility: Narcosis. *Journal of Mental Science, 91,* 301–10.

Eysenck, M.W., & Eysenck, H.J. (1980). Mischel and the concept of personality. *British Journal of Psychology, 71,* 191–209.

Gheorghiu, V.A. (1989). The development of research on suggestibility: Critical considerations. In V.A. Gheorghiu, P. Netter, H.J. Eysenck, & R. Rosenthal (eds.), *Suggestion and suggestibility: Theory and research* (pp. 3–55). New York: Springer-Verlag.

Gheorghiu, V.A., Grimm, M., & Hodapp, V. (1978). Standardisierung einer skala zur erfassung der sensorischen suggestibilität (indirekte variante) an schülern der sekundarstufe II. *Diagnostica, 14,* 350–61.

Gheorghiu, V.A., Netter, P., Eysenck, H.J., & Rosenthal, R. (eds.). (1989). *Suggestion and suggestibility: Theory and research.* New York: Springer-Verlag.

Gudjonsson, G.H. (1987). Historical background to suggestibility: How interrogative suggestibility differs from other types of suggestibility. *Personality and Individual Differences,* 8, 347–55.

Hammer, A.G., Evans, F.J., & Bartlett, M. (1963). Factors in hypnosis and suggestion. *Journal of Abnormal and Social Psychology, 67,* 15–23.

Haniotes, C.J. (1977). Hypnosis and breast enlargement—a pilot study. *Journal of the International Society of Professional Hypnosis, 6,* 8–12.

Ikemi, Y., & Nakagawa, S. (1962). A psychosomatic study of contagious dermatitis. *Kyushu Journal of Medical Science, 13,* 335–52.

James, W. (1890). *Principles of psychology.* New York: Holt.

Le Cron, L.M. (1969). Breast development through hypnotic suggestions. *Journal of the American Society of Psychosomatic Dentistry and Medicine, 16,* 58–61.

Mischel, W. (1968). *Personality and assessment.* London: Wiley.

Otis, M.A. (1924). A study of suggestibility of children. *Archives of Psychology, 11*(70).

Pearce, H.J. (1902). Experimental observations upon normal motor suggestibility. *Psychological Review, 9,* 329–56.

Prioleau, L., Murdoch, M., & Brody, N. (1983). An analysis of psychotherapy vs. placebo studies. *Behavioural and Brain Sciences, 6,* 275–85.

Rachman, S., & Hodgson, R. (1980). *Obsessions and compulsions.* Englewood Cliffs, NJ: Prentice-Hall.

Rachman, S.J., & Wilson, G.T. (1980). *The effects of psychological therapy.* London: Pergamon Press.

Scott, W.D. (1910). Personal differences in suggestibility. *Psychological Review, 17,* 147–54.

Smith, M.L., Glass, G.V., & Miller, T.I. (1980). *The benefits of psychotherapy.* Baltimore, MD: The Johns Hopkins University Press.

Staib, A.R., & Logan, D.R. (1977). Hypnotic stimulation of breast growth. *American Journal of Clinical Hypnosis, 19,* 201-08.

Stukat, K.G. (1958). *Suggestibility: A factorial and experimental analysis.* Stockholm: Almqvist and Wiksell.

Town, C.H. (1916). An experimental study of the suggestibility of twelve and fifteen-year old boys. *Psychological Clinic, 10,* 1–12.

Weitzenhoffer, A.M. (1957). *General techniques of hypnotism.* New York: Grune and Stratton.

White, L., Tursky, B., & Schwartz, G.E. (eds.). (1985). *Placebo: Theory, research and mechanisms.* New York: Guilford.

Willard, R.D. (1977). Breast enlargement through visual imagery and hypnosis. *American Journal of Clinical Hypnosis, 19,* 195–200.

Williams, E. (1974). Stimulated breast growth by hypnosis. *Journal of Sex Research, 10,* 316–26.

Young, H.F., Bentall, R.P., Slade, P.D., & Dewey, B.A. (1987). The role of brief instructions and suggestibility in the elicitation of auditory and visual hallucinations in normal and psychiatric subjects. *Journal of Nervous and Mental Disease, 175,* 41–48.

PART TWO

THEORETICAL PERSPECTIVES

4

SUGGESTIBILITY, ABSORPTION, AND DISSOCIATION:
An Integrative Model of Hypnosis

Etzel Cardeña and David Spiegel

"They'll take suggestion as a cat laps milk."
—Antonio in *The Tempest* by Shakespeare

In *The Tempest,* Shakespeare describes the ploys of Prospero to frighten his enemies through his "high charms." He leads them to distraction, enhances their suggestibility and, lastly, gains insight into the workings of their souls. Prospero has been described as a prototypical Renaissance therapist who works on his victims' imagination (and attentional focus) to achieve therapeutic goals (Schleiner, 1987). However, specific theories on the explicit connections between attention, imagination, and increased suggestibility were not developed until the nineteenth century, particularly in relation to the budding literature on the phenomena and processes that we now call "hypnosis."

As Gheorghiu (1989a) has so aptly summarized, the fates of hypnosis and suggestibility have been very closely linked, although an account of their relationship remains unclear. In practice, the scales of hypnotic susceptibility are almost entirely based on the ability to follow a hypnotist's suggestions to distort perceptions and engage in specific motor actions. This approach has recently been criticized by one of the creators of the widely used Stanford scales as being insensitive to the distinction between voluntary and nonvoluntary compliance with a suggestion (Weitzenhoffer, 1980). In theory, hypnosis has been tautologically explained as enhanced suggestibility or, more currently, as a multidimensional occurrence that includes enhanced suggestibility as one of its core components (Gheorghiu, 1989a). Our approach in this paper is to discuss enhanced suggestibility as one of the three main phenomenal components of hypnosis, the other two being absorption and dissociation. We propose that the usual circularity of the theoretical discussions on hypnosis and enhanced suggestibility can be avoided by resorting to the more basic processes of attention deployment and processing of information. We will review current findings and related concepts on the nature of "ordinary" conscious experience and how it changes during a typical hypnotic event. We will propose that changes in cognitive processing during hypnosis facilitate the influence of suggestive communications through a diminution of alternative and self-reflective ideation.

Ordinary conscious experience

At any point, we receive information from at least three different and constant sources: the physical and social surroundings, the stimuli generated endogenously by the body, and the vast network of related associations and stimuli generated by the brain/mind. The idea that conscious experience is a filtered version of a much larger number of processes occurring at any one point has a longstanding history in psychology, certainly including the models of unconscious and dissociative processes espoused, respectively, by Freud and Janet. Nonetheless, and perhaps because of a misunderstanding of James's notion of the continuity of the stream of thought, it has frequently been assumed that conscious experience has greater thematic continuity than it actually does.

The account of our ongoing conscious experience as a smooth and thematically congruent process was dealt a devastating blow by Nietzsche at the end of last century. Since then, this notion has been challenged by fiction writers such as James Joyce and Virginia Woolf. In their writings, the ordinary "stream" of awareness is but a collection of brief, ever-changing associations whose claim to continuity, rationality, and "reality orientation" is tenuous. More recent empirical work has confirmed that our account of ordinary experience as possessing thematic continuity and rationality is a false reconstruction rather than an accurate portrayal of the ongoing stream of thought. Further, the capacity to suppress unbidden mentation and maintain a continuous reflective stance is profoundly limited (Uleman & Bargh, 1989), as every meditation practitioner knows.

In a systematic study of thought sampling with University of Minnesota students, Klinger (1978) found that their thoughts tended to be very brief (median of about 5 seconds). These thoughts were commonly related to the immediate situation, including periodic evaluation of goal attainment, and were "reality-oriented." But there was also a substantive proportion of thoughts that included some strangeness and distortion (about 1/5 of the samples). In a series of experiments using signal detection and other paradigms, Singer and collaborators (Singer, 1988) reported that about 50% of their respondents' mentation was unrelated to the specific task in which they were involved. It was also found that, at least in the case of adolescents, a high proportion of their unrelated mentation dealt with unresolved conflictual issues.

Extrapolating from this body of literature, we propose that, under ordinary circumstances, a given "primary" suggestion (see below) might become but one of the number of ever-changing thoughts and images and, at that, one that might be in competition with more urgent issues. Further, the possible impact of a suggestion would probably be intermittently monitored and reflected upon by the thinker. This is not to say that the intended suggestion might not result "in the acceptance with conviction of the communicated proposition in the absence of logically adequate grounds for its acceptance," as McDougall (1908; in Gheorghiu, 1989b, p. 104) would phrase it. Rather, we are proposing that, other things being equal, the disjointed, competitive, stimulus-loaded, and intermittently reflective nature of ordinary processing would not be as conducive to following a suggestion as the hypnotic context. Although suggestibility in occurrences other than hypnosis is not the topic of this paper, it is significant that enhanced suggestibility has been reported in connection with light sleep and drowsiness (Budzynski, 1986), restricted environmental stimulation (Barabasz, 1989), and an exhaustion period following strong emotional expression after pharmacologically induced arousal (Greenberg and Safran, 1987). In all of these procedures, the amount of competition from external sources of stimulation is reduced in comparison with the ordinary mode of consciousness.

Hypnotic processes and suggestibility

Hypnosis and enhanced suggestibility

Suggestion and suggestibility are complex and multilayered concepts with a long history that is only partially related to hypnosis (Gheorghiu, 1989a). In this paper, we are exclusively concerned with a theoretical account of enhanced suggestibility within the hypnotic context. In a very influential, although not uncontroversial distinction, Eysenck and Furneaux proposed in 1945 (see Eysenck, 1989) that there were two main types of suggestibility: primary (involving ideomotor tasks and closely correlated with hypnotizability) and secondary (involving indirect sensory procedures and not correlated with hypnotizability). Gheorghiu (1971, 1989a) has clarified this distinction by declaring that "primary" suggestibility involves direct, overt suggestions, whereas "secondary" suggestibility involves indirect, concealed suggestions.

Less controversial, and in Weitzenhoffer's view "unquestionable" (1980, p. 132), have been the experiments showing that hypnotic induction increases direct suggestibility (Weitzenhoffer & Sjoberg 1961; Barber & Glass, 1962; Hilgard & Tart, 1966). Weitzenhoffer (1980) has further characterized the increase in suggestibility following induction procedures as involving only an enhancement of nonvoluntary compliance with the suggestions. This is contrasted with a deliberate, voluntary effort to follow the instructions. In agreement with this position, Bowers (1982) has reported a high correlation between the criterion of behavioral responsiveness to suggestion experienced *nonvolitionally* and the Stanford Hypnotic Susceptibility Scale (Form C). Bowers, Laurence, and Hart (1988) also found that a substantial number of participants (approximately 80%: Table 2, p. 341) passing a test item experienced the enactment of the suggestions as involving some degree of non-voluntariness. Fully 32.2% of their participants reported that their response had been experienced as "happening by itself." Arguably, the ability to experience suggestion as nonvoluntary, which is highly correlated with "objective" indices of hypnotizability, is a personality trait that is rather impervious to training procedures (Crouse & Kurtz, 1984).

A common increase in direct suggestibility following induction procedures is uncontroversial, as Hilgard and Tart (1966) pointed out. However, this does not imply that suggestibility is synonymous with a hypnotic state, which includes other basic phenomena. They further speculated that enhanced suggestibility to some suggestions might disappear in "deeper states of hypnosis." Consistent with this speculation, Hilgard (1986) reports that some of his respondents would lose contact with the hypnotist during self-assessed very deep hypnotic states until the hypnotist would lower the level of depth by placing a hand on the participant's shoulder. A more direct example of this phenomenon can be found in a recent project investigating the phenomenology of self-assessed very deep hypnosis (Cardeña, 1988a). After a procedure minimizing any explicit suggestion other than to go as deeply as possible into hypnosis, the following exchange in reference to a homonyms test took place during a session with a usually very cooperative hypnotic virtuoso:

Hypnotist: I would like you to tell me the first word that comes to your mind. . . . "Arch."

Participant: That's not a word.

H: "A-r-c-h."

(*Long pause during which the participant is silent.*)

H: O.K., let me try another one. "Beat."

P: That's not important.

Rather than a deliberate attempt to resist a request to which the participant had previously acquiesced, the exchange shows that during very deep states the participant's experiences are very unusual. They seem to be spontaneous, out of the ordinary, and reflect a much greater investment in "internally" generated phenomena. Or, as the participant just quoted stated with regards to the items of the homonyms test, "these things aren't here, they're somewhere else. They're only where you are." In a certain sense, in very deep hypnosis the respondents seem to disregard some specific suggestions that may not be meaningful within their current experience. At another level, though, they are actually enacting the higher-order suggestion of going into as deep a state as possible.

The nature of hypnosis

As mentioned, an increase in primary suggestibility commonly follows a hypnotic procedure. Furthermore, it has been well established theoretically (e.g., Hilgard, 1986) and empirically (e.g., Bowers, 1982) that, in addition to perceived nonvoluntary actions, an increase in the vividness and conviction of imaginal experiences are common aspects of the hypnotic experience. It is also clear, for example, that the prominence and characteristics of the imaginal experiences depend on individual factors (Pekala, 1989) and variations in level of depth (Cardeña, 1988a). In agreement with a multidimensional consideration of hypnosis, we will consider the factors that—theoretically or empirically—have been associated with the hypnotic experience.

Shor considered suggestibility to be a common but not characteristic phenomenon of hypnotic experience. The three main factors of hypnosis that he originally proposed are: a) trance (the fading of the "generalized reality orientation," which gives context and perspective to ongoing contents of consciousness); b) nonconscious involvement (the nonconscious fulfilling of a role as a hypnotized participant); and c) archaic involvement (the "transferential" relationship toward the therapist) (Shor, 1962, 1970). Hence, Shor pointed to the nonconscious aspects of cultural socialization (i.e., nonconscious involvement), personal psychodynamics (i.e., archaic involvement), and cognitive (i.e., trance) elements of a hypnotic occurrence.

Kihlstrom, et al. (1989) recently conducted a factorial analysis of those three factors, plus five other "dimensional variables" (drowsiness, relaxation, vividness of imagery, absorption, and access to the unconscious) that Shor (1979) later developed. They demonstrated that 6 out of the 8 scales loaded in a general factor similar to the absorption construct. The two scales loading poorly with this factor were archaic involvement and relaxation. It is not surprising that archaic involvement, which deals with transferential-laden patterns of response, would be independent from more purely cognitive processes. Certainly the perceived relationship with the hypnotist is basic to the person's trust (or lack of it) to go under hypnosis, but it can be considered more of a requirement to engage in an alternate mode of awareness, rather than an integral part of it.

The finding concerning the factorial independence of relaxation merits a lengthier comment, given Edmonston's (1989) declaration that relaxation is a defining component of hypnosis. The arguments against Edmonston's position are very strong and involve historical, cross-cultural, and experimental evidence. Historically, the association between hypnotic-like occurrences and relaxation was not a part of Mesmer's method, but rather a later development by his disciple, the Marquis de Puysegur. Congruent with this far from inevitable development is the cross-cultural literature on the phenomenology of possession and shamanic events, which bears a close correspondence with reported hypnotic experiences (Cardeña, 1988b, 1989). Also, there is scant but consistent literature showing that *tension* enhancement verbalizations can induce trance experiences (Ludwig & Lyle, 1964), and that strenuous physical activity coupled with a hypnotic induction can enhance suggestibility (Banyai & Hilgard, 1976; Malott, 1984). Lastly, hypnotic virtuosos are able to achieve very deep states while engaged in pedaling an ergometer, even though they may take slightly longer in achieving those states than while relaxed (Cardeña, 1988a). This is probably because of the greater difficulty to engage fully in imaginal experiences while maintaining an active body. Relaxation is a culturally incidental, rather than necessary and sufficient, condition of hypnosis. What the usual relaxation induction does share with other modalities is the prolonged and continuous narrowing of attention on the same type of (e.g., somatic) events, with an associated neglect of much of the usual competing environmental stimulation.

In addition to the theoretically derived factors of Shor, a number of factorial studies give support to at least three common dimensions of a hypnotic experience: a) lack of reflective awareness, b) a sense of compulsion and enhanced suggestibility, and c) unusual phenomenal occurrences, including effortless experiencing and increase in imagery, changes in body image and somatic sensations, and others (Evans, 1963; Ås & Ostvold, 1968; Field & Palmer, 1969; see also Cardeña, 1988a; Bowers, Laurence, & Hart, 1988). The first factor is similar to the construct of absorption: the second factor directly addresses the findings of enhanced primary suggestibility. Although less overtly, dissociation, which has also been proposed as an experiential and/or theoretical construct underlying hypnotic experience (Hilgard, 1986; Spiegel, 1990) would be a constituent of the "classic suggestion" effect and of other phenomenal occurrences (e.g., a sensation of losing contact with the body). We turn now to a consideration of the relationship between enhanced suggestibility, absorption, and dissociative processes.

Absorption and suggestibility

The construct of absorption has been defined as "a disposition for having episodes of single 'total' attention that fully engages one's representational (i.e., perceptual, imaginative and ideational) resources" (Tellegen & Atkinson, 1974). An absorption scale devised by Tellegen has shown a consistent, albeit moderate, correlation with hypnotizability. In contrast with the usual broken stream of ordinary experience mentioned above, absorption is characterized by focal, undivided attention to an event, either internal or external. Attention can be engaged by a relatively simple stimulus (e.g., a spot on the ceiling) or a complex stimulus (e.g., a beautiful landscape). Along these lines, preliminary analyses suggest that absorption can be conceptualized along two dimensions: internal versus external focus, and narrow versus expansive object of attention (A. Tellegen, personal communication, Fall 1987). What is important is that the individual maintains his/her attention in a certain type of event, which therefore achieves particular salience, rather than doing a frequent sampling of different types of experiential events (e.g., constantly shifting attention from perceptual to imaginal events, etc.). The reduced sampling also implies that frequent changes from a merely conscious to a reflectively conscious stance will be less probable.

In contrast with the frequent appearance of unbidden thoughts and the conscious monitoring of goal acquisition, the absorbed individual becomes fully engaged in a self-initiated activity (e.g., artistic performance) or a passive one (e.g., watching an engaging movie). In the specific case of the hypnotized individual, O'Shaughnessy (1972) has characterized his/her experience as being "necessarily and continuously unselfconsciously conscious of the hypnotizer, and intermittently conscious of his voice; but he is not conscious of the world. . . . His consciousness of these items *in* the world is a merely *regional or non-connective consciousness.*" The person lacks (in the case of a deeply hypnotized individual), or has greatly diminished (in a less absorbing experience) meta-consciousness (i.e., the awareness of being aware).

The exclusive and continuous concentration on a type of event is incongruous with the actively maintained frame of reference and context that Shor (1959) called "generalized reality orientation." This is defined as a structured frame of reference in the background of attention which supports, interprets and gives meaning to all experiences" (p. 291). The similarity between Shor's concept and "absorption" is borne out not only conceptually, but also by a recent study showing a high correlation between an operationalization of Shor's concept and the absorption scale devised by Tellegen (Kihlstrom, et al., 1989).

The maintenance of perspective and context in any situation should not be considered a given. Rather, it is one of many sources of internal and external stimulation. Baars (1988) has proposed an influential model of cognitive processing that is congruent with current computational models (Spiegel, 1990). It posits multiple levels of cognitive processing and simultaneous sources of nonconscious information. In Baars's model, the "generalized reality orientation" could be regarded as one of the main (unconscious) contexts that is in continuous competition to access the "global workspace" (i.e., consciousness). Enhancing another context (e.g., one affecting internally generated imaginal experiences) through conscious focusing of attention would lower the probability of the "generalized reality orientation" becoming part of the foreground of conscious awareness. This model does not preclude the general "unreflected on" reality orientation from affecting behavior as in the case, for example, of avoiding a negatively hallucinated chair. What happens, rather, is that the behavior is not reflected on and subjected to a perspectival, critical inquiry, as is the case with the more usual form of (fractured) experiencing. It is not that hypnotic experience implies the unavailability of contextual information. Instead, this background information is not accessed and does not become part of a consciousness that is mostly occupied with an absorbing, continuous experience. In Gheorghiu's terms (1989a), "the conscious monitoring authority is bypassed" (p. 42). This discussion does not contradict the notion of strategic, planned enactment of a hypnotic suggestion, but it does imply that these plans are tacitly, unreflectively carried out.

From this perspective, it should be clear that the general increase in suggestibility after a hypnotic induction would be the natural outcome of the changes in relating to the information conveyed. In the ordinary modality of experiencing, a suggestion might be one of a number of events occupying the person's attentional resources. Because of the continuous flux in the contents of consciousness, the suggestion would not only be in competition with other sources of stimulation, but might also be the subject of reflective, critical analysis. In contrast, hypnosis fosters an absorbing, unself-conscious processing of information in which a suggestion might play a more predominant role in the mental life of the individual. Because of the diminished competition with other sources of stimulation, and because of the continuity of unreflective mentation that absorption implies, a suggestion during hypnosis would have greater salience and receive a more intense and enduring focus of attention.

James (1890, pp. 387–88) provides a poignant example of the nature of mental competition. Holding, as he did, that ideas were invitations to action, he wondered why his ideas about getting up and getting dressed on a cold morning did not prevent him from lying in bed for a long period. His answer was that, given the circumstances, every idea/image of getting up, lighting a fire, etc., was counterposed by strong competing ideas about the cold and discomfort associated with getting up. In a hypnotic context, the number of shifts in mental contents is greatly reduced, which may account for the common observation that hypnotized individuals commonly underestimate the amount of time spent in hypnosis (Gheorghiu, 1989a). Because fewer mental shifts occur during hypnosis than during waking, the hypnotized individual might therefore assume that, at least subjectively, fewer changes have occurred and, hence, less time has elapsed.

The effects of a diminished critical process on suggestibility is exemplified by the recent work by Malott, Bourg, and Crawford (1989). The authors found that, in contrast with a nonhypnotic condition, during hypnosis their respondents agreed more and gave fewer counterarguments to persuasive communication. In agreement with an interactionist approach, the authors also report that, during "waking" and hypnotic conditions, highly hypnotizable individuals were in greater agreement with the communication and produced more favorable thoughts than low hypnotizables.

Absorption in a hypnotic context occurs mostly through the interaction between the general cognitive disposition to become absorbed and a specific situation that purposefully seeks to engage the individual's concentration capacities. It is not particularly controversial that hypnotic techniques commonly involve the focusing and narrowing of attention. Thus, breadth and a shifting focus are exchanged for continuity of attention and an ensuing intensity of the mental events receiving attention. The typical induction procedure usually proceeds by eliminating sources of stimulation (e.g., restricting sensorial stimulation) and directing the attentional resources to one or at most two foci of attention.

Alternatively, induction techniques using confusion and uncertainty may confuse or overwhelm limited attentional resources onto a "contentless" context that the organism is motivated to resolve (Baars, 1988). In addition to hypnotic forms of induction, indigenous practices (e.g., drumming, dancing) commonly involve forms of stimulation that help focus and maintain attention on one or two specific sources of stimulation. A source of particular interest in recent years has been the very high hypnotizability of clinical populations, such as post-traumatic stress disorder and multiple personality disorder (Spiegel, Hunt, & Dondershine, 1988; Spiegel & Cardeña, 1990). These results might represent a "natural experiment" in which predisposed individuals exposed to a traumatic event have their attention automatically drawn by, and focused on, an event that demands immediate organismic response. Later on, given specific internal or external triggers, these individuals may automatically engage themselves in these processes even though they may no longer be adaptive.

Consistent with this view, experimental work suggests that the central characteristics of a laboratory-induced traumatic event may be well retained in memory, to the detriment of specific and peripheral details (Christianson & Loftus, 1987; Loftus & Burns, 1982). It does not take a big speculative leap to propose that, during a traumatic event, the individual engages in a narrower and more focused attentional process, and become more absorbed in the event. This style of cognitive processing would also imply a diminished capacity to process in conscious awareness the context and "generalized reality orientation" of that event (Spiegel & Cardeña, 1990).

Dissociation and suggestibility

In his pioneering work, Janet anticipated much of the present argument by discussing the relationship between narrowing of attention and dissociation (van der Hart & Horst, 1989). The connections between dissociative processes and hypnotic phenomena in general have historical and theoretical underpinnings that are beyond the scope of this paper (Hilgard, 1986; Spiegel, 1990). The notion of dissociation has been used to describe seemingly autonomous psychological systems. These range from a simple "split off" idea with its associated affect, body state, etc. (what Janet called idée fixe), to experienced alternate identities within the same individual (i.e., multiple personality disorder). We will concentrate our discussion on explaining why suggested and, at times, spontaneous actions are experienced during hypnosis as dissociated from the usual sense of self-control.

To start with, we should point out that the enactment of not fully deliberate acts is a constant occurrence in everyday life. As we engage in any activity, such as writing a paper, there is a constant variety of physical movements (including "classical" hypnosis behaviors such as arms rising and falling) as well as other events that happen without any *deliberate* planning or implementation by the actor. Of course, these actions are usually not regarded as impersonal except in rare modes of experiencing such as depersonalization. In the hypnotic context, however, changes in attentional processes bring about a different relationship to these same behaviors. The "classical suggestion effect," implying an experience of involuntariness, can be accounted for by three factors: the lack of competition of the suggestion with other mental contents, its resulting salience, and the continuous focus of attention placed on it.

As explained above, a hypnotic suggestion gains its importance by the lack of shifts of attention and the lack of competing ideas and contexts. Another implication of the narrowing of attention and disregard of competing stimulation is that a suggestion will achieve particular salience in a person's ongoing experience (or remain as a powerful plan to be instantiated later, in the case of a posthypnotic suggestion). Due to its being paid more and more continuous attention, hypnosis is experienced differently than most other mental states, which are usually of a shifting and discontinuous nature.

To explain the increased experience of involuntariness associated with a hypnotic suggestion, we need only discuss three associated elements. In hetero-hypnosis, the source of the stimulation (i.e., invitation to act) is *not* initiated by the individual himself/herself, but rather by the hypnotist. Consequently, the act does not have the quality of self-referentiality that an overtly planned and implemented action would have. In this sense, the experience of dissociation from a particular action is more veridical than we ordinarily tend to think. The individual did not initiate the action and its continued implementation has some of the automaticity that is common to many of our behaviors and experience. This automaticity, however, might be experienced (correctly, we might add) as being of a more intense and salient nature than that of other behaviors. The reason for this, of course, is that such behavior does not have to compete with as many other equally strong plans and ideas as is usually the case in ordinary experience.

The last element that helps to explain the experience of involuntariness is that the person is led to pay continuous attention to the unfolding implementation of a behavior, thought, etc. As mentioned earlier, many of our acts and mental events in ordinary experiencing could be considered to be nonvoluntary. Ordinarily, we do not pay attention to these events, being as we are drawn by a variety of other events. In the hypnotic context, the hypnotist initiates an action (or takes advantage of a naturally occurring behavior such as tired eyelids), and implicitly or explicitly requires the participant to retain his/her attention on that action. Even if the respondent has to initiate the action voluntarily (i.e., if the "invitation" is not strong enough by itself), by being asked to maintain it and pay attention to it he/she may come to experience it as having some associated involuntariness (Bowers, et al., 1988). Other putative dissociative processes in hypnosis (e.g., amnesia and analgesia) would require a separate discussion, but one that could be framed in terms of the changes in attentional focus and process, and of the diminution of consciousness shifts and reflectivity that we have outlined. Lastly, it should be stated that some experiences during hypnosis (e.g., complex imaginal experiences) are not exclusively or mainly dissociative in nature and deserve a systematic discussion beyond the scope of this paper.

Conclusion

We have presented a theoretical model that seeks to integrate the three concepts that are commonly used to describe hypnotic occurrences: suggestibility, absorption, and dissociation. We propose that changes in attentional continuity and focus are the bases on which hypnotic cognition is built. Whereas the ordinary form of conscious processing is characterized by constant shifts of contents, hypnotic cognition commonly involves a greater moment-to-moment continuity of conscious experience coupled with a diminution of self-reflective processes. Because of the nature of the hypnotic context, competing contexts (including a critical function of the ongoing activities) are neglected in favor of the experiences and behaviors suggested by the hypnotist. And because of the diminished competition with other types of mental occurrences (including self-reflective appraisal), hypnotic suggestions entail greater salience, influence, and perceived involuntariness. Increased suggestibility can thus be seen as the natural outcome of cognitive changes in the way that the individual relates to the information conveyed. Hypnotic cognition can thus be seen as both different from, but explainable in terms of, ordinary cognition.

References

Ås, A., & Ostvold, S. (1968). Hypnosis as subjective experience. *Scandinavian Journal of Psychology, 9*, 33–38.

Baars, B.J. (1988). Momentary forgetting as a "resetting" of a conscious global workspace due to competition between incompatible contexts. In M.J. Horowitz (ed.), *Psychodynamics and cognition*. Chicago: University of Chicago Press.

Banyai, E., & Hilgard, E.R. (1976). A comparison of active-alert hypnotic induction with traditional relaxation induction. *Journal of Abnormal Psychology, 85(2)*, 218–34.

Barabasz, A.F., & Barabasz, M. (1989). Effects of restricted environmental stimulation: Enhancement of hypnotizability for experimental and chronic pain control. *International Journal of Clinical and Experimental Hypnosis, 37*(3), 217–31.

Barber, T.X., & Glass, L.B. (1962). Significant factors in hypnotic behavior. *Journal of Abnormal and Social Psychology, 64*, 222–28.

Bowers, P. (1982). The classic suggestion effect: Relationship with scales of hypnotizability, effortless experiencing, and imagery vividness. *International Journal of Clinical and Experimental Hypnosis, 30*(3), 270–79.

Bowers, P., Laurence, J.R., & Hart, D. (1988). The experience of hypnotic suggestions. *International Journal of Clinical and Experimental Hypnosis, 36*(4), 336–49.

Budzynski, T. (1986). Clinical application of non-drug induced states. In B.B. Wolman and M. Ulman (eds.), *Handbook of states of consciousness*. New York: Van Nostrand Reinhold.

Cardeña, E. (1988a). *The phenomenology of quiescent and physically active deep hypnosis*. Unpublished doctoral dissertation, University of California, Davis.

Cardeña, E. (1988b). Deep hypnosis and shamanism: Convergences and divergences. In R.I. Heinze (ed.), *Proceedings of the Fourth International Conference on the Study of Shamanism and and Alternate Modes of Healing* (pp. 289–303). California: Independent Scholars of Asia.

Cardeña, E. (1989). Varieties of possession experience. *AASC (Association for the Anthropological Study of Consciousness) Quarterly, 5*(2–3), 1–17.

Christianson, S.A., & Loftus, E.F. (1987). Memory for traumatic events. *Applied Cognitive Psychology, 1*, 225–39.

Crouse, E., & Kurtz, R. (1984). Enhancing hypnotic susceptibility: The efficacy of four training procedures. *American Journal of Clinical Hypnosis, 27*(2), 122–36.

Edmonston, W.E. (1989). Conceptual clarification of hypnosis and its relationship to suggestibility. In V.A. Gheorghiu, P. Netter, H.J. Eysenck, & R. Rosenthal (eds.), *Suggestion and suggestibility: Theory and research* (pp. 69–78). New York: Springer-Verlag.

Evans, F.J. (1963). *The structure of hypnosis: A factor analytic investigation*. Unpublished doctoral dissertation, University of Sydney, Australia.

Eysenck, H.J. (1989). Personality, primary and secondary suggestibility, and hypnosis. In V.A. Gheorghiu, P. Netter, H.J. Eysenck, & R. Rosenthal (eds.), *Suggestion and suggestibility: Theory and research* (pp. 57–68). New York: Springer-Verlag.

Field, P.B., & Palmer, R.D. (1969). Factor analysis: Hypnotic inventory. *International Journal of Clinical and Experimental Hypnosis, 22*(1), 50–61.

Gheorghiu, V.A. (1971). Relations between the direct and indirect forms of the body sway test. *International Journal of Clinical and Experimental Hypnosis, 19*(3), 134–39.

Gheorghiu, V.A. (1989a). The development of research on suggestibility: Critical considerations. In V.A. Gheorghiu, P. Netter, H.J. Eysenck, & R. Rosenthal (eds.), *Suggestion and suggestibility: Theory and research* (pp. 99–112). New York: Springer-Verlag.

Gheorghiu, V.A. (1989b). The difficulty in explaining suggestion: Some conceivable solutions. In V.A. Gheorghiu, P. Netter, H.J. Eysenck, & R. Rosenthal (eds.), *Suggestion and suggestibility: Theory and research* (pp. 3–56). New York: Springer-Verlag.

Greenberg, L.S., & Safran, J.D. (1987). *Emotion in psychotherapy.* New York: Guilford.

Hilgard, E.R. (1986). *Divided consciousness.* (Expanded edition). New York: Wiley.

Hilgard, E.R., & Tart, C.T. (1966). Responsiveness to suggestions following waking and imagination instructions and following inductions of hypnosis. *Journal of Abnormal Psychology, 71,* 196–208.

James, W. (1890). *The principles of psychology.* New York: Holt.

Kihlstrom, J.F., Register, P.A., Hoyt, I.P., Albright, J.S., Grigorian, E.M., Heindel, W.C., & Morrison, C.R. (1989). Dispositional correlates of hypnosis: A phenomenological approach. *International Journal of Clinical and Experimental Hypnosis, 37*(3), 249–63.

Klinger, E. (1978). Modes of normal conscious flow. In K.S. Pope & J.L. Singer (eds.), *The stream of consciousness.* New York and London: Plenum.

Loftus, E., & Burns, T.E. (1982). Mental shock can produce retrograde amnesia. *Memory and Cognition, 10*(4), 318–23.

Ludwig, A.M., & Lyle, W.H., Jr. (1964). Tension induction and the hyperalert trance. *Journal of Abnormal and Social Psychology, 69*(1), 70–76.

Malott, J.M. (1984). Active-alert hypnosis: Replication and extension of previous research. *Journal of Abnormal Psychology, 93*(2), 246–49.

Malott, J.M., Bourg, A.L., & Crawford, H.J. (1989). The effects of hypnosis upon cognitive responses to persuasive communication. *International Journal of Clinical and Experimental Hypnosis, 37*(1), 31–40.

McDougall, W. (1908). *An introduction to social psychology.* London: Methuen.

O'Shaughnessy, B. (1972). Mental structure and self-consciousness. *Inquiry, 15,* 30–63.

Pekala, R.J. (1989, November). A cluster analysis of the phenomenology of hypnotized individuals: The presence of subtypes. Presented at the 40th Annual Meeting of the Society for Clinical and Experimental Hypnosis, St. Louis, Missouri.

Schleiner, W. (1987). Prospero as a Renaissance therapist. *Literature and Medicine, 6,* 54–60.

Shor, R.E. (1959). Hypnosis and the concept of the generalized reality orientation. *American Journal of Psychotherapy, 13,* 582–602.

Shor, R.E. (1962). Three dimensions of hypnotic depth. *International Journal of Clinical and Experimental Hypnosis, 10,* 23–38.

Shor, R.E. (1970). The three-factor theory of hypnosis as applied to the book-reading fantasy and to the concept of suggestion. *International Journal of Clinical and Experimental Hypnosis, 18,* 89–98.

Shor, R.E. (1979). A phenomenological method for the measurement of variables important to an understanding of the nature of hypnosis. In W. Fromm & R.E. Shor (eds.),

Hypnosis: Developments in research and new perspectives. (Revised 2nd edition.) New York: Aldine.

Singer, J.L. (1988). Sampling ongoing consciousness and emotional experience: Implications for health. In M.J. Horowitz (ed.), *Psychodynamics and cognition.* Chicago: University of Chicago Press.

Spiegel, D. (1990). Hypnosis, dissociation and trauma: Hidden and overt observers. In J.L. Singer (ed.), *Repression and dissociation: Defense mechanisms and personality styles* (pp. 121–42). Chicago, University of Chicago Press.

Spiegel, D., & Cardeña, E. (1990). Dissociative mechanisms in PTSD. In M.E. Wolf & A.D. Mosnaim (ed.), *Post-traumatic stress disorder: Biological mechanisms and clinical aspects* (pp. 22–34). Washington, D.C.: American Psychiatric Press.

Spiegel, D., Hunt, T., & Dondershine, H.E. (1988). Dissociation and hypnotizability. *American Journal of Psychiatry, 145*(3), 301–5.

Tellegen, A., & Atkinson, G. (1974). Openness to absorbing and self-altering experiences ("absorption"), a trait related to hypnotic susceptibility. *Journal of Abnormal Psychology, 83,* 268–77.

Uleman, J.S., & Bargh, J.A. (eds.) (1989). *Unintended thought.* New York: Guilford Press.

van der Hart, O., & Horst, R. (1989). The dissociation theory of Pierre Janet. *Journal of Traumatic Stress, 2*(4), 397–412.

Weitzenhoffer, A.M. (1980). Hypnotic susceptibility revisited. *American Journal of Clinical Hypnosis, 22*(3), 130–46.

Weitzenhoffer, A.M., & Sjoberg, B.M., Jr. (1961). Suggestibility with and without "induction of hypnosis." *Journal of Nervous and Mental Disease, 132,* 204–20.

5

THE ADAPTIVE VALUE OF SUGGESTIBILITY AND DISSOCIATION

John F. Schumaker

Boris Sidis, in his pioneering work, *The Psychology of Suggestion,* made the accurate observation that the human being is, first and foremost, a "*suggestible animal*" (Sidis, 1898, p. 17). Nothing is, in fact, more uniquely human than the intriguing class of behavior that is broadly defined as "suggestibility." A global perspective will reveal that suggestibility is one of the very few categories of behavior that is *universal* by strict definition. The eminent anthropologist Melford Spiro (1965) drew attention to another universal category of behavior, namely religiosity. In fact, he recommended a new name for our species—"*homo religiosus.*" However, I assert that suggestibility rivals religiosity as the most ubiquitous class of human behavior. We find suggestibility, just as we do religiosity, in virtually all cultures of the world. Sexual motivation, as a class of behavior, cannot even compete with suggestibility and religiosity in this regard (see Heider, 1976). Our name might require modification once again—maybe *homo suggesto-religiosus*!

Almost every type of question has been asked in the attempt better to understand the slippery phenomenon of suggestibility. But curiously, the least asked question is the most obvious and potentially fruitful one: *why* are human beings suggestible? As H. J. Eysenck writes in chapter 3 of this book, a preliminary discussion of the essential nature of suggestibility provides the requisite foundation for empirical investigations. As Gheorghiu (1989a) also points out, very little discourse has actually surfaced regarding the essential nature of suggestibility in the human being.

In trying to uncover *why* we are suggestible, I will argue that there is *adaptive* value in our capacity to accept and act upon suggestions. I will even maintain that our species could not exist in its present form if it were not for our suggestive (and, as we will see, our dissociative) capabilities. While this may seem a bold claim for a type of behavior that commands so little of our interest and attention, one might try to imagine what would happen if human beings were totally *nonsuggestible.* The consequences would be enormous. At the very least, there would be chaos. In all likelihood, we would not, in fact, resemble ourselves in our present form, if we existed at all. And we would certainly not be a "social" animal. There are very good reasons why we became the "suggestible animal" of which Sidis spoke. I will attempt to show that suggestibility serves the individual, and society, in several important ways.

However, before proceeding with this macroscopic view of the value of our faculty for suggestive responding, it is necessary to delimit "suggestibility." I would also like to introduce the concept of dissociated consciousness into this discussion, since dissociation and suggestion must be understood conjointly.

The nature of suggestibility and dissociation

At its simplest level, the term "suggestion" usually connotes a *type* of influential communication, while "suggestibility" typically refers to differences between people in the propensity to respond to suggestions. But beyond this, there exists a formidable tangle of terms that clash with partially overlapping meanings. There is even considerable debate over what does and does not constitute a "response" to suggestion. Then there is also the highly problematic term "hypnosis," which finds its way into any discussion of the suggestibility process. Furthermore, the words "suggestion" and "suggestibility" are themselves loaded with an inordinate number of meanings, so much so that some have questioned the usefulness of the construct of suggestibility.

Rather than abandon the concepts of suggestion and suggestibility, I feel that it would be better to proceed with a much narrower and tightly circumscribed definition of these terms. We might start by looking at some of the earliest definitions of the suggestion process in order to decide how to set limits on the constructs of suggestion and suggestibility. Sidis (1898) described a suggestion as an "intrusive idea" that was accepted in an *uncritical* and *automatic* fashion. McDougall (1908) referred to the process of suggestion as a method of communication "resulting in the acceptance with conviction of the communicated proposition *in the absence of logically adequate grounds for its acceptance*" (p. 100, my emphasis). This particular definition highlights the essentially *nonrational,* or irrational, characteristics of the suggestion process. Later, people like Gordon Allport (1961) made specific reference to the rational and critical thinking operations which are conspicuously *disengaged* during the suggestion process.

This point regarding the irrationality of the suggestibility process is very important, since it helps to specify what a suggestion is *not.* A suggestion is *not* a rational response. It is a class of behavior that is *not* the result of our higher levels of cognitive monitoring and control. In order to retain the usefulness of terms such as "suggestion" and "suggestibility," I feel that we must keep in mind the latter part of McDougall's definition. That is, we can only say that a behavior was the result of suggestion if the acceptance of the "suggestion" was made *without an adequate logical basis.*

Suggestibility, however, is not a passive feature of cognition. The act of responding to a suggestive communication requires that the individual actively *overrides* or *inhibits* the mental faculties involved in logic and critical analysis. Charles Tart (1986) reiterates this position when he describes the behavior of individuals in a "trance" state. A trance, he says, "need not be merely passive stupidity, but can include an active, organized pursuit of the wrong things" (p. 70). I will argue later in this paper that our suggestive capacities are very useful and important, as they allow us to accept and abide by these "wrong" (i.e., inaccurate) things. Allport (1961) also realized that, during the act of suggestive responding, there is a distinct absence of the thought and judgment processes which *should* otherwise be in place. Gheorghiu (1989b) is another who seems to advocate a rather strict definition of suggestion and suggestibility. He goes a bit beyond McDougall in this sense when he states that a response to suggestion is *uncontrolled* to the extent that the person must disregard the possibility that he/she can respond in ways other than that prescribed by the suggestion itself.

At certain times (e.g., during "hypnotic" suggestion), one cannot help noticing the suspension of judgment and critical thought that occurs during suggestive responding. Let us say that my "hypnotist" points to a pencil and suggests that it is an extremely heavy piece of lead. Let us also say that, after being offered the chance to pick up the pencil/lead, I cannot begin to do so because of its great "weight." In this case, it must be said that my resolute belief that the pencil is super-heavy is *without an adequate logical foundation.* We should then be justified in saying that my behavior was a result of suggestion. An objective outsider (even an intelligent chimpanzee) would undoubtedly be struck by my apparent *mindlessness* (i.e., absence of "executive" cognitive control). Even so, I maintain that suggestive responding (strictly defined) is a very difficult, sophisticated, and complicated task. We could never get a chimpanzee genuinely to believe, and act as if, a banana were anything but a banana. My dog Katie could never be convinced that the slipper she likes to chew is actually her favorite brand of dog biscuit. The problem goes beyond that of a language barrier that exists between them and us. As clever as they might be, they are not smart enough to be so stupid! For good reason, suggestibility and the potential for active "mindlessness" evolved in the only earthly creature to be endowed with greatly amplified intelligence and consciousness (Schumaker, 1990). Shortly, I will discuss the value of suggestibility, some of which is directly related to the problems connected with our *degree* of intelligence and consciousness.

Dissociation revisited (yet again)

I feel that a concept such as dissociation, or dissociated consciousness, is required in order to comprehend the nonrational nature of suggestive responding. This particular concept has a long history and dates back to the work of Pierre Janet (1889). More recently, Ernest Hilgard (1986/1977) attempted to breathe new life into this construct in the form of his well-conceived neo-dissociation theory. This latter model views consciousness as operating along multiple pathways. It assumes a hierarchical system of cognitive control, with largely independent modes of information processing. It is thought that the highest level of control is typically associated with awareness, volition, and self-initiative. Certain conspicuous changes are apparent when consciousness becomes greatly dissociated, as it might during "trance" (including "hypnotic" trance) or in pathological dissociative disorders. As Bowers (1982) observes, there is a dramatic reduction in the extent to which behavior is *controlled* by higher levels of cognition. Also, there are distinct changes in the way a person *experiences* him-self/herself. In this regard, Bowers finds it useful to make a distinction between dissociative control and dissociative experience. In describing dissociation as "the secret of hypnosis," Hilgard (1965, p. 71) made reference to the subsidence of "the planning function" that is a feature of dissociated consciousness.

Neo-dissociation theory has been used to explain a variety of behavioral phenomena, including hypnotic analgesia, multiple personality disorder, "hysteria," post-traumatic stress disorder, fugue, possession, glossolalia, shamanistic healing, and so on. But our understanding of dissociation has been hampered by a tendency to associate it only with pathological syndromes. Fortunately, some thinkers are beginning to appreciate the more subtle aspects of dissociation, as well as the role that dissociation plays in the maintenance of health, and the prevention of psychological disturbances. For example, Beahrs (1983) writes that "dissociation can no longer be viewed as a pathological entity to be gotten 'rid of,' but rather as a basic *given* which should be used more effectively" (p. 100). Even so, despite periodic resurgences of interest in dissociation, it is still viewed with a certain amount of skepticism. This is despite the growing body of psychophysiological research that is consistent with a multi-modal conception of consciousness.

While the concept of dissociation needs further refinement, it helps us to account for the varying degrees of irrationality that are associated with suggestive responding. Edmonston (1989) touches on that key feature of suggestibility when he refers to the suggestion process as the central mechanism by which incoming sensory information becomes *distorted.* He echoes the early view of William James (1981/1890) in saying that "suggestion is a directive which informs the senses to distort or change the interpretation of the sensed stimuli" (Edmonston, 1989, p. 69). He states that suggestibility enables a person to create "illusions" which are "facsimiles of the real world" (p. 70). However, there is no evidence to indicate that people in any way question the veracity of these suggestion-based "facsimiles" of reality. Therefore, we have a curious situation wherein suggestions can distort incoming information and construct an alternative reality *outside of a person's awareness.* Such a paradoxical situation begins to make some sense if we can speak of *multiple* modes of information processing.

My theoretical position does not view hypnosis as a unique entity that should be understood and studied in its own right. Rather, it is but one of many possible ways that dissociation and suggestion can interact and operate as a distortive mechanism. This can be seen in Martin Orne's (1959) outline of the essential features of the "hypnotic" state. These include a) an altered state of consciousness; b) a compulsion to follow cues from external sources; c) the by-passing of objective reality; d) the potential to experience perceptual and memory distortions as real; and e) the ability to tolerate faulty logic. (It would be interesting to determine how long a "hypnotic" subject could tolerate *nondistortive* suggestions. Not for long, I would guess.) Gheorghiu (1989a) makes the cogent observation that an understanding of suggestibility is rooted in the *contradictory* nature of the human being. Nothing could be more true. For me, the most fascinating contradiction is the way that we can flit between varying degrees of rationality and irrationality. In *Pensées,* Pascal (1973/1670) was so taken with our chimera-like natures that he called the human being "a depository of truth, yet a cesspool of uncertainty and error." Each of us, he added, is "the judge of all things, yet a stupid earthworm" (p. 65). I believe that our contradictory and paradoxical natures are, in fact, closely tied to the way we operate as creatures of suggestion.

As a *prerequisite* to suggestive responding, we must somehow be able to neutralize or override our rational and critical thinking capacities.

Gheorghiu makes this point when he describes "substitution" as the essence of suggestibility, defining this as a "process by which the conscious monitoring authority is bypassed" (1989a, p. 42). I feel that our capacity for dissociation makes it possible to render our critical and analytical thought process largely inoperative. That is, dissociation allows us to isolate and suppress our "conscious monitoring authority" (Gheorghiu's phrase) in such a way (and to such a *degree*) that we become *potentially* responsive to suggestions that would otherwise be rejected by that "authority."

Therefore, while adhering to a stringent definition of suggestion and suggestibility, I would maintain that the suggestion process operates conjointly with dissociation. More specifically, I feel that it is our ability to dissociate that makes suggestive responding possible. Dissociation must *precede*, and pave the way for, suggestibility. Consequently, if the conditions are not right for dissociation, they are not right for suggestive responding. Suggestions, properly defined, involve conclusions about or interpretations of reality which would not be made if a person were enjoying (or suffering from!) the workings of his/her critical and analytical mental faculties. If not *initially* dissociated, a chair could not be "suggested" into a horse. A person would not respond to the suggestion that he/she would feel no pain while undergoing major surgery. Likewise, there would be no angels, devils, or holy ghosts. While functioning under "dissociative control," as Bowers (1982) terms it, we are able to override logic and reason. In turn, we are able to accept (or believe) what would be unacceptable or unbelievable if those "executive" cognitive processes were operative. We are then free to misperceive the world and ourselves, something that is of great value to us.

Gheorghiu (1989b) qualifies his thesis that suggestion is a largely nonrational process by stating that one cannot automatically assume that the suggested (or "substitute") reality is of no use to the individual, or even that it is false. I would agree on both counts. The entire point of this chapter is to highlight the adaptive value of suggestion. And even though these suggestions are accepted without involvement from the "conscious monitoring authority," there is the *chance* that they could be true. All we can say is that a response to suggestion is made without the assistance of the higher-order faculties which greatly increase the likelihood that our perceptions will be accurate and in accordance with objective reality. In some respects, responses to suggestions are exercises in pure "faith," since they are incorporated without consideration of evidence or verification. Therefore, the suggester is removed from the issue of veracity.

The above discussion also does not require that dissociation be viewed in an all-or-nothing way. In fact, dissociation is probably an *ongoing regulatory mechanism.* It is not an arbitrary feature of cognition. At some preconscious level, "decisions" are made regarding the *degree* of "dissociative control" that is required in light of intrapersonal, interpersonal, and situational factors. I agree with Rhue and Lynn (chapter 10 in this book) who regard dissociation as a *goal-directed* activity aimed at regulating internal experiences. They add that, through dissociation, the person is able to reduce negative affect, and to renounce problematic aspects of the self. They discuss dissociation as it is involved in the generation of adaptive "fantasy" that is used in various ways as a coping mechanism.

In some respects, dissociation resembles "reification," a process described by the Harvard sociobiologists Lumsden and Wilson (1981) as "a diagnostic activity of human consciousness" (pp. 107-08). They argue that the human brain is equipped to *filter* through vast quantities of incoming information and to "diagnose" what might prove "noxious" for the individual. In a simplistic sense, "reification" allows the individual to simplify or reduce the complexity of incoming information in such a way that "chaos" can be transformed into some artificial order. According to Lumsden and Wilson, this artificial order takes the form of "mentifacts" which are fictitious categorizations or understandings of the world. The pivotal aspect of this theory is that culture *co-evolves* with this feature of cognition. The "mentifacts" upon which we rely for the illusion of order need *content* and *structure.* Those are a product of *cultural* evolution.

In a similar manner, dissociation can be seen as a "diagnostic" activity. The brain seems to "know" how and when to regulate degree of dissociation. But, like "reification," dissociation is usually part of a reconstruction process whereby the reality of the individual is effectively and positively transformed. In and of itself, dissociation does nothing except neutralize "executive" control and thereby enhance suggestibility. The person is potentially able to receive, accept, and incorporate logic-defying information. But that is only the beginning of the process. Dissociated consciousness is a vacuous state that is rendered meaningful through the process of suggestion. Without suggestions, a "dissociated" person is directionless (and "mentifactless"). Suggestions give structure to dissociated states. A good "hypnotic" subject, for example, achieves a dissociated state via the "induction" procedures of the "hypnotist." But unless the "hypnotist" offers some suggestions, the person will remain disengaged, or suspended, until the dissociated state fades of its own accord.

Dissociation, like "reification," must also be understood in the context of culture, since culture is what typically determines the *content* of our suggestions and our altered (or "mentifactual") constructions of reality. This will become very apparent when we look at the content of "religious" belief/practice, as well as certain types of dissociative disorders. Usually, culture also plays a primary role in prescribing the *procedures* that should be used in achieving a workable degree of dissociation. Given the many cultures of the world, it is not surprising that these methods are great in number and impressive in their diversity. Historically, most of these dissociative procedures became part of a culture's "religious" rituals. Likewise, most cultures throughout history provided a set of suggestions which became translated into "religious" beliefs. But let us first look at dissociation as it can operate independently of suggestion.

Neurological conservation and economy of effort

This particular adaptive function relates to dissociation as it operates with "absorption" (Tellegen & Atkinson, 1974) in a *preventative* role. This assumes that, whereas suggestive responses are necessarily reliant on a certain degree of dissociation, it is possible for dissociation to serve us without the involvement of the suggestion process. The "common everyday" trances of which Rossi (1986) speaks are instances of mild dissociation. He cites examples such as "highway" hypnosis, the glassy-eyed student who drifts off during a lecture, the housewife staring vacantly into her cup of coffee, and so on. In these cases, a person facilitates dissociation by channeling complete attention in a highly focused and *all-absorbing* manner. It is not unlike the absorption techniques employed by designated people (e.g., shamans, hypnotists, priests, etc.) who promote dissociative states in others. The primary differences are that the "common everyday" dissociative trance is self-generated, and also that suggestions are not introduced in order to engage and direct behaviors.

Often, after I leave university committee meetings, I realize that I must have been in some sort of dissociative state for much of the previous hour or so. From the little I remember of these meetings, I believe that my technique is to tap my pen very lightly on the table while concentrating only on the pen and the tapping sound. During brief periods of awareness, I have observed different techniques by other staff members. One staff member prefers to focus on his right shoe as he bounces it up and down, while another takes a clump of her long hair and blankly sorts through individual strands of hair. Without knowing it, people fade in and out of mild dissociative trances throughout the day. This serves a very important function, one that

Ludwig (1983) refers to as *neurological conservation*. By dissociating ourselves from sources of external stress (and this includes boredom!), we effectively reduce the amount of strain that is placed on our autonomic nervous systems. This also gives us a break from mental activity that, while not stressful in itself, is of a prolonged nature. By taking advantage of these periods of mild dissociation, we conserve ourselves neurologically and reduce the risk of cognitive overload and eventual nervous exhaustion. Also, these periods of being on "automatic pilot" enable us to function more efficiently at a limited number of mental tasks that demand our undivided attention.

Another related adaptive feature of the dissociative capacity is *economy of effort*. With reference to the importance of economy of action, Gheorghiu (1989a) writes that people often cannot afford "a confrontation with the pros and cons" (p. 42). It can be useful to feel *as if* there is only one course of action as situations and events present themselves. Ludwig (1983) comments on the value of being able to *automize* behavior. This enables the individual to arrive at a state of "*single-mindedness*" wherein that person can reduce the vast amount of extraneous stimuli that would constitute cognitive static. That is, dissociation can serve as a "cognitive filter" that provides us with the opportunity to compartmentalize our mental functions. With this done, we can operate single-mindedly on the basis of these dissociated "compartments." Our behavior is thus more economical in the sense that we can remain removed from stimuli and other mental functions that could reduce productivity. Ludwig (1983) writes that dissociation improves the efficiency of energy expenditure because "by not weighing *all* contingencies and probabilities, individuals are in a better position to act" (p. 96).

Reality-transcendence

In writing specifically about the psychobiology of dissociation, Rossi (1987) estimates that 80% or 90% of information contained in the human mind is *false*. Even if he is only half correct in that calculation, it is extremely impressive that creatures as intelligent as ourselves can manage to get so many things so very wrong. But Harold Sackeim (1983) comes to our defense in his essay on the adaptive value of "lying to oneself." He speaks on behalf of our misperceptions. In fact, he writes that our misperceptions are highly adaptive and that "fostering falsity may be the most effective strategy for promoting psychological health" (p. 135).

Ludwig (1983) cites some of the psychobiological functions of the dissociation process, all of which contribute to what he calls "the great survival value" offered by this dimension of cognition. He describes dissociation as a large *unitary* process which reveals itself in many ways. Some of these reflect the needs and conflicts of the individual, while others are associated with social forces and cultural factors. Ludwig writes that, "given an individual's capacity for dissociation, these molding influences will determine whether the outward manifestations will be hypnosis, mediumistic trance, arctic hysteria, fugue, or multiple personality" (p. 95). But if suggestions become operative during dissociated states, it is reasonable to speak of the functions of our dissociative and suggestive capabilities as they operate conjunctively.

One of these functions is to enable the human being to escape from "the constraints of reality" (Ludwig, 1983, p. 96). Amplified intelligence and self-consciousness made reality into a distinct problem for members of our species. In his classic book *The Denial of Death,* Ernest Becker (1973) envisioned the *terror* that would derive from an undistorted view of reality. He saw the evolutionary idea of a self-conscious animal as "ludicrous, if not monstrous" since it made us potentially aware that "we are food for worms" (p. 87). He described our extensively developed associative cortex as an "unintended evolutionary *mistake.*" Intelligence of a high magnitude complicates survival. For example, Dobzhansky, Ayala, Stebbins, and Valentine (1977) spoke of death awareness as one of the unfortunate byproducts of the evolution of the elevated intelligence (and concomitant self-consciousness), while even suggesting that amplified intelligence could be "an evolutionary dead end." Sheldon (1975) addressed the affective consequences of consciousness in relation to the functions of "religious" cognition. He wrote that "traditionally, religions have . . . allayed the pain of conflict by selling out to the *seemingly* remoter evil of *almost certain* error" (p. 26). Error has, in fact, been a historical bedfellow of the conflict-ridden, self-conscious animal that Becker exposed as an evolutionary clanger.

Once our evolution took us across what Passingham (1982) called the "cerebral Rubicon," it became necessary to adapt to our own intelligence. That is, we needed some cognitive mechanism that would allow us to take advantage of our awesome intellectual powers, while at the same time keeping us potentially ignorant (as in "ignore") of certain unpalatable dimensions of reality. In *The Two Sources of Morality and Religion,* Henri Bergson (1935) referred to this secondary adaptation as "counter-intelligence." He described it as "a defensive reaction against what might be depressing for the individual and dissolvent for society in the exercise of intelligence" (p. 194). Bergson added that "counter-intelligence" could "guard against certain dangers of intellectual activity without compromising the future of intelligence" (p. 99). The complex capacity for this type of cognition made it possible for the human being to regulate both degree and content of consciousness. From that point on, we were to live in a "translated world," as Rainer Maria Rilke (1977/1955) termed it, destined "to be opposites, always, and nothing else but opposites" (p. 57). We could synchronously live in and out of reality, a curious feature of behavior that served our species in a crucial way.

There are obvious parallels between Bergson's concept of "counter-intelligence" and that of the dissociative ability. In the same way that Bergson viewed "counter-intelligence" as the mental process which made nonrational belief possible, I feel it is reasonable to regard dissociation as a prerequisite to belief that defies one's own logic and reason.

Here we must again make a distinction between dissociation and the suggestion process. As an example, let us use my former belief in "holy water." I needed to achieve a certain degree of dissociation before I could genuinely believe that a bowl of water was "holy water." Certainly, a "holy water" belief qualifies as a suggestive behavior since it requires that I accept a communicated proposition, with conviction, without adequate grounds for acceptance (McDougall, 1908). Beyond that, I had adequate grounds for *nonacceptance,* since our priest could be seen drawing the water from an ordinary tap! Regardless, the "holy water" belief was the result of a suggestion that I absorbed while in a dissociated state. The emotional chanting of the choir, the priest's monotonous voice, the gold incense burner swinging on its chain, the endlessly repeated rituals—I went "under" in no time at all. But, even though in a receptive dissociated state, a suggestion was still necessary if I was to come away with that "holy water" belief.

The *content* of "religious" and other reality-defying beliefs varies according to the cultural context from which the suggestions derive. One group of aboriginal Australians believe that tree spirits can make women pregnant. Some groups in Southern Africa believe that their departed ancestors live on in the bodies of dead hyenas. A recent Gallup Poll revealed that 54% of American adults believe in angels, while 40% believe in devils (Lopreato, 1984). A survey by the Australian National University recently showed that 88% of Australians believe in some sort of god. Wallace (1966) estimates that, over the course of its history, the human being has conjured up at least 100,000 different religions, and at least as many deities. Were it not for our capacity to dissociate and to absorb reality-snubbing suggestions while in such a state, I dare say that none of the above beliefs would be possible. And to the extent that such beliefs (usually classified as "religious") are good for us, we can say that our dissociative and suggestive abilities are adaptive in nature.

The coping value of religion is well documented in the literature. In my recent book *Wings of Illusion* (Schumaker, 1990), I review the literature on this subject and conclude that religious belief/practice can be understood as a mental health prophylactic. With some exceptions, research has shown that culturally patterned religious beliefs are associated with reduced death anxiety, increased life satisfaction, social adjustment, a sense of well-being, fewer reports of emotional distress and disturbance, less risk of suicide, a facilitation of the enculturation process, and so forth. My own research revealed that psychopathology, especially of a psychosomatic nature, was more prevalent among atheists than their strongly religious counterparts (Schumaker, 1987). While some thinkers have made reference to the potential "side-effects" of religion (e.g., guilt, sexual inhibitions, intolerance, etc.), the *composite* influence of religion has been positive from a survival standpoint.

As obvious as the connection seems between suggestibility and religious belief, very few investigators have explored this relationship. Argyle and Beit-Hallahmi (1975) do summarize a relatively small body of research and conclude that there is a link between religious belief and degree of suggestibility. Some studies in their survey used measures of "psychomotor" suggestibility, while others assessed "primary" suggestibility. Still others gauged religious belief in relation to measures of "social" suggestibility, and placebo responsiveness. One research team found that religious experiences were significantly more common in people scoring high on the Harvard Group Scale of Hypnotic Susceptibility (Gibbons & DeJarnette, 1972). They explain their findings by claiming that, in most cases, religious experience (like religious belief) is a response to suggestion. But we must again keep in mind the crude and ill-conceived nature of our tests of suggestibility, and also remember that they are locked conceptually into the largely misunderstood phenomenon of "hypnosis." Even so, it is almost self-apparent that religious beliefs are the consequence of culturally-based suggestions which have historically been incorporated by large segments of the population. Simple logic tells us that a person must be suggestible in order to accept such suggestions. However, we must not fall into the same trap as is possible with regard to "hypnosis." Religion is only one of many *procedures* for utilizing our dissociative and suggestive capacities in the service of reality-transcendence. And while it is an inevitable procedure of all workable cultures, not all people respond to such suggestions. Most religious ceremonies are intended to assist people in the task of achieving a dissociated state in which suggestions can be implanted. Still, just as some people do not respond to "hypnotic" procedures, some people do not respond to religious procedures. This does not change the fact that virtually all people have the *potential* to accept religious beliefs, or suggestions.

Wijeyewardene (1986) theorizes that, throughout premodern times, religion was a *total* way of life for members of our species. To the extent that this is true, we must appreciate the highly adaptive nature of nonrational conceptions of the world. In the same vein, we would need to concede that our dissociative and suggestive faculties are of great value in that they allow us to achieve major distortions of reality which act in the service of our personal well-being and our overall ability to function productively. It happens that, over the past few centuries, there has been an erosion of traditional religious beliefs/practices. Despite some exceptions, the age-old religious methods for promoting dissociation and instilling health-giving suggestions have dwindled, not only in number, but in their effectiveness as well. The consequences of this trend have far-reaching social and clinical implications, but they are well beyond the scope of this chapter. But let me conclude this section by saying that the study of suggestion, dissociation, and "hypnosis" belongs at least as much to theology as it does psychology, psychiatry, and medicine.

Social cohesion and social control

If we were totally *nonsuggestible,* and unable to circumvent our "conscious monitoring authority," we could not function as a *social* animal. It is quite obvious that our survival was, and remains, dependent on our "social" nature. But what is not so obvious is the role that our suggestive and dissociative abilities play in this enormously important process.

In his treatise on the evolutionary advantages of dissociation, Ludwig (1983) states that "the dissociative capacity . . . represents the main means whereby man becomes united to his fellow man" (p. 97). He denounces the notion that it is rationality and reason that bind us to our fellow human beings. Becker (1973) describes the actual manufacture of irrationality and illusion as an important "cultural project." He felt strongly enough about this to define culture quite simply as a "*macro-lie*!" These shared misperceptions serve the important purpose of *homogenizing* human perception. Ludwig states that the "enhancement of the herd sense" is the result of our ability to dissociate which, in turn, allows us to embrace non-Aristotelian beliefs or conclusions (i.e., suggestions) about the world. I believe that the same is true of the social control process generally, which is reliant on the mechanisms of suggestion and dissociation.

In some ways, this takes us back to a discussion of *homo religiosus*, since many of "non-Aristotelian" beliefs we hold are institutionalized under the heading of religion. But Ludwig also theorizes that dissociated consciousness enables us to follow earthly authority figures, charismatic leaders, and other "alpha" individuals, as he calls them. Just as dissociation and suggestion, together, allow one to believe in "holy water," or "Holy Ghosts," they also allow one to attach an enormous amount of unwarranted meaning and importance to a flag, or the "state" (or maybe even to the concept of a "side" or a "team"). Lopreato (1984) writes specifically about religious dissociations in describing them as "a mechanism that *subordinates the individual to the group* by sanctifying group values and morality" (p. 298). Kurtz (1986) also makes reference to the moral functions of religious beliefs, noting that "they provide a system of rules and commandments guiding action" (p. 468). However, this can also be said of dissociations and concomitant suggestions which relate to less conspicuously religious ideology and ritual.

Scheibe (1974, 1983), one of the foremost thinkers on social control, describes this process as one in which individuals are obedient and conforming to prescribed values, norms, and standards. He maintains that social control is an all-pervasive and ongoing operation that dominates and suppresses *individual* dispositions toward independent thought or action. But Scheibe also believes that one can understand the workings of social control in the same way one can understand hypnosis, suggestibility, and related phenomena. In fact, it only stands to reason that we must be creatures of suggestion and "trance" if we can be de-individualized and controlled in ways which are sometimes extreme.

Scheibe shows us that social control functions in such a way that aggression will be perceived as legitimate. People, acting in accordance with their "social identity" and the social ideology of which they are disciples, will engage in acts of violence and cruelty that are without bounds. Even though "legitimized aggression," as Scheibe terms it, has taken a considerable toll over the lifespan of our species, one can only surmise that it somehow acted in the service of the group. Either way, it seems unlikely to me that aggression could be "legitimized" as it has been throughout history if we were not suggestible animals.

In a reverse sense, it is probable that social pandemonium would result if we had large numbers (or even small numbers) of highly intelligent, self-conscious creatures who maintained *personalized,* or single, world views. Social cohesion and social control is only possible if a *common* "reality" is somehow invented and propagated. We might call these conventions, or conventional understandings of the world. In the preface to his play *Our Town,* Thornton Wilder (1957) gives an excellent definition of a convention. It is "*an agreed-upon falsehood, an accepted untruth.*" These function to unite masses of people around a limited number of "truths" which, in turn, guide action in *coordinated* fashion.

The conventional "truths" that allow us to understand ourselves and the world in similar ways are almost inevitably myths that also add positive bias to objective reality. Therefore, in order for us to become "social," we needed a brain-level mechanism that would allow us to *agree* that certain untruths and falsehoods are true. During the course of our evolutionary development, an ability emerged that allowed us to become removed from logical and critical thought and to absorb and maintain valuable misperceptions of the world.

Kantor (1972), in a discussion of factors which contribute to social cohesion, comments on the importance of *transcendence* and *communion.* Ideally, reality-transcendence and self-transcendence is achieved via a leader who specifies the content that the transcendent reality will have. By "communion" is meant the ceremonies, rituals, etc. which provide a *context* for the dissemination and reinforcement of "*mentifacts,*" or fictitious constructions of reality. In Kantor's model, the group "leader" might be compared to a "hypnotist," while the "communion" (rituals, ceremonies, etc.) could represent the hypnotic induction procedure under which the reality-transcending suggestions are provided. As Tart (1986) wrote, enculturation is very much a "hypnotic" procedure. In *Wings of Illusion,* I refer to culture as the "master hypnotist" (Schumaker, 1990). Culture and enculturation, if one can conceptualize these abstract forces, can be seen to be completely dependent upon our dissociative and suggestive aptitudes. The ways that we are united and controlled at the level of culture are virtual extensions of these extraordinary cognitive attributes.

Emotional discharge

With reference again to the adaptive value of our dissociative ability, Ludwig (1983) observes that dissociation makes it possible for individuals to discharge a range of volatile emotions that might otherwise remain in a pent-up form. Most of these emotional discharge systems take the form of culturally constituted group practices. Ludwig cites examples such as orgiastic ritual practices, trance dances, highly charged "possession" states, group "revivals," ebullient religious ceremonies, and so forth. According to Ludwig, these are group-sanctioned forms of catharsis, all of which utilize the human potential for dissociation.

While I agree with Ludwig's assertion that group-endorsed dissociative catharsis is beneficial, one should not disregard the suggestion process in such a discussion. In fact, the types of dissociative catharsis described by Ludwig can only become a *patterned* part of a culture if people are able to agree on the *content* and *mode of expression* for a dissociative discharge. If dissociative catharsis was acted out on an *individual* basis, these individuals would be perceived as raving lunatics. For instance, speaking in "tongues" is an exercise in dissociation that allows a therapeutic discharge of emotions. But it should be remembered that all forms of dissociative catharsis are reliant upon a *suggested* context. If someone was speaking in "tongues" on a street corner and no one had ever heard of the "Holy Ghost," that person would be mercifully taken away for psychiatric observation.

Suggestions, and people's suggestibility (i.e., ability to absorb suggestions) are essential in order to construct an agreed-upon foundation of illogical "logic" that will allow large segments of the population to make nonsensical "sense" of these healthy actions. The "Holy Ghost," as a suggestion, makes it possible for numerous people to take advantage of a health-enhancing dissociative catharsis. The same holds true for the vast array of other group dissociations that we see around the world. In all cases, the suggestion process functions in concert with dissociative procedures in enabling the construction and ratification of modified versions of reality that are recognizable and "true" (however likely it is that they are false).

The therapeutic nature of dissociation is thus released when the content and mode of its expression is given shape through the mechanism of suggestion. The two processes operate as a continuous feedback system, with dissociation making possible the absorption of logically unfounded suggestions, and those suggestions enabling the *meaningful* acting out of dissociative behaviors.

Escape from self, conflict, and trauma

Flight from self

Taylor and Brown (1988) review an interesting body of research which shows that mental health is largely a function of *self-illusion.*

As these researchers conclude, people tend to be happier, less depressed, and more productive if they are skilled at *misperceiving* themselves and their relationship to the world around them. In chapter 9 of this book, Frederick Gibbons gives a detailed analysis of this line of research in the context of human suggestibility. He maintains that heightened suggestibility is the result of *external focus,* as compared to internal focus (which reduces suggestibility).

Gibbons describes a process in which external focus and elevated suggestibility make it possible for people to respond *selectively* to suggestions that impose *positive* cognitive bias on their self-perceptions. He acknowledges that these self-illusions are self-serving and generally healthy for the individual. He also mentions the conditions under which suggestibility will be decreased to the extent that the self-illusion process becomes unworkable. According to Gibbons, they are the same conditions under which hypnosis and placebo become less effective. In all cases, this involves the person engaging in *self-focusing* mental activity. It appears that self-consciousness and suggestibility are largely incompatible. Simple logic would allow us to state that suggestibility and accuracy of perception are incompatible, which takes us back to Edmonston's (1989) conception of suggestibility as our "central distortive mechanism."

In light of the above, we should not find surprising the conclusions of Groth-Marnat's review of the relationship between psychopathology and suggestibility during "hypnotic" procedures (see chapter 11 of this book). He found that people with high levels of "hypnotic" suggestibility were better able to manage their anxiety levels. Affective disturbances, including depression, were more common in less suggestible individuals. Taken together, one is again led to conclude that suggestibility is part of a mental health prophylactic process. If that is the case, one must accept that suggestibility is adaptive, and that it operates on behalf of the individual, even if illusions, distortions, and cognitive biases are the end products.

In my earlier discussion of reality-transcendence, I described the way in which dissociation and suggestion operate together in providing a needed escape from the crisis of existence, or what Victor Frankl (1963) called "the universal existential crisis." Just as our relationship to existence (and nonexistence) can generate anxiety, so can our relationship to ourselves. As Gibbons points out in his chapter, the accurate perception of ourselves is potentially disturbing and depressing. I have made the case that dissociation must be included in an understanding of suggestive processes as they operate as distortive mechanisms. I believe that this holds true regarding the healthy self-illusions mentioned above. While Gibbons does not employ the term "dissociation," I would argue that a certain degree of dissociated consciousness must be in place before a person can absorb suggestions that lead to inaccurate and distorted pictures of oneself. The "external focus" method for sustaining the necessary degree of suggestibility to self-delude may be the same procedure that yields a sufficient degree of dissociation. In other words, people who must suffer the depression that stems from an unbiased conception of self are not only failing to maintain adequate levels of suggestibility, but they are also failing to dissociate sufficiently for distortive suggestions to take root.

Coping with conflict and trauma

Dissociation and suggestion are also involved in a "reification" process that allows us to escape from *situational* conflicts at the level of our everyday lives. Ludwig (1983) states that, as an evolutionary adaptation, our capacity to dissociate is ideally suited to resolve irreconcilable conflicts. This is so despite the obvious contradiction here, namely that *irreconcilable* conflicts are ones that cannot be reconciled, or resolved. That is, there is no *real* solution. Dissociation enables us to "solve" such conflict situations by separating the sources of conflict. Ludwig (1983) argues that, in cases of extreme conflict, dissociation provides the option to "relegate one set of attitudes, wishes and values to one state of consciousness and a conflicting set to another" (p. 96). The person is thereby freed from a paralyzing conflict and provided with the basis for concerted action.

Conflicts can also arise when two drives are in direct opposition to one another. Dissociation creates the opportunity to isolate those drives and to forego the guilt and the sense of responsibility that would result from a person acting on a drive he/she deems to be wrong. Ludwig (1983) speaks of the "trance logic" that is accessed via the dissociation process. With this dissociative form of "logic," a person can bypass critical thought while becoming temporarily, or permanently, disengaged from one source of conflict.

To illustrate this, we might take the example of a young girl who was traumatized by her sexually abusive father. Recurrent memories of her previous encounters with her father would represent an ongoing source of emotional distress. If effective cognitive defenses are not found, people who were severely abused as children can fall prey to a host of emotional and psychological ills which can follow them through life. This is further indicated by the greatly increased rates of suicide among victims of extreme child abuse.

Spiegel, Hunt, and Dondershine (1988) describe the potential value of dissociation as a method of coping with trauma. They state that dissociation can serve as "a defense against the painful affect associated with memories of the traumatic experience" (p. 301). More specifically, they view dissociation as a cognitive mechanism that enables a person to achieve a "polarization of consciousness." Through the process of dissociation, the person is then able to arrive at a "pseudo normality," as Spiegel, et al. call it. In such a state, the person can maintain at least a partial, or periodic "polarization of experience" with amnesia for earlier traumatic events. In commenting that victims of severe trauma are more likely to make use of dissociative defenses, Spiegel, et al. draw attention to the "on-off" quality of post-traumatic defensive dissociation. For some reason, the amnesia occasionally gives way to highly intense, vivid, and frightening memories and images of the earlier trauma(s).

An understanding of the defensive use of dissociation as a vehicle for conflict "resolution" must also take into account the suggestion process. In psychogenic fugue, for example, we see more than dissociation in the form of drastic diminishment of the usual integrative functions of consciousness. We also see the establishment of an *alternative* identity which necessarily involves the absorption and consolidation of a complex set of suggestions. While one might argue that there are instances of "pure" defensive dissociation (e.g., psychogenic amnesia) these tend to be rare and of short duration (Sackeim & Vingiano, 1984). Depersonalization, wherein people typically complain that "nothing seems real," might also be cited as an example of "pure" dissociation. But there are many problems with the diagnosis of depersonalization, a major one being that it is frequently a component of affective disorders, schizophrenia, and a range of organic syndromes. Therefore, aside from possible rare exceptions, most defensive dissociations involve the incorporation of suggestions (made possible through dissociation) which enable a person to *reconstruct* reality in a meaningful alternative manner. The source of these suggestions may be external or internal.

Multiple personality disorder is one of the most widely discussed dissociative disorders, especially in light of recent findings which show that most of those affected were severely battered and/or otherwise abused as children (Andorfer, 1985; Brassfield, 1983). As an adaptive maneuver, consciousness becomes dissociated and operates on the basis of multiple modes of control, each separated by "amnesic barriers" (Hilgard 1986/1977). Through the various fictional identities, the conflict becomes "resolved" or dissipated to the extent that it is portioned up and assigned to satellite personalities.

The interaction of dissociation and the suggestion process is very complex in multiple personality disorder, and we might turn to anorexia nervosa to illustrate the way in which suggestion operates conjointly with the dissociation process. Mordecai Kaffman (1983; also chapter 15, this volume) is most convincing in his thesis that anorectic symptomatology is the result of autosuggestion and absorption. According to Kaffman, it is quite possible for certain predisposed individuals to "hypnotize" themselves into anorectic patterns of thought and behavior. This is done via monotonous, monothematic one-way self-communication that is repeated over and over again. This is not unlike the self-hypnotic procedure described by Hilgard in this volume (chapter 1). My own clinical work in the area of anorexia nervosa has convinced me that these people are, in fact, in a self-generated trance state. This is consistent with others who have described the anorexic as "programmed" and "robot-like" (Bruch, 1975; Selvini, 1971). Beyond that, there is evidence that the anorectic person may be exceptionally suggestible in the formative *pre-onset* condition (Groth-Marnat & Schumaker, 1990; also see chapter 11 by Gary Groth-Marnat in this book).

I prefer not to describe the anorectic syndrome as "self- hypnotic" in nature because of the above-mentioned problems inherent in the word "hypnosis." However, I would be inclined to describe anorexia as an *auto-dissociative* disorder, as well as an autosuggestive disorder. Let me explain, especially since anorexia nervosa is not typically regarded as a classic dissociative disorder.

The most commonly accepted etiological formulation of anorexia nervosa is that it is a desperate and urgent attempt to escape the realities associated with approaching adulthood. As a consequence of family "enmeshment" and other predisposing situational and developmental factors, the would-be anorexic is very ill-equipped to face adult demands and responsibilities. It is an *adaptive* dissociation that allows these people completely to ignore the bulk of "generalized reality," a term used by Shor (1959); again, see Kaffman's chapter for more details. It seems very plausible that anorexia nervosa is an autosuggestive phenomenon. But I would also add that dissociated consciousness must be achieved before the person would respond to such wildly distortive self-suggestions. And they are massive distortions of reality that the anorexic manages to accomplish. Not only does she/he dispose of the bulk of objective reality, but she/he becomes totally self-deluded about the nature and merits of thinness. These people are able to achieve body-image distortions which continually convince them that they are grossly obese when, in fact, they might be nothing but skin and bones. Their unwavering *devotion* to thinness leads Kaffman (in his chapter) to compare these individuals to those who have been "brainwashed" by fanatical religious cults.

If Kaffman is right, we may have a peculiar situation in which the potential anorexic is actually using the self-directed "be thin" monologue as a basis for "absorption," not unlike some hypnotists of old who used a metronome, or a ball on a string. Endless repetitions of this message (or almost any stimulus for that matter) are sufficient *for some people* to establish a dissociative trance. In such a state, a person is able to override logic and critical thought in order to be able to accept suggestions for which there is *no logical foundation*. This *procedure* results in a state of *dissociation*. In the absence of such a prerequisite dissociative state, the "be thin" message could not become translated into suggestive (i.e., distortive) behavior. Therefore, anorexia nervosa is a coping mechanism that exemplifies the way a person can achieve a sufficient degree of dissociated consciousness in order to believe and act upon self-administered suggestions.

It is beyond the scope of this chapter to explore other very important aspects of the interaction of dissociation, suggestion, and symptom formation. One might ask, for example, why it is that anorexia nervosa is a culture-bound syndrome, and why it is in our culture that 90% of people with anorexia nervosa are women (but also why the percentage of men is increasing). I believe that we can improve our understanding of the suggestion process by searching out culture-bound dissociative syndromes in one culture which appears to be etiologically identical, but symptomatically different, from culture-bound disorders in other cultures. Some readers might be interested, for example, in the close relationship between anorexia nervosa as it appears in the West, and *koro* (an intense fear of penis shrinkage) that exists in Southern China. In his chapter in this book, Kaffman mentions *koro* in relation to anorexia nervosa and other "monoideistic" disorders. He also mentions that "witch doctor" therapies can be expected to work better than conventional therapies with these "hypnotic" types of disorders. I take up these points in considerable detail in my earlier mentioned book (Schumaker, 1990).

Conclusion

I have argued here that our suggestive and dissociative capacities are an aspect of our biological endowment, and that they have distinct adaptive value in many areas of our lives. To them we owe our potential to transcend reality, to function as "social" creatures, to find refuge from conflict and self, and also to operate in an economical and energy-conserving fashion. Some of these are complex defensive functions, while others play a basic preventative part in safeguarding the overall integrity of our nervous systems. Dissociation can operate independently of the suggestion process, as occurs when "absorption" facilitates dissociation for the everyday purposes of neurological conservation and economy of effort. However, it was shown that suggestive responses, strictly defined, are always reliant on a certain degree of dissociated consciousness. This latter process makes a person *potentially* responsive to suggestion by effectively disengaging higher order cognitive functions. Suggestion and dissociation have an additional interaction with culture. This can be seen in healthy as well as pathological expressions of this dimension of behavior.

As we grow in our knowledge of our suggestive and dissociative abilities, we will hopefully appreciate the important place they hold in our past and our future.

References

Allport, G.W. (1961). *Pattern and growth in personality*. New York: Holt, Rinehart and Winston.

Andorfer, J.C. (1985). Multiple personality in the human information processor: A case history and a theoretical formulation. *Journal of Clinical Psychology, 41*, 309–24.

Argyle, M., & Beit-Hallahmi, B. (1975). *The social psychology of religion*. London: Routledge and Kegan Paul.

Beahrs, J.O. (1983). Co-consciousness: A common denominator in hypnosis, multiple personality, and normalcy. *American Journal of Clinical Hypnosis, 26*, 100–12.

Becker, E. (1973). *The denial of death*. New York: The Free Press.

Bergson, H. (1935). *The two sources of morality and religion*. Westport, Conn: Greenwood Press.

Bowers, K.S. (1982). Unconscious influences and hypnosis. Paper presented at the 1982 annual meeting of The American Psychological Association, Washington, D.C..

Brassfield, P.A. (1983). Unfolding patterns of multiple personality through hypnosis. *American Journal of Clinical Hypnosis, 26*, 146–52.

Bruch, H. (1975). How to treat anorexia nervosa. *Roche Reports: Frontiers of Psychiatry*.

Dobzhansky, T., Ayala, F.J., Stebbins, G.L., & Valentine, J.W. (1977). *Evolution*. San Francisco: W.H. Freeman.

Edmonston, W.E. (1989). Conceptual clarification of hypnosis and its relationship to suggestibility. In V.A. Gheorghiu, P. Netter, H.J. Eysenck, & R. Rosenthal (eds.), *Suggestion and suggestibility: Theory and research*. Berlin: Springer-Verlag.

Frankl, V. (1963). *Man's search for meaning*. New York: Pocket Books.

Groth-Marnat, G., & Schumaker, J.F. (1990). Hypnotizability, attitute toward eating, and concern with body size in a female college population. *American Journal of Clinical Hypnosis, 32*, 194–200.

Gheorghiu, V.A. (1989a). The development of research on suggestibility: Critical considerations. In V.A. Gheorghiu, P. Netter, H.J. Eysenck, & R. Rosenthal (eds.), *Suggestion and suggestibility: Theory and research* (pp. 3–55). Berlin: Springer-Verlag.

Gheorghiu, V.A. (1989b). The difficulty in explaining suggestion: Some conceivable solutions. In V.A. Gheorghiu, P. Netter, H.J. Eysenck, & R. Rosenthal (eds.), *Suggestion and suggestibility: Theory and research* (pp. 99–112). Berlin: Springer-Verlag.

Gibbons, D., & DeJarnette, J. (1972). Hypnotic suggestibility and religious experience. *Journal for the Scientific Study of Religion, 11,* 152–56.

Heider, K. (1976). Dani sexuality: A low energy system. *Man, 11,* 188–201.

Hilgard, E.R. (1965). *Hypnotic susceptibility.* New York: Harcourt, Brace and World.

Hilgard, E.R. (1986/1977). *Divided consciousness: Multiple controls in human thought and action.* New York: Wiley.

James, W. (1981). *The principles of psychology,* Volume II. Cambridge, MA: Harvard University Press (originally published in 1890).

Janet, P. (1889). *L'automatisme psychologique.* Paris: Felix Alcan.

Kaffman, M. (1983). Inflexible belief constructs in families of paranoid patients. *International Journal of Family Psychiatry, 3,* 487–500.

Kantor, R.M. (1972). *Commitment and community.* Cambridge, MA: Harvard University Press.

Kurtz, P. (1986). *The transcendental temptation: A critique of religion and the paranormal.* New York: Prometheus Books.

Lopreato, J. (1984). *Human nature and biocultural evolution* (p. 278). Boston: Allen and Unwin.

Ludwig, A.M. (1983). The psychobiological functions of dissociation. *American Journal of Clinical Hypnosis, 26,* 93–99.

Lumsden, C.J., & Wilson, E.O. (1981). *Genes, mind, and behavior: The coevolutionary process.* Cambridge, MA: Harvard University Press.

McDougall, W. (1908). *An introduction to social psychology.* London: Methuen.

Orne, M. (1959). The nature of hypnosis: Artifact and essence. *Journal of Abnormal and Social Psychology, 58,* 277–99.

Pascal, B. (1973). *Pensées: Notes on religion and other subjects.* Translated by John Warrington. London: J.M. Dent and Sons (originally published in 1670).

Passingham, R.E. (1982). *The human primate.* Oxford: W.H. Freeman.

Rilke, R.M. (1977/1955). *Duino Eligies.* Boston: Houghton Mifflin.

Rossi, E.L. (1986). Altered states of consciousness in everyday life. In B. Wolman & M. Ullman (eds.), *Handbook of states of consciousness* (pp. 97–122). New York: Bantam Books.

Rossi, E.L. (1987). The psychology of dissociation. *Canadian Psychology, 28,* 112–13.

Sackeim, H.A. (1983). Self-deception, self-esteem and depression: The adaptive value of lying to oneself. In J. Masling (ed.), *Empirical studies of psychoanalytic theories* (pp. 329–69). Hillsdale, NJ: Erlbaum.

Sackeim, H.A., & Vingiano, W.A. (1984). Dissociative disorders. In S. Turner & M. Hersen (eds.), *Adult psychopathology and diagnosis* (pp. 329–69). New York: Wiley.

Scheibe, K.E. (1974). Legitimized aggression and the assignment of evil. *American Scholar, 43,* 575–92.

Scheibe, K.E. (1983). The psychology of national identity. In T.R. Sarbin & K.E. Scheibe (eds.), *Studies in social identity*. New York: Praeger.

Schumaker, J.F. (1987). Mental health, belief deficit compensation, and paranormal beliefs. *Journal of Psychology, 121*, 451–57.

Schumaker, J.F. (1990). *Wings of illusion*. Cambridge, UK: Polity Press (also, Buffalo, NY: Prometheus Books).

Selvini, M. (1971). Anorexia nervosa. In S. Arieti (ed.), *World biennial of psychiatry and psychotherapy*, Vol. I. New York: Basic Books.

Sheldon, W.H. (1975). *Prometheus revisited*. Cambridge, MA: Schenkman.

Shor, R.E. (1959). Hypnosis and the concept of generalized reality orientation. *American Journal of Psychotherapy, 13*, 582–602.

Sidis, B. (1898). *The psychology of suggestion*. New York: D. Appleton and Company.

Spiegel, D., Hunt, T., & Dondershine, H.E. (1988). Dissociation and hypnotizability in post-traumatic stress disorder. *American Journal of Psychiatry, 145*, 301–05.

Spiro, M. (1965). Culturally constituted defense mechanisms. In M.E. Spiro (ed.), *Context and meaning in cultural anthropology*. New York: The Free Press.

Tart, C.T. (1986). *Waking up: Overcoming the obstacles to human potential*. Boston: Shambhala.

Taylor, S.E., & Brown, J.D. (1988). Illusion and well-being: A social psychological perspective on mental health. *Psychological Review, 103*, 193–210.

Tellegen, A., & Atkinson, G. (1974). Openness to absorbing and self-altering experiences ("absorption"), a trait related to hypnotic susceptibility. *Journal of Abnormal Psychology, 83*, 268–77.

Wallace, A.F.C. (1966). *Religion: An anthropological view*. New York: Random House.

Wijeyewardene, G. (1986). *Place and emotion in northern Thai ritual behaviour*. Bangkok: Pandora Press.

Wilder, T. (1957). *Three plays*. New York: Harper and Row.

6

SUGGESTIBILITY: A Social Psychological Approach

Graham F. Wagstaff

What is suggestibility?

The task of devising some central definition of the term "suggestibility" is not an easy one. Marcuse (1976) argues that the terms "suggestibility" and "suggestion" have a multiplicity of possible definitions. These include the influence of one person on another without his or her consent, the implanting of an idea, possessing a submissive tendency, and appealing to the unconscious. Moreover, he remarks, "The definitions which have been proffered are varied, confusing and incomplete" (p. 85).

Suggestibility is often linked with hypnosis, but opinions differ as to whether hypnotic phenomena are simply manifestations of suggestibility or whether hypnosis involves something other than suggestibility. For example, Wilson and Barber (1983) tend to use the terms "responsiveness to suggestions" and "hypnotic responsiveness" interchangeably. On the other hand, others have argued that it is meaningful to differentiate between "hypnotic" and "waking" suggestibility and that hypnotic responsiveness is more than simple responsiveness to suggestion (Evans, 1967; Hilgard, 1973; Sheehan & Perry, 1976). Bowers (1983) actually favours a tripartite division: hypnotic suggestibility, waking suggestibility, and hypnotic *susceptibility*. The link between hypnosis and suggestibility has given rise to a series of suggestibility tests which some allege can be presented in the "hypnotic" and "waking" states, thus enabling comparisons to be made between "hypnotic" and "waking" suggestibility. Such tests include suggested body-sway, arm lowering, arm levitation, eye-closure, arm rigidity, hands moving together, hands locked together, positive and negative hallucinations (which can be gustatory visual, tactile or olfactory), amnesia, and anaesthesia. But according to Bowers (1983), purer tests of hypnotic *susceptibility* are those which measure "tranceability" independently of suggestibility, such as hypnotic depth reports.

The problems of defining and measuring suggestibility are made more complex by the existence of another set of classic suggestion tests which are not usually, if ever, administered in the context of hypnosis. One of the most famous of these is Chevreul's pendulum. In this, the subject is asked to hold steady a bob suspended on a thread, and one assesses the swing of the bob when the subject is told that the bob is swinging. Other "non-hypnotic" tests include the progressive weights, contradictory information, and ink-blot tests. (For further descriptions and examples, see Eysenck & Furneaux, 1945; Stukat, 1958).

The phenomena associated with these tests would seem heterogenous enough, but there are even more phenomena which, at one time or another, have been associated with suggestion. For example, theorists and researchers have recently turned their attention to the concept of "interrogative suggestibility" (Gudjonsson, 1987), including false confessions to crimes (Coid, 1981), and incorporating misleading information into eyewitness accounts (Powers, Andriks, & Loftus, 1979). Also included as evidence of the alleged influence of suggestion have been automobile fatalities following publicized suicides (Phillips, 1979), conformity with group aesthetic preferences (Mohan & Kumar, 1975), placebo responding (Strupp, 1974), the "voodoo death" phenomenon (Hall, 1986), and yawning when others yawn (Marcuse, 1976).

Categories of suggestibility

In an attempt to make sense of this range of diverse tests and associated behaviors, a number of investigators have attempted to intercorrelate various measures of suggestibility to establish whether any meaningful groupings and common mechanisms can be identified. Unfortunately, results have been equivocal.

One grouping (in fact the only grouping) which has been reported fairly consistently has been labelled "primary suggestibility." Eysenck (1947) describes this as "the execution of a motor movement by the subject consequent upon the repeated suggestion by the experimenter that such a movement will take place, without conscious participation in the movement on the subject's part" (p. 165). This factor is purportedly best measured by tests such as body-sway, arm levitation and lowering, and Chevreul's pendulum. However, while various researchers have claimed to identify further types of suggestibility, results are inconsistent (see for example, Eysenck & Furneaux, 1945; Stukat, 1958; Duke, 1964; Evans, 1967). In general then, different measures of suggestibility seem to relate, at best, weakly with each other, with the exception of those purported to indicate primary suggestibility.

Sometimes this failure of different measures of "suggestibility" to relate consistently may seem surprising. For example, if we conceive of suggestibility as some kind of potential to respond to ideas or beliefs placed in the mind (the Oxford Dictionary defines a suggestion as the "insinuation of a belief or impulse into the mind"), one might expect that a very good measure of suggestibility would be *placebo responsiveness;* that is, a person's tendency to respond positively to inert substances, or innocuous therapeutic contexts, when led to believe they will be beneficial. Indeed, some writers have assumed that suggestion lies at the heart of the placebo effect (see for example, Shapiro, 1973; Strupp, 1974). Nevertheless, Evans (1974) concludes "most studies have found no significant relationship between suggestibility and the placebo response" (p. 72).

Even the construct of primary suggestibility is not without its problems. Most supporters of this construct seem to accept the definition by Eysenck (1947). They assume that the responses that characterize primary suggestibility have an automatic quality. For example, Evans (1967) argues that responsiveness to these tests is "passive." He says: "the direct suggestion of the desired movement implies that the subject plays no overt role in producing the movement, but rather passively awaits its occurrence" (p. 118). But what is the mechanism behind this "passive" response? Some have argued that ideomotor action theory provides a reasonable explanation. According to ideomotor theory, the thought or image of a movement may result in that movement occurring. For example, Hull (1933) concluded that imagination may result in the "feeble execution of acts customarily performed in connection with the situation being imagined" (p. 46). Hull also concluded that this could be offered as a mechanism to account for hypnotic responding. However, more recent evidence indicates that hypnotic subjects will still respond to suggestion even if the suggestions are *contrary* to their imaginings. For example, if subjects are asked to *imagine* their arms are heavy, while it is suggested that their arms are rising, they will raise their arms (Zamansky, 1977; Spanos, Weekes, & de Groh, 1984). Further, Evans (1967) argues that ideomotor action cannot adequately account for primary suggestibility because it cannot account for performance on the pendulum test in which the imagining processes are directed towards an inanimate object. Perhaps, instead, such findings could be interpreted in accordance with an alternative view that it is a capacity for *dissociation* which accounts for primary suggestibility; maybe subjects high on primary suggestibility display dissociations between conscious awareness and the systems controlling responsiveness to suggestion (Evans, 1967). However, others imply that it is the employment of dissociation which essentially distinguishes *hypnotic* suggestion (Hilgard & Hilgard, 1983). That leaves us with possibly a two-tier system, with the use of imagination operating in suggestibility and dissociation in hypnotic suggestibility. But this makes little sense to those who argue that hypnotic and waking suggestibility are not qualitatively different. Others have attempted to associate suggestibility with conditioning. It has been proposed that the automatic quality that defines responsiveness to suggestion may be due to the fact that such responses are conditioned responses. Again, results have been inconsistent (see for example, Evans, 1967; Lohr & Souheaver, 1981).

The task of finding a mechanism for primary suggestibility has been made more difficult by findings which indicate that classic primary suggestion measures can show significant correlations with social influence measures which appear to bear little obvious resemblance to a concept which is supposed to be restricted to non-volitional motor activity. For example, Stukat (1958) identified three tests which could be used as a measure of primary suggestibility: the body sway, arm lowering, and pendulum tests. However, in a sample of 80 adults, the correlation between the pendulum test and a test of susceptibility to leading questions (0.35) was little different from the correlation between the pendulum test and the arm levitation suggestion (0.37). This would seem to conflict with Gudjonsson's (1987) view that interrogative suggestibility bears little resemblance to traditional conceptions of suggestibility. Moreover, Stukat (1958) identified a general second order factor of suggestibility which related positively to his tests of primary suggestibility, as well as a tendency to conform to the opinions of a majority.

Some of the most puzzling findings have come from attempts to find correlates of hypnotic susceptibility. Some writers have argued that hypnotic susceptibility is related only to direct suggestions, such as those involved in the body-sway test. They maintain that other kinds of suggestion, such as the odor test, are not related to hypnosis. For example, Hilgard (1985) argues that "only primary suggestibility (is) closely related to hypnosis" (p. 32), a view which also seems to be shared by writers such as Eysenck and Furneaux (1945), Gibson (1987), and Marcuse (1976). However, evidence pertaining to this proposal is far from conclusive. For example, Hajek and Spacek (1987) found a small but significant relationship between hypnotic responsiveness and a social influence test in which subjects were asked to estimate the increase of brightness in a light which actually had not increased in brightness. Also, Moore (1964) found a low but significant relationship between hypnotic responsiveness and a test of "influencibility" which involved judgements given after false peer-group norm feedback (0.21). Most importantly, however, in Moore's study, the correlation between this influencibility test and body-sway was 0.66, a correlation which exceeded any of the correlations between the individual hypnosis scale items themselves. In addition, Graham and Green (1981) reported a significant relationship between hypnotic responsiveness and alumni annual giving, while Shames (1981) found significant correlations of 0.41 and 0.66 between hypnotic responsiveness and measure of conformity to majority group opinion in the judgement of lines.

Given results such as these one might be inclined to argue, as does Marcuse (1976), that "the many different psychological processes involved in the term suggestibility are often confused, and the word "suggestion" is frequently nothing more than a wastepaper basket for vague and ambiguous concepts" (p. 84). It may also be of some significance that the terms "suggestion" and "suggestibility" do not even appear as entries in the recent, much celebrated, *Oxford Companion to the Mind* (Gregory, 1987). This is perhaps a measure of the present confusion which surrounds the term.

A social psychological approach

Has the concept of suggestibility reached a dead end? Has it outlived its usefulness? I think not. But I believe that if we are to understand the reasons behind the multitude of confusions and contradictions, and make some progress in the area of suggestibility, we may need to challenge and revise certain basic assumptions.

The concept of suggestibility first came to the fore in the nineteenth century as a concept which might explain automatism and, later, hypnotic phenomena. It was very much seen as a "normal" phenomenon to be found in everyone and operating in everyday situations. This was vastly different from such explanations of hypnotic effects as magnetic fluids, or abnormal states.

Nevertheless, the prevailing *zeitgeist* of perceiving many human behaviors as automatic remained. This probably stemmed from the zealous application of the still comparatively new scientific notion of mechanistic cause to human behavior. Thus suggestibility, though mundane, was still used to refer to manifestations of automatic, nonvolitional behavior in response to communications. It seems that a number of psychologists and sociologists then climbed on the bandwagon and a whole range of disparate phenomena were viewed as automatic. However, it is very likely that these earlier investigators, who had little knowledge of the problems of experimental design, also overestimated the automatic quality of the behaviors they observed. This may be significant in that many of our classic suggestion tests were devised in this era (for a useful historical review see Stukat, 1958). Consequently, the possibility exists that many researchers *still* overestimate the degree of automatism that occurs in response to communications labelled as "suggestions."

I propose, therefore, that we challenge the utility of our "classic suggestion tests" as they are usually presented. We should not assume that they necessarily tap *automatic* responding of various kinds. Rather, we should recognise that suggestibility tests and other situations associated with suggestibility are primarily *social situations* in which participants are more likely to be *active* participants than *passive* recipients. In this respect, research on suggestibility *per se* has lagged behind developments in the field of hypnosis. So, a brief look at some of these developments may provide us with some important insights into what probably happens when we administer most classic tests of suggestibility.

Research into hypnotic phenomena over the past half century or so has given rise to a number of theories of hypnosis which could loosely be called "social psychological" in orientation (see, for example, Sarbin & Coe, 1972; Spanos, 1982, 1986; Wagstaff, 1981, 1986). These differ from more traditional concepts of hypnosis by rejecting the utility of the terms such as "hypnotic state," "trance," "altered state of consciousness," and "waking state." They stress instead terms such as attitudes, beliefs, expectations, conformity, compliance, imagination, and relaxation. From a social psychological perspective, hypnosis is not seen as some kind of physiological state, genetically transmitted. Rather it is viewed as a *social invention,* culturally transmitted. It is assumed that most hypnotic situations are social situations in which hypnotist and subject act out roles. The role of the subject is to present himself or herself as "hypnotized" according to previous expectations and cues given indirectly or directly by the hypnotist and the immediate context. This does not necessarily mean, however, that the hypnotic subject is "faking" (though he or she may be). Instead, it is assumed that the subject may actually try very hard to enact the hypnotic role and may attempt to use a variety of techniques or strategies to bring about various effects. For example, when it is suggested to subjects that their arms are heavy, they may try very hard to make their arms heavy by thinking along with the suggestions. Or, when it is suggested that no pain will be felt, the subject may try distraction, or imagining a pleasant scene. Such strategies may be deemed successful by the subject depending on his or her expectations. According to my own version of this approach (Wagstaff, 1986), most hypnotic responding can be seen as involving three stages. First, the subject figures out what is expected on the basis of previous experience, the situational context, and the hypnotist's instructions. Second, the subject may employ imaginative and other deliberate activities to try to bring about the suggested effects. Third, if the strategies fail, or are not used, the subject either gives up, or reverts to behavioral compliance or shaming.

Initially, it may seem a ridiculous idea that subjects would act out a role involving pain, distress or embarrassment, and even sham or fake effects. However, there is now significant literature which indicates that subjects who enter experiments or comparable situations have a strong desire to cooperate and appear as good, helpful subjects. For example, Milgram (1974) found that a majority of subjects seemed prepared to give lethal doses of electric shock to an innocent victim if instructed to do so by an experimenter. Of course, the shocks in Milgram's experiment were not actually real, though the subjects said they believed they were. However, in a follow-up study by Sheridan and King (1972), they used *real* shocks and a *real* victim; a puppy. All female subjects in this study obeyed the command to administer the painful doses of shock to the suffering animal. Orne (1962) has also demonstrated that people will agree to perform the most nonsensical requests if instructed to do so. In one study, subjects were required to perform additions on sheets filled with random digits. Subjects were given 2,000 sheets to complete, with 224 additions on each sheet. The subjects were then told by the experimenter "Continue to work; I will return eventually." The result was that, five and a half hours later, the *experimenter* gave up! The subjects seemed willing to go on for hours rather than let the experimenter down. Importantly, it seems that this desire to cooperate with the experimenter is such that subjects can be quite willing to tell lies rather than let the experimenter down. For example, in a study by Levy (1967) subjects were recruited to take part in a verbal learning experiment. However, the success of the particular experiment depended on subjects *not* knowing of the experimental hypothesis. Nevertheless, Levy arranged for an accomplice to tell subjects of the hypothesis before they performed the task. Levy found that not one subject spontaneously volunteered his or her knowledge to the experimenter during the experiment, and on further questioning 75% denied any prior knowledge of the experiment.

The term *compliance* refers to the phenomenon of responding in a manner which is contrary to one's beliefs or private convictions, in order to achieve accord with the views, wishes, or expectations of others (Tedeschi, Lindskold, & Rosenfeld, 1985). Compliance has an important place in the social psychological literature largely due to the experiments of Asch (1956). His research showed that people would make clearly erroneous judgments of the lengths of lines when confronted with the judgments of others briefed to give incorrect responses.

However, it was Orne (1970) who really brought the problem of compliance to the center stage of hypnosis research by pointing out how necessary it was to control for the effects of conformity to *demand characteristics* in hypnosis research. That is, one must ascertain whether a hypnotic phenomenon is "real" or "genuinely" experienced, or whether subjects have simply complied with the demands of experimental situations and faked or shammed to create the appropriate impression. There is now a great deal of evidence to indicate that hypnotic subjects often do simply comply with experimental demands. For example, there are individual cases where subjects have admitted as much. Certain effects such as amnesia can be eliminated if subjects are given an opportunity to "own-up" to compliance (Wagstaff, 1977, 1981). Other phenomena disappear when the hypnotist is absent, only to reappear on his or her return (Spanos, et al., 1987). Also, subjects classified as highly hypnotizable often claim a history of "pretending" (Wilson & Barber, 1982).

Nevertheless, not even the most ardent supporter of the view that compliance may operate in hypnotic situations would attempt to argue that *all* hypnotic phenomena can be accounted for in terms of compliance only. The general principle is not that all hypnotic phenomena are manifestations of compliance. Rather, the general principle is that one does not need to postulate any unique property of hypnosis, such as a "state," or "trance," in order to explain hypnotic effects. Thus, for example, supporters of the social psychological position also stress that there is still no definitive support for a physiological indicator of a hypnotic state. Moreover, hypnotic induction procedures do not enable one to transcend one's capacities in equivalent non-hypnotic situations on a variety of tasks involving memory, muscular endurance, and pain tolerance. They also point out that a number of more subtle phenomena once thought possibly unique to hypnosis (e.g., disorganized and source amnesia, and "incongruous" experiences such as transparent hallucinations) are readily explicable in terms of "normal" processes and repeatable by non-hypnotic control groups given appropriate instructions (Spanos, 1982, 1986; Wagstaff, 1981, 1986, 1987).

If we adopt this social psychological perspective, then there appear to be a number of important implications for the study of suggestibility *per se*. First, the distinction between so-called "hypnotic" and "waking" suggestibility becomes simply a matter of procedure. Hypnotic tests of suggestibility are "waking" tests dressed up in extra social ritual. When differences emerge between hypnotic and waking suggestibility, it is thus not because one involves a special altered state and the other does not. It is because the hypnotic ritual engenders extra expectations and contextual demands. For example, subjects may "try harder" or attempt to report more bizarre experiences when a situation is defined as "hypnosis" (Wagstaff, 1981). Second, most responses to suggestions, hypnotic or otherwise, are primarily *deliberate* and *strategic,* not passive and automatic. This does not mean that subjects are necessarily lying when they say their actions feel involuntary. Rather, subjects often deliberately try to bring about responses so they can *interpret* their responses as involuntary. For instance, if you try hard to imagine that your arm is heavy and moving down, you may eventually feel it is moving of its own accord (Lynn, Rhue, & Weekes, 1989). Third, if we define "suggestibility" as "the tendency to respond to suggestions," then differences in standardized measures of suggestibility are more likely to reflect differences in attitudes, expectancies, and possibly even role skills. There is no need to try to understand these in terms of some physiologically based capacity to respond to stimuli without conscious volition (indeed, Spanos and his associates have modified hypnotic susceptibility by teaching appropriate attitudes and strategies; see Bertrand, 1989). Fourth, certain responses to suggestion may not be as dramatic as a researcher may at first think. For example, in hypnotic situations, subjects *if given the choice* prefer to describe so-called "hallucinated" phenomena as "imagined" rather than "seen" (Spanos, 1982). So, it is probable that misinterpretations of subjects' mundane experiences also occur in non-hypnotic tests of suggestibility. Finally, fifth, tests of suggestibility are likely to be biased by behavioral compliance, just like other tests which involve social interactions. Therefore we cannot necessarily assume that subjects are telling the truth when they report seeing, smelling, tasting, or feeling something. They may be lying to help out the experimenter, to appear cooperative, or even to show off.

Whither suggestibility?

Given the range of social and cognitive variables that are likely to interact and affect responding to any particular standard suggestibility test, it is not really surprising that attempts to isolate a global trait of suggestibility have not been very successful. We should perhaps not even get too excited by the notion of "primary suggestibility." It is a feature of psychological testing that, as task similarity increases, there is a greater likelihood that performance on one will correlate with performance on another. It is the case that certain tests (e.g., arm levitation, body-sway, arm lowering, and to a lesser extent, the pendulum) tend to correlate significantly with each other. But this could simply reflect the fact the attitudes, expectancies, and strategies required to perform these tasks are similar. We cannot assume that they tap some special capacity to produce motor responses from images without conscious participation. Furthermore, the mere fact that these tests relate weakly to measures of social influence does not allow one to assume that they are somehow independent of social influence processes. After all, different measures of constructs such as conformity and persuasibility correlate only weakly with each other (McGuire, 1968).

A major problem seems to be that many tests of suggestibility, as presently devised and presented, are simply not sufficiently sensitive to differentiate between the following four classes of phenomena.

1. To be affected by a communication or expectation such that certain responses are overtly enacted, or subjectively experienced, without volition, as in automatism.
2. *Deliberately* to use one's imagination or employ strategies to bring about effects (even if interpreted, eventually, as involuntary) in response to a communication or expectation.
3. To accept what people say consciously, but uncritically, and to believe or privately accept what is said.
4. To conform overtly to expectations or the views of others, without the appropriate private acceptance or experience; that is, to exhibit behavioral compliance without private acceptance or belief.

There is little doubt that, historically, it is only category 1 which really encompasses the true domain of suggestibility, although there is perhaps some overlap with category 3. But I suspect that category 1 *still* encompasses what to many is the defining characteristic of suggestibility. That is, a true response to suggestion is not a response brought about at any stage by volition, but rather a true nonvolitional response, perhaps even brought about *despite* volition. However, in my view, I doubt very much whether any of the classic studies of suggestibility have ever actually managed to measure this characteristic in an accurate way. Indeed, if we really do wish to measure automatic behavior, this may require a new, more sophisticated approach. For example, investigators might do well to look at the techniques developed by Hull (1933) more than fifty years ago. In one ingenious study, Hull asked a naive male subject to demonstrate how long he could stand with his eyes closed. Under the pretext of placing him in the right position, a pin with a hook on it was tagged on to the subject's collar, unbeknown to him. From the pin a thread ran back to a recording apparatus. The subject was told not to move whilst he saw another subject being tested. Another subject, a woman, then proceeded to reach for the wall, with all her might. The results showed that the unsuspecting male swayed backwards and forwards as he saw the female move backwards and forwards. Hull's elaborate procedure seems a far cry from the standard body-sway test in which subjects are usually given direct suggestions for movement. But Hull seemed to be far more aware that one could not infer "automatism" unless an attempt is made to eliminate other sources of responding.

A new look at suggestibility might also involve investigating afresh certain phenomena which at present have been excluded from some mainstream conceptions of suggestibility. For example, the phenomenon of the placebo response has been prematurely rejected by some from the central domain of suggestibility because of the failure of placebo responding to correlate significantly with other alleged tests of suggestibility. However, we have yet to establish whether these latter tests even reliably tap "suggestibility" as it was originally conceived.

The overall conclusion to be drawn from this analysis is thus as follows: if we conceive of "suggestibility" as a label which refers to a cross-situational capacity to respond automatically, or even empathically to expectations or the communications of others, and to do this possibly even despite active conscious efforts to do otherwise, then *research has really yet to begin.*

References

Asch, S.E. (1956). Studies of independence and conformity: A minority of one against a unanimous majority. *Psychological Monographs, 70,* 9 whole no. 416.

Bertrand, L.D. (1989). The assessment and modification of hypnotic susceptibility. In N.P. Spanos & J.F. Chaves (eds.), *Hypnosis: The cognitive behavioral perspective.* Buffalo, NY: Prometheus Books.

Bowers, K.S. (1983). *Hypnosis for the seriously curious.* New York: Norton.

Coid, J. (1981). Suggestibility, low intelligence and a confession to crime. *British Journal of Psychiatry, 139,* 436–38.

Duke, J.D. (1964). Placebo reactivity and tests of suggestibility. *Journal of Personality, 32,* 227–35.

Evans, F.J. (1967). Suggestibility in the normal waking state. *Psychological Bulletin, 67,* 114–29.

Evans, F.J. (1974). The placebo response in pain reduction. In L.V. DiCara, et al. (eds.), *Biofeedback and self-control* (pp. 72–79). Chicago: Aldine.

Eysenck, H.J. (1947). *Dimensions of personality.* London: Routledge and Kegan Paul.

Eysenck, H.J., & Furneaux, W.D. (1945). Primary and secondary suggestibility. *Journal of Experimental Psychology, 25,* 485–503.

Gibson, H.B. (1987). Is hypnotherapy a placebo? *British Journal of Experimental and Clinical Hypnosis, 4,* 149–56.

Graham, K.R., & Green, L.D. (1981). Hypnotic susceptibility related to an independent measure of compliance—alumni annual giving: A brief communication. *International Journal of Clinical and Experimental Hypnosis, 29,* 351–54.

Gregory, R.L. (1987). *The Oxford companion to the mind.* Oxford: Oxford University Press.

Gudjonsson, G.H. (1987). Historical background to suggestibility. How interrogative suggestibility differs from other types of suggestibility. *Personality and Individual Differences, 8,* 347–55.

Hall, H. (1986). Suggestion and illness. *International Journal of Psychosomatics, 33,* 24–27.

Hajek, P., & Spacek, J. (1987). Territory, hypnotic susceptibility and social influence: A pilot study. *British Journal of Experimental and Clinical Hypnosis, 4,* 115–19.

Hilgard, E.R. (1973). The domain of hypnosis. *American Psychologist, 28,* 972–82.

Hilgard, E.R. (1985). Conscious and unconscious process in hypnosis. In D. Waxman, P. Misra, M. Gibson, & M.A. Basker (eds.), *Modern trends in hypnosis.* New York: Plenum.

Hilgard, E.R., & Hilgard, J.R. (1983). *Hypnosis in the Belief of Pain.* New York: W. Kaufmann.

Hull, C.L. (1933). *Hypnosis and suggestibility: An experimental Approach.* New York: Appleton-Century-Crofts.

Levy, L.H. (1967). Awareness of learning and the beneficent suspect as expert witness. *Journal of Personality and Social Psychology, 6,* 365–70.

Lohr, J.M., & Souheaver, G.T. (1981). Primary waking suggestibility and classical conditioning of word meaning. *Psychological Reports, 48,* 119–26.

Lynn, S.J., Rhue, J.W., & Weekes, J.R. (1989). Hypnosis and experienced nonvolition: A social cognitive integrative model. In N.P. Spanos & J.F. Chaves (eds.), *Hypnosis: The cognitive behavioral perspective.* Buffalo, NY: Prometheus Books.

Marcuse, F.L. (1976). *Hypnosis: Fact and fiction.* Hammondsworth: Penguin Books.

Milgram, S. (1974). *Obedience to authority.* London: Tavistock.

McGuire, W.J. (1968). Personality and susceptibility to social influence. In E.F. Borgatta & W.W. Lambert (eds.), *Handbook of personality theory and research.* Chicago: Rand McNally.

Mohan, V., & Kumar, D. (1975). Semantic differential measurement of the effect of suggestion on aesthetic choices in different personality groups. *Studia Psychologica, 17*, 224–47.

Moore, R.K. (1964). Susceptibility to hypnosis and susceptibility to social influence. *Journal of Abnormal and Social Psychology, 68*, 282–94.

Orne, M.T. (1962). On the social psychology of the psychological experiment: With particular reference to demand characteristics and their implications. *American Psychologist, 17*, 776–83.

Orne, M.T. (1970). Hypnosis motivation and ecological validity of the psychological experiment. In W.J. Arnold & M.M. Page (eds.), *Nebraska symposium on motivation* (pp. 187–265). Lincoln, Nebraska: University Nebraska Press.

Phillips, D. (1979). Suicide, motor vehicle fatalities, and the mass media: Evidence toward a theory of suggestion. *American Journal of Sociology, 84*, 1150–74.

Powers, P.A., Andriks, J.L., & Loftus, E.F. (1979). Eyewitness accounts of females and males. *Journal of Applied Psychology, 64*, 339–47.

Sarbin, T.R., & Coe, W.C. (1972). *Hypnotic behavior: The psychology of influence communication.* New York: Holt.

Shames, M.L. (1981). Hypnotic susceptibility and conformity: On the mediational mechanism of suggestibility. *Psychological Reports, 49*, 563–65.

Shapiro, A.K. (1973). Contribution to a history of the placebo effect. In N.E. Miller, et al. (eds.), *Biofeedback and self-control* (pp. 217–43). Chicago: Aldine.

Sheehan, P.W., & Perry, C.W. (1976). *Methodologies of hypnosis: A critical appraisal of contemporary paradigms of hypnosis.* Hillsdale, NJ: Laurence Erlbaum.

Sheridan, C.L., & King, R.G. (1972). Obedience to authority with an authentic victim. *Proceedings, Eightieth Annual Convention, American Psychological Association*, 165–66.

Spanos, N. P. (1982). A social psychological approach to hypnotic behavior. In G. Weary & H.L. Mirels, (eds.), *Integrations of clinical and social psychology.* New York: Oxford University Press.

Spanos, N.P. (1986). Hypnotic behavior: A social psychological interpretation of amnesia, analgesia, and "trance logic." *The Behavioral and Brain Sciences, 9*, 449–502.

Spanos, N.P., Menary, E., Brett, P.J., Cross, W., & Ahmed, Q. (1987). Failure of posthypnotic responding to occur outside the experimental setting. *Journal of Abnormal Psychology, 96*, 52–57.

Spanos, N.P., Weekes, J.R., & de Groh, M. (1984). The "involuntary" countering of suggested requests: A test of the ideomotor hypothesis of hypnotic responsiveness. *British Journal of Experimental and Clinical Hypnosis, 1*, 3–11.

Strupp, H.H. (1974). Effects of suggestion on total respiratory resistance in mild asthmatics. *Journal of Psychosomatic Research, 18*, 337–46.

Stukat, K.G. (1958). *Suggestibility: A factorial and experimental analysis.* Stockholm: Almqvist and Wiksell.

Tedeschi, J.T., Lindskold, S., & Rosenfeld, P. (1985). *Introduction to social psychology.* St. Paul, MN: West Publishing.

Wagstaff, G.F. (1977). An experimental study of compliance and posthypnotic amnesia. *British Journal of Social and Clinical Psychology, 16*, 225–28.

Wagstaff, G.F. (1981). *Hypnosis, compliance and belief.* Brighton: Harvester Press/New York: St. Martin's Press.

Wagstaff, G.F. (1986). Hypnosis as compliance and belief: A socio-cognitive view. In P.L.N. Naish (ed.), *What is hypnosis?* Milton Keynes: Open University Press.

Wagstaff, G.F. (1987). Hypnosis. In H. Beloff & A. Colman (eds.), *Psychology Survey 6* (pp. 234–54). Leicester: British Psychological Society, and Cambridge, MA: MIT Press.

Wilson, S.C., & Barber, T.X. (1983). The fantasy-prone personality: Implications for understanding imagery, hypnosis and parapsychological phenomena. In Anees A. Sheikh (ed.), *Imagery: Current Theory Research and Application* (pp. 340–87). New York: Wiley.

Zamansky, H.S. (1977). Suggestion and countersuggestion in hypnotic behavior. *Journal of Abnormal Psychology, 86,* 346–51.

7

SUGGESTIBILITY: A Reversal Theory Perspective

Michael J. Apter

In recent years a general theory of motivation, emotion, and personality has been emerging which is centrally concerned with intra-individual differences and the states of mind between which people move in the course of everyday life. This theory, known as "reversal theory" (Apter, 1982, 1989), may be seen as embodying what has been called a "structural-phenomenological" approach to psychology. By this is meant that the starting point of all its analyses is the structure and dynamics of conscious experience. Since suggestibility, especially in the dramatic form of hypnosis, would appear to involve one or another kind of special experiential state, it is natural to ask whether reversal theory might throw any new light on the nature of such states. The aim of the present chapter is to examine this question.

Reversal theory

For a variety of cogent reasons which cannot be elucidated here (see Apter, 1989), one of the fundamental propositions of reversal theory is that there are four pairs of "metamotivational modes" such that, for each pair, one or the other member of the pair is always operative during waking life. The members of a pair represent opposite ways of experiencing some aspect of one's motivation and, since they are opposite, a switch from one to the other represents a phenomenological *reversal* (hence the name of the theory). In normal people such reversals are expected to happen reasonably frequently in the course of everyday life, so that mental health is supposed to go with a certain kind of instability rather than stability. In this respect there is, according to the theory, an inherent inconsistency in normal human experience and behavior. Understanding the individual person necessitates understanding the factors which induce reversals in that individual, the natural biases which the individual may have toward one or the other member of each pair (these are referred to in the theory as *dominances* to distinguish them from conventional traits), and the strategies, tactics, and specific behaviors which for that individual tend to be associated with each mode. To understand an individual's behavior at a given moment it is necessary to know which member of each pair is operative at that moment, how the operative modes are articulated, and which of those which are operative at that moment is the most phenomenologically *salient*.

Adopting this perspective gives us a new and potentially powerful way of looking at not only normal but also abnormal behavior (e.g., Murgatroyd & Apter, 1984, 1986), and of understanding various types of experience including, for example, aesthetic experience (Apter, 1984), religious experience (Apter, 1985), and humor (Svebak & Apter, 1987).

The four pairs of metamotivational modes, or states of mind alluded to above can be described briefly as follows:

1. *Telic and paratelic*

The telic mode is a serious-minded one in which the individual sees what he or she is doing as being important beyond itself. Indeed, in this state of mind the ongoing behavior is performed for the sake of significant goals which the behavior might lead to in the future—perhaps even the distant future. An example might be studying for an examination.

The paratelic mode is a more casual, light-hearted, and playful one. Behavior is engaged in for its own sake, and for the immediate pleasures that go with it, rather than for future purposes. An example might be spending the evening drinking or watching television.

High arousal in the telic mode would appear to be experienced as "bad," typically as anxiety. In the paratelic mode, on the contrary, it is experienced as "good"—as exciting or thrilling.

2. *Negativism and conformity*

In the conformist mode one prefers to respect all salient social rules and conventions and not to discomfort others by being impolite or "difficult." An example would be the typical state of mind of people at a church service or a tea party.

In the less frequently occurring negativistic mode one prefers to behave in a way that one can perceive as breaking rules, defying conventions, and generally being rebellious and doing what one should not do. An example would be behaving in a deliberately provocative way on a polite social occasion.

3. *Mastery and sympathy*

In the mastery mode one perceives one's interpersonal transactions as power struggles, with all those involved attempting to achieve dominance and control over each other. Playing sport would be a good example, or bargaining with a salesman.

In the sympathy mode, in contrast, one construes interpersonal transactions as having to do with caring and nurturing. Those taking part hope to experience friendship with each other and sentiments of liking. While the mastery mode is to do with taking through strength, or yielding through weakness, the sympathy mode is about giving, or being given, through kindness. Giving a friend or relative a birthday present would be an example of this mode.

4. *Autic and alloic*

In the autic mode it is what happens to oneself that matters most. For example, whether one perceives the outcome of a business negotiation to be good or bad depends on whether one has profited or not.

In the alloic mode one identifies with another person (or group) so that it is what happens to this other that counts most— even at one's own expense. An example would be looking after a sick relative where one is doing so out of love rather than duty.

Before turning specifically to see how these ideas might relate to suggestibility, and to put matters in context, it should be added that reversal theory as a whole has generated an increasing amount of psychometric, experimental, psychological, and psychophysiological research over the last decade. It has also been used for clinical purposes. Representative papers will be found in two edited collections: Apter, Fontana, and Murgatroyd (1985) and Apter, Kerr, and Cowles (1988).

This brief description of reversal theory, although by no means comprehensive, is sufficient for present purposes. However, an exception concerns the autic and alloic states, which we will need to look at in more detail as a preliminary to discussing hypnosis later in the chapter.

The autic and alloic states are defined, as we have seen, in terms of the "emotional center" of the individual. In the autic case this center is the individual himself or herself—it is what happens to self that, phenomenologically, matters most. In the alloic case the center lies outside the individual—it is what happens to another person or group that, phenomenologically for that individual, matters most. In other

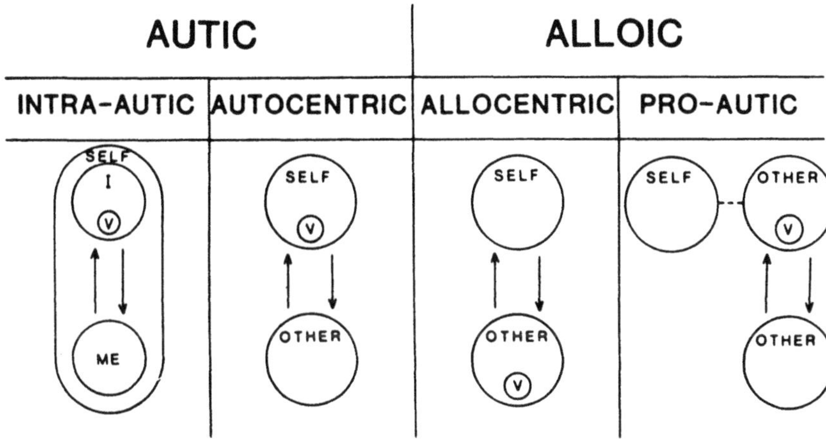

Figure 7.1.

words, in the latter case the individual is identifying or empathizing with the other, and is therefore likely to behave in an unselfish or altruistic way toward that other.

In each of these two modes there are two versions (see Figure 7.1). In the first version self and other are *interacting* directly. This occurs, for example, in a business negotiation, when a nurse cares for a patient, or two tennis players play against each other. In the autic mode we can refer to this as *autocentric* and in the alloic mode as *allocentric*. In these cases, the outcome for self and the outcome for the other tend to be inversely related. When A gives to B, then A loses something and B gains something. Whether A experiences this as good or bad depends on whether A is in the autic or alloic mode.

In the second version of these two modes, the individual is *not* directly interacting with another in this kind of way. In the alloic case we have those situations in which A's loss is *not* B's gain. These situations occur when B is interacting with another "other" C, and A is either cooperating with B in this interaction or simply empathizing with, or "rooting" for him. For example, A and B may be members of the same team, so that it is what happens to the team that matters most. This alloic form of situation in which A's center of concern is the team rather than himself can be thought of as involving the experience of having an "extended self." Alternatively, A may identify with the hero in a film, with B here acting as a "surrogate self" for A. Both extended self and surrogate self, then, are different forms of the alloic case. Both differ from the allocentric in that they do not involve direct interaction between A and B of the "I win, you lose" type. Let us call this version of the alloic mode the *pro-autic* state, because the other here is a representative of self.

In the autic mode we also have the possibility of a type of experience in which self is not interacting with another. That is, we have to recognize that there may be no other person or group in the individual's mind at a given moment at all—because the individual may be looking inwards at herself or himself. For example, a man might be worrying about his weight, or a woman making up or choosing what to wear. In these sorts of situations there is indeed still a duality, which may be captured in terms of Mead's (1934) celebrated distinction between "I" and "Me"—where "I" is the self that observes and "Me" is the self which is observed by "I." Thus when I look in a mirror the face that I see is "Me" whereas it is "I" that sees "Me." Let us call such an inward-looking version of the autic mode the *intra-autic* state. (Note that it is still autic since, a fortiori, it is self which matters most.)

These versions of these states have been described and discussed in more detail in Apter (1988). But, in order to get a better idea of how they relate to each other, it may be helpful to examine Figure 7.1. In doing so, we may note the following. (1) The position of the marker "v" represents the center of concern. On the autic side "v" is in "self" whereas on the alloic side it is in "other." This is how autic and alloic are defined. (2) The two inner parts of the diagram, representing autocentric and allocentric, show direct dyadic interactions between self and other, and this distinguishes them from the two outer parts of the diagram. (3) The autocentric and allocentric both involve self and other being at the focus of awareness. However, there is a sense that, in the intra-autic case, only self is salient (albeit in dual form). In the pro-autic case only "otherness" is salient (specifically the identified-with-other relating to yet another other).

Metamotivation and suggestibility

People obviously manipulate and influence each other in a whole variety of ways, generally through the promise of mode-specific rewards. These include help toward long-term achievement to people in the telic mode, immediate fun to people in the paratelic mode, sympathy to people in the autic sympathy mode combination, and so on. But the term "suggestibility" implies that the individual concerned is especially vulnerable to, or wants to be influenced by, another person or group of people. That is, suggestibility is a term which relates to the propensity of the individual to be influenced irrespective of particular extrinsic rewards and punishments.

From the reversal theory perspective there are at least three different ways in which this might arise, and therefore, in a sense, at least three types of suggestibility. This implies, incidentally, that suggestibility of each of these types may come and go under different conditions since each relates to different metamotivational modes or mode combinations. In other words, in this view suggestibility is more state-like than trait-like.

The weakest form of suggestibility is that in which individuals are simply in the conformist mode. These people have a desire or need, at the time in question, to go along with salient requirements, rules, social expectations, etc. which are perceived to govern a particular situation. This is weak in the sense that most of us, most of the time, are presumably in this comfortable conformist state of mind. In this state of mind, we would generally avoid causing unnecessary trouble or embarrassment. We would like to keep social relations riding along smoothly, and prevent ourselves from committing *faux pas*. Also, we prefer to appear to others as polite and "nice," to avoid "ruffling feathers," and so on. (This is another way of saying that for most of us the negativistic mode, with its rebelliousness, awkwardness, rudeness, and provocativeness, is a less frequently occurring state of mind). Now when we are in the conformist mental state we tend to be sensitive to the needs of the situation as we perceive them and, other things being equal, tend to comply with them. We will therefore be likely to comply with polite requests, go along with the way other people are doing things, attempt to meet expectations, or even obey orders provided they are not too bizarre or unethical. This kind of suggestibility is, then, the kind of minimal "background" suggestibility which we all experience for much of our lives.

The second type of suggestibility is much stronger and involves the combination of the alloic and mastery metamotivational modes. It will be recalled that in the alloic mode the "emotional center" of the individual is in the other with whom he or she identifies; and the mastery mode involves the general situation being interpreted as a struggle for dominance, power, and control. Putting these two together we can say that in the alloic mastery mode one wants the other to feel strong and powerful.

In the allocentric version of this (i.e., the version in which there is a direct competitive interaction between self and other), the individual is willing to submit to other, and be dominated and subservient to other. This makes the other appear stronger, and paradoxically, since self is identifying with other, self will also feel stronger (albeit vicariously). As a consequence there will be a tendency to do, or even feel, those things suggested by the other. Thus the schoolchild may be suggestible in this sense to the identified-with teacher, the soldier to his sergeant, the religious neophyte to his or her guru, the masochistic woman to her "lover," a crowd to a rabble-rouser. The latter example reminds us that demagogues ride to power not only on fear but on the popular support of masses who are willing to abase themselves in order to experience power at second hand. Power breeds power in that, the stronger the "leader," the more powerful the followers feel themselves to be, and the more likely they are to provide the leader with even more power and control over themselves—a dangerous mechanism indeed.

In the second, pro-autic, version of the alloic/mastery mode combination we see the situation in which the individual no longer feels himself/herself to be interacting directly with the other. Instead, such people support the other's power struggle with a third party. Here the individual might be particularly prone to feel those emotions called on by the other in his struggle. One thinks here of the war leader addressing mass rallies, as Hitler did so effectively at Nuremberg. Indeed a great orator can move people to experience him/her as a "surrogate self," and to experience the whole mass (including the leader) as an "extended self." The individual feels himself/herself to be part of an overwhelming and irresistible force, and exults vicariously in its transcendent power. "Mass suggestibility" seems to depend on this crude ability to induce such a combination of other-centeredness and a lust for power. This appears to be used by some religious leaders as well as politicians and military generals.

We can turn now to the third general type of suggestibility mentioned earlier. Whether it is stronger than mass suggestibility—to which it bears, as we will see, some resemblance—is a moot point. In any case it is the type to which the term "suggestibility" is perhaps most often applied. It is that complex and enigmatic phenomenon known as hypnotism.

The paradoxical nature of hypnosis

When we turn to hypnosis we see a special hybrid state which involves elements of both the intra-autic and, in a sense, the pro-autic states of mind. The best way to understand this is to look at what happens in the course of a typical hypnotic induction procedure. Let us look at such a procedure in a step-by-step manner.

1. The subject lies down, in comfort, in a safe and reassuring context. He or she therefore experiences a "protective frame" (Apter, 1989) which filters out threat from the real world and encourages the emergence of the *paratelic* mode. By lying down the subject is also placed in a passive position in which the expectation is that he or she will be an *observer* rather than an actor. That is, the subject is placed in the same state as someone about to watch a film on television. The first step therefore is designed to produce someone who is both paratelic and a passive observer.
2. The hypnotist next draws attention to different parts of the subject's body, for example, by "relaxing" each part of the body in turn. This not only further increases the subject's passivity, but more crucially brings about the *intra-autic* state. That is, attention is concentrated inwards toward the self, thus setting up the "I/Me" split, with "I" observing "Me" in the form of "Me" as a body. Alternatively, the subject is asked to imagine self in some safe and pleasant setting such as lying on a beach. Like the relaxation technique, such imaging also has the dual effect of consolidating the subject's paratelic passivity and inducing the intra-autic state.
3. We now come to a critical stage in which the hypnotist attempts to *uncouple* "I" from "Me" by removing the subject's feeling of being in total voluntary control of "Me." In the case where attention is being focused on the subject's body, parts of the body are described in ways which seem to demonstrate its independence. For example, saying that "you can hardly move" is likely to be true following the relaxation procedure. Or saying that "your eyelids are closing" may be true if during the earlier part of the induction process the subject has been fixating some point which requires that he or she needs to strain a little to look upwards. Alternatively, if the subject has been placed in some imaginary exotic setting, the hypnotist might describe the subject as doing novel things. While it may not have occurred to the subject to create these images voluntarily, the subject can hardly avoid doing so following a suitably vivid description. The effect is that "I" and "Me" come to be experienced as "self" and "other" in the sense that "Me" increasingly seems not to be part of self. (It is presumably at this step that the occasional reports by subjects of depersonalization and body-distortion are likely to occur).
4. As the subject's feelings and actions continue to be described in this way, so a narrative is set up concerning the "other" (i.e., the erstwhile "Me") for the passive self to observe. And as happens in the face of narrative, self tends inevitably to identify with the main protagonist. In other words, the intra-autic state, paradoxically, becomes a kind of pro-autic state in which the individual identifies with himself or herself! That is, following an uncou-

> pling in the intra-autic state, we have a recoupling in this pseudo-pro-autic state. But the recoupling does not bring "Me" under normal voluntary control. It rather involves "I" *identifying* with "Me" in the same way as self might empathize with the character in a film and have the same feelings and emotions as that character is perceived to have. But the feelings and emotions are in fact being determined by the hypnotist. In turn, these feelings and emotions lead to tendencies to action. In a truly pro-autic case, these tendencies are inhibited since they can accomplish nothing. One cannot, by taking action, help the hero or heroine in a film (although one may still display startle reactions or tears, grip the seat, etc.). But this is not a truly pro-autic case: it is really intra-autic. The hypnotist can play on this by suggesting not only emotions but actions that may flow from them and encourage an automatic "acting-out." (Of course such "play-acting" must, in fact, be under voluntary control; but the point is that, in this situation, it is not experienced as such.) Another way of putting all this would be to say that, as occurs in response to all "fictional narrative" situations, disbelief tends to be suspended. Whatever actions are described are believed to occur. But the actions are those of "Me" and therefore they may be automatically produced to fit the description. In other words the subject temporarily believes the descriptions to be veridical and therefore acts in such a way as to make them so. (Incidentally, the earlier induction of the paratelic state may also help to encourage the subject to experience what is happening as entertaining narrative to which the suspension of disbelief is an appropriate reaction).

It will be noticed that, in the above account, the hypnotist is not experienced as a third party, another "other," or as a controlling force. Rather, the hypnotist is experienced merely as the narrator, the medium of information. One consequence of this is that any negativism which the subject might feel is unlikely to be directed against the hypnotist. The reason is that the situation is not experienced as one of compliance to the hypnotist any more than watching a film is experienced as compliance to the projectionist. This is consistent with evidence that the hypnotist is experienced as a narrating voice rather than a person and that the experience of reading fiction is like that of hypnosis (Hilgard, 1979).

It will also be noticed that there is no suggestion in any of this that hypnosis involves, as the popular view has it, some form of sleep. This is supported by evidence which shows that the hypnotic state is associated with waking EEG records (e.g., Tart, 1964; Barber, 1969).

This account fits, and makes sense of, a number of obvious characteristics of hypnotism. For example:

1. The hypnotist's speech is concentrated on the subject's feelings, sensations, emotions, and actions, and not on those of the hypnotist or other people. This is so obvious that it usually goes unremarked. But it is an essential feature of hypnotism and is needed in order to set up the "bubble" of self-centeredness that is described by the term intra-autic.
2. The hypnotist typically does not order or command the subject. Usually the language used is one of description: "Your left hand is rising," "You are now five years old," "You feel a band of heat around your head," etc. In other words, the hypnotist adopts the style of a narrator.
3. Hypnotized subjects lack foresight, initiative, and planning. This makes sense if the subject is merely a passive consumer of a narrative (even if, paradoxically, this narrative concerns his or her own actions).
4. Subjects appear to be "under the spell" of the hypnotist and relatively unaware of potential distractions. But the same kind of selective attention would be true of someone watching a film or a sporting event.
5. Fantasizing appears to be relatively easy under hypnosis. This is not surprising if the whole hypnotic phenomenon is based on a kind of fantasy.
6. There is little "reality testing" by the subject so that he or she will uncritically accept ideas that might normally seem untrue or absurd. But if one is enjoying a narrative, one does tend to suspend one's disbelief and "enter into the spirit of things."

The present argument is not entirely inconsistent with the views of such researchers as Barber (1969) and Sarbin (1950, 1956) who argue that hypnosis is no more than imaginative involvement and role playing. Thus the results of Barber and Wilson's (1977) experiment are very understandable in terms of the argument just presented. In that study, subjects displayed typical hypnotic responses after being "induced" by instructions to imagine that they were watching a television program. However, reversal theory implies that hypnosis is more than "ordinary" imaginative involvement and role play since it also involves that special form of intra-autic self-identification which has been described. Whether this may be said to make hypnosis a "special state of consciousness" (which both Barber and Sarbin would wish to deny) is then simply a matter of preferred terminology rather than a substantive issue.

The view being presented here is also not inconsistent with Hilgard's (1968, 1973, 1977) neo-dissociation theory. The reversal theory account, like Hilgard's, draws attention to a division of consciousness which occurs during hypnosis. Also, there is more than a passing resemblance between the observing "I" of reversal theory and that of Hilgard's "hidden observer." The same similarity exists between reversal theory's observed "Me" and Hilgard's hypnotized part of consciousness. But reversal theory extends beyond Hilgard's neo-dissociation theory in suggesting that one part of consciousness not only observes but identifies with another "objectified" part. Indeed it is this which, more than anything else, constitutes the core feature of the phenomenon of hypnosis. We might take the example of Hilgard's pain-analgesia experiments in which the hypnotized part of consciousness did not feel pain but the hidden observer did (Hilgard & Hilgard, 1975). Reversal theory would suggest that "I" is aware of the pain, but at the same time identifies and empathizes with a "Me" which does not feel pain. This is not unlike someone who, while sitting in a cinema, may actually feel cold while empathically experiencing the heat of a desert in the film. Furthermore, the empathic experience may be more phenomenally salient than the real one.

The hypnotist may therefore be systematically causing some element of confusion. But this confusion is not, as some investigators (e.g., Miller, Galanter, & Pribram, 1960; Kubie & Margolin, 1944) have claimed, a confusion by the subject of the hypnotist's words for his own thoughts. This would be too simple. Rather, the subject, with the help of the hypnotist, confuses himself with himself or herself with herself! To achieve this the hypnotist makes use of, and embellishes, a paradox inherent in the very structure and logic of conscious experience itself—the reflexive paradox involved in the perception of self by self.

Conclusion

This brief chapter has shown that, by focusing on the structure of conscious experience, reversal theory provides a novel framework for examining the various phenomena which are referred to by the term "suggestibility." Certainly reversal theory does not yet give answers to all the important questions that are raised in this area. The "suggestions on suggestibility" that it does provide are tentative and no doubt open to objections. But they are distinctive and not implausible. And they come from a general theory which is gaining increasing empirical support in a number of areas of psychology.

References

Apter, M.J. (1982). *The experience of motivation: The theory of psychological reversals.* London and New York: Academic Press.

Apter, M.J. (1989). *Reversal theory: Motivation, emotion and personality.* London: Routledge.

Apter, M.J. (1984). Reversal theory, cognitive synergy and the arts. In W.R. Crozier & A.J. Chapman (eds.), *Cognitive processes in the perception of art* (pp. 411–26). Amsterdam: North-Holland (Elsevier).

Apter, M.J. (1985). Religious states of mind: A reversal theory interpretation. In L.B. Brown (ed.), *Advances in the psychology of religion* (pp. 62–75). Oxford: Pergamon Press.

Apter, M.J. (1988). Beyond the autocentric and the allocentric. In M.J. Apter, J. Kerr & M. Cowles (eds.), *Progress in reversal theory.* Amsterdam: North-Holland Press (Elsevier).

Apter, M.J., Fontana, D., & Murgatroyd, S. (eds.) (1985). *Reversal theory: Application and developments.* Cardiff: University College Cardiff Press and New Jersey: Lawrence Erlbaum.

Apter, M.J., Kerr, J.H., & Cowles, M. (eds.) (1988). *Progress in reversal theory.* Amsterdam: North-Holland Press (Elsevier).

Barber, T.X. (1969). *Hypnosis: A scientific approach.* New York: Van Nostrand Reinhold.

Barber, T.X., & Wilson, S.C. (1977). Hypnosis, suggestions and altered states of consciousness: Experimental evaluation of the new cognitive behavioral theory and the traditional trance-state theory of hypnosis. In W.D. Edmonston, Jr. (ed.), *Conceptual and investigative approaches to hypnosis and hypnotic phenomena.* Annals of the New York Academy of Sciences, Vol. 296, 34–47.

Hilgard, E.R. (1968). *The experience of hypnosis.* New York: Harcourt Brace Jovanovich.

Hilgard, E.R. (1973). A neodissociation interpretation of pain reduction in hypnosis. *Psychological Review, 80,* 396–411.

Hilgard, E.R. (1977). *Divided consciousness: Multiple controls in human thought and action* (expanded ed.). Chichester: Wiley.

Hilgard, E.R., & Hilgard, J.R. (1975). *Hypnosis in the relief of pain.* Los Altos, CA: W. Kaufmann.

Hilgard, J.R. (1979). *Personality and hypnosis: A study of imaginative involvement.* Chicago: University of Chicago Press (pp. 34–40, 252–55).

Kubie, L.S., & Margolin, S. (1944). The process of hypnotism and the nature of the hypnotic state. *American Journal of Psychiatry, 100,* 611–22.

Mead, G.H. (1934). *Mind, self and society.* Chicago: University of Chicago Press.

Miller, G.A., Galanter, E., & Pribram, K.M. (1960). *Plans and the structure of behavior.* New York: Holt.

Murgatroyd, S., & Apter, M.J. (1984). Eclectic psychotherapy: A structural phenomenological approach. In W. Dryden (ed.), *Individual psychotherapy in Britain* (pp. 389–414). London: Harper and Row.

Murgatroyd, S., & Apter, M.J. (1986). A structural-phenomenological approach to eclectic psychotherapy. In J. Norcross (ed.), *Handbook of eclectic psychotherapy* (pp. 260–80). New York: Brunner/Mazel.

Sarbin, T.R. (1950). Contributions to role-taking theory: 1. Hypnotic behavior. *Psychological Review, 57,* 255–70.

Sarbin, T.R. (1956). Physiological effects of hypnotic stimulation. In R.M. Dorcus (ed.), *Hypnosis and its therapeutic applications.* New York: McGraw-Hill.

Svebak, S., & Apter, M.J. (1987). Laughter: an empirical test of some reversal theory hypotheses. *Scandinavian Journal of Psychology, 28,* 189–98.

Tart, C.T. (1964). A comparison of suggested dreams occurring in hypnosis and sleep. *International Journal of Clinical and Experimental Hypnosis, 12,* 263–89.

8

RELIGIOUS EXPERIENCES, ALTERED STATES OF CONSCIOUSNESS, AND SUGGESTIBILITY: Cross-Cultural and Historical Perspectives

Colleen Ward and Simon Kemp

Although psychologists have conventionally been reluctant to approach the study of religion and religious experiences, recently these phenomena have come under scientific scrutiny. Research on religious experiences has documented their frequency among "ordinary" people, elaborated their characteristics and effects, and even offered a classification system in relation to psychological processes and outcomes (Valla & Prince, 1989). Given the nature of the subject matter, however, a major problem faced by investigators in this field is the management of divergent explanatory frameworks for these events. On the one hand is a variety of the precise, scientific approaches which may interpret religious experiences in terms of mental health and illness, stress and coping, cognitive processing, and/or social role enactment. These approaches must be reconciled, on the other hand, with the popular and influential interpretation of these conditions in terms of supernatural causality and divine or diabolical consequences. The interplay between scientific and popular explanations of these occurrences becomes even more complex when religious experiences are viewed over time and across cultures.

This paper examines a variety of unusual religious experiences in different historical and cultural contexts with emphasis on their relationship to suggestibility. Spirit possession and visionary experiences are highlighted as examples of altered states of consciousness whose manifestation is shaped by motivational, social, and political factors. The psychological framework for this analysis acknowledges the significance of popular explanations of these altered states and incorporates this into the examination of suggestibility and religious experiences.

In both cross-cultural and historical literature the characteristics of spirit possession have often been likened to those of hypnotic responding (Prince, 1982). Comparisons frequently highlight the similar manifestations of altered states of consciousness in the form of hypnotic and possession trance. Sargant's (1974) analysis of contemporary ceremonial spirit possession in Zambia, Nigeria, Brazil, and the West Indies, as well as demon possession in seventeenth-century Europe, exemplifies this approach with a focus on the physiological bases of trance induction, central nervous system responses, and experiential elements of altered states of awareness in the possession experiences. More commonly, however, researchers have emphasized the heightened suggestibility characteristic of possession and hypnotic states. This is evidenced by Walker's (1972) study of ceremonial possession in Africa, Kane's (1982) examination of possession by the Holy Spirit and ritual fire handling in the Appalachia, and Lindstrom's (1978) discussion of possession and exorcism in charismatic churches.

Given the speculative link between the two phenomena, it is likely that an analysis of human suggestibility and spirit possession may draw on resources from and reflect common themes in the clinical and social psychological literature on hypnosis. Indeed, cross-cultural and historical descriptions of ritual possession phenomena have mirrored to some extent the prominent states vs. nonstate debate in the psychological research on hypnotic responding (Spanos & Barber, 1974). Advocates of the former position assert that hypnosis entails a special condition, generally referred to as trance, which is intrinsically different from ordinary states of consciousness. Proponents of the latter maintain that good hypnotic subjects are fundamentally the same as normal individuals responding to the demands of particular social situations. It has been pointed out that both perspectives are concerned with shifts in cognitive processing and that they are converging in contemporary theory and research. However, Spanos and Barber (1974) argue that state theorists have been neither clear nor consistent about the relationships between trance and suggested imaginings. It has remained ambiguous as to whether the trance state is a synonym for suggestion-related imagining, an antecedent condition, or a superordinate construct that encompasses suggestibility and imagining together with other unspecified processes. Efforts to clarify the relationship between these factors in an attempt to examine human suggestibility becomes even more complex with reference to spirit possession which incorporates culture-specific attributions of causality to conditions that may or may not appear to involve unusual states of consciousness. Nevertheless, the relationship between trance, possession, and altered states of consciousness in a cross-cultural and historical context must be elucidated as a preliminary to the examination of human suggestibility.

Altered states of consciousness (ASCs) can be said to involve qualitative shifts in the ordinary mode of mental functioning. This is the characteristic, habitual pattern that adapts an individual to survive successfully in her/his culture's consensus reality (Tart, 1980). Krippner (1972) has identified some 20 types of ASCs, including trance states which are purportedly characterized by focused attention and hypersuggestibility. Shor (1959) referred to trances as states of functional non-awareness, "a detachment from the structured frame of reference in the background of attention which supports, interprets and gives meaning to experience" (p. 583).

Although trance has been conventionally considered an unusual state of consciousness, it has been institutionalized and is widespread on a cross-cultural and historical basis. Bourguignon and Evascu (1977), for example, reported that in a world-wide sample of 488 societies, 90% (437) displayed naturally occurring trance and/or possession states. There are some difficulties, however, in the clarification of the relationship between altered states of consciousness, trance, and possession. A major difficulty arises from the defining characteristics of the phenomena. Possession occurring in various forms and fashions is primarily defined by laypeople through the attribution of causality. For example, abnormal behavior shown by some individual may be attributed by onlookers to possession by an evil spirit, whereas trance is primarily defined by psychologists with somewhat more precision in terms of its signs and symptoms (e.g., focused attention or unresponsiveness to external stimuli).

Figure 8.1 below illustrates the relationship between trance and possession when considered in conjunction with the distinction of central and peripheral possession advanced by Lewis (1971) and expanded by Ward (1980). From an anthropological perspective Lewis defines central or ritual possession as experiences whose prime function is to uphold a society's official morality and established power. The salient characteristics may shift from macrosocial factors to individual psychological ones when ritual possession is viewed as a temporary, generally voluntary and reversible form of trance behavior that is exhibited in the context of religious ceremonies and attributed to the power of sympathetic spirits (S. Walker, 1972). Central possession is supported and encouraged by cultural beliefs; it may provide therapeutic benefits; and despite the associated non-ordinary states of consciousness, it is not perceived as unusual or pathological by members of the host culture. Examples of central possession include Voodoo or Shango ceremonial possession in the West Indies (Kiev, 1961; Ward, 1979–80), possession by the Holy Spirit in charismatic Christian churches (Kane, 1982), Hauka and Sasale possession dances in the Songhay of Mali and Niger (Stoller, 1989), Umbanda trance and possession in Brazil (Pressel, 1974), possession and ceremonial fire-walking in India (Malhotra & Khomne, 1980), ritual possession in the Shona of Zimbabwe (Garfias, 1979–80), and ecstatic possession in early modern Europe (e.g., Teresa of Avila, 1982/1577).

Peripheral possession, by contrast, is taken to denote experiences which provide no direct support of the society's moral code, usually include spirits outside the central religious cult, and are typically found in persons with low status or marginal positions in society. Adding a psychological dimension to the anthropological definition, peripheral possession may be seen as a relatively stable and long-term state in which the individual believes that s/he is unwillingly possessed by one or more intruding spirits, and exhibits contingent behavioral responses which are attributed to the spirits' influence (Ward & Beaubrun, 1980). Peripheral possession is long-term and involuntary and is negatively evaluated both by the culture and the individual, who subjectively experiences the condition as distressing. Cross-cultural and historical literature indicates that peripheral possession is often viewed as maladaptive and curatives are sought for the discomfort, often in the form of exorcism. Examples of peripheral possession might include demon possession in medieval and contemporary Christian settings (Kemp, 1989; Kemp & Williams, 1987; Ward, 1989; Ward & Beaubrun, 1981), Zar possession in Muslim North Africa (Lewis, 1971), possession and bride sickness in India (Freed & Freed, 1964), and possession epidemics in Malay factory workers (Ackerman & Lee, 1978). Occasionally individuals are referred to mental health professionals for treatment of conditions that they ascribe to possession, as evidenced by Warner's (1977) study of Spanish American clients in a community mental health setting and Yap's (1960) investigation of institutionalized patients in Hong Kong. It is important to note that the manifestation of peripheral possession may be punctuated by altered states of consciousness within or without a religious context but that the condition itself, unlike that of central possession, extends beyond the duration of an altered state of awareness. In relation to Figure 8.1, then, it may be summarized that possession of the central/ritual type involves an altered state of awareness in the form of trance whereas peripheral possession may or may not include an altered state of awareness, and this ASC may or may not be trance (e.g., some psychotic states are attributed to possession).

Visions and other apparent revelatory phenomena are also religious experiences that appear to involve ASCs. Religious visions have not been frequently studied by psychologists, although hallucinations have been subjected to clinical investigations. Most studies of these experiences, however, have concentrated on hallucinations in circumstances where they rather commonly occur, in schizophrenia, for ex-

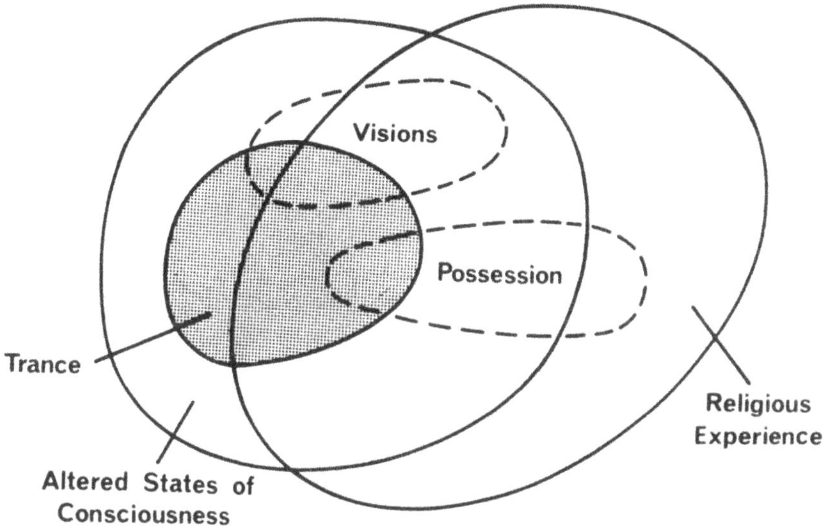

Figure 8.1. Schematic of the relationship between religious experience, altered states of consciousness, trance, visions, and possession.

ample, or in sensory deprivation experiments (e.g., Asaad & Shapiro, 1986). These studies may be dealing with somewhat different phenomena than those occurring, say, in religious mystics.

It is not always easy to ascertain the state of consciousness of someone reporting a religious vision, but it seems likely that most if not all such experiences take place when the visionary is in a trance or dissociative state. This is certainly the case for the visions reported by Teresa of Avila (1982/1565). It is also true, for example, in the Spiritual Baptist community of Trinidad and Tobago, which relies alternately on sensory bombardment and deprivation techniques to induce religious visions in their mourning practices (Ward & Beaubrun, 1979). In some cases the dissociative state is probably linked to some recognizable physical disorder or psychological distress. For example, the revelation of eight-year old Jaume Cirosa in 1458 occurred seven days before the boy died of plague (Christian, 1981). Julian of Norwich's (1966/1393) visions occurred after she had actually received last rites. In contemporary Canadian research Valla and Prince (1989) describe religious experiences linked to emotional distress, such as grief over the death of a loved one or ambivalence about interpersonal relationships. In other cases a dissociative state suitable for visions or for heightened and controlled mental imagery may be induced or conditioned by a period of training (Noll, 1985).

On initial consideration, it might appear that revelatory experiences such as visions, which refer to something or someone apparently outside the observer, are quite a different category of experience from possession states, in which an individual is apparently taken over by some other entity. In fact, however, there are clear links between the two kinds of experience (see Figure 8.1). In the first place, the two states are frequently experienced, at different times, by the same person. For example, Teresa of Avila reports both visual and auditory experiences of God, and a "Prayer of Union" in which she was left with the conviction that God had been within her (Teresa of Avila, 1982/1577, pp. 251–56). The daughter of a medieval clergyman who was subsequently cured at St. Bartholomew's church was first overheard speaking with the devil, although her nurse could see no one. After some repetitions of this behavior, the girl finally became possessed by the devil (Moore, 1923, p. 49). Similarly, West Indian Spiritual Baptists who experience symbolic visions during mourning practices are also likely to become possessed by the Holy Spirit at charismatic church services. A second link between possession and visions is that the two kinds of experience are not always easy to distinguish. Consider, for example, a present-day Christian who describes him/herself as "filled with the spirit of the Lord" following a visionary experience.

Attempts to relate suggestibility to ASCs involving possession and visionary experiences, then, involve a number of considerations. It is maintained here that central possession as well as many forms of peripheral possession and revelatory experiences do involve altered states of consciousness which can be described as trance or dissociation. With these conditions, certain mental functions which are ordinarily integrated with other functions operate in a more compartmentalized or automatic way, typically outside the sphere of conscious awareness, memory recall, or responsiveness to most external stimuli (Ludwig, 1983). While trance and dissociative states have conventionally been assumed to reflect states of hypersuggestibility, this is arguably due to their contextualization in research on hypnosis and clinical practice with multiple personality disorders. Although Sargant (1974) asserts that individuals experiencing possession trance are hypersuggestible, and Wilson and Barber (1983) make the same case for fantasy-prone individuals, it is argued here that this is not a profitable position to adopt—primarily because of the difficulty in distinguishing what is hypersuggestible from the usual levels of social demands affecting behaviors in specific situations. A more fruitful approach, the trance states notwithstanding, is to concentrate on social and cultural factors which precipitate religious experiences and influence their manifestation.

It is also possible that individuals in different cultures or different historical periods vary in suggestibility. It could be, for example, that suggestibility is increased in uncertain times or disintegrating societies (Alcock, 1981). However, the problems of comparing suggestibility across cultures or eras and of quantifying variables such as societal uncertainty or disintegration make this a difficult proposition to test. Again, we have preferred to concentrate on the identification and examination of social forces operating within different societies.

The following section examines central and peripheral forms of possession and revelatory religious experiences in historical and cross-cultural perspectives. While precipitation of ritual possession trance can be interpreted in terms of specific sensory and physical inductors of altered states of awareness, emphasis is placed on social, cultural, and political factors which act as demand characteristics. These serve as implicit and explicit social cues that communicate which behaviors are expected in a situational display of possession or from one who has had a religious vision. These demand characteristics may derive from the individual, group, or societal influences, and the resultant behaviors may afford advantages on each of these levels.

Cross-cultural and historical perspectives

Although trance, possession, and visions are widespread in both cross-cultural and historical contexts, approaches to the examination of these states have varied. Anthropologists, cross-cultural psychologists, and transcultural psychiatrists have offered an abundance of literature on religious rituals and activities in "exotic" cultures and subcultures. As fieldwork has allowed for the direct observation of trance and possession states, the literature includes data on the experience, manifestation, and precipitation of altered states of consciousness. Immediate access to these phenomena has permitted researchers to analyze suggestibility in terms of both the altered states of awareness and the social demand characteristics. Historical approaches, by contrast, have been shaped by the limitations of archival resources and inaccessibility of possessed or visionary subjects. Despite these constraints, the following sections demonstrate common themes about suggestibility and religious experiences across cultures and over time. These themes are elaborated through the analysis of ritual possession and self-mortification practices in the Hindu celebration of Thaipusam in Malaysia and the examination of visionary experiences and demonic possession in medieval and early modern Europe.

Thaipusam in Malaysia

In honor of the deity Murugan, the festival of Thaipusam is observed during the tenth month of the Tamil calendar by South Indians in Malaysia. During this time Hindu devotees offer prayer, sacrifice, and thanksgiving in fulfillment of vows for divinely granted favors. Although offerings may be simple, worship most often involves kavadi-bearing, where devotees permit their bodies to be pierced and decorated with skewers, hooks, and needles in an expression of faith and purity. Despite extensive piercing, devotees rely on ritual possession trance for the control of pain and bleeding and are able to complete temple pilgrimages, carrying kavadis weighing up to forty pounds, to fulfill vows and offer thanksgiving.(1)

Analysis of suggestibility in the Thaipusam performance may be undertaken with reference to individual, social, and cultural components and may incorporate diverse factors from biological and motivational responses, on one hand, to socio-political influences, on the other. While the research reported here emphasizes the social and cultural elements which facilitate trance and possession, this is not intended to imply that these states are in any way reducible to mere role enactment as postulated by Spanos (1989). Ritual possession involves altered states of awareness, defined by subjective experience and supported by external observations. These states are dependent upon biological as well as social factors. Indeed, research has demonstrated that both specific biological responses and social demands or suggestions are necessary prerequisites for the ASC experience (Walsh, 1974). This perspective on ritual possession is comparable to Shor's (1969) analysis of hypnosis, which entails both ASC and role-taking dimensions.

On the most basic level, participation in Thaipusam requires motivation and commitment, as the decision to bear kavadi is based on a vow. The vow may be prompted by favors received or anticipated, with requests commonly pertaining to health, occupational and educational endeavors, marriage, children, financial difficulties, domestic problems, and/or psychological pressures. Participation may also be a gesture of love, devotion, or pursuit of religious merit (Ward, 1984). Although personal motivation is a significant component of the Thaipusam performance, environmental factors exert considerable influence over the ceremonial activities.

With respect to external or public factors, Lee (1989) has offered a valuable dramaturgical framework for the analysis of ritual possession, with emphasis on social markers which define and influence the manifestation of possession trance. In his analysis of spirit mediums in Malaysia he presents three components which are central to the possession performance and cue both the medium and the audience as to what is expected in the ritual. He refers to these factors as the "rules of the ceremony": status distance, altered states of consciousness, and display of power.

With respect to status distance, Thaipusam devotees are distinguished on a number of counts from their audience and attendants. Most fundamentally, participation in the festival is the culmination of ritual purification which begins much earlier. This includes food and sleep deprivation as well as abstinence from alcohol, smoking, sexual intercourse, and social activities. A major aim of the preparation period is cleansing and the attainment of purification. This serves to separate the devotee from other members of the community, particularly unclean individuals such as menstruating women and people who have had recent deaths in their families, who are not allowed to fulfill vows during Thaipusam.

The separation is reiterated on Thaipusam day when the devotee rises early for a ritual bath, is dressed in yellow garments, symbolizing purity, and makes offerings including coconut, banana, flowers, lime, milk, incense, and betelnut with prayer at the temple. These activities are consistent with Hindu traditions which emphasize the importance of physical acts of religious devotion—bathing, fasting, clothing, dancing, care of images, and gifts. All of this represents a means of expiating sins, acquiring merit, and attaining mental serenity (Bhattacharyya, 1953). The yellow garments, particularly, serve to set the devotee apart and to attract attention from the audience who expect the display of ceremonial trance, possession, and self-mortification.

Expectations regarding Thaipusam performances are often made explicit, and in some cases there are direct attempts to train individuals in trance induction (Prince, 1987). Many devotees reside in the temple during the preparation period and may also receive informal guidance with respect to the practices and the experience of the religious trance. Additionally they may have the opportunity to observe outbursts of trance during group prayer sessions. It is important to note that ritual trance is learned, and most devotees acknowledge that it is easier to enter, sustain, and control trance during their second or third kavadi-bearing experiences (Ward, 1984). In addition to direct training, devotees will have had the experience of observing numerous Thaipusam celebrations as well as the opportunity to model their trance behaviors on these observations. Most importantly, devotees are explicitly assured that those who complete the preparation period and are pure of heart will easily enter a sacred altered state and will not experience pain during piercing. Expectations are particularly influential in these performances; Council, Kirsch, Vickery, and Carlson (1983), for example, have demonstrated substantial correlations between expectations and subsequent behavioral reactions in hypnotic responding.

Consistent with Lee's notion that altered states of consciousness are important in the expression of spirit possession, ritual trance plays a central part in the Thaipusam festivities. The dissociative state, an example of central possession, is temporary and voluntary and attributed to the power of sympathetic Shiva family deities.(2) The induction of trance, however, is facilitated by a combination of complex factors, which include physiological and psychological variables as well as social and cultural ones.

A major precipitant of trance is an increase of exteroceptive stimulation and the presence of somatopsychological factors which affect biochemistry and neurophysiology. Sensory bombardment of repetitive stimuli—olfactory, auditory, and kinesthetic—plays an important role in evoking dissociation. Stimulation includes the chanting of Sanskrit prayers by temple priests with refrains from the attendants, inhalation of pungent incense, and in some cases repetitive stroking of the skin. Trance is further aided by fasting, contributing to hypoglycemia, and occasionally by hyperventilation practices. There is also some evidence of enhanced endorphin levels during the trance state (Prince, 1987). The sensory bombardment and ceremonial preparation are similar to techniques used in the rituals of other cultures, including those of North American Indians (Jilek, 1982; Lex, 1975), Afro-Christian cults in South America and the Caribbean (Pressel, 1974; Ward, 1979–80; Ward & Beaubrun, 1979), and animistic groups in Africa (Sargant, 1974) and Asia (Wirz, 1954).

From a cognitive perspective, the role of attention is important in trance induction and maintenance. Devotees are able to tune into relevant religious stimuli (e.g., repetitive chanting) while remaining relatively insensitive to most aspects of the surrounding environment. Concentration is sharply focused, usually on prayer and divine concerns. Psychologically, the experience constitutes an altered state of consciousness, which may be referred to as trance. Subjective experience of the possession trance includes dissociation from most external stimuli, selective attention, unusual bodily sensations and dissolution of body boundaries, sensations of lightness and "blank feelings," alterations in body image, analgesia to pain, internal orientation, concentration, alteration in the quality of thought, diminished logic, intense emotions including euphoria, temporal and spatial disorientation, selective amnesia, detachment from the external environment, and gross, uncontrollable muscular movements such as tremors and rigidity (Ward, 1984).

But the altered state of awareness and the physical factors which aid in trance induction, are not the only salient components of ritual possession. Devotees are also sensitive to a number of social cues which affect trance behavior and pain control. This may be illustrated by the rule-bound procedures used in the trance induction and piercing practices, in particular the changes in ceremonial chants. For example, religious songs are initially directed to request the gods' acceptance and protection of the devotee. At the appropriate moment when the priest recognizes divine acceptance, the prayers are altered to more joyful chants. The devotee, then, receives a clear message, and the piercing commences with the assurance of benevolent protection.

The devotee is also supported by a group of family members or friends who continue on the pilgrimage. They may provide drinks or massage tired legs. They always chant and sometimes play drums and wind instruments to sustain trance. They also make offerings, such as cutting limes and breaking coconuts at intersections to prevent the meddling of any mischievous spirits. Support by the attendant group is magnified by the community at large. The atmosphere of Thaipusam celebrations resembles a carnival, the streets lined with thousands of brightly dressed folks on the pilgrimage route, roadside stalls playing religious music, mobile vendors of food and drink. People come to participate in the religious ceremony, but also to observe the dramatic presentation of self-mortification practices displayed without evidence of pain. The behaviors of the crowd and the devotees are mutually reinforcing—the devotee perceives the demand to perform in a particular way and is rewarded with attention and support for doing so. The crowd members experience reinforcement of their religious and spiritual beliefs through the evidence that the deities do, indeed, protect their followers.

With respect to Lee's (1989) final criterion, the display of power is also significant in the customs of Thaipusam festivities. This occurs in the tolerance of flesh-piercing, which may be quite dramatic. Devotees frequently exhibit cheek skewers over eight feet long. Many have dozens of hooks inserted in their backs and pulled as if on reins by attendants. There have even been cases of individuals who are paraded through the streets suspended from hooks on mobile apparatuses. Such dramatic feats are performed without any indication of or admission to pain or evidence of profuse bleeding. This may be aided by expectations, motivations, altered states of consciousness, the sharpness of the hooks and needles, superficial piercing by experts, and the administration of holy ash when the hooks and skewers are removed (Ward, 1984). The analgesic effect of the endorphins present should also be noted (Prince, 1987). Finally, there is a symbolic element of significance. The skewers are traditionally capped with spade-shaped edges resembling the vel, a lance that the Hindu deity Murugan utilized in his victory over the forces of evil. Symbolically, then, Murugan's armaments are empowered to dispel the evil and to protect the devotee.

Given that demand characteristics are operative in the Thaipusam celebrations, attention might be turned to any "punishments" inflicted on those who do not conform to expectations. The vow to take kavadi is regarded as a very serious commitment, both personal and social. The decision is typically supported by family, friends, and the community at large. Neglect of one's commitment evokes shame and guilt and is believed to precipitate retaliation from the deities. Frivolous or half-hearted participation is also punished. The most obvious method is the infliction of pain. During chants, trance induction, and piercing rituals, the priests expect and await divine signs of the devotee's acceptance, usually demonstrated by the appropriate altered state of consciousness. If this is not apparent after a certain time, however, sacred songs will change from requests for protection to entreaties for forgiveness, with the devotee being instructed to increase prayers and concentration. The piercing will, nevertheless, proceed although the devotee may be offered lime to diminish pain. The inability to endure pain introduces a secondary punishment in that it also demonstrates that the devotee is not pure of heart. That is a powerful social stigma in a close-knit, collectivist, religious society.

Successful participation in Thaipusam, by contrast, affects positive psychological and social rewards for both the individual and the community. For the individual who has withstood the ordeal, purity of heart has been demonstrated and status has been achieved in the community. The devotee obtains praise and support from family and friends. The display of invincibility and power enhances self-concept, and there is often a feeling of self-satisfaction over a job well done and a bargain completed. The Thaipusam festivities also offer a respite from the harsh conditions of daily life experienced by participants who come primarily from lower socio-economic backgrounds. It has been further suggested that ritual ceremonies such as Thaipusam provide cathartic emotional benefits and feelings of rejuvenation which extend from the individual to the larger group (Bourguignon, 1972). For the community the festivities positively enhance the visibility of a relatively disadvantaged minority group in culturally plural Malaysia (Wiebe & Mariappen, 1978). The celebrations also function to reaffirm religious beliefs and traditions and to promote cohesion in the Hindu community.

Visions and possession in medieval and early modern Europe

In this section, we examine the attitudes of medieval and early modern Christianity to a variety of religious activities. This will include claims of visions, revelations, and demonic possession, in both religious mystics and lay individuals. We then attempt to consider how these attitudes may have functioned as socio-political influences on the expression of such religious experiences. Serious limitations are involved in the use of historical material to provide insight into how social forces affect trance, visions, and possession states. The social forces themselves, and their impact on the individual, are often not specified by the contemporary observers in the kind of detail that we should like. Thus the kind of information given by a present-day psychologist or anthropologist describing, say, the ceremonies of Thaipusam is usually unavailable. A further problem is that the records now available are very likely a biased sample of medieval or early modern ASC experiences. There are two obvious sources of bias: firstly, that religious experiences which might have led the visionary into trouble are less likely to have been reported to anyone; and secondly, that the written sources which have survived have done so in part because they were acceptable to, and often illustrated, the doctrine of the Church. Therefore, in comparison to the contemporary investigation of religious experiences, it becomes even more difficult in historical research to disentangle the role of social and political factors in producing or influencing the content of ASCs from the role played by these factors in the reporting of these experiences. It is very likely, indeed, that these processes were tangled almost from the outset.

Some compensation for these limitations is provided by the fact that historical material provides the opportunity to investigate the possible effects of long-term societal and political changes on trance and possession. As we will show, there is suggestive evidence that the social and political changes of the sixteenth-century Reformation that followed Martin Luther's rebellion against the Church did accompany, and perhaps effect, changes in the kinds of individual trance and possession experiences that were reported.

Very broadly, in medieval or early modern Europe an ASC experience might be attributed to one of three kinds of influence: it might be due to a visitation from God or one of His saints, it might be a work of the devil, or it might be the consequence of some physiological process. Distinguishing between these three possibilities was generally held by both observers and participants to be difficult, not least because of the widely recognized possibility of causal interaction. The devil, for example, might be particularly zealous in trying to corrupt a holy person. Or he might take advantage of an existing tendency to mental disorder to possess or tempt someone. It was also recognized that too much prayer or fasting and not enough sleep, as often occurred in monasteries, could produce ASC experiences that appeared to be divinely caused, but actually had a physiological origin (e.g., Teresa of Avila, 1982/1577, pp. 245–46).

Throughout its history, the Christian Church has been unwilling to accept ritual possession or trance as necessarily involving divine intervention. The historical origins of this scepticism are easy to identify. The rival religious cults of the Roman Empire often involved ritual trance or possession. When the early Christians observed such behavior, they were unwilling to concede the existence of other gods than their own and simply attributed it to demonic activity. According to Tertullian (1931/197–98), for example, people who "claim to be god-possessed, who by sniffing at altars inhale a divine power" (p. 125) are in reality possessed by demons who can be made to confess their real nature by a true Christian.

It might be expected that in the later Middle Ages, when Christianity had practically a religious monopoly over Europe, ritual possession or trance would have been generally regarded as divinely caused. Hence, it would be encouraged by the Church authorities. Many enthusiastic religious movements were not proscribed, and individual mystics were usually free from persecution. However, there was never any official encouragement of charismatic movements, and generally the official attitude remained one of suspicion. Part of the reason for this scepticism derived from that of the Church Fathers, who continued to be widely read. A more important reason, however, was the perceived threat of heresy. Individuals who claimed to have visions or other divinely caused experiences often had religious ideas which conflicted with those of the Church. The Church's ideological response to this threat to its authority was simply to claim that such visions were either the work of the devil or of some mental weakness or disorder.

Not surprisingly, then, the question of whether the content of revelatory experience was consistent with scripture and the doctrine of the Church was of fundamental importance. This determined whether a particular experience should be ascribed to divine causes or not. Julian of Norwich, for example, remarks in the course of describing her revelations that "I shall always believe what is held, preached, and taught by Holy Church" (Julian of Norwich, 1966/1393, pp. 75–76). In the trial of Joan of Arc her interrogators viewed with particular suspicion the unconventional demand of her voices that she should wear men's clothing (e.g., Lucie-Smith, 1976).

Another widely used criterion was that trances of divine origin were expected to have beneficial effects. Thus Teresa of Avila (1982/1577) and the medieval author of *The Cloud of Unknowing* both stress that awareness of God should produce tranquillity. Some novices may be deceived by the devil, and then "the eyes of some of them are so set in their heads as though they were sheep suffering from brain disease, and were near death's door" (Walsh, 1981, p. 221). Religious authorities interrogating apparent visionaries about miraculous apparitions in late medieval Spain often asked them to describe their feelings about the apparition in some detail (Christian, 1981).

Neither these nor the other criteria occasionally maintained to determine the real cause of an ASC experience were capable of rapid employment. In general, would-be visionaries had to be prepared to convince sceptical audiences, even if composed of family or fellow villagers, of the divine or saintly origin of their experience. The initial reaction to such reports was often hostile. Thus when young Juan Gonzalez in 1455 told his father about his vision, his father told him he was lying and threatened to beat him if he told anyone else (Christian, 1981, p. 96). Often such visionaries were only believed if they could provide a more or less objectively verifiable sign of some kind, and many visionaries reported repeat visions in which they asked the appearing saint for a sign. These requests were frequently granted. Sometimes the sign was the indication of some hidden relic. A sign with a more psychological content was provided in 1436 by Ines Martinez whose hand was temporarily paralysed with her thumb lying over her bunched fingers so as to form a rough cross (Christian, 1981, pp. 64–65).

The authority of the Church in questioning and frequently denying the genuineness of claimed religious experiences seems to have been exercised through a number of different but interrelated channels. It is clear from the example of Juan Gonzalez that even the local peasantry were unlikely to greet visionary claims with much enthusiasm. Perhaps this attitude was in part based on their knowledge of the scepticism of the Church authorities and fear of the possible consequences of inquisition. One consequence of the attitude was that reports of revelatory experiences seem to have been comparatively rare (Christian, 1981).

The use by the Church of the inquisitorial procedure to investigate unorthodox beliefs or heresies dates from the thirteenth century. To have an ASC experience was not in itself heretical, even if the experience contained unorthodox doctrine. For example, in the case of Joan of Arc, the visionary was instructed to wear men's clothing and fight the English. What was heretical, however, was firm belief in the sanctified nature of unorthodox visions or any attempt to persuade or preach to others on the basis of them. As the penalties for heresy could be severe—Joan of Arc was one of many burned at the stake—the inquisition naturally acted as a check on people spontaneously reporting ASC experiences. It is also noticeable that most of the experiences that were reported, for example those from late medieval Spain, were characterised by both blameless orthodoxy and a tendency for independent visionaries to report very similar experiences (Christian, 1981). Clearly the content of these visions reflects the suggestibility of the visionaries.

A very different form of social control appears to have operated within monasteries and convents, and to a certain extent in wealthy lay society. Here the key figure seems to have been the individual's confessor. It is important to realize that monks or nuns in contemplative orders were supposed to confess completely and frequently to their chosen confessor, who then, in turn, advised them on their conduct. The importance of the relationship between confessor and penitent, which has many parallels to that between psychiatrist and patient, is underlined by its frequent mention in medieval and early modern mystical writing. *The Cloud of Unknowing,* for example, stresses the importance for young disciples of obeying the instructions of their confessors, and not simply following their own impulses.

Religious advisers in the Middle Ages seem to have often acted as a voice of caution. One of the afflictions of St. Lidwyna (1380–1433) was the refusal of her curate, Andrew of Marienward, to take her visions and prophecies seriously. Instead he seems to have regarded her as mentally disordered or tempted by a devil, and asked the local congregation to pray for her (Baring-Gould, 1914, Vol. 4, p. 197).

Teresa of Avila illustrates both the importance of the confessor-penitent relationship and the complexity of its effects. At several points she discusses how important it is to have a confessor. She notes how one should go about choosing a confessor, preferably one who is well-educated, and how one should then follow his instructions (e.g., Teresa of Avila, 1982/1565, pp. 27, 167, 293). It was also important to her that at least some of her confessors believed in the divine nature of her revelations and encouraged her in them (e.g., Teresa of Avila, 1982/1565, pp. 151–52, 228–29). At the same time, however, these relationships did not always run smoothly. Her confessors sometimes feared the influence of the devil in her visions. Or, even more discouraging, they were unable to decide on the nature of the experience (e.g., Teresa of Avila, 1982/1577, pp. 310–13).

It is plain from Teresa of Avila's writings that the confessors themselves often came under pressure to judge her experiences in particular ways. Thus one of her confessors, Baltasar Alvarez, was reportedly advised to beware "lest the devil should deceive him into believing anything [Teresa] might say to him" (Teresa of Avila, 1982/1565, p. 185). On a later occasion, the attitude of her confessor altered when a change in his Jesuit superior led to a new policy. Teresa (1982/1565, p. 227) remarks that the Jesuits "are extremely particular about the virtue of never doing the slightest thing save in conformity with the will of those set over them." Clearly, then, confessors frequently acted as the agents of Church policy in their attitude to the experiences of their penitents and are, therefore, likely to have exerted influence over the penitent's religious experiences.

Many aspects of late medieval attitudes to ASC and the influences upon their manifestation can be seen in the autobiography of Margery Kempe (1944/1436). She was a merchant's wife who, possibly because she acquired a distaste for sex with her husband after fourteen children, took up a life of piety. In her book, she reports numerous visitations from God, Mary, and the saints. She also describes a pilgrimage to the Holy Land, and appears to have periodically resorted to different regimes of fasting. Generally, she was fortunate in her confessors, or perhaps they were awed by her forthright personality as well as her piety. Either way, they seem to have reacted to news that God had ordered a change in fasting, or what clothes she should wear by duly approving. Margery was, however, careful to obtain such approval, and made a point of mentioning it when at one stage she was under investigation for heresy.

Margery is of special interest to us, as well as to her contemporaries, because of her loud weeping and sobbing at occasions or in places of religious significance. Margery describes herself as having no control over these crying fits. Although early on she prayed for "a well of tears" (Kempe, 1944/1436 p.70), it is clear that over the years they became a source of embarrassment to her. Her crying fits seem to have caused very mixed reactions in both religious and lay onlookers. Many seem to have regarded them as divinely caused and regarded Margery herself as a religious figure. She reports being frequently summoned to pray at the beds of the dying. On the other hand, many did not believe "it was the work of God, but rather some evil spirit, or a sudden sickness, or else simulation and hypocrisy" (p. 71). She was several times accused of heresy and imprisoned, but each time she was freed after convincing her examiners, who included the Archbishop of York, of the orthodoxy of her beliefs. On another occasion two priests tried to test the effect of social factors on her crying by taking her to a church where there was no audience but themselves. Particularly annoying for others seems to have been her crying during sermons. One friar in her own town banned her from attending his sermons because of the disturbance, but many preachers seem to have patiently endured it. Finally, when her confessor pointed out to her that he was practically her last supporter, she was told by God her crying would stop and it did. The apparent success of social disapproval at stopping the crying did not pass unnoticed by contemporaries, many of whom attributed the cessation to the hostile friar or to hypocrisy on Margery's part.

It is unlikely that Margery Kempe would have been able to persist in her unusual behavior for so long—the crying fits endured for ten years—if she had been born a century or so later. A consequence of the Reformation of the early sixteenth century and the Catholic Church's reaction to it seems to have been an increased reluctance to credit individual revelation of any kind. One outcome of this change was a marked drop in the number of reported visionary experiences in early modern Spain. Another was the punishment of even doctrinally orthodox reports of visions. Francisca la Brava, for example, received a hundred lashes in public in 1523 for reporting an apparition of the Virgin Mary (Christian, 1981).

A curious accompaniment, perhaps even a consequence, of the scepticism towards and repression of ASC experiences involving sanctified figures seems to have been an increased interest in ASC experiences involving diabolical figures. Particularly interesting are cases of demonic possession. Demonic possession had been a reasonably common attribution for certain classes of mental disorder in the Middle Ages (e.g., Kemp, 1989; Kemp & Williams, 1987). In general, however, no particular fuss seems to have been made about the victims. For example, public exorcisms seem to have been rarely employed. Also there is not much evidence of systematic questioning of the allegedly possessing devils. In turn, the possession experiences in the Middle Ages do not seem to have been characterized by particularly florid behavior. Medieval demons, for example, do not seem to have frequently prophesied or displayed clairvoyance. (For some collected medieval examples see Clarke, 1975; Habig, 1973; Kramer & Sprenger, 1971/1486; Moore, 1923).

Towards the end of the Middle Ages and in the sixteenth century, however, more attention was paid to alleged possession victims. One cause of the change was the increasing tendency to attribute possession to witchcraft, and hence a move toward interrogating the possessing demon in an attempt to find the witch. Another was the tendency by both Catholics and Protestants to use successful public healings of the possessed as propaganda for their own religion (Kramer & Sprenger, 1971/1486; Thomas, 1971; D.P. Walker, 1981). This augmented attention, coupled with an increased desire to distinguish true possession victims from those who were merely mentally disordered or faking the symptoms (D.P. Walker, 1981), seems to have suggested the development of more florid behavior on the part of the possessed. For example in 1582, Nicolas Facquier was possessed by a devil called Cramoisy who "claimed to belong to an order of spirits who lived in the limbo of unbaptised infants and visited Paradise three times a year. He was possessing Facquier in order that three of his cousins who were Huguenots should return to the true Church" (D. P. Walker, 1981, p. 31).

An interesting feature of some of these early modern diabolical possessions is that, although the nature of the possessing entity clearly labels them as peripheral possessions, they also have some of the features of central possession. In the first place, these possessions were often confronted by elaborate ritual exorcisms, ritual developed at least partly for the purpose of impressing the onlookers. Secondly, and more importantly, the possessed often made pro-social rather than antisocial pronouncements: Facquier's three cousins, incidentally, were converted to Catholicism.

Perhaps these diabolical possessions shared some of the features of central possession because attempts to report a vision of God or one of the saints were, at this time, often more harshly dealt with than attempts to report visions of the devil or even apparent demonic possession. In general, apparent possession victims were kindly treated and, on occasion, listened to attentively. In fact, as D.P. Walker points out, many of the pronouncements of the self-confessed sixteenth century demons, like that possessing the thirteen-year old Thomas Darling in 1596, contain strong elements of piety.

Although Lee's (1989) "rules of ceremony" were proposed in the context of ritual possession trance in Malaysia, they have some applicability to historical European religious experiences. The importance of status distance, for example, is shown in the fact that the officially approved mystics, like Teresa of Avila or Julian of Norwich, were members of contemplative religious orders. The "amateur" performances of Margery Kempe or the Spanish peasantry were less encouraged. Moreover, the visionary experiences of low-status Spaniards, for example married women, were less likely to be credited than those of individuals of higher status, in part because they were held by contemporaries to be more suggestible (Christian, 1981). The importance of altered states of consciousness is hard to determine for some of the experiences reported. Even so they are clearly important for members of monastic orders in which prayer, fasting, physical penances, and isolation were commonplace. Finally, some display of power, by means of a miracle or claivoyance, was often exhibited by the lay visionaries or the allegedly demoniacally possessed, although not invariably by members of the contemplative orders.

Conclusion

Our accounts of Thaipusam in present-day Malaysia and the religious experiences of medieval and early modern Europe clearly highlight rather different aspects of the way in which ASCs are affected by social factors. In part the differences arise because the present-day study of Thaipusam provides greater opportunity for detailed anthropological and psychological investigation of the social forces and their effects. More elaborate information can be gleaned about the characteristics of ASCs in religious experiences, the significance for the individual, and the contemporaneous situational factors which affect the manifestation of trance and possession. But the differences also arise from diversities in the societies themselves. Christianity maintained enormous secular as well as religious influence in medieval and early modern Europe. The historical approach is therefore able to assess longitudinally the macrosocial and political forces which have affected the manifestation of possession and visions in religious experiences.

Broadly speaking, similar social ends seem to have been served by religious experiences over time and across cultures. For the individual, successful participation may enhance not only personal psychological well-being, which we have not considered here in depth, but also provides a source of social recognition and status. For the society, the ceremonies of Thaipusam or of ritual exorcism may serve as sources of enjoyment for the spectators. More importantly, perhaps, the experiences may foster a sense of cultural unity and furnish a channel for the transmission and reinforcement of religious and cultural beliefs. However, as is clear from the European example, the social importance of the religious experiences can, in turn, make them a natural target for political and social control.

In conclusion, then, it is natural to think that ASC experiences, in which someone is apparently possessed by or has a vision of some supernatural being, are essentially private events that concern only the individual and are only peripherally affected by social factors. However, the cross-cultural and historical study of these experiences reveals a quite different picture. Suggestibility plays a significant role in the generation and manifestation of religious experiences. The production of trance and related experiences is heavily affected by social factors that range from the micro level, in which the experience of a Thaipusam devotee is conditioned by the expectations and beliefs of family and friends, to a macro level, in which the conflict between Catholic and Protestant can be seen to have affected the reported visions and possessions of individuals throughout Europe. Furthermore, the process of suggestibility appears to affect both when or how often an ASC experience occurs and the nature of the experience itself.

Notes

The authors would like to thank Ken Strongman for his helpful comments on an earlier draft of this manuscript.

1. The size and structures of kavadis vary in contemporary practice, but all are linked to the offering of a pot of holy milk. Originally kavadis were wooden bars with semicircular attachments supported on the shoulder and decorated with feathers and flowers. Larger, more modern kavadis are decorated metal structures which are carried with support from the waistband and shoulder rests, usually with metal spikes extending upward and outward from the supports (Ward, 1984).

2. Informants have varied in their interpretations of the trance state. Most indicate that they are possessed by deities, while others claim that the deities are merely watching over and protecting them. Although the festival is in honor of Murugan, it is appropriate for devotees to become engaged with other members of his family—Shiva and Shakti, the father and mother, and Ganesh, the brother.

References

Ackerman, S.E., & Lee, R.L.M. (1978). Mass hysteria and spirit possession in urban Malaysia: A case study. *Journal of Sociology and Psychology, 1*, 24–34.

Alcock, J.E. (1981). *Parapsychology: Science or magic.* Oxford: Pergamon.

Asaad, G., & Shapiro, B. (1986). Hallucinations: Theoretical and clinical overview. *American Journal of Psychiatry, 143*, 1088–97.

Baring-Gould, S. (1914). *The lives of the saints.* Edinburgh: John Grant.

Bhattacharyya, S. (1953). Religious practice of Hindus. In K. Morgan (ed.), *The religion of Hindus* (pp. 154–205). New York: Ronald Press.

Bourguignon, E. (1972). Trance dance. In J. White (ed.), *The highest state of consciousness* (pp. 331–43). Garden City, NJ: Doubleday.

Bourguignon, E., & Evascu, T. (1977). Altered states of consciousness within a general evolutionary perspective: A holocultural analysis. *Behavior Science Research, 12*, 197–216.

Christian, W.A. (1981). *Apparitions in late medieval and early modern Spain.* Princeton, NJ: Princeton University Press.

Clarke, B. (1975). *Mental disorder in earlier Britain.* Cardiff: University of Wales.

Council, J.R., Kirsch, I., Vickery, A.R., & Carlson, D. (1983). "Trance" vs. "skill" hypnotic inductions: The effects of credibility, expectancy and experimenter modeling. *Journal of Consulting and Clinical Psychology, 51,* 432–40.

Freed, S.A., & Freed, R.R. (1964). Spirit possession in a north Indian village. *Ethnology, 3,* 152–71.

Garfias, R. (1979–80). The role of dreams and spirit possession in the Mbira Dza Vadzimu music of the Shona people of Zimbabwe. *Journal of Altered States of Consciousness, 5,* 211–34.

Habig, M.A. (1973). *St. Francis of Assisi: Writings and early biographies.* London: Society for Promoting Christian Knowledge.

Jilek, W.G. (1982). Altered states of consciousness in North American Indian ceremonials. *Ethos, 10,* 326–43.

Julian of Norwich. (1966). *Revelations of divine love.* (C. Wolters, ed.) Harmondsworth: Penguin. (Original work written ca. 1393.)

Kane, S. (1982). Holiness ritual fire handling: Ethnographic and psychophysiological considerations. *Ethos, 10,* 369–84.

Kemp, S. (1989). "Ravished of a fiend": Demonology and medieval madness. In C. Ward (ed.), *Altered states of consciousness and mental health: A cross-cultural perspective* (pp. 67–79). Newbury Park, CA: Sage.

Kemp, S., & Williams, K. (1987). Demonic possession and mental disorder in medieval and early modern Europe. *Psychological Medicine, 17,* 21–29.

Kempe, M. (1944). *The book of Margery Kempe* (W. Butler-Bowden, ed.) New York: Devin-Adair. (Original work written 1436.)

Kiev, A. (1961). Spirit possession in Haiti. *American Journal of Psychiatry, 118,* 133–38.

Kramer, H., & Sprenger, J. (1971). *Malleus maleficarum* (M. Summers, trans.) New York: Arrow. (Original work written ca. 1486.)

Krippner, S. (1972). Altered states of consciousness. In J. White (ed.), *The highest state of consciousness* (pp. 1–5). Garden City, NJ: Doubleday.

Lee, R.L.M. (1989). Self-presentation in Malaysian spirit seances: A dramaturgical perspective on altered states of consciousness in healing ceremonies. In C. Ward (ed.), *Altered states of consciousness and mental health: A cross-cultural perspective* (pp. 251–66). Newbury Park, CA: Sage.

Lewis, I.M. (1971). *Ecstatic religion: An anthropological study of spirit possession and shamanism.* Middlesex: Penguin.

Lex, B. (1975). Physiological aspects of ritual trance. *Journal of Altered States of Consciousness, 2,* 109–22.

Lindstrom, L.G. (1978). Religious faith healing and its psychological conditions: A methodological study. In T. Kallstad (ed.), *Psychological studies on religious man* (pp. 211–42). Stockholm: Almqvist and Wiksell.

Lucie-Smith, E. (1976). *Joan of Arc.* London: Allen Lane.

Ludwig, A.M. (1983). The psychobiological functions of dissociation. *American Journal of Clinical Hypnosis, 26,* 93–99.

Malhotra, K.C., & Khomne, S.B. (1980). Fire walk ceremony at the village of Hauman Takli, Maharashtra. *Eastern Anthropologist, 33,* 83–88.

Moore, N. (ed.) (1923). *The book of the foundation of St. Bartholomew's Church in London.* London: Early English Text Society, o.s. 163.

Noll, R. (1985). Mental imagery cultivation as a cultural phenomenon: The role of visions in shamanism. *Current Anthropology, 26*, 443–61.

Pressel, E. (1974). Umbanda trance and possession in São Paulo, Brazil. In F. Goodman, H.H. Henney, & E. Pressel (eds.), *Trance, healing and hallucination* (pp. 113–225). London: Wiley.

Prince, R. (1982). Shamans and endorphins: Hypotheses for synthesis. *Ethos, 10*, 409–23.

Prince, R. (1987, February). Trance, trance-training and the endorphin hypothesis: New approaches to shamanism. Paper presented at the Fourth International Institute for Systems Science Oberwallis Conference, Brig, Switzerland.

Sargant, W. (1974). *The mind possessed.* New York: Penguin.

Shor, R.E. (1959). Hypnosis and the concept of generalized reality orientation. *Journal of Psychotherapy, 13*, 582–602.

Shor, R.E. (1969). Hypnosis and the concept of reality orientation. In C.T. Tart (ed.), *Altered states of consciousness* (pp. 233–50). New York: Wiley.

Spanos, N.P. (1989). Hypnosis, demon possession, and multiple personality: Strategic enactments and disavowals of responsibility for actions. In C. Ward (ed.), *Altered states of consciousness and mental health: A cross-cultural perspective* (pp. 96–124). Newbury Park, CA: Sage.

Spanos, N.P., & Barber, T.X. (1974). Toward a convergence in hypnosis research. *American Psychologist, 29*, 500–11.

Stoller, P. (1989). Stressing social change and Songhay possession. In C. Ward (ed.), *Altered states of consciousness and mental health: A cross-cultural perspective* (pp. 267–84). Newbury Park, CA: Sage.

Tart, C.T. (1980). A systems approach to altered states of consciousness. In J.M. Davidson & R.J. Davidson (eds.), *The psychobiology of consciousness* (pp. 243–70). New York: Plenum.

Teresa of Avila, St. (1982). Interior castle. (Original work written 1577.) In E.A. Peters (ed. and trans.), *The complete works of Saint Teresa of Jesus. Vol. 2* (pp. 199–351). London: Sheed and Wood.

Teresa of Avila, St. (1982). The life of the Holy Mother Teresa of Jesus. (Original work written 1565.) In E.A. Peters (ed. and trans.), *The complete works of Saint Teresa of Jesus. Vol. 1.* (pp. 10–300). London: Sheed and Wood.

Tertullian (1931). *Apology.* (T.R. Glover, trans.). London: Heinemann. (Original work written 197–198 AD.)

Thomas, K. (1971). *Religion and the decline of magic.* London: Weidenfeld and Nicolson.

Valla, J.P., & Prince, R. (1989). Religious experiences as self-healing mechanisms. In C. Ward (ed.), *Altered states of consciousness and mental health: A cross-cultural perspective* (pp. 149–66). Newbury Park, CA: Sage.

Walker, D.P. (1981). *Unclean spirits.* London: Scolar.

Walker, S. (1972). *Ceremonial spirit possession in Africa and Afro-America.* Leiden: Brill.

Walsh, D.H. (1974). Interactive effects of alpha feedback and instructional set on the subjective state. *Psychophysiology, 11*, 428–35.

Walsh, J. (ed.) (1981). *The cloud of unknowing.* London: SPCK. (Original work written ca. 1350–1400.)

Ward, C. (1979–80). Therapeutic aspects of ritual trance: The Shango cult in Trinidad. *Journal of Altered States of Consciousness, 5,* 19–29.

Ward, C. (1980). Spirit possession and mental health: A psycho-anthropological perspective. *Human Relations, 33,* 149–63.

Ward, C. (1984). Thaipusam in Malaysia: A psycho-anthropological analysis of ritual trance, ceremonial possession and self-mortification practices. *Ethos, 12,* 307–34.

Ward, C. (1989). Possession and exorcism: Psychopathology and psychotherapy in a magico-religious context. In C. Ward (ed.), *Altered states of consciousness and mental health: A cross-cultural perspective* (pp. 125–44). Newbury Park, CA: Sage.

Ward, C., & Beaubrun, M.H. (1979). Trance induction and hallucination in Spiritual Baptist mourning practices. *Journal of Psychological Anthropology, 2,* 479–88.

Ward, C., & Beaubrun, M.H. (1980). The psycho-dynamics of demon possession. *Journal for the Scientific Study of Religion, 19,* 201–07.

Ward, C., & Beaubrun, M.H. (1981). Spirit possession and neuroticism in a West Indian Pentecostal community. *British Journal of Clinical Psychology, 20,* 295–96.

Warner, R. (1977). Witchcraft and soul loss: Implications for community psychiatry. *Hospital and Community Psychiatry, 28,* 686–90.

Wiebe, P.W., & Mariappen, S. (1978). *Indian Malaysians: The view from the plantation.* New Delhi: Manohar.

Wilson, S.C., & Barber, T.X. (1983). The fantasy-prone personality: Implications for understanding imagery, hypnosis and parapsychological phenomena. In A.A. Sheik (ed.), *Imagery* (pp. 340–87). New York: Wiley.

Wirz, P. (1954). *The art of healing.* Leiden: Brill.

Yap, P.M. (1960). Possession syndrome. *Journal of Mental Science, 106,* 114–37.

PART THREE

RESEARCHING SUGGESTIBILITY

9

SELF-PERCEPTION AND SELF-DECEPTION
The Role of Attention in Suggestibility Processes

Frederick X. Gibbons and Sue Boney McCoy

In 1962, Stanley Schachter and Jerome Singer published a study in *Psychological Review* that has come to be recognized as a classic in social psychology, not so much because of its specific results but because of the impact it had on the field. The research was based on a theoretical assumption with a long history in social psychology, which is that, being "social animals," people rely heavily on other people for information. That includes information about the world around them, about subjective and objective reality, and about themselves. The process is called social comparison (Festinger, 1954), and the extent to which it occurs varies as a function of both situational and dispositional factors. Some people do it more than others, and sometimes people do it more than other times. But the fact is that we all do it, and it is the primary reason why the social environment has such a profound effect on our behavior.

With this assumption in mind, Schachter and Singer speculated that they could, in effect, influence individuals' interpretations of their own emotional states by providing them with false information from an external source, specifically, another person. Although the procedure they used was a complicated one, it can be described briefly. They injected all of their subjects with a stimulant similar to adrenaline. Only half of the subjects were told the truth about the drug and what effect it would have on them, however. The other half received false information. This meant that when the drug started to take effect on these subjects, and their hearts started to race, hands to become jittery, and so forth, they did not know exactly what was happening to them, or why it was happening. Schachter and Singer then placed an actor in the room whose job it was to provide the subjects with information, via his behavior (i.e., emotional "cues"), that would help them decide how to identify or label their emotional state. In one case he acted quite pleased, stating clearly that he was enjoying the experiment, whereas in the other condition he did just the opposite.

Schachter and Singer's reasoning was that the subjects who had received incorrect information about the effects of the drug would be confused by their arousal reaction and would, consequently, look to available external sources to help them figure out what was going on. Sure enough, when later asked how they felt, the misinformed subjects in the presence of the happy actor reported experiencing considerable enjoyment, whereas those who responded in the presence of the angry one did the opposite. The Schachter and Singer study made one point very clearly, which is the fact that people do use external information in order to help them understand internal responses. In fact, this point is a fundamental one in social psychology, which underlies many psychological phenomena including, of course, social influence, but also conformity, self-perception, and impression formation. According to the reasoning that we will develop in this chapter, a key element in the social influence process—and therefore a key component of suggestibility—is focus of attention. Our primary hypothesis is this: directing one's attention outside the self increases the likelihood that one will rely on external information to interpret internal states. As a result, behavior becomes much more responsive to external cues. Directing attention back on the self, on the other hand, increases awareness of internal states and reduces the tendency to look for and react to external information.

We will first present empirical evidence supporting our contentions, including specifically the role that focus of attention plays in reducing suggestibility and increasing self-knowledge. Then we will discuss the advantages and disadvantages associated with enhanced self-knowledge. Finally, we will discuss the broader implications of both augmented and diminished suggestibility.

Self-awareness theory

The theoretical basis of our work is Duval and Wicklund's theory of objective self-awareness (1972). Self-Awareness (SA) theory, as it is usually called, has two primary postulates: (a) attention may be directed either outward toward the environment or inward toward the self; (b) directing attention inward initiates a self-evaluation process whereby the individual compares his/her current behavior or a salient dimension of the self (e.g., physical appearance) with a "standard" or ideal for that dimension that the individual maintains (i.e., the way the person feels s/he "should be"). In a recent update of the theory (Gibbons, 1990), one of us suggested a slightly different conceptualization. That is, directing attention toward the self results in the "accessing of the self-schema" (Carver & Scheier, 1981). The self-schema is a cognitive representation of the self. In other words, it is the dynamic, exceptionally complex image of the self that constitutes the self-concept in its entirety, including all of its physical, emotional, and dispositional components. As a result of this accessing, the individual not only becomes more cognizant of a variety of self-dimensions, ranging from minor aches and pains to major role performance (e.g., parenting, career progress), but is also more likely to report accurately on these dimensions. As Gibbons (1990) suggested, the SA person is "one who becomes more careful in deliberating his or her own behavior and its consequences. The result is a significant strengthening in the link between internal response and overt behavior" (p. 262).

Focus of attention and suggestibility

Two self-dimensions that have received considerable empirical attention from SA theorists are arousal and affect. The hypothesis in the early research in this area was simply that awareness of affect or arousal should be enhanced by self-awareness when those internal states are amplified. For example, a person who has been provoked is more likely to retaliate when his attention is directed back upon the self, and less likely to respond if attention is distracted externally.(1) The same applies to emotional arousal. When a male college student looks at pictures from *Playboy* magazine and then is encouraged to self-focus, his awareness of the emotional response is increased. As a result, he likes the pictures more (Scheier and Carver, 1977). The opposite holds true as well. When there is no amplification of internal response, then focusing attention internally should increase awareness of the *absence* of activity. And that should be true whether *external* information suggests there is internal reactivity or not.

Self-focus and placebo response

We tested this latter hypothesis in a series of studies involving self-focused attention and placebo reactivity. Specifically, our assumption was that if self-focused attention increases awareness of internal states, it should reduce reliance on external information about those states—when that information is incorrect or misleading—thereby reducing suggestibility. In the first experiment (Gibbons, Carver, Scheier, & Hormuth, 1979), we gave our subjects a large gelatin capsule filled with bicarbonate of soda. Presentation of the "drug," which we called "Cavanol," was accompanied by the suggestion that it would produce three specific arousal symptoms (e.g., heart rate increase). Subjects then worked on a simple task during which half of them were made self-aware by means of a large mirror. When questioned subsequently as to the extent of the drug's general effects, those who had been encouraged to self-focus reported significantly less reactivity. In addition, when asked which symptoms they had and had not experienced, significant differences between the SA and non-SA subjects appeared only on the three symptoms that we had ascribed to the drug. Both groups reported some elevated experience of some other symptoms that had not been specifically mentioned (e.g., dizziness, headache). In short, SA subjects appeared to be "looking internally" for the symptoms described to them, and when they found no evidence that those symptoms were elevated, they reported as such. In contrast, those whose attention had not been focused internally did report a more or less standard placebo response.

Similar results were found in a follow-up study (Scheier, Carver, & Gibbons, 1979). In the first of two experiments, male subjects were asked to view moderately arousing slides of nude women after they had been led to believe that the slides would be either very arousing or not at all arousing. In the second experiment, subjects were again given false expectations, this time with regard to the intensity of a particular flavor they were asked to taste. Both experiments produced essentially the same pattern of results: those whose attention was self-directed were significantly less influenced by the false suggestion than were those who were not encouraged to self-focus. Moreover, the self-focused subjects were also more accurate in assessing their actual internal states.

The veracity hypothesis

The results of these two studies, plus those of a third, were instrumental in developing what we have called the veridicality or "veracity" hypothesis (Gibbons, 1983). The hypothesis states that reports about self-dimensions will be more accurate when they are made while attention is self-focused. The third experiment that contributed to that hypothesis involved a different kind of suggestibility, namely conformity behavior. What we attempted to do in that study (Gibbons & Wright, 1983) was to alter the sexual attitudes of a group of college students by presenting them with false information suggesting that their peers' attitudes had become much more liberal over the last four or five years (which was not true). When we compared the self-reported sexual attitudes of our students before and after they had received this bogus information, it became apparent that our persuasion attempt had worked. Subjects adopted a much more "progressive" stance on such issues as the advisability of pre-marital sex, masturbation, and adultery, after they found out that their peers had become more liberal on these issues. But that was the case only if their attention had not been self-focused during the second response. Those who had been SA when reporting did alter their opinions, as might be expected, but not nearly as much, so that the correlation between their pre-and post-manipulation reports was higher than the comparable correlation for their nonself-focused counterparts (r=.79 vs. .57).

Encouraged by this series of studies and these results, we became interested in exploring what at the time appeared to be an obvious clinical implication of SA theory and of our veracity hypothesis. We sought to determine whether self-focused attention might increase the accuracy with which psychiatric patients report on their psychological problems (Gibbons, Smith, Ingram, Brehm, Pearce, & Schroeder, 1985). We asked alcoholics and people with personality disorders to tell us about their problem, including how serious it was, how long they had had it, and so forth. The results were consistent with expectations: those who reported while their attention was internally-directed presented a less flattering but also much more accurate description of their problems; accuracy was determined by comparing subjects' responses with hospital records and evaluations provided by hospital staff.

Similar results were obtained when we asked incarcerated women to tell us about their criminal behavior (Gibbons & Gerrard, 1986). Once again the reports of the self-focused women were more accurate, primarily because the non-SA women were much more given to exaggeration or understatement, depending on which approach presented the most favorable image to the experimenter. One other finding from this research is worth mentioning. Besides self-reports of their problem behavior, we also assessed the mood states of the psychiatric patients and the prisoners, and in both cases found that the accurate self-reports among the SA subjects were accompanied by significantly worse mood states. The "somber but sincere" demeanor of these subjects is a common characteristic of the state of self-awareness.

Self-Focus and Self-Presentation. The pattern of error among the non-SA subjects in these self-report studies was clearly not random and suggested a motivated distortion that would best be described as a type of impression management. When given the opportunity to bolster or embellish their images and avoid embarrassment, without fear of discovery (subjects were not aware that we had access to their actual case histories), they took advantage. Thus, once again the behavior of the non-SA subjects reflected an orientation toward others, in this case a desire to please and/or look good in the eyes of those observing them. Toward that end they were willing to embellish and in some cases fabricate their self-reports, whereas the self-focused subjects were not. The reason is not because self-attention eliminates the desire to present a favorable image to others; it does not. What it does do is to prevent the impression management process from going too far, by inhibiting misrepresentation of the self (what some theorists have called "assertive impression-management": Tetlock & Manstead, 1985). Thus, although the SA person may be quite interested in presenting a favorable image to others, s/he is not willing to distort that image, or lie, in order to do it. In sum, the accuracy that is produced is attributable to a large extent to two factors: (a) increased attention to, and awareness of, internal states; and (b) less concern with the opinions of others.

Limits of self-knowledge

Before discussing the implications of the veracity hypothesis, one additional placebo study should be mentioned because it is relevant. The procedure in that study (Gibbons & Gaeddert, 1984) was similar to that of our original "Cavanol" study, but with a slightly different twist. Self-aware and non-SA subjects were given a placebo prior to working on a series of mathematical problems. The problems were said to be a good measure of mathematical and general intellectual ability. This time, however, instead of just telling subjects that the drug would be arousing, we also suggested that it would affect their performance on the mathematics set. Half the subjects were led to believe the drug would facilitate their performance, half that it would interfere. Our expectation was that the "utility" of the placebo would influence the amount of activity which subjects ascribed to it, with greater effects attributed to the inhibiting drug. Such a pattern would be generally consistent with an impression-management motive, and, in fact, that is the pattern we obtained from the non-SA subjects. However, even though the SA subjects certainly realized their mathematical performance would look more impressive if they overidentified the inhibiting drug and underidentified the facilitating drug, they did not distinguish between the two. As expected, while working on the evaluative task, the SA subjects reported enhanced arousal, and they attributed some of that arousal to the drug they had taken regardless of the particular benefits associated with it. In short, SA subjects' self-reports were an accurate reflection of their internal arousal states (elevated by the evaluative task), but they could not distinguish between two equally plausible sources of that arousal, one being task anxiety and the other the drug. They simply did not have access to that type of internal information.

Initially, our veracity results appeared encouraging from a clinical perspective. In fact, the conventional wisdom in psychology for many years—actually until quite recently—has maintained that self-knowledge is the *sine qua non* of mental health. Numerous psychologists, from Freud to Jahoda to Beck, have suggested that self-misperception is associated with pathology. Among persons with mental health problems, an increase in self-knowledge has typically been taken as evidence of improvement. Indeed, this accuracy/health perspective is the basis for what was once a fairly popular technique in psychotherapy, called self-confrontation. The process involves having the client view videotapes of him/herself in different (usually social) situations, with the explicit goal of enhancing self-knowledge. But the notion goes back a lot further than that. Beginning with Solon (c. 600 BC), the adage "Know thyself" has been considered a fundamental injunction, which is why the recent provocative work on the relation between self-*deception* and mental health may end up being recognized as one of the most dramatic paradigm shifts in late twentieth century psychology.

Self-illusion and self-knowledge

One of the earliest empirical works indicating that the relation between mental health and accurate self-knowledge is not necessarily positive was done by Alloy and Abramson (1979). These authors found that depressed persons' perceptions of the contingency between their instrumental behavior and their outcomes was much more accurate than were the same perceptions of nondepressed students. What was particularly noteworthy about this study was the fact that it was the nondepressed subjects whose perceptions were marked by inaccuracy; they tended to overattribute responsibility to the self when they succeeded and underattribute to the self when they failed. A series of studies followed shortly thereafter demonstrating essentially the same phenomenon in different ways. For example, it has been shown that people will view themselves more favorably than other people view them, remember positive information about the self better than they do negative information, and believe that positive characteristics are much more descriptive of the self than are negative (see Taylor & Brown, 1988). Along the same lines, people generally believe that the future is likely to hold almost exclusively positive outcomes for the self, to the point where negative events, such as illness, are thought to be extremely unlikely and much less likely to happen to the self than to others (Weinstein, 1984).

Once again, however, each one of these illusion examples is much more typical of persons who are not depressed, or low in self-esteem, or self-aware. Those individuals tend not to be overly optimistic about the future (Pyzsczynski, Holt, & Greenberg, 1987) and are less likely to perceive themselves more favorably than others do.

So who is kidding whom? In general, the research suggests that it is nondepressed persons who are deceiving themselves, and in fact, there is direct evidence to support this conclusion. Several studies have demonstrated a positive correlation between measures of depression and self-deception. For example, the Self-Deception Questionnaire (SDQ; Sackeim & Gur, 1978) has been shown to correlate significantly with the Beck Depression Inventory (Ingram & Johnson, 1990). The SDQ assesses the extent to which an individual denies certain feelings that are potentially threatening but nonetheless quite common. By the same token, the tendency to deceive the self appears to be inversely related to chronic self-focus, whereas chronic self-focus is positively related to depression (Smith & Greenberg, 1981).

Our contention is that it is essentially the same mediating factor that underlies the relations between self-focused attention and suggestibility, between self-focus and negative affect, and between self-focus and self-knowledge. That factor is the tendency to look inward for information about the self, and to rely less on external cues or information. Thus, nondepressed persons are less knowledgeable about themselves *and* less truthful with themselves, at least in part because they tend to be less introspective. But, strangely enough, they benefit from that lack of integrity. As Taylor and Brown (1988) suggest, the individual who self-deludes "will be happier, more caring, and more productive than the individual who perceives (this same) information accurately and integrates it into his or her view of the self" (p. 205). One is reminded here of Tolstoy's (1978/1890) insight from *Kreutzer Sonata:* "Both salvation and punishment for man lie in the fact that he can befog himself so as not to see the misery of his position" (p. 564).

Suggestibility and personal interest

Hypnotism, placebo responsivity, and conformity, like other forms of suggestibility, are results of social influence. But they are not passive responses to influence attempts. Rather, they involve some active degree of amenability to the suggestion. People are willing to enhance the self at the expense of accuracy or veracity, and the more beneficial the expected effects, the more likely people are to be persuaded by a particular suggestion. Indeed, Plotkin (1985) has argued that the placebo effect is the "direct achievement of the patient himself or herself" (p. 245). Placebos that offer pain relief, or those that are expected to produce a desirable or "pleasant" effect, will typically elicit more of a reaction than those that do not (Gibbons & Gaeddert, 1984; Ross & Olson, 1981). Similarly, a review of literature in the hypnosis area suggests that hypnotic suggestion is less effective when it is inconsistent with the personal interests and self-perceptions of the individual. Generally speaking, people are more persuaded by external information about the self—whether relevant to personality or physical state—when that information has a positive message.

Summary. By now it would be safe to say that the weight of the evidence supports the claim that illusions and optimistic biases are health-promoting and beneficial. People are quite willing to believe what others say about them, *and* they are capable of sorting through that information, selectively attending to and encoding some of it, while filtering out what seems irrelevant or unflattering. Positive information is encoded, while negative information is distorted or forgotten, in much the same way that favorable suggestions produce more reaction. Underlying both phenomena is the consistent factor of external focus. In contrast, the ability to self-delude, like other types of suggestion, is inhibited by internal focus. As a consequence of this inhibition, the benefits of self-delusion, as well as many of the benefits associated with placebos and hypnosis, and suggestion in general, are lost.

The advantages of accurate self-perception

Taylor and Brown (1988) make a cogent argument outlining the benefits of self-illusion. A similar message can be found in another review article by Snyder and Higgins (1988), who claim that self-focus tends to short-circuit many of the salutary effects of "excuse-making" (i.e., creating external causal attributions for unfavorable outcomes). One reason for this, they suggest, is that self-focus makes one "accountable" for one's own behavior, thereby inhibiting the self-deception that is necessary for excuse-making to be effective.

Still, it would be misleading to suggest that accurate self-perception is necessarily "depressogenic," or that there are not, in fact, some benefits associated with self-knowledge. In both review articles, Taylor and Brown, and Snyder and Higgins allude to the possibility that the increased self-knowledge associated with self-directed attention can enhance well-being. We agree, and in fact would suggest that there are a number of reasons why self-knowledge, and especially accurate self-knowledge, can enhance subjective well-being at the individual level, and perhaps more importantly, increase quality of life at the societal level as well.

Health. Several theories of health behavior (e.g., the health belief model: Janz & Becker, 1984) are based on the assumption that prophylactic behaviors are generally prompted by a belief in personal vulnerability. People who do not think they are likely to contract a particular illness are much less likely to take precautions against that occurrence. One reason for this has to do with self-perception and recall of previous behavior. When considering their own vulnerability, people are more likely to recall risk-reducing behavior selectively, while ignoring or forgetting risk-increasing behavior (Gerrard, Gibbons, & Warner, 1990). In essence, this is a type of self-illusion that is once again a symptom of poor self-knowledge. This being the case, it should be counteracted by internal focus of attention, and there is some evidence to support this. Research by Suls and Fletcher (1985) has indicated that people who are chronically self-focused are more willing to admit having physical problems or ailments of one kind or another and, apparently, are more likely to seek medical assistance when those problems are detected.

Of course, what happens after that assistance is sought is an interesting question. Many health psychology researchers recognize the importance of the doctor-patient relationship and the role that the patient's faith in the therapeutic technique plays in the healing process (e.g., Plotkin, 1985). According to Evans (1985), a doctor's belief in the power of a particular treatment "presumably communicates itself to the anxious patient, and legitimizes a plausibility and expectation that it will work" (p. 226). Diminished reliance on external sources of information in such a setting could pose an obstacle to therapy. Thus, chronic self-focus could prove to be a handicap. On the other hand, although we are not physicians, we suspect that many medical doctors, including psychiatrists, would usually prefer to treat patients who have a realistic conception of their own physical and mental status.

Personal Values. The primary reason why the recent work on illusion and self-deception has received so much attention is because it is clearly counterintuitive. Not just clinical psychology and psychiatry, but Western and Eastern philosophies in general maintain that self-knowledge and self-integrity are to be valued. Leading figures in social psychology, such as Festinger and Heider, and many others in psychology have argued that behavioral consistency (i.e., attitudes with behavior, behavior with behavior) impresses both external and internal audiences. And self-attention promotes this type of consistency. Unfortunately, self-focus also functions as a *monitor* of attitude/behavior and behavior/behavior congruence, and that often results in some discomfort. In short, some self-attention is necessary to monitor actions and keep behavior in line with personal values and standards. By the same token, that monitoring process can often be disconcerting, and too much self-focus can be debilitating.

Self-focus in a societal context

Looking at the *overall* impact that self-focus has on behavior presents a somewhat different perspective. It can be seen, then, that while the individual "pays the price" associated with self-focus, there are also a number of benefits that accrue at a societal level. To illustrate, we will again rely on research from social psychology, beginning with a clever study involving children and Halloween candy. In that study (Diener, Fraser, Beaman, & Kelem, 1976), trick-or-treaters were surreptitiously observed while they took advantage of an unguarded candy display. An adult first told the children they could have only one candy bar, and then left the room. The children were either identified individually or made anonymous, and they either acted individually or in groups. Results indicated that the anonymous children and those in groups helped themselves to more treats than did the identified (SA) or individual children.

Deindividuation

Based in part on this research, and several other studies showing less aggressive behavior among people who were individually identified, Diener (1979) developed a theory of deindividuation that is based on focus of attention. He argues that deindividuation is a psychological state that occurs among individuals involved in very active groups. Its primary characteristic is a lack of personal identity attributable to the fact that attention has been drawn away from the self and into the environment. When that happens, self-awareness is replaced with a strong group identity, and behavior becomes almost totally disinhibited. In essence, suggestibility and social influence are maximized. Thus, the usual (personal) values, standards, and convictions that serve to constrain behavior, or to keep it in line, are ignored. The individual becomes immersed in the group and its collective behavior, engaging in various acts that would not even be considered if the person were alone or if attention were self-focused. These behaviors may range from the innocent, such as taking an extra candy bar or two, to the malicious, such as verbal aggression against an outgroup member, to the deadly, such as riots, looting, and lynch mobs.

Contagion and Inhibition. Under these circumstances we would argue that self-confrontation therapy, despite its drawbacks, would be effective at deterring behavior, and also, at a different level, in preventing certain behaviors from occurring in the first place. The soccer fan who is confronted on the eleven o'clock news with the ugly reality of his stadium riot behavior is likely to experience considerable discomfort, and perhaps make some commitment not to become involved in such activities again. The opposite response—but for essentially the same reasons—might be expected from the inactive bystanders in Latane and Darley's (1970) helping research, or from the 38 witnesses to the 1963 murder of Kitty Genovese that prompted the Latane and Darley studies. In one case behavior that is inconsistent with personal standards is elicited from the individual, a process called behavioral contagion. In the other case a value-consistent behavior is "prevented" from occurring—what would be considered behavioral inhibition. In both instances, however, the reason why appropriate behavior does not occur is because attention is directed away from the self, and external factors are "controlling" behavior.

Elsewhere one of us has suggested (Gibbons, in press) that focus of attention is the "remote control" that a society "maintains" over its members. It encourages some actions and discourages others, but generally it works to keep behavior in line with endogenous motives and goals. In so doing, it presents an interesting paradox: self-focused attention brings behavior in line with societal or social goals, while it reduces social influence or susceptibility to social stimuli. Thus, it promotes civilized behavior by bringing actions into line with internalized values. The value structure that serves as a guide to behavior when attention is self-directed (similar to what symbolic interactionists have called the "generalized other") develops through social experience. Recently, Wicklund and Gollwitzer (1987) have suggested that this value system is an "accumulation of perspectives," which reflects years of interacting with and learning from other people. But the structure itself is *internally* based, and as Duval and Wicklund stated, it is in no way dependent on other persons. Thus, although others are instrumental in developing the personal value structure (and modifying it), ultimately the control over behavior comes from within, when attention is self-focused.

Conclusion

The paradox that we have presented might best be viewed as a dilemma of sorts. At an individual level, self-awareness promotes and inhibits behavior, and it often does both in a constraining manner. Moreover, there is a burden that comes with self-focus. That is because there are many things about the self that we do not wish to know, and many self-dimensions that we would just as soon not contemplate or deliberate upon. When we do, the knowledge can be disturbing; in many ways the truth (about the self) hurts. When we direct attention outside the self, however, we can rely on others for positive feedback without acknowledging that that feedback may be tempered to please us. At the same time, information that we do not like or do not want to hear will not be processed. Or, if it is processed, it can be distorted upon recall, or simply forgotten. Thus, part of the increased suggestibility that comes with external focus is a willingness to be misled, sometimes even fooled, about the self. As a result, we remain happy, though misinformed.

When our attention is self-directed, self-illusions or self-delusions become much more difficult to maintain—we may be unhappy, but nonetheless accurate. Our motives are endogenous, and our behavior is controlled more by personal values than by external influence. Thus, both suggestibility and persuasibility are reduced. At a societal level, however, self-attention plays an important role. It may make us uncomfortable as individuals, but it is necessary to maintain structure as a group. Without it, some form of anarchy would develop; social discourse as we know it would be impossible. In this sense the "burden" of self-focus becomes a facilitator of social structure.

Note

(1) Theoretically, anything that serves to focus attention back on the self should bring about a "state" of self-awareness. Empirically, the most commonly used and most effective device has been a mirror (although tape recorders, name tags, and introspective instructions have all been used). In addition, some researchers have selected subjects based on a *dispositional* tendency toward chronic self-focus or introspection (a trait called "private self-consciousness").

References

Alloy, L.B., & Abramson, L.Y. (1979). Judgement of contingency in depressed and nondepressed students. *Journal of Experimental Psychology: General, 108*, 441–85.

Carver, C.S., & Scheier, M.F. (1981). *Attention and self-regulation: A control theory approach to human behavior.* New York: Springer-Verlag.

Diener, E. (1979). Deindividuation: The absence of self-awareness and self-regulation in group members. In P. Paulus (ed.), *The psychology of group influence.* Hillsdale, NJ: Erlbaum.

Diener, E., Fraser, S.C., Beaman, A.L., & Kelem, R.T. (1976). Effects of deindividuating variables on stealing by Halloween trick-or-treaters. *Journal of Personality and Social Psychology, 33,* 178–83.

Duval, S., & Wicklund, R.A. (1972). *A theory of objective self-awareness.* New York: Academic Press.

Evans, F.J. (1985). Expectancy, therapeutic instructions, and the placebo response. In B. Tursky & G.E. Schwartz (eds.), *Placebo* (pp. 215–28). New York: Guilford.

Festinger, L.A. (1954). A theory of social comparison processes. *Human Relations, 7,* 117–40.

Gerrard, M., Gibbons, F.X., & Warner, T. (1990). Effects of reviewing risk-relevant behavior on perceived vulnerability. (Submitted for publication.)

Gibbons, F.X. (1983). Self-attention and self-report. The "veridicality" hypothesis. *Journal of Personality, 51,* 517–42.

Gibbons, F.X. (1990). Self-attention and behavior: A review and update. In M. Zanna (ed.), *Advances in experimental social psychology* (Vol. 23, pp. 249–303). San Diego: Academic Press.

Gibbons, F.X. (In press). The impact of focus of attention and affect on social behavior. In R. Crozier (ed.), *Shyness and embarrassment: Perspectives from social psychology.* New York: Cambridge University Press.

Gibbons, F.X., Carver, C.S., Scheier, M.F., & Hormuth, S.E. (1979). Self-focused attention and the placebo effect: Fooling some of the people some of the time. *Journal of Experimental Social Psychology, 15,* 263–74.

Gibbons, F.X., & Gaeddert, W.P. (1984). Focus of attention and placebo utility. *Journal of Experimental Social Psychology, 20,* 159–76.

Gibbons, F.X., & Gerrard, M. (1986). Self-awareness and the truth-as-standard hypothesis. Paper presented at the American Psychological Association Convention, Washington, D.C.

Gibbons, F.X., Smith, T.W., Ingram, R.E., Pearce, K., Brehm, S.S., & Schroeder, D.J. (1985). Self-awareness and self-confrontation: Effects of self-focused attention on members of a clinical population. *Journal of Personality and Social Psychology, 48,* 622–75.

Gibbons, F.X., & Wright, R.A. (1983). Self-focused attention and reactions to conflicting standards. *Journal of Research in Personality, 17,* 263–73.

Ingram, R.E., & Johnson, B. (1990). Vulnerability to distress: Cognitive and emotional reactivity in chronically self-focused individuals. (Submitted for publication).

Janz, N.K., & Becker, M.H. (1984). The health belief model: A decade later. *Health Education Quarterly, 11,* 1–47.

Latane, B., & Darley, J.M. (1970). *The unresponsive bystander: Why doesn't he help?* New York: Appleton-Century-Crofts.

Plotkin, W.B. (1985). A psychological approach to placebo: The role of faith in therapy and treatment. In B. Tursky & G.E. Schwartz (eds.), *Placebo* (pp. 237–54). New York: Guilford.

Pyszcynski, T., Holt, J., & Greenberg, J. (1987). Depression, self-focused attention, and expectancies for positive and negative future life events for self and others. *Journal of Personality and Social Psychology, 52,* 944–1001.

Ross, M, & Olson, J.M. (1981). An expectancy-attribution model of the effects of placebos. *Psychological Review, 88,* 408–37.

Sackeim, H.A., & Gur, R.C. (1978). Self-deception, self-confrontation, and self-consciousness. In G.E. Schwartz & D. Shapiro (eds.), *Consciousness and self-regulation: Advances in research* (Vol. 2, pp. 139–97). New York: Plenum.

Schachter, S., & Singer, J.E. (1962). Cognitive, social, and physiological determinants of emotional state. *Psychological Review, 69,* 379–99.

Scheier, M.F., & Carver, C.S. (1977). Self-focused attention and the experience of emotion: Attraction, repulsion, elation, and depression. *Journal of Personality and Social Psychology, 35,* 625–36.

Scheier, M.F., Carver, C.S., & Gibbons, F.X. (1979). Self-directed attention, awareness of bodily states and suggestibility. *Journal of Personality and Social Psychology, 37,* 1576–88.

Smith, T.W., & Greenberg, J. (1981). Depression and self-focused attention. *Motivation and Emotion, 5,* 323–31.

Snyder, C.R., & Higgins, R.L. (1988). Excuses: Their effective role in the negotiation of reality. *Psychological Bulletin, 104,* 23–25.

Suls, J., & Fletcher, B. (1985). Self-attention, life stress, and illness: A prospective study. *Psychosomatic Medicine, 47,* 469–81.

Taylor, S.E., & Brown, J.D. (1988). Illusion and well-being: A social psychological perspective on mental health. *Psychological Bulletin, 103,* 193–210.

Tetlock, P.E., & Manstead, A.R. (1985). Impression management vs. intrapsychic explanations in social psychology: A useful dichotomy. *Psychological Review, 92,* 59–77.

Tolstoy, L. (1978). *Kreutzer Sonata.* In J. Bayley (ed.), *The Portable Tolstoy.* Harmondsworth, UK: Penguin. (Originally published in 1890.)

Weinstein, N.D. (1984). Why it won't happen to me: Perceptions of risk factors and susceptibility. *Health Psychology, 3,* 431–57.

Wicklund, R.A., & Gollwitzer, P.M. (1987). The fallacy of the private-public self-focus distinction. *Journal of Personality, 55,* 491–522.

10

FANTASY PRONENESS, HYPNOTIZABILITY, AND MULTIPLE PERSONALITY

Judith W. Rhue and Steven Jay Lynn

Carla's parents were downstairs discussing her college prospects. Carla was upstairs playing with her dolls, Barb, Kathy, and Becky. As the scenario unfolded, Barb argued that Carla, a straight-A student, would be stupid to spurn the generous scholarship offered by the school of her choice. Kathy argued that Carla should capitalize on her musical talents and join a rock band before committing herself to years of grueling education. Becky finally struck a hard-won compromise: Carla would go to college and join a campus rock band. Carla thanked her dolls, gently placed them in a box, locked it and went downstairs to tell her parents that after careful deliberation she had decided to accept the scholarship. Carla is a classic fantasy-prone personality (Lynn & Rhue, 1985).

So too was the famous spiritual medium Eileen Garett. As her autobiography reveals, she lived a great part of the time in a world of make-believe, had imaginary playmates who looked and felt like ordinary children, had visitations from dead relatives, and had difficulty distinguishing fantasized from nonfantasized events and persons. As an adult, she was an excellent hypnotic subject.

Other fascinating examples of fantasy-prone persons can be found in science, the arts, and literature. Parrish (1897) described a phenomenon that he termed "the waking hallucinations of healthy persons." Purdy (1936), Vogt and Sultan (1977), Luria (1968), and Schatzman (1980) described "gifted" individuals with dramatic, highly unusual hallucinatory ability. Despite historical descriptions of persons with extraordinary fantasy talents, only in recent years has the constellation of personality attributes that comprises the syndrome of fantasy proneness been identified and studied in depth.

In this chapter we will present a summary of our research (Lynn & Rhue, 1985, 1986, 1987, 1988; Rhue & Lynn, 1985, 1987a, b, c, 1989 a, b; Rhue, Lynn, Henry, & Buhk, 1987, 1989) on people like Carla and Eileen Garett, with a particular focus on the developmental characteristics of fantasy-prone persons and the relation between psychopathology, multiple personality, and fantasy proneness. We will argue that many fantasy-prone persons can be described as receptive to internal and external events, as open to experience, and as sensitive to suggestion in a variety of contexts.

The examples of Carla and Eileen Garett only hint at the richness of fantasy-prone persons' imaginal lives. In a series of fascinating articles, Wilson and Barber (1981, 1983) described their serendipitous discovery of a group of individuals whom they alternately termed "fantasy addicts," "fantasy-prone personalities," and "fantasizers." Whereas fantasizers differed in many respects, they shared a deep, profound, and longstanding involvement in fantasy and imagination. Wilson and Barber contended that fantasizers' intense imaginal involvements represent manifestations of adaptive fantasy abilities at the extreme end of the continuum of the trait of fantasy proneness. Nevertheless, they estimated that fantasy proneness was evident in as much as 4% of the population.

Wilson and Barber discovered fantasizers in the context of an intensive interview study of excellent hypnotic subjects. In describing the characteristics of fantasy proneness, the researchers noted that their 27 excellent hypnotic subjects reported certain experiences with greater frequency than did the 25 nonexcellent (poor, medium, and medium-high susceptible) hypnotic subjects with whom they were compared. What sorts of experiences did their fantasizers report?

Fantasizers' most outstanding feature is their profound involvement in fantasy. Many reported spending at least half of their waking life fantasizing. They also reported the ability to hallucinate objects and to experience fully what they fantasize "as real as real." This included rich and vivid imagery before sleep, vivid recall of personal experiences, the achievement of orgasm in the absence of physical stimulation, and physical reactions, such as anxiety and nausea, to observed violence on television. Sixty percent of Wilson and Barber's female subjects reported that they had a false pregnancy at least once. Like Eileen Garett, many fantasizers also reported psychic and out-of-body experiences, and the occasional difficulty in differentiating fantasized events and persons from nonfantasized ones. Finally, fantasizers exhibited a sensitivity to social norms that resulted in a secret fantasy life to which few were privy. Many of the fantasizers interviewed felt that a burden of secrecy was lifted when they shared the details of their secret fantasy lives.

Fantasizers described their fantasies as vivid and creative. For instance, during a social conversation they might report that they typically see, hear, smell, and feel what is being described. When they became bored at a social gathering, they might escape by imagining that the people were clowns or by fantasizing themselves alone with a lover on an exotic tropical island.

Specific stimuli also set off correlated fantasies. For example, when a fantasizer heard the word "Egypt" she might imagine in detail her life as the wife of a pharaoh. While performing routine tasks at home or at work, they tended to fantasize that they were doing something else or were somewhere else. When fantasizers had free time, they would sit down or lie down and fantasize for fifteen minutes, or one or two hours. Many also set aside a special place solely for fantasizing. And when they were doing something unpleasant, many rewarded themselves with a sexual fantasy. In fact, Wilson and Barber reported that fantasizers' sexual fantasies were so real that 75% of the fantasizers reported that they have had orgasms produced solely by sexual fantasies.

Fantasizers who were asked what their lives would be like if they were never able to imagine or fantasize again found this question extremely distressing; they just could not imagine life without fantasizing. Many said they could not live more than a few hours without fantasizing; they compared the loss of fantasy to the loss of one or more of the senses, especially vision—it would be like going blind. In short, fantasy appeared to be an integral part of fantasizers' identities and their everyday lives.

These descriptions of fantasy-prone persons were so fascinating that we initiated an intensive research program to extend Wilson and Barber's exploratory research. Over the past eight years we have screened more than 7,000 college students in order to obtain seven samples of more than 200 fantasy-prone subjects. There was much to be learned: Wilson and Barber's sample was a select one (i.e., women) who were largely postgraduate professionals recruited from the ranks of participants in workshops the authors conducted, and from personal or professional relationships such as therapy clients. Also, Wilson and Barber did not use objective and empirically validated measures, the nature and administration of hypnotic suggestions was not standardized, and the precise hypnotizability levels of subjects were not reported. And finally, they did not have a comparison group of subjects who were truly low in hypnotizability or fantasy proneness.

Because Wilson and Barber believed that there was a close association between fantasy proneness and responses to suggestion, we investigated the relation between fantasy proneness, hypnotizability, and waking suggestion. Hypnotic suggestions invite subjects to focus directly on the hypnotist's communications, to engage in fantasy, and to give free rein to the imagination in line with suggested experiences. Wilson and Barber argued that fantasizers' lifetime history of intense fantasy, as well as their ability to have vivid images of past personal experiences, allow them quickly and easily to experience classical hypnotic phenomena (e.g., age regression and visual hallucinations).

Fantasizers, then, have well-practiced talents that are conducive to the successful experience of hypnosis.

There is ample support for the proposition that excellent hypnotic subjects are able to fantasize and imagine in accordance with hypnotic suggestions. However, they also seem able to respond to nonhypnotic activities that require a temporary diminution of rational, reality-bound analytical thinking. The concept of fantasy proneness derives from, and encompasses, the construct of imaginative involvement as elaborated by Josephine Hilgard (1970, 1974). Hilgard felt that imaginative involvement represented a central dimension underlying hypnotic responsiveness. She also found evidence to support her belief that the capacity for imaginative involvement facilitated a temporary absorption in satisfying experiences in which fantasy plays a prominent role. Allied to the concepts of fantasy proneness and imaginative involvement is the construct of "absorption" (Tellegen & Atkinson, 1974). Tellegen and Atkinson (1974) contended that the capacity for "absorbed" and self-altering attention represents an essential component of hypnotic susceptibility.

A number of studies support the dual constructs of absorption and imaginative involvement. These derive from early studies using inventories that documented an association between hypnotic susceptibility and imaginative involvements which were characterized by deep absorption and concentration, pleasure, and loss of awareness of external reality (Baum & Lynn, 1981). More recent studies using scales specifically designed to measure "absorption" have also provided confirmatory data (for reviews see Council, Kirsch, & Hafner, 1986; Spanos, 1986). These studies have documented a modest association ($r=.25-.40$) between hypnotic susceptibility and absorption.

At the outset we argued that there exists a relation between suggestibility and fantasy proneness. In addition to the research just cited, our studies of fantasizers support this association. In each of the studies that selected subjects on the basis of fantasy proneness, we used the Inventory of Childhood Memories and Imaginings (ICMI of Wilson & Barber, 1981) as a screening instrument. This questionnaire was adapted from the interview schedule used by Wilson and Barber in their research. To conform with Wilson and Barber's estimates of the prevalence of fantasy-prone persons in the population, we selected fantasizers who scored in the upper 2% to 4% of our sample. We contrasted the performance of these subjects with nonfantasizers who scored in the lower 2% to 4% and also with medium fantasy-prone subjects who scored in the range between the fantasizers' and the nonfantasizers' scores.

In our first study, we conducted an interview to validate subjects' fantasy-prone status. We also administered measures of hypnotizability, imagination, personality, and play and punishment history. In the interview, fantasy proneness was defined in terms of Wilson and Barber's (1983) definition of being able to establish a theme, and then create an imaginative scenario that unfolds with some of the characteristics of a dream, or sometimes a motion picture.

Subjects were screened in groups for fantasy proneness with the ICMI. Subjects who were invited to participate were informed that the 8–10 hour "study of personality" would be divided into five sessions. No set sequence of sessions was adhered to. In the first session, subjects were hypnotized using the Harvard Group Scale of Hypnotic Susceptibility (HGSHS: A; Shor & Orne, 1962). They also received the MMPI, a measure of personality functioning and adjustment. As a means of gauging the subjects' ability to function in an academic environment, subjects' official grade-point averages were obtained from the registrar.

In the second session, we examined subjects' responses to waking suggestions (Creative Imagination Scale of Wilson and Barber, 1978) and administered a measure of creativity (Barron-Welsh Revised Arts Scale, 1952) and a vividness of mental imagery scale (Sheehan, 1967). In the third session, subjects received the Rorschach Inkblot test. In the fourth session, they participated in a semi-structured interview for 1–5 hours; subjects were asked to be objective, and strong demands for honesty were made. In the fifth session, subjects participated in a reading absorption task.

Hypnotizability, imagination, and creativity

Our first study (Lynn and Rhue, 1986) supported the idea that fantasy-prone subjects are high hypnotizable, imaginative, and creative. Fantasizers outperformed less fantasy-prone subjects on measures of hypnotizability and vividness of imagery. However, fantasy proneness was not a perfect predictor of hypnotizability. In fact, more than a third of the nonfantasizers (35.29%) scored as high hypnotizables, and nonfantasizers were just as hypnotizable as medium fantasy-prone subjects. Nevertheless, an impressive number of fantasizers (nearly 80%) passed at least 9 of 12 suggestions and scored in the high-susceptible range. In addition, compared with less fantasy-prone subjects, fantasizers were more responsive to suggested experiences while awake.

Another finding of interest was that fantasizers were more creative than medium and nonfantasy-prone subjects, as measured by a test of subjects' preference for visual complexity of line drawings (Barron-Welsh Revised Arts Scale, 1952). In a recent study (Buhk, Rhue, Henry, & Lynn, 1988), we repeated this measure and replicated our earlier finding. We also found that fantasizers were more creative than nonfantasizers when tested with The Alternate Uses Test of Guilford (1978). This measure indexes divergent thinking ability by requiring subjects to generate multiple uses for well-known objects. In summary, fantasizers exhibited a facility for responding to suggestions, regardless of whether they were administered in a hypnotic or waking context. As documented by convergent measures, fantasizers were also more creative than less fantasy-prone subjects.

To examine the robustness of our hypnotizability findings, we (Rhue & Lynn, 1989a) varied the subject selection procedures and the conditions of testing. Rather than participating in an intensive, multisession interview study, subjects participated in a single-session group hypnosis experiment. Even when the conditions of testing were radically altered, the majority of fantasizers tested as high hypnotizable. Although fantasizers were more hypnotizable than nonfantasizers, fantasizers were no more hypnotizable than medium fantasy-prone subjects. Nonfantasizers emerged as the group distinctly lower in hypnotizability. This pattern of results was recently replicated by Huff and Council (1987) and by Siuta (in press) in Poland.

Wilson and Barber marshalled evidence that virtually equated high hypnotizability and fantasy proneness: 96% of their highly hypnotizable subjects were described as fantasizers. The fact that they selected subjects on the basis of their hypnotic talent rather than on the basis of their fantasy proneness could account for this impressive degree of association. To examine this possibility, we (Green, Rhue, Lynn, Williams, & Mare 1989) tested so-called hypnotic "virtuosos"—subjects who were required to pass at least 11 of 12 suggestions on both the Harvard Group Scale of Hypnotic Susceptibility and on the individually administered Stanford Hypnotic Susceptibility Scale (SHSS: C of Weitzenhoffer & Hilgard, 1962). These subjects scored within the upper 5% of our population. We compared these subjects' scores on our index of fantasy proneness with subjects who passed at least 11 or 12 suggestions on the Harvard Scale, but who were not screened on the SHSS: C. These subjects scored within the upper 10% of our population. These two groups were contrasted with subjects who scored in the 9–10 suggestion (high hypnotizable/nonstringently screened) range on the Harvard Scale, and finally, with subjects who scored in the 0–3 suggestion (low hypnotizable) range on the Harvard Scale.

The majority of subjects who scored at the extreme end of the hypnotizability distribution failed to conform to the profile of the fantasy-prone subject, as defined by scoring in the upper 4% of the distribution on the ICMI. In fact, only 2 of our 12 virtuosos (16.66%) scored as fantasizers on the ICMI. A similar frequency of subjects (12.82%; 5/39 subjects) who passed 11 or 12 Harvard Scale suggestions could be classified as fantasizers. In short, we were unsuccessful in approximating Wilson and Barber's findings. We found no evidence for an intimate connection between hypnotizability and fantasy proneness.

Although the majority of high hypnotizable subjects were not aptly described as fantasy-prone, high hypnotizable subjects were found to be more fantasy-prone than low hypnotizable subjects. However, only the subjects who passed at least 11 suggestions on the Harvard Scale were more fantasy-prone than the medium hypnotizable subjects. Subjects who were high hypnotizable but were nonstringently screened (passed 9 and 10 Harvard Scale suggestions) were no more fantasy-prone than were medium hypnotizable subjects. Finally, medium hypnotizable subjects were no more fantasy-prone than low hypnotizable subjects.

Our research secured evidence for only a modest degree of association between fantasy proneness and hypnotizability. The obtained correlation between hypnotizability and fantasy proneness ($r=.29$) is consistent with the results of many studies. Less correspondence exists between fantasy proneness and hypnotizability than Wilson and Barber's preliminary research suggested. Negative attitudes, lack of motivation, atypical interpretation of suggestions, and poor rapport with the hypnotist dampen responding in even highly imaginative subjects.

Developmental aspects of fantasy proneness

In addition to examining the relation between fantasizers' responsiveness to suggestion in waking and hypnotic contexts, we were also interested in addressing the following questions: if fantasizers' imaginal life is particularly gratifying, are there childhood antecedents that predispose subjects to use fantasy in adulthood? Despite the healthy emotional functioning attributed to fantasizers, do fantasy involvements represent an autistic retreat into a fantasy world as a result of an inability to cope effectively with reality? Or are there compensatory and adaptive functions of deep fantasy involvement?

If fantasy proneness serves an adaptive function in adulthood, then there ought to be ample evidence for its adaptive function in childhood. In fact, two developmental pathways to fantasy proneness have been identified. The first is encouragement to fantasize by a significant adult: We found that some fantasizers reported that a significant adult, such as a parent, grandparent, teacher, or friend encouraged and reinforced their fantasies, imaginal activities, and make-believe play experiences. Along with J.R. Hilgard (1970, 1974) and Wilson and Barber (1981), we found that these "encouraging" adults frequently read their children fairy tales and treated the child's dolls and stuffed animals "as if they were alive."

We (Rhue & Lynn, 1987c) measured parental encouragement to fantasize (e.g., direct encouragement to imagine and to read stories; parents' reading of stories, poems, or fairy tales) and also examined special life situations presumed to foster extensive fantasy involvement (e.g., music, art, dance, acting lessons). Only one factor was able to discriminate fantasizers from less fantasy-prone subjects; fantasizers reported more parental encouragement to read stories. Nevertheless, more than a third of our 21 subjects (38%) reported that their fantasy activities were encouraged by adults; this statistic is in close agreement with that reported by Wilson and Barber.

Freud (1959/1908) noted that "unsatisfied wishes are the driving power behind fantasies; every separate fantasy contains the fulfillment of a wish, and improves an unsatisfactory reality." More recently, researchers and writers (Fraiberg, 1968; Overstaad, 1981; Piaget, 1951; Singer, 1973) have underscored the adaptive and defensive function that fantasy serves in children who experience significant failure or frustration. This suggests that a second developmental pathway to fantasy proneness in later life is the use of fantasy and imaginative involvements in childhood as an escape from an aversive environment.

The finding by Rhue and Lynn (1987c) concerning physical punishment suggests that developmental pathway. In that study, 6 of the 21 fantasizers studied reported being severely abused as children (e.g., bruises, bleeding, or broken bones); none of the other subjects reported comparable punishment. Only 2 of these subjects also reported being encouraged to imagine by an adult. Relative to less fantasy-prone subjects, fantasizers reported a greater frequency and severity of physical punishment. They also reported being hit more even if they were good.

These findings harmonize with Wilson and Barber's reports that some fantasizers' histories included physical abuse and a parent who either deserted the family or had severe emotional problems. Earlier, Josephine Hilgard (1979) reported that hypnotic susceptibility and the more general trait of imaginative involvement were related positively to severity of childhood punishment. Recently Rhue, Lynn, Henry, Buhk, and Boyd (1990) contrasted groups of college students who reported being physically and sexually abused during childhood with comparison groups of students who reported the loss of a parent before age ten, and another group who reported that they were from an intact family. The groups of students who reported being physically and sexually abused had higher scores on the measure of fantasy proneness than the two comparison groups.

The fantasizers in our interview study reported a greater use of imagination to cope with pain and had more thoughts of revenge toward the punisher. However, they did not differ from other subjects in their ratings of the positivity of their early home environment. Imaginative abilities, then, may serve a functional role in minimizing physical and psychic pain and in preserving a relatively positive view of the abusive environment (Rhue & Lynn, 1987c).

The fantasizers we studied also reported greater loneliness, greater enjoyment of imaginary games, and greater enjoyment of solitary play and less enjoyment of playing with friends. This is consistent with the hypothesis that deep fantasy involvement has adaptive and perhaps compensatory functions.

Fantasy proneness and psychopathology

If fantasy proneness serves as an adaptive coping mechanism for certain individuals, it does not necessarily follow that all fantasizers are paragons of adjustment. Indeed, profound fantasy involvement might jeopardize psychological adjustment or pose special risks. For instance, psychological disorders might be byproducts of a chaotic, unregulated, or overly rigid and inflexible use of fantasy (Lynn & Rhue, 1988). Furthermore, fantasizers report experiences associated with psychotic or schizophrenic conditions. Hallucinatory experiences and the inability to distinguish fantasy from reality characterize many mental hospital inpatients with schizophrenic diagnoses. For certain persons, fantasy may assume gradually increasing importance and lead to a disengagement from everyday activities.

Many psychological disorders have a cognitive component that includes imagery and fantasy (e.g., phobias, schizophrenia, obsessive-compulsive disorder). So it is notable that the majority of Wilson and Barber's (1981) fantasy-prone subjects were described as creative, well-adjusted, high-functioning professionals who had earned post-graduate degrees in psychology, law, and medicine. Only a minority of the fantasizers were described as psychologically maladjusted.

To clarify the relation between fantasy proneness, psychological adjustment, and symptom report, we conducted five studies. Our first study (Rhue & Lynn, 1987b) was based on our initial sample of fantasizers who were interviewed and received the Rorschach and MMPI tests. Consistent with the construct of fantasy proneness, fantasizers scored higher than comparison subjects on measures of ideation thought to be associated with fantasy proneness. Their high scores on the MMPI schizophrenia (T=83.80) and F(T=71.42) scales are consonant with their willingness to report atypical experiences, including hallucinatory and paranormal experiences, and their occasional problems differentiating fantasy from reality. Fantasizers' reports of a rich fantasy life were consistent with Rorschach findings of high productivity of ideation and associative abilities.

The clinical elevations on the Schizophrenia and Hypomania (T =77.95) scales produced a modal MMPI profile with an 8/9 code type. This code-type was replicated in a study using the MMPI–168 (Lynn & Dudley, 1987). Rhue and Lynn (1989b) and Huff and Council (1987) found that fantasizers produced clinical elevations on scale 8, with the conditions of testing varying somewhat across studies. In the Rhue and Lynn (1989b) study, there also was a subclinical elevation on the Hypomania (9) scale, with it being the second highest elevation. Thus, MMPI scale 8 (Schizophrenia) consistently discriminates fantasizers and nonfantasizers in a college population.

Given that our sample was comprised of college students, these elevations can be interpreted as reflecting ideational productivity, unconventional and peculiar thinking, and perhaps greater alienation and preoccupation with an internal world of fantasy (Rhue & Lynn, 1987b). We believe that fantasizers' life histories of intense and gratifying fantasy involvements become associated with a heightened tolerance for unusual or atypical perceptions, experiences, and thoughts. Indeed, fantasizers perceived themselves as unique, creative, and at times, nonconforming individuals. As a group, fantasy-prone subjects did not show signs of severe psychopathology. They were successful in negotiating the academic demands of college and there were no indications of pathological or bizarre ideation in the interviews. Furthermore, Rorschach test data indicated that fantasizers displayed adequate reality testing, a rich affective and cognitive life, and a versatility of perceptual and associative cognitive processes (Rhue & Lynn, 1987b).

Our findings are consistent with the hypothesis that fantasy serves an adaptive and compensatory function in relatively nondefensive individuals. Fantasizers in our MMPI studies had higher elevations on MMPI Scale 6 (Paranoia) than the comparison groups. Their ideation also reflected greater projected hostility on the Rorschach-based Elizur Hostility Scale (Elizur, 1949) compared to the medium fantasy-prone subjects, with a strong trend toward greater hostility relative to the nonfantasizers (Rhue & Lynn, 1987b). The elevated paranoia scores just failed to reach the clinical range. This suggests the use of projective defenses, an interpretation complemented by "projected" hostility scores that fell within the neurotic range.

Given that two childhood pathways to fantasy proneness were abuse and isolation, it is not surprising that fantasy proneness occurs in individuals who show less ego strength and defensiveness (relatively low K MMPI scores) than do their less fantasy-prone counterparts. In the interviews, fantasizers reported using fantasy as an escape, as an outlet for anger, and as a means of regulating their internal life. Our results are consistent with Kris's (1952) hypothesis that some individuals use fantasy adaptively to modulate and channel ego dystonic impulses. This process promotes the integration of fantasy and imagination into everyday life (Lynn & Rhue, 1988).

Our initial study of adjustment did not examine fantasizers' self-perceptions, social relationships, and psychiatric history. Rhue and Lynn (1988) studied high, medium, and low fantasy-prone subjects and found that fantasizers were comparable to subjects in the comparison groups in terms of the number of close friends that they reported, the positivity of their self-concept, and their academic performance. Although fantasizers reported more problems, most fantasizers rated themselves in the range of extremely-to-moderately well-adjusted, and believed that others would rate them similarly. Fantasizers are apparently able to incorporate the perception of having relatively more problems into their broader self-concept and identity as fantasy-prone persons. We believe that fantasy proneness is adaptive in the sense that it may promote and preserve a positive self-concept.

Despite this picture of positive adjustment, adaptive imaginative tendencies and more pathological functioning appear to overlap, at least in a subset of fantasizers. For example, three fantasizers reported a history of psychiatric hospitalizations and a fourth rated himself as having "many psychological problems/poorly adjusted." In contrast, none of the subjects in the comparison groups reported such problems. Furthermore, 5 of the 23 fantasizers in the Rhue and Lynn (1987b) study showed signs of severe psychopathology on the personality tests. The common thread that runs through these fantasizers' backgrounds is a reported history of harsh and frequent childhood punishment. What these findings suggest is that a history of abuse, when combined with fantasy proneness, may predispose fantasizers to severe adjustment problems in adult life.

Our third study in this series provided additional evidence that a subset of fantasizers are more maladjusted than the general population (Lynn & Dudley, 1990). Fantasizers had relatively high scores on measures of psychosis proneness, magical thinking (Eckblad & Chapman, 1983), and what is termed perceptual aberration (Chapman, Chapman, & Raulin, 1976). Magical thinking is defined as the belief in conventionally invalid forms of causation, and perceptual aberration encompasses five kinds of schizophrenic body-image aberrations. Of the 13 fantasizers identified in our sample, 5 had extreme scores on the measures of psychosis proneness and unusual perceptions. In short, some degree of overlap exists between relatively healthy imaginative tendencies and pathological ideational processes in the fantasy-prone population.

Is fantasy proneness a byproduct or prominent feature of a personality disorder, or is it a distinct syndrome? Huff and Council (1987) found that fantasizers, relative to nonfantasizers, exhibited signs of greater personality pathology, including schizoid and borderline personality organization. The consistent findings of a link between measures of schizotopy and fantasy proneness, as well as our evidence for an association between fantasy proneness and measures of paranoia and projected hostility, suggest that at least some fantasizers might be appropriately classified as schizotypal and paranoid personalities. Wilson and Barber speculated that, in addition to exhibiting signs of regressed or primitive thought processes, fantasizers exhibit qualities characteristic of hysterics diagnosed during the nineteenth century. Our discussion suggests that it is worthwhile to examine whether the incidence of personality disorders is greater in fantasy-prone versus nonfantasy-prone populations.

To address these questions, we recruited a sample of 18 fantasizers and 12 subjects who scored within half a standard deviation above and below the mean of the ICMI screening instrument. Subjects were given a structured diagnostic interview (SCID-II; Spitzer, Williams, & Gibbon, 1987) designed to provide information required to diagnose personality disorders. Prior to the administration of the interview, acceptable diagnostic reliabilities were established.

Based on the interview, none of the nonfantasizers had personality disorders. In contrast, 2 of the fantasizers had one personality disorder (obsessive-compulsive and paranoid), and 2 other fantasizers had two or more personality disorders (paranoid and histrionic; histrionic, narcissistic, and borderline). Thus, 22.22% of the fantasizers exhibited symptoms of personality disorders. Our research suggests that there is no single personality disorder that universally accompanies fantasy proneness. Also fantasy proneness is generally not melded with, or confounded by, other longstanding, ingrained, cognitive-behavioral patterns of adaptation. The fact that two of the fantasizers had paranoid personality features is consistent with our previous MMPI findings. Along with the Rorschach data concerning projected hostility, the structured interview suggests that projection can be incorporated into fantasizers' cognitive activity as a distinct mode of adaptation. The fact that two of the subjects had histrionic features is consistent with impressionistic interview observations that a minority of fantasizers were flamboyant and had childlike, playful qualities (Lynn & Rhue, 1987).

The majority of fantasizers do not exhibit signs of maladjustment, although a minority of fantasizers exhibit signs of psychopathology. Whereas our research suggests that fantasy proneness is by no means a necessary precursor or concomitant of psychopathology, between 20–35% of the fantasizers we studied exhibited signs of maladjustment, psychopathology, or deviant ideation.

Fantasy proneness and multiple personality

It is conceivable that fantasizers' developmental history and attributes predispose them to certain disorders, psychological symptoms, or diagnoses. It is tempting to speculate that fantasizers are more likely to receive a diagnosis of dissociative disorder, particularly multiple personality. Child abuse is a developmental antecedent common to both fantasy proneness and multiple personality (Lynn, Rhue, & Green, 1988). The literature on multiple personality is replete with reports of discordant parental relations, childhood abuse, incest, and other types of trauma (Wilbur, 1984). Under these circumstances, certain persons may use fantasy as a psychic safety valve to minimize dysphoric affect, while developing an avoidant style of conflict and conflict resolution. This can extend to the creation of "believed-in-selves" that are nonetheless segregated from core aspects of the personality that escape the taint of abuse and maltreatment.

"Dissociation" has frequently been implicated as an important mechanism in the genesis and maintenance of multiple personality disorder (Spiegel, 1984). Dissociation can be thought of as an imagination-based cognitive strategy that involves the use of imagination and attentional strategies (e.g., amnesia, distraction, motivated forgetting). It creates a credible feeling of distance or separation from aversive events outside the realm of personal control or from feelings that generate guilt, anger, or anxiety. Dissociation is often viewed as an automatic process. However, we contend that it is an essentially creative process which is automatized only in the sense that much imagination and fantasy is experienced as spontaneous and not premeditated. Imagination, fantasy, and dissociation are goal-directed. They serve an active yet functional role in disavowing negative affect, disowning aspects of the self, and more generally, regulating internal experiences.

Given their imaginative proclivities, fantasizers are particularly likely to create believed-in-personas in childhood in order to buffer feelings of guilt, anger, and anxiety. Or it can simply be a form of recreational activity. This activity can be thought of as a dissociative cognitive strategy that is foremost a fantasy-based creative activity. Recently, Lynn, Rhue, and Green (1988) examined the characteristics of fantasy-prone subjects culled from a large sample of college students. Fantasizers indicated that their childhood make-believe world extended to the creation of imaginary friends and to imbuing stuffed animals and dolls with "life." Moreover, they created credible selves or characters that took on a life of their own in their childhood imaginations.

We have argued that a fine line exists between the creation of a pretend self and the development and elaboration of a persona that eventually comes to be viewed as a separate self (Lynn, Rhue, & Green, 1988). In fact, as we noted above, many physically abused and/or sexually abused children are probably well-practiced in the cultivation of a sense of separateness from their core self, one that they hope to preserve despite maltreatment. Fantasizers' reports of out-of-body experiences and a lack of awareness of engaging in seemingly goal-directed activities, such as writing stories, also suggest the use of imagination-based dissociative strategies.

There are many parallels between the attributes and developmental characteristics of fantasizers and multiples (Lynn, Rhue, & Green, 1988). Multiples are described as highly hypnotizable (see Bliss, 1984a; Spiegel, 1984). They frequently report imaginary playmates that were "every bit as real as friends or parents" (see Bliss, 1984a, p. 138; Fagan & McMahon, 1984). They also complain about an inability to distinguish between events and the hypnotic world (a "self-hypnotic trance" that they "withdraw into," Bliss, 1984b). Multiples report being lonely as children (Fagon & McMahon, 1984). The names given to their various personalities are frequently derived from personalities or fantasy characters from childhood (Stern, 1984). The most common feature of the multiple is a "very difficult childhood" (Hilgard, 1977). Additionally, multiples (Stern, 1984) and fantasizers (Council & Huff, in press; Wilson & Barber, 1981) both profess belief in paranormal experiences, and both report having out-of-body experiences and hysteric symptoms (Fagan & McMahon, 1984). Finally, research using the MMPI indicates that both adult multiple personalities (Bliss, 1984b; Solomon, 1983) and fantasizers score highest on the schizophrenia scale.

We have hypothesized that a harsh childhood environment, combined with fantasy proneness, increases the likelihood that a person will be diagnosed as a multiple (Lynn, et al., 1988). It may be the case that multiple personalities emerge in childhood as fantasy-based creations, along the lines we described. However, a different possibility is that certain cases of multiple personality are shaped or created by social forces in adulthood, including the use of hypnosis and suggestive procedures on the part of therapists who treat multiples (see also Spanos, Weekes, & Bertrand, 1985).

Which clients would be most prone to such influence? We maintain that fantasizers would be particularly vulnerable. This is because of the fluid boundaries between their senses of fantasy and reality, their ability to create diverse "believed-in selves," their use of fantasy for adaptive and defensive purposes, and their responsivity to hypnotic and suggestive procedures. This may be the reason why there exists such a high degree of commonality between the "multiple personality" and the fantasy-prone person.

Concluding comments

Research on fantasy-prone persons suggests that, in addition to sharing a history of imaginative involvements that may serve an adaptive and compensatory function, fantasizers can also be described as creative, suggestible, and open to experience. Nevertheless, our understanding of the role and function of profound fantasy and imagination in everyday life is at a very preliminary stage. For instance, it is necessary to investigate the validity and generalizability of our findings by assessing subjects' fantasies and imaginings in mundane, ecologically valid everyday life situations.

Questions can be raised about the representativeness of the population of fantasy-prone subjects who participate in experimental research. Fantasizers screened in studies like ours might be willing to endorse items that subjects, concerned about portraying a conventional image, are reluctant to endorse. An example would be a history of child abuse. In research we plan to undertake, we will examine the effects of different methods of recruiting fantasy-prone subjects.

Like other research in this area, the reliability of our developmental findings is limited by the retrospective nature of our research. It can also be argued that the reports of fantasizers are less reliable because their fantasy proneness is conducive to distortions and elaborations of their experiences. This is a distinct possibility that should be evaluated in future research. However, many of our findings are consonant with those of other studies in this research area and have a high degree of internal consistency.

It is important to resist the temptation to generalize the present results beyond the population tested. Fantasy-prone college students may represent a particularly well-adapted group of individuals who manifest an extensive history of imaginative involvements, yet retain a measure of cognitive control of their fantasy lives. We intend to examine the antecedents and concomitants of fantasy proneness in diverse populations, including patient groups, abused versus non-abused children, and the elderly.

We continue to be impressed by the diversity exhibited by fantasizers. Indeed, the term "fantasy-prone person" is misleading if used to denote a unified syndrome of affective, cognitive, and behavioral attributes. Fantasizers vary widely in their hypnotizability level, developmental history, and psychological adjustment. It is important to understand the determinants of fantasy in day-to-day life better, as a function not only of enduring qualities of the person but also of classes of situations that initiate or terminate fantasy and imaginal activities.

References

Barron, F., & Welsh, G. (1952). Artistic perception as a possible factor in personality style: Its measurement by a figure preference test. *Journal of Psychology, 33*, 199–203.

Baum, D., & Lynn, S.J. (1981). Hypnotic susceptibility level and reading involvement. *Journal of Clinical and Experimental Hypnosis, 29*, 366–74.

Bliss, E.L. (1984a). A symptom profile of patients with multiple personalities including MMPI results. *Journal of Nervous and Mental Disease, 172*, 197–202.

Bliss, E.L. (1984b). Hysteria and hypnosis. *Journal of Nervous and Mental Disease, 172*, 203-06.

Buhk, K., Rhue, J.W., Henry, S., & Lynn, S.J. (1988). Fantasy prones: Are their word associations richer? Meeting of the Society of Clinical and Experimental Hypnosis, Ashville, North Carolina.

Chapman, L.J., Chapman, L.P., & Raulin, M.L. (1976). Scales for physical and social anhedonia. *Journal of Abnormal Psychology, 85*, 374–82.

Council, J.R., & Huff, K.D. (in press). Hypnosis, fantasy activity, and reports of paranormal experiences in high, medium and low fantasizers. *British Journal of Clinical and Experimental Hypnosis.*

Council, J.R., Kirsch, I., & Hafner, L. (1986). Expectancy versus absorption in the prediction of hypnotic responding. *Journal of Personality and Social Psychology, 50,* 182–89.

Eckblad, M., & Chapman, L.J. (1983). Magical ideation as an indicator of schizotype. *Journal of Consulting and Clinical Psychology, 51,* 215–25.

Elizur, A. (1949). Content analysis of the Rorschach with regard to anxiety and hostility. *Rorschach Research Exchange, 13,* 247–84.

Fagan, J., & McMahon, P.P. (1984). Incipient multiple personalities in children. Four cases. *Journal of Nervous and Mental Disease, 172,* 26–36.

Fraiberg, S. (1968). *The magic years.* New York: Scribner's.

Freud, S. (1959/1908). Creative writers and daydreaming. In J. Strachey (ed.), *The standard edition of the complete works of Sigmund Freud* (Vol. XII, pp. 141–54). London: Hogarth.

Green, J., Rhue, J.W., Lynn, S.J., Williams, B., & Mare, C. (1989). Fantasy proneness in highly hypnotizable subjects. Meeting of the American Psychological Association, New Orleans.

Guilford, J.P., Christensen, P.R., Merrifield, P.R., & Wilson, R.C. (1978). *Alternate Uses, Forms B and C: Manual of instructions and interpretations.* Orange, CA: Sheridan Psychological Services, Inc.

Hilgard, E.R. (1977). *Divided consciousness: Multiple controls in human thought and action.* New York: Wiley.

Hilgard, J.R. (1970). *Personality and hypnosis: A study of imaginative involvement.* Chicago: University of Chicago Press.

Hilgard, J.R. (1974). Imaginative involvement: Some characteristics of the highly hypnotizable and nonhypnotizable. *International Journal of Clinical Experimental Hypnosis, 22,* 238–56.

Hilgard, J.R. (1979). Imaginative and sensory-affective involvement in everyday life and in hypnosis. In E. Fromm & R. Shor (eds.), *Hypnosis: Developments in research and new perspectives* (pp. 483–518). New York: Aldine Publishing.

Huff, K., & Council, J. (1987, August). *Fantasy proneness and psychological coping.* Paper presented at the meeting of the American Psychological Association, New York.

Kris, E. (1952). *Psychoanalytic explorations in art.* New York: International Universities Press.

Luria, A.R. (1968). *The mind of mnemonist.* New York: Basic Books.

Lynn, S.J., & Dudley, K. (1987). *The Magical Ideation Scale: A construct validation study.* Unpublished manuscript, Ohio University.

Lynn, S.J., & Dudley, K. (1990). Unpublished raw data.

Lynn, S.J., & Rhue, J.W. (September, 1985). Daydream believers. *Psychology Today,* 14–15.

Lynn, S.J., & Rhue, J.W. (1986). The fantasy-prone person: Hypnosis, imagination, and creativity. *Journal of Personality and Social Psychology, 51,* 404-08.

Lynn, S.J., & Rhue, J.W. (1987). Hypnosis, imagination, and fantasy. *Journal of Mental Imagery, 11,* 101–12.

Lynn, S.J., & Rhue, J.W. (1988). Fantasy-proneness: Hypnosis, developmental antecedents, and psychopathology. *American Psychologist, 43,* 35–44.

Lynn, S.J., Rhue, J.W., & Green, J.P. (1988). Multiple personality and fantasy proneness:

Is there an association or disassociation? *British Journal of Experimental and Clinical Hypnosis, 5,* 138–42.

Overstaad, B. (1981). *Bibliotherapy: Books to help young children.* St. Paul, MN: Toys 'n Things Press.

Parrish, J. (1987). *Hallucinations and illusions, a study of the fallacies of perception.* London: Scott.

Piaget, J. (1951). *Play, dreams and imitation in childhood.* New York: Norton.

Purdy, D. (1936). Eidetic imagery and plasticity of perception. *Journal of General Psychology, 15,* 437–54.

Rhue, J.W., & Lynn, S.J. (1985). *Correlates of fantasy proneness.* Paper presented to the meeting of the Midwest Psychological Association, Chicago.

Rhue, J.W., & Lynn, S.J. (1987a). *Fantasy proneness, absorption and hypnosis: A reexamination.* Unpublished manuscript.

Rhue, J.W., & Lynn, SJ. (1987b). Fantasy proneness and psychopathology. *Journal of Personality and Social Psychology, 53,* 327–36.

Rhue, J.W., & Lynn, S.J. (1987c). Fantasy proneness: Developmental antecedents. *Journal of Personality, 55,* 121–37.

Rhue, J.W., & Lynn, S.J. (1988). Fantasy proneness and extrasensory ability. 12th American Imagery Conference, San Diego.

Rhue, J.W., & Lynn, S.J. (1989a). Fantasy proneness, hypnotizability, and absorption—A reexamination. *The International Journal of Clinical Experimental Hypnosis, 37,* 100–06.

Rhue, J.W., & Lynn, S.J. (1989b). Hypnosis and beyond: Research on the fantasy prone person. *Hypnos, Swedish Journal of Hypnosis in Psychotherapy and Psychosomatic Medicine, 16,* 175–87.

Rhue, J.W., Lynn, S.J., Henry, S., & Buhk, K. (1987). Abuse during childhood: Does it facilitate the development of imaginative involvement? Meeting of the Southeastern Psychological Association.

Rhue, J.W., Lynn, S.J., Henry, S., & Buhk, K. (1989). Hypnosis, imagination, and child abuse: An update. Paper presented at The Society for Clinical and Experimental Hypnosis, St. Louis, Missouri.

Rhue, J.W., Lynn, S.J., Henry, S., Buhk, J., & Boyd, P. (1990). *Child abuse, imagination, and hypnotizability.* Unpublished manuscript.

Schatzman, M. (1980). *The story of Ruth.* New York: Putnam.

Sheehan, P.W. (1967). A shortened form of Betts' Questionnaire Upon Mental Imagery. *Journal of Clinical Psychology, 23,* 386–89.

Shor, R.E., & Orne, E.C. (1962). *Harvard Group Scale of Hypnotic Susceptibility, Form A.* Palo Alto, CA: Consulting Psychologists Press.

Singer, J. (1973). *The child's world of make-believe.* New York: Academic Press.

Siuta, J. (in press). Fantasy proneness in a Polish sample. *British Journal of Clinical and Experimental Hypnosis.*

Solomon, R. (1983). Use of the MMPI with multiple personality patients. *Psychological Reports, 53,* 1004-06.

Spanos, N.P. (1986). Hypnotic behavior: A social-psychological interpretation of amnesia, analgesia, and "trance logic." *Behavioral Brain Science, 9,* 442–502.

Spanos, N.P., Weekes, J.R., & Bertrand, L.D. (1985). Multiple personality: A social psychological perspective. *Journal of Abnormal Psychology, 9,* 362–76.

Spiegel, D. (1984). Hypnosis with medical/surgical patients. *General Hospital Psychiatry, 5,* 265–77.

Spitzer, R.L., Williams, J.B.W., & Gibbon, M. (1987). Structured clinical interview for DSM-III-R-Personality Disorders. New York: New York State Psychiatric Institute.

Tellegen, A., & Atkinson, G. (1974). Openness to absorbing and self-altering experiences ("absorption"), a trait related to hypnotic susceptibility. *Journal of Abnormal Psychology, 83,* 268–77.

Vogt, D., & Sultan, G. (1977). *Reality revealed: The theory of multidimensional reality.* San Jose, CA: Vector Associates.

Weitzenhoffer, A.M., & Hilgard, E.R. (1962). *Stanford Hypnotic Susceptibility Scale, Form C.* Palo Alto, CA: Consulting Psychologists Press.

Wilbur, C.B. (1984). Treatment of multiple personalities. *Psychiatric Annals, 14,* 27–31.

Wilson, S.C., & Barber, T.X. (1978). The Creative Imagination Scale as a measure of hypnotic responsiveness: Applications to experimental and clinical hypnosis. *American Journal of Clinical Hypnosis, 20,* 235–49.

Wilson, S.C., & Barber, T.X. (1981). Vivid fantasy and hallucinatory abilities in the life histories of excellent hypnotic subjects ("somnambules"): Preliminary report with female subjects. In E. Klinger (ed.), *Imagery, Volume 2: Concepts, results, and applications* (pp. 158–72). New York: Plenum.

Wilson, S.C., & Barber, T.X. (1983). The fantasy-prone personality: Implications for understanding imagery, hypnosis, and parapsychological phenomena. In A.A. Sheikh (ed.), *Imagery: Current theory, research, and application* (pp. 340–87). New York: Wiley.

11

HYPNOTIZABILITY, SUGGESTIBILITY, AND PSYCHOPATHOLOGY:

An Overview of Research

Gary Groth-Marnat

Some of the earliest discoveries of modern psychology were inspired by attempts to understand the relation between hypnosis and psychopathology. Charcot (1890) and Janet (1920) both emphasized the dissociative aspects of hypnotic states and believed that hypnosis was characteristic of severe neurological and mental dysfunction. In contrast, Bernheim (1888) emphasized the importance of suggestion and associated hypnosis with normal psychological function. Numerous outmoded concepts have also been used to explain hypnotizability and psychopathology, including animal magnetism, somnambulism, magical forces, monomania, vapors, lunacy, and frenzy. This has resulted in what Sarbin and Coe (1979) have referred to as a "graveyard of abandoned beliefs." Despite continued controversy in many areas, recent empirical research has more clearly established the extent and importance of hypnotizability among different diagnostic groups. The purpose of the following overview is to summarize relevant research related to these groups, develop generalizations suggested by the results of the research, and suggest future directions.

Understanding hypnotizability and psychopathology has relevance in helping to reveal more fully the different causative factors as well as the most effective means of treating some types of disorders. For example, persons who are naturally hypnotizable might be predisposed to develop post-traumatic stress disorder (Spiegel, Hunt, & Dondershine, 1988) or bulimia (Groth-Marnat & Schumaker, 1990; Pettinati, Horne, & Staats, 1985). Dissociative abilities might be an important factor in the maintenance of some disorders, such as multiple personality (Brassfield, 1983) and hysterical psychosis (Steingard & Frankel, 1985). The effective treatment both of pain and of a wide number of psychophysiological conditions has also been related to hypnotic responsiveness (see Bowers & Kelly, 1979; Hilgard & Hilgard, 1983; Perry, Gelfand, & Marcovitch, 1979). A positive outcome in psychotherapy has often been predicted based on high levels of hypnotizability even when hypnosis was not used as the method of treatment (Nace, Warwick, Kelly, & Evans, 1982). Furthermore, hypnotic suggestibility has been used as a model to investigate experimentally different psychopathological processes such as delusions, hallucinations, and dissociation (see Blum & Barbour, 1979; Kihlstrom, 1979).

Suggestibility and psychopathology

The research on suggestibility has centered on (1) its relationship to hypnosis, (2) a trait of personality, and (3) suggestibility as a psychosocial phenomenon (Gheorghiu, 1989). Despite these different approaches to suggestibility, nearly all the work on suggestibility and psychopathology has been done within the context of hypnotizability. Indeed, very few studies have been performed on specific diagnostic categories and their relation to nonhypnotic suggestibility such as conformity, social suggestibility, placebo response, gullibility, persuasion, and interrogative suggestibility. This paucity of studies is due, in part, to the lack of a fully developed composite test of nonhypnotic suggestibility. Tests of nonhypnotic suggestibility appear to measure widely varying, and possibly unrelated types of behavior, such as susceptibility to suggestions for body sway (body sway test), or the degree to which a person is influenced by interrogation (interrogative suggestibility). On the other hand, an extensive body of research has accumulated around carefully developed tests of hypnotizability.

The research that has been performed on psychopathology and nonhypnotic suggestibility has often produced contradictory results. For example, it was initially found that neurotics responded more to body sway than normals (Eysenck, 1947; Furneaux, 1952; Ingham, 1954). Stukat (1958) countered this by his findings that neurotics were not highly susceptible to motor suggestibility tests such as body sway, but were more susceptible than normals to social influence. Barber (1964) reviewed and contradicted all of the above findings by concluding that neurotics did not differ from normals on either tests of suggestibility or tests of hypnotizability. More recent studies have found that neurotics and persons with low self-esteem were more susceptible than normals to interrogative suggestibility (Gudjonsson, 1983; Gudjonsson & Lister, 1984).

The distinction between hypnotic and nonhypnotic suggestibility is difficult to draw. Implied in any discussion of hypnotizability is the central issue of suggestibility. However, hypnotizability is a complex group of related skills involving not only suggestibility, but also absorption, dissociation, control of mental imagery, fantasy proneness, role enactment, and attention (see Evans, 1967, 1989; Gheorghiu, 1989; Hilgard, 1987). Equally important are such factors as rapport, expectation, motivation, persuasion, previous experience with hypnosis, and the context of induction. Furthermore, suggestion is not a necessary feature of hypnosis (Hammer, Walker, & Diment, 1978) and the relation between hypnotizability and waking suggestibility is not clearly understood (Evans, 1967, 1989; Miller, 1980). Thus any review of hypnotizability and psychopathology needs to take into account the multidimensionality of measures of hypnotizability.

Hypnotizability and general measures of adjustment

Early research failed to find a clear relationship between hypnotizability and specific personality features, including level of adjustment (Sarbin & Madow, 1947; Schafer, 1947). However, Barber (1956) and Levitt, Brady, and Lubin (1963) reported that hypnotizability was related to greater emotional stability and lower levels of anxiety. A more recent comparison between high and low susceptible college students indicated that the students who were most susceptible to hypnosis had higher self-regard, greater sensitivity to nuance, and were more likely to focus on unusual details. In addition, they were found to be more introverted. In contrast, low susceptibles had lower self-regard, a more global mode of perception, greater anxiety, and were more extroverted (Zlotogorski, Hahnemann, & Wiggs, 1987). The authors concluded that people who are anxious, guarded, and have low self-regard would have a more difficult time with hypnotic tasks. While fantasy proneness is not identical to hypnotizability, moderate correlations have been found between the two constructs (Lynn & Rhue, 1986). Similarly, fantasy-prone groups have been found to have a more positive self-concept and be relatively healthy when compared with low fantasizers (Lynn & Rhue, 1986, 1988). However, there is a subgroup of high fantasizers who appear to have significantly more personal difficulties than the general population (Lynn & Dudley, 1987).

Most groups of psychiatric patients have lower levels of hypnotizability than non-psychiatric controls. The more severe the disorder, the lower the level of hypnotizability. For example, Spiegel, Detrick, and Frischolz (1982) supported earlier studies (Spiegel & Spiegel, 1978; Spiegel, Fleiss, & Bridger, 1975) in their assessment of the hypnotizability of psychiatric patients. These included patients with thought disorders, generalized anxiety, affective disorders, and miscellaneous disorders. None of the clinical groups were as hypnotizable as the normal controls. Spiegel and his colleagues concluded that the anxious preoccupation associated with many psychiatric difficulties disrupts the concentration required for hypnotic dissociation, a view shared by Zlotogorski, et al. (1987). Furthermore, trance-type states may work as an effective coping mechanism to defend against anxiety. Persons who lack this ability are thus likely to be more vulnerable to anxiety.

Hypnotizability among psychotics

Although the issue is both controversial and complex, studies of psychotics have generally found them to be one of the least hypnotizable of any group (Lavoie & Sabourin, 1980; Spiegel, et al., 1982). This has been found to be particularly true for chronic schizophrenics (Lavoie & Sabourin, 1980). Even among psychotics, those who were most hypnotizable in relation to other psychotics were found to be relatively healthy. Specifically, the relatively hypnotizable psychotics had fewer behavioral deviations, greater adaptive regression, and less involvement with primary process thinking (Lavoie, Sabourin, & Ally, 1976). Many studies have been performed attempting to establish the hypnotizability of psychotics. But conclusions should be made cautiously, since most studies have not taken into account such crucial factors as age, chronicity of the illness, accuracy of diagnosis, repeated measures of hypnotizability throughout the course of the illness, degree of contact with reality, and level of patient cooperativeness (Pettinati, 1982).

Although psychotics may not have high scores on hypnotizability, they still may have significant hypnotic-like processes such as dissociation, absorption, vivid internal imagery, and fantasy proneness. Indeed, schizophrenia has sometimes been conceptualized as a hypnotic suggestion from within, which results in the patient becoming a passive (hidden) observer who is dissociated (split) from his or her experience (i.e., Bowers, 1961; King, 1970). Psychotics' low scores on formal tests of hypnotizability might be due simply to difficulties in controlling these processes, as well as deficiencies regarding rapport, communication, attention, and motivation.

Disorders characterized by high hypnotizability

Despite the finding that most disorders have relatively low levels of hypnotizability, a subgroup of disorders are characterized by unusually high hypnotizability. These include hysteria, multiple personality, post-traumatic stress disorder, anorexia/bulimia, and phobias. Most of these disorders involve dissociation, relatively low levels of anxiety, good concentration, relatively intact communication skills, the ability to develop good rapport, and high motivation.

Hysteria

Historically, hysteria has always maintained close links with hypnosis. This link was inevitable, given that both hysteria and hypnosis involve dissociation, rapport with another person, a field of interaction, and the interdependence of psychological and physiological processes (Chertok, 1974). Furthermore, most hysterical symptoms can be developed in normal hypnotizable subjects through hypnotic suggestion (i.e., Sackeim, Nordlie, & Gur, 1979). Charcot, Freud, Breuer, and Janet all used hypnosis as a means of understanding and treating hysteria. Knowledge relating to hysteria was then used to conceptualize general principles of the unconscious, and to understand the role of dissociation in psychiatric illness. The early treatment of hysteria was primarily by means of hypnosis. However, Freud's abandonment of hypnosis resulted in a loss of interest among later generations of psychoanalysts.

Numerous case histories extending over the past hundred years provide extensive anecdotal evidence of the presence of high hypnotizability among hysterics. Despite this, surprisingly few studies have been performed using formal hypnotic susceptibility scales with samples of hysterics (or the DSM-III variants of conversion reaction or histrionic personality). Noteworthy exceptions are studies by Bliss (1983, 1984) and Bendefeldt, Miller, and Ludwig (1976), who found high levels of hypnotizability among samples of patients with conversion symptoms. Similarly, Bliss (1984) found high levels of hypnotizability among a sample of severe hysterics (Briquet's Syndrome). In addition, hysterical psychosis has been found to be both an extreme expression of a hysterical personality disorder, and has been isolated as a clearly different diagnostic category than psychosis. One of the major distinguishing features of hysterical psychosis is a high level of hypnotizability, whereas other groups of psychotics have markedly low levels of hypnotizability (Steingard & Frankel, 1985; Spiegel & Fink, 1979).

Multiple personality disorder

Similar to hysteria, most of the evidence for high hypnotizability among multiple personalities comes from extensive case histories.

Quantitative studies also reveal that multiple personalities have heightened hypnotizability levels (Bliss, 1980, 1983, 1984). In addition, Bliss (1984) has noted a wide diversity of symptoms among multiple personalities, including obsessions, phobias, depression, hysteria, hyperactivity, and sociopathy.

Case studies of multiple personalities have typically been used to illustrate the dramatic extent to which the personality can be dissociated into different components. Dissociation has often been sufficiently complete for psychophysiological changes to be different for each of the discrete personalities (Braun, 1983). The histories typically reveal an extremely high level of child abuse to which the patient has originally adapted through fantasy and dissociation (Brassfield, 1983; Horton & Miller, 1972). The dissociation is adaptive in that it allows for denial, as well as a discharge of unacceptable rage through another "portion" of the personality. It also conceals guilt related to anger, and grief stemming from the perceived loss of a loved person. A person's sense of helplessness may also be reduced. Beahrs (1983) has argued that the heightened levels of dissociative abilities, in and of themselves, do not create the person's difficulties. It is rather the transfer of control of these abilities. Thus therapy has typically capitalized on the individual's heightened levels of hypnotizability to integrate the different levels of personality. Ideally the treatment paradigm becomes that of taking dissociative phenomenon from the realm of the dysfunctional to that of healthy co-consciousness, so that "what was once a symptom becomes a skill" (Beahrs, 1983, p. 105).

Post-traumatic stress disorder

Post-traumatic stress disorder (PTSD) has been studied much more recently than either hysteria or multiple personalities. However, many of the dynamics between multiple personality and PTSD are quite similar. Both disorders involve dissociation as a means of adaptive protection from unacceptable memories. These memories are then discharged during spontaneous trance states. Spiegel (1984) has even argued that multiple personality can be conceptualized as a type of PTSD. He points out that both types of patients have been victims of trauma. They experience extreme helplessness, surrender to the situation, and have a constriction of mental processes. Both disorders are also characterized by heightened levels of hypnotizability (Bliss, 1984, 1985; Spiegel, 1984; Spiegel, et al., 1988). Spiegel, et al. (1988) theorize that actual traumas experienced by multiple personalities and persons with PTSD are typically experienced in a dissociated state. Later spontaneous trance states produce a recovery of the experience. The trance states help to explain both the intrusiveness of the recollections, as well as their intense, abreactive quality (state-dependent learning). This may result in extremes of experience in which the victims "alternate between intense, vivid, and painful memories and images associated with the traumatic experience and a kind of pseudonormality in which the victims avoid such memories using traumatic amnesia, other forms of dissociation, or repression, with a reduction in adaptive capacity and a constriction of the range of affective response" (Spiegel, et al., 1988, p. 301). Accompanying symptoms frequently include depersonalization, amnesias, and hallucinations (Spiegel, et al., 1988).

Anorexia nervosa and bulimia

Anorexia nervosa and bulimia are caused and maintained by a complex number of interacting factors, including a culture which emphasizes thinness, family enmeshment, repetitive thoughts related to food intake, entry into an eating disorders subculture, satisfaction of sensation needs, biological predispositions, and adaptive resolution of the challenges of adolescence (see Bruch, 1977; Schumaker, Groth-Marnat, Small, & Macaruso, 1986; Striegel-Moore, Silberstein, & Rodin, 1986). In addition, hypnotizability may be a significant factor. From a rational perspective, anorexia nervosa and bulimia can be conceptualized as an overincorporation of Western society's all-pervasive suggestion to "be thin." These disorders can therefore be classified as "culture bound syndromes" (Schumaker & Groth-Marnat, 1988; Swartz, 1985). These suggestions might then become incorporated as a result of repetitive autosuggestions regarding weight regulation and food intake. The disorder could then become self-maintaining and based on the single ruling motivation for weight regulation, or what Kaffman (1989) has referred to as a "monoideism" (see Kaffman's chapter in this volume). In addition, clinical observations have noted hypnotic-like phenomena involved with the perceptual distortions regarding body size and the involuntary behaviors associated with binging and purging. Moshe (1986) has suggested that there is a subgroup of persons with eating disorders who express a wide variety of dissociative behaviors.

Formal research supports the view that anorexia nervosa and bulimia involve heightened levels of suggestibility. Pettinati, et al. (1985) reported that bulimics were highly hypnotizable, whereas anorexics were only slightly more hypnotizable than a normative group. However, anorexics who purged were more hypnotizable than either restricting anorexics or normative controls (Pettinati, Kogan, Margolis,

Shrier, & Wade, 1989). In contrast, Bliss (1982, 1983) found greater hypnotizability among anorexics when compared with normative groups. A possible difficulty with Bliss's study might have been that the diagnostic criteria for anorexia nervosa was not clearly specified and it might have included a number of bulimics. Increased hypnotizability was also found among college females with unusually high concerns about food regulation and weight control (Groth-Marnat & Schumaker, 1990). In addition, high school females who reported the greatest tendency to engage in extreme dieting behaviors also showed the greatest reduction in these attitudes following a videotape presentation depicting the dangers associated with radical weight control measures (Schumaker, Groth-Marnat, & Harris, 1987).

The above findings implicate high levels of hypnotizability in bulimics, and possibly in anorexics as well. Theoretically, the waking suggestibility component of hypnotizability might be significant in the preonset stages of anorexia nervosa and bulimia. This is consistent with the observation that the "enmeshed" families of anorexics (and many bulimics) limit the patient's individuation, and demand excessive conformity (Attie & Brooks-Gunn, 1989; Bruch, 1977; Minuchin, Rosman, Baker, & Leiberman, 1978). Families which demand excessive conformity appear to produce persons with high levels of hypnotizability (Long, 1968; Shames, 1981). Thus the pre-onset anorexic would be highly responsive to the acceptance or overacceptance of shared beliefs ("be thin") within their family and culture. The pre-onset anorexic is typically described as compliant, suggestible, obsessive, perfectionistic, and introverted (Bruch, 1977). On the other hand, the post-onset anorexic has been described as stubborn, resistant, secretive, rebellious, and difficult to treat. Thus the disorder seems to become self-maintaining, which is consistent with Kaffman's formulation of it as a monoideistic disorder perpetuated through autohypnosis. Perceptual distortions of body image might also help to perpetuate the disorder. The involuntary behaviors associated with binging and purging in bulamarexics and bulimics are consistent with dissociative states and could also be important reinforcing factors. In addition, hypnosis has been effectively used for treating anorexia nervosa by correcting distorted body images, fostering appropriate autonomy, reducing perfectionistic tendencies, reinforcing a healthy self-image, reducing hyperactivity, enhancing self-esteem, and educating the person regarding his or her spontaneous dissociative states (Baker & Nash, 1987; Gross, 1984; Pettinati, et al., 1989). Thus different aspects of hypnotizability, including waking suggestibility, autosuggestion, perceptual distortions, and dissociation might be important in the development, maintenance, and treatment of anorexia nervosa and bulimia.

Phobic disorder

It has been speculated that highly hypnotizable persons who have difficulty coping with stress might more easily develop phobic disorders. The phobic beliefs can be conceptualized as perceptual distortions reinforced by autosuggestion occurring during spontaneous dissociative states. This is consistent with the majority of studies on phobics, which have found that they have high levels of hypnotizability (Foenander, Burrows, Gerschman, & Horne, 1980; Frankel & Orne, 1976; John, Hollander, & Perry, 1983). However, Frischolz, Spiegel, Spiegel, Balma, and Markell (1982) did not find higher levels of hypnotizability among phobics when they were compared with comparison groups of smokers and pain patients.

Miscellaneous disorders

A number of additional difficulties have been sporadically researched and found to be associated with hypnotizability. The occurrence of non-physically based persistent medical symptoms might in part be unknowingly produced and maintained through direct or indirect suggestions on the part of physicians (Haberman, 1987). This is likely to occur among persons who are highly hypnotizable and who are unconsciously seeking to legitimize their difficulties. Conflicting results have been reported regarding obesity. Whereas Thorne, Rasmus, and Fisher (1976) reported high levels of hypnotizability, Deyoub (1978) reported levels which did not differ from normal controls. In addition, sexual offenders (rape, pedophilia, incest) have been found to be above average in hypnotizability (Bliss & Larson, 1985). Finally, suggestibility may be one of a variety of factors in the development and maintenance of *folie à deux* (Soni & Rockley, 1974).

Difficulties related to group effects on behavior are beyond the scope of this review, but are worth noting since they all involve suggestion. This includes the spread of hysterical symptoms in work environments (i.e., Kerchoff & Back, 1968), the spread of individual suicides following a highly publicized suicide (Phillips, 1974), and deindividuation in crowds leading to antisocial behavior (i.e., Mann, 1981; Festinger, Newcomb, & Pepitone, 1952). Each of these areas has been thoroughly researched and conceptualized within a social psychological context.

Discussion and conclusion

A central issue relating to hypnotizability and psychopathology is the significance of hypnotizability in relation to each disorder. But is it a mere epiphenomenon, or a central aspect of the disorder? For example, dissociation may be the core feature in multiple personalities and would therefore be essential to the development and maintenance of the disorder. Or, hypnotizability might be relatively less important in bulimia since the person's family, media images, entry into an eating disorders subculture, and developmental crises might be relatively more important. Hypnotic-like states might also serve as coping mechanisms which allow for the discharge of negative affect such as in multiple personalities. PTSD might involve state-dependent learning, which occurs during the trauma and is vividly recovered when the person later develops spontaneous trance states. Of particular importance is the cause-effect relation of hypnotizability; does a predisposition to become easily hypnotized make a person more susceptible to certain types of disorders, or do the events which cause the disorders also cause increased hypnotizability? Would this then mean that some persons were more resistant to a disorder such as combat stress if they were relatively unhypnotizable? The above issues need to be integrated into a clear theory of hypnotizability, both in relation to the specific disorders as well as to psychopathology in general. This should include longitudinal and experimental research designs, as well as the usual approaches measuring differences between groups.

Whereas the association between hypnotizability and specific types of disorders is relatively well established, the relation between nonhypnotic suggestibility has been only minimally investigated. For example, are bulimics or persons with PTSD also more susceptible to social compliance, placebo response, or interrogative suggestibility? If so, why might this be the case? Furthermore, how do such constructs as fantasy proneness and absorption relate to specific psychopathologies? Do they relate in similar or different ways as hypnotizability, and if so, why?

Very few studies have taken into consideration the implications of the context of the assessment or the nature of hypnotizability tests themselves. Thus different results might have been achieved within a classroom as opposed to clinic, hospital, or military facility. Little attention has also been paid to the importance of motivation, rapport, expectation, prestige of the examiner, or rationale for the experiment as perceived by the subjects. For example, a schizophrenic might potentially have excellent hypnotic-like abilities but, due to difficulties with interpersonal rapport, might have difficulties expressing these abilities. Likewise, competitive, controlling patients might resist the benevolent authoritarian approach inherent in most formal tests of susceptibility. More permissive, indirect wording might produce quite different results regarding either hypnotic or nonhypnotic suggestibility (Barber, 1980). This underscores the larger issue that most research on hypnotizability is imbedded in mechanistic linear thinking rather than an interacting systems approach (Fourie & Lifschitz, 1988; Sarbin & Coe, 1979). Hypnotizability (or psychopathology itself) is seen as existing within the person rather than within the context or interface between people. Changing the context or mode of interaction might result in quite different levels of hypnotizability, especially among patient groups.

The material contained in this overview proceeds from the perspective that people with different types of pathology have varying levels of hypnotizability. Again, it needs to be stressed that high hypnotizability, in and of itself, does not suggest psychopathology. In fact, there is good evidence that higher hypnotizability among nonpatient groups is associated with positive mental health (Zlotogorski, Hahnemann, & Wiggs, 1987).

Despite the above controversies and unanswered questions, there are a number of generalizations which can be made regarding hypnotizability and psychopathology. Persons with low hypnotic susceptibility tend to be anxious, guarded, constricted, and to have difficulties controlling their internal images, absorbing themselves in tasks, or establishing interpersonal rapport. Thus psychotic disorders (especially chronic schizophrenia), generalized anxiety disorders, and affective disorders are associated with low levels of hypnotic susceptibility. Higher levels of hypnotizability are found in disorders in which the person can concentrate effectively, understand communication accurately, develop a good level of rapport, become highly motivated, and maintain lower levels of anxiety. The disorders themselves might have been the result of specific hypnotic abilities such as waking suggestibility, autosuggestion, dissociation, spontaneous trance, or perceptual distortions. As a result, multiple personality, PTSD, hysteria (conversion reaction, Briquet's syndrome, hysterical psychosis, histrionic personality), phobias, bulimia, and possibly anorexia nervosa all show high levels of hypnotizability. Although the differences in hypnotizability among different clinical populations has become more clearly established, the significance of these disorders requires much further investigation.

References

Attie, I., & Brooks-Gunn, J. (1989). Development of eating problems in adolescent girls: A longitudinal study. *Developmental Psychology, 25*, 70–79.

Baker, E.L., & Nash, M.R. (1987). Applications of hypnosis in the treatment of anorexia nervosa. *American Journal of Clinical Hypnosis, 29,* 185–93.

Barber, J. (1980). Hypnosis and the unhypnotizable. *American Journal of Clinical Hypnosis, 23,* 4–9.

Barber, T.X. (1956). A note on "hypnotizability" and personality traits. *International Journal of Clinical and Experimental Hypnosis,* 109–14.

Barber, T.X. (1964). Hypnotizability, suggestibility, and personality: A critical view of research findings. *Psychological Reports, 14,* 299–320.

Beahrs, J.O. (1983). Co-consciousness: A common denominator in hypnosis, multiple personality, and normalcy. *American Journal of Clinical Hypnosis, 26,* 100–13.

Bendefeldt, F., Miller, L.L., & Ludwig, A.M. (1976). Cognitive performance in conversion hysteria. *Archives of General Psychiatry, 33,* 1250–54.

Bernheim, H. (1888). *Hypnosis and suggestion in psychotherapy.* (Repr. New York: University Books, 1964.)

Bliss, E.L. (1980). Multiple personalities : A report of 14 cases with implications for schizophrenia and hysteria. *Archives of General Psychiatry, 37,* 1388–97.

Bliss, E.L. (1982). The psychology of anorexia nervosa. In M. Gross (ed.), *Anorexia nervosa.* Lexington, MA: Collamore Press.

Bliss, E.L. (1983). Multiple personalities, related disorders and hypnosis. *American Journal of Clinical Hypnosis, 26,* 114–23.

Bliss, E.L. (1984). Hysteria and hypnosis. *Journal of Nervous and Mental Disease, 172,* 203–06.

Bliss, E.L., & Larson, E.M. (1985). Sexual criminality and hypnotizability. *Journal of Nervous and Mental Disease, 173,* 522–26.

Blum, G.S., & Barbour, J.S. (1979). Selective inattention to anxiety-linked stimuli. *Journal of Experimental Psychology: General, 108,* 182–224.

Bowers, K.S., & Kelly, P. (1979). Stress, disease, psychotherapy, and hypnosis. *Journal of Abnormal Psychology, 88,* 490–505.

Bowers, M.K. (1961). Theoretical considerations in the use of hypnosis in the treatment of schizophrenia. *International Journal of Clinical and Experimental Hypnosis, 9,* 39–46.

Brassfield, P.A. (1983). Unfolding patterns of the multiple personality through hypnosis. *American Journal of Clinial Hypnosis, 26,* 146–52.

Braun, B.G. (1983). Neurophysiologic changes in multiple personality due to integration: A preliminary report. *American Journal of Clinical Hypnosis, 26,* 84–92.

Bruch, H. (1977). Psychological antecedents of anorexia nervosa. In R. A. Vigersky (ed.), *Anorexia nervosa.* New York: Raven Press.

Charcot, J.M. (1890). *Oeuvres completes, tome IX.* Paris: Lecrosnier et Babe.

Chertok, L. (1974). Hysteria, hypnosis, and psychopathology. *Medicina Psicosomatica, 19,* 341–51.

Deyoub, P.L. (1978). Relation of suggestibility to obesity. *Psychological Reports, 43,* 175–80.

Evans, F.J. (1967). Suggestibility in the normal waking state. *Psychological Bulletin, 67,* 114–29.

Evans, F.J. (1989). The cognitive and interpersonal components of suggestibility. In

V.A. Gheorghiu, P. Netter, H.J. Eysenck, & R. Rosenthal (eds.), *Suggestion and suggestibility: Theory and research.* New York: Springer-Verlag.

Eysenck, H.J. (1947). *Dimensions of personality.* London: Routledge and Kegan Paul.

Festinger, L., Pepitone, A., & Newcomb, T. (1952). Some consequences of de-individuation in a group. *Journal of Abnormal and Social Psychology, 47,* 382–89.

Foenander, G., Burrows, G.D., Gerschman, J., & Horne, D. (1980). Phobic behavior and hypnotic susceptibility. *Australian Journal of Clinical and Experimental Hypnosis, 8,* 41-46.

Fourie, D.P., & Lifschitz, S. (1988). Not seeing the wood for the trees: Implications of susceptibility testing. *American Journal of Clinical Hypnosis, 30,* 166–77.

Frankel, F.H., & Orne, M.T. (1976). Hypnotizability and phobic behavior. *Archives of General Psychiatry, 33,* 1259–61.

Frischolz, E.J., Spiegel, D., Spiegel, H., Balma, D.L., & Markell, C.S. (1982). Differential hypnotic responsivity of smokers, phobics, and chronic-pain control patients: A failure to replicate. *Journal of Abnormal Psychology, 91,* 269–72.

Furneaux, W.D. (1952). Primary suggestibility and hypnotic suggestibility in a group situation. *Journal of General Psychology, 46,* 87–91.

Gheorghiu, V. A. (1989). The development of research on suggestibility: Critical considerations. In V.A. Gheorghiu, P. Netter, H.J. Eysenck, & R. Rosenthal (eds.), *Suggestion and suggestibility: Theory and research.* New York: Springer-Verlag.

Gross, M. (1984). Hypnosis in the therapy of anorexia nervosa. *American Journal of Clinical Hypnosis,* 175–81.

Groth-Marnat, G., & Schumaker, J.F. (1990). Hypnotizability, attitude toward eating, and concern with body size in a female college population. *American Journal of Clinical Hypnosis, 32,* 194–200.

Gudjonsson, G.H. (1983). Suggestibility, intelligence, memory recall and personality: An experimental study. *British Journal of Psychiatry, 142,* 35–37.

Gudjonsson, G.H., & Lister, S. (1984). Interrogative suggestibility and its relationship with self-esteem and control. *Journal of the Forensic Science Society, 24,* 99–110.

Haberman, M.A. (1987). Spontaneous trance as a possible cause for persistent symptoms in the medically ill. *American Journal of Clinical Hypnosis, 29,* 171–76.

Hammer, A.G., Walker, W.L., & Diment, A.D. (1978). A nonsuggested effect of trance induction. In F.H. Frankel & H.S. Zamansky (eds.), *Hypnosis at its bicentennial.* New York: Plenum.

Hilgard, E.R. (1987). Research advances in hypnosis: Issues and methods. *International Journal of Clinical and Experimental Hypnosis, 35,* 248–64.

Hilgard, E.R., & Hilgard, J.R. (1983). *Hypnosis in the relief of pain* (2nd ed.). Los Altos, CA: Kaufman.

Horton, P., & Miller, D. (1972). The etiology of multiple personality. *Comprehensive Psychiatry, 18.*

Ingham, J. G. (1954). Body-sway suggestibility and neurosis. *Journal of Mental Science, 100,* 432–41.

Janet, P. (1920). *The major symptoms of hysteria.* New York: Macmillan.

John, R., Hollander, B., & Perry, C. (1983). Hypnotizability and phobic behavior. *Journal of Abnormal Psychology, 92,* 390–92.

Kaffman, M. (1989). Anorexia nervosa in the kibbutz: Factors influencing the development of a monoideistic fixation. *International Journal of Eating Disorders*, 33–53.

Kerchoff, A.C., & Back, K.W. (1968). *The June bug: A study of hysterical contagion.* New York: Appleton-Century-Crofts.

Kihlstrom, J.F. (1979). Hypnosis and psychopathology. *Journal of Abnormal Psychology, 88*, 459–73.

King, P.D. (1970). Ego development and the hypnosis theory of schizophrenia. *Psychoanalytic Review, 57*, 647–56.

Lavoie, G., & Sabourin, M. (1980). Hypnosis and schizophrenia: A review of experimental and clinical studies. In G.D. Burrows & L. Dennersein (eds.), *Handbook of hypnosis and psychosomatic medicine.* Amsterdam: Elsevier.

Lavoie, G., Sabourin, M., & Ally, G. (1976). Hypnotizability as a function of adaptive regression among chronic psychotic patients. *International Journal of Clinical and Experimental Hypnosis, 24*, 238–57.

Levitt, E.E., Brady, J.P., & Lubin, B. (1963). Correlates of hypnotizability in young women: Anxiety and dependency. *Journal of Personality, 31*, 53–57.

Long, T.E. (1968). Some early life stimulus correlates of hypnotizability. *International Journal of Clinical and Experimental Hypnosis, 16*, 61–67.

Lynn, S.J., & Dudley, K. (1987). *Magical ideation: A validation study.* Unpublished manuscript, Ohio University.

Lynn, S.J., & Rhue, W.J. (1986). The fantasy prone person: Hypnosis, imagination, and creativity. *Journal of Personality and Social Psychology, 51*, 404–08.

Lynn, S.J., & Rhue, W.J. (1988). Fantasy proneness: Hypnosis, developmental antecedents, and psychopathology. *American Psychologist, 43*, 35–44.

Mann, L. (1981). The baiting crowd in episodes of threatened suicide. *Journal of Personality and Social Psychology, 41*, 703–09.

Miller, R.J. (1980). The Harvard group scale of hypnotic susceptibility as a predictor of nonhypnotic suggestibility. *International Journal of Clinical and Experimental Hypnosis, 28*, 46–52.

Minuchin, S., Rosman, B.L., Baker, L., & Leiberman, H. (1978). *Psychosomatic families: Anorexia nervosa in context.* Cambridge, MA: Harvard University Press.

Moshe, T. (1986). Dissociative states presenting as an eating disorder. *American Journal of Clinical Hypnosis, 29*, 137–42.

Nace, E.P., Warwick, A.M., Kelly, R.L., & Evans, F.J. (1982). Hypnotizability and outcome in brief psychotherapy. *Journal of Clinical Psychiatry, 43*, 129–33.

Perry, C., Gelfand, R., & Marcovitch, P. (1979). The relevance of hypnotic susceptibility in the clinical context. *Journal of Abnormal Psychology, 88*, 592–603.

Pettinati, H.M. (1982). Measuring hypnotizability in psychotic patients. *The International Journal of Clinical and Experimental Hypnosis, 30*, 404–16.

Pettinati, H.M., Horne, R.L., & Staats, J.M. (1985). Hypnotizability in patients with anorexia nervosa and bulimia. *Archives of General Psychiatry, 42*, 1014–16.

Pettinati, H.M., Kogan, L.G., Margolis, C., Shrier, L., & Wade, J.H. (1989). Hypnosis, hypnotizability, and the bulimic patient. In L.M. Hornyak & E.K. Baker (eds.), *Experiential therapies for eating disorders.* New York: Guilford Press.

Phillips, D. (1974). The influence of suggestion on suicide. *American Sociological Review, 39,* 340–54.

Sackeim, H.A., Nordlie, J.W., & Gur, R.C. (1979). A model of hysterical and hypnotic blindness: Cognition, motivation, and awareness. *Journal of Abnormal Psychology, 88,* 474–89.

Sarbin, T.R., & Coe, W.C. (1979). Hypnosis and psychotherapy: Replacing old myths with fresh metaphors. *Journal of Abnormal Psychology, 88,* 506–26.

Sarbin, T., & Madow, L. (1947). Predicting the depth of hypnosis by means of the Rorschach test. *American Journal of Orthopsychiatry, 12,* 268–71.

Schafer, R. (1947). A study of personality characteristics related to hypnotizability. Unpublished masters thesis, University of Kansas.

Schumaker, J.F., & Groth-Marnat, G. (1988). The role of suggestibility in the understanding and treatment of anorexia nervosa. *Corrective and Social Psychiatry, 35,* 24–27.

Schumaker, J.F., Groth-Marnat, G., & Harris, T. (1987). The prevention of anorexia nervosa in an adolescent female population. In J.L. Sheppard (ed.), *Advances in behavioral medicine* (Vol. 4). Lidcombe, NSW: Cumberland College of Health Sciences.

Schumaker, J.F., Groth-Marnat, G., Small, L., & Macaruso, P.A. (1986). Sensation seeking in a female bulimic population. *Psychological Reports, 59,* 1151–54.

Shames, M.L. (1981). Hypnotic susceptibility and conformity: On the mediational mechanisms of suggestibility. *Psychological Reports, 49,* 563–66.

Soni, S.D., & Rockley, J.G. (1974). Socio-clinical substrates of folie à deux. *British Journal of Psychiatry, 125,* 230–35.

Spiegel, D. (1984). Multiple personality as a post-traumatic stress disorder. *Psychiatric Clinics of North America, 7,* 101–10.

Spiegel, D., Detrick, D., & Frischolz, E. (1982). Hypnotizability and psychopathology. *American Journal of Psychiatry, 139,* 431–37.

Spiegel, D., & Fink, R. (1979). Hysterical psychosis and hypnotizability. *American Journal of Psychiatry, 136,* 777–81.

Spiegel, D., Hunt, T., & Dondershine, M.D. (1988). Dissociation and hypnotizability in post-traumatic stress disorder. *American Journal of Psychiatry, 145,* 301–05.

Spiegel, H., & Spiegel, D. (1978). *Trance and treatment: Clinical uses of hypnosis.* New York: Basic Books.

Spiegel, H., Fleiss, J.L., & Bridger, A. A. (1975). Hypnotizability and mental health. In S. Arieti (ed.), *New dimensions in psychiatry: A world view.* New York: John Wiley & Sons.

Steingard, S., & Frankel, F.H. (1985). Dissociation and psychotic symptoms. *American Journal of Psychiatry, 142,* 953–55.

Striegel-Moore, R.H., Silberstein, L.R., & Rodin, J. (1986). Toward an understanding of risk factors for bulimia. *American Psychologist, 41,* 246–63.

Stukat, K.G. (1958). *Suggestibility: A factorial and experimental analysis.* Stockholm: Almqvist and Wiksell.

Swartz, L. (1985). Anorexia nervosa as a culture-bound syndrome. *Social Science and Medicine, 20,* 725–30.

Thorne, D.E., Rasmus, C., & Fisher, A.G. (1976). Are "fat girls" more hypnotically susceptible? *Psychological Reports, 38,* 267–70.

Zlotogorski, Z., Hahnemann, L.E., & Wiggs, E.A. (1987). Personality characteristics of hypnotizability. *American Journal of Clinical Hypnosis, 30,* 51–56.

12

HOW SUGGESTION PLAYS TRICKS WITH MEMORY

Kelly Toland, Hunter Hoffman, and Elizabeth Loftus

Consider two versions of the events that occurred in China's Tiananmen Square in June of 1989:

Version 1

Demonstrators for democracy, many of them students, were occupying the square when the "People's Liberation Army," with machine guns poised, poured into the square and fired on the crowd. This massacre of civilians in Beijing turned a late-spring Sunday into one of the bloodiest days in the history of Communist China. One witness, a Beijing bus driver, recalled his own fragments of experience amid the slaughter of hundreds, perhaps thousands, of unarmed protesters: ". . . I was going up and down the western part of Changan Avenue. . . . At every intersection, people were slaughtered. . . . The man next to me was hit in the eye. When we loaded him onto a tricycle to take him to the hospital, I saw his eye fall out of the socket . . ." (*Newsweek,* June 19, 1989, p. 22).

Version 2

When the People's Liberation Army came into the square, the student protesters left peacefully. In other parts of Beijing, some thugs stole guns from the soldiers and tried to overthrow the government. When soldiers tried to get their guns back from the thugs, shots were fired. Unfortunately, innocent bystanders and brave soldiers were killed.

Is it possible to suggest to the Chinese people a version like #2, one so flagrantly inaccurate, and succeed in altering what people actually remember? The Chinese government is trying.

Research into the suggestibility of human memory offers insights into the circumstances under which the Chinese government can succeed in changing the memories of its citizens. Many experiments in the area of suggestibility of memory utilize a simple paradigm (see Loftus, 1979a). Subjects witness some event such as a simulated car accident or a burglary, via a slide presentation or a film. Half of these subjects later receive misleading information about some critical details in the presentation and the other half, control subjects, do not. When tested on their memory for the critical details, misled subjects typically perform poorly relative to those who received no misleading post-event suggestions. For instance, in one such study, subjects viewed a slide presentation depicting a traffic accident. Subsequently, all subjects received written information about the accident, but for half of these subjects a stop sign in the presentation was inaccurately described as a yield sign. When tested on their memory for the traffic sign, subjects who had received the misleading suggestion were significantly less accurate.

Misleading post-event suggestions can do more than alter people's memory for objects. Subjective recollections for aspects such as the overall emotional context of an event can also be altered. For example, in one study, subjects were shown a three-minute segment taken from the film *Diary of a Student Revolution,* in which eight demonstrators noisily, but nonviolently disrupt a class. After viewing this film clip, subjects received either a neutral/passive questionnaire or an emotional/aggressive questionnaire. Other than the emotionality of the words used, the meanings of the questions were analogous for the two versions.

One week later the subjects were asked a series of questions about various aspects of the disruption. Those who had previously answered questions that were worded in an emotional/aggressive manner were more likely to report that the disruption was noisier and more violent, that the student demonstrators were more belligerent, and that the students in the classroom reacted more antagonistically than were those whose questionnaires were neutral and passive. This result demonstrates that the wording of a post-event interrogation profoundly influences the subjective recollections of witnesses.

Impaired memory performance due to post-event suggestions has been referred to as the "misinformation effect." In the last two decades, scores of studies conducted all around the world have documented the power of misinformation. By delineating the circumstances under which the misinformation effect prevails, researchers are able to make inferences about the way human memory works. Of particular interest are the factors that influence suggestibility, the implications of the findings for the permanence of our memories, and whether or not reports of misinformation are true reflections of people's memories.

Factors influencing suggestibility

Several situational factors affect the likelihood that post-event suggestions will distort a person's recollection. These include the strength of a person's original memory for the event about which they receive misleading suggestions, whether or not they are warned about misleading information, (as well as the explicitness of any warning), the amount of time elapsed since witnessing the event, the blatancy of the misinformation, prior commitment to an inaccurate memory, and the believed expertise of the source of the misleading suggestions. Experiments focusing on each of these variables reveal conditions that might lead Chinese citizens to accept the information being imposed on them by their government.

Strength of memory

The strength of a person's original memory for an event is one critical factor involved in suggestibility. In a study by Shaughnessy and Mand (1982), subjects were shown an event either once or twice. Mock witnesses who had seen an event twice were less likely to accept misinformation than those who had seen the event only once. Thus, the stronger the original event memory, the more resistant it was to post-event contamination.

Warnings

Another factor is the presence of a warning about misleading information. In several studies subjects have been warned about the possibility of misleading information prior to its presentation. The warning diminished the misinformation effect (Greene, Flynn, & Loftus, 1982). However, only warnings given before, but not after the presentation of misinformation worked. One explanation is that warned subjects scrutinize the misinformation and then notice discrepancies between it and their previously stored memory.

Blatantly false information

When the misinformation contained in a misleading suggestion blatantly contradicted previous information, subjects were highly resistant to its damaging influence (Loftus, 1979b). In one experiment, subjects received misleading information about the color of a wallet that had been highly visible and central to the event depicted in the slide presentation. Very few subjects accepted this suggestion on a subsequent test. In addition, the presentation of blatantly false information enhanced performance on other details about which subjects received more subtle misleading suggestions. Apparently, the blatantly false information alerted subjects to discrepancies between the two sources of information, and caused them to scrutinize the post-event information more than they normally would.

Authority of information provider

The authority or expertise of the person who presents misinformation can affect suggestibility. Smith and Ellsworth (1987) manipulated this variable by having two types of questioners asking misleading questions about an event: knowledgeable and naive. They found that when the questioner presenting the misleading suggestions was thought to be knowledgeable, subjects were more likely to accept misinformation than when the questioner was thought to be naive.

Other research on the importance of the interrogator has been conducted using children as subjects (Ceci, Ross, & Toglia, 1987). The suggestibility of children's memory was greater when the person providing the misinformation was an adult rather than another child. Apparently then, suggestibility in children results in part from children's desire to comply with the demands of an authority figure.

Commitment to a distractor

In a study by Schooler, Foster, and Loftus (1988), one group of subjects received only incorrect alternatives on a forced-choice recognition test, and thereby were forced to commit to an incorrect response. On a subsequent recognition test including both the correct and other incorrect alternatives, subjects who had previously committed to an incorrect response showed decreased accuracy relative to control subjects who had not previously so committed themselves. This result suggests that committing to an inaccurate response may impair the ability to accurately recall aspects of previously witnessed events.

Delay before presentation of postevent information

One last factor relevant to suggestibility is the amount of time elapsed between the original event and the presentation of the misleading suggestion. A study done by Loftus, Miller, and Burns (1978) manipulated this variable by presenting subjects with misleading, consistent, or neutral post-event information at intervals varying from twenty minutes to one week. In addition to demonstrating the usual impaired performance for misled subjects relative to control, results of a recognition test on the original information showed that the proportion of subjects responding correctly decreased significantly as the delay interval increased. This effect is consistent with the interpretation that memories are more suggestible after a time period because the strength of the original memory trace fades over time, thereby making a discrepancy between the original and post-event information less detectable (Tousignant, Hall, & Loftus, 1986).

Several factors bear on the suggestibility of the memories of Chinese citizens. First, those who have no strong memory for the events in Tiananmen Square would be the most likely to accept the misinformation being imposed on them by the Chinese government. The vast majority of the Chinese population are highly susceptible to suggestion by virtue of the fact that they never witnessed the original event. For them, no original memory for the event ever existed in the first place. Thus, the misleading information provided serves not to impair a memory, but to create a belief. In contrast, those who actually witnessed the slaughter of thousands of pro-democracy demonstrators might have a strong memory to begin with, and might not be readily misled by immediate attempts to deceive with blatantly false information. As the memories fade over time, however, memories for certain details of the originally witnessed event could become increasingly susceptible to misinformation. For instance, although it seems unlikely that a massacre witness would come to believe the suggestion that no massacre occurred at all, it does seem plausible, given the factors that influence suggestibility, that someone could, over time, come to remember the clothing on the man who was shot in the eye as being a green soldier's uniform. If the source of this suggestion were an authority figure, the original memory would run an even greater risk of contamination. And if forced to report a memory as if it were true, a person's ability to retrieve an accurate memory may actually be impaired.

The Permanence of memory

Research has clearly demonstrated that post-event misinformation can alter a person's memory report. Why this effect occurs, however, is disputed. For instance, consider a person who witnesses an accident involving a stop sign, is subsequently misinformed that the sign was a yield sign, and ultimately reports having seen a yield sign. What happened to the original memory? Was the memory altered? Could the original memory be recovered at some later time? If it can be recovered, how would this be done? These questions bear on a fundamental issue about human memory, namely, the permanence of memory traces.

Several hypotheses have been offered regarding the mechanism responsible for the misinformation effect, two of which are the alteration hypothesis and the coexistence hypothesis. The alteration hypothesis proposes that misleading information actually alters the original memory representation. The coexistence hypothesis, on the other hand, assumes that the original information and the misleading information coexist in memory. The misleading information renders the original information inaccessible, without damaging the original memory. These two hypotheses share the assumption that erroneous reports are the result of interference with the original memory due to the presentation of misleading information. However, they differ with respect to the types of interference occurring, as well as in what they imply about the retrieval of originally witnessed memories. If one takes the view that memories are altered by misinformation, then recovery of the ancestral information may not be possible. However, if one believes that the original memory is simply rendered inaccessible due to misinformation, then attempts to access the original information could prove fruitful. The findings of studies addressing this issue have not been fully consistent.

Alteration of memory traces

The alteration hypothesis derives support from failed empirical attempts to recover original memories. Recovery attempts have been made by giving subjects incentives for accurate reporting, "second guess" techniques, and even hypnosis.

Loftus (1979a) acknowledged that people may not access and report the original information because they lack incentive to do so. To test this possibility, subjects were offered various amounts of money for correct responses. Presumably, if one could gain up to 25 dollars for giving a correct response, one would be motivated to do so. However, results showed that despite monetary incentive, subjects were still highly susceptible to the impairing effects of misinformation—as susceptible as those who did not stand to gain economically.

Attempts to motivate subjects with verbal incentives have met a similar fate. In one study, subjects were told that "most intelligent people can pick out the slide they saw before, despite any distracting information they have been exposed to." As with monetary incentives, verbal incentives failed to increase levels of accurate performance (Loftus, 1979a).

Second-guess techniques have also been developed to explore the existence of the original memory trace. With this technique, when a subject's first report of memory is incorrect, he or she is given a second chance to recall. Presumably, if any trace of the original information remained in memory, performance on the second guesses would be above chance. Results, however, provided no evidence for the existence of the original memory trace.

Finally, researchers have utilized hypnosis in attempts to uncover an original memory trace. Presumably, if hypnosis allows access to original perceptions, such techniques could recover an original memory trace. However, results of such studies have failed to do this. In one such study (Sheehan, 1989), more rather than less memory distortion occurred when subjects were hypnotized at the time they were tested.

Coexistence of memory traces

Coexistence theories derive support from successful attempts to recover the original information after exposure to misinformation has presumably altered that information in memory. Results of such studies demonstrate that although not all memories are necessarily recoverable in this way, it is possible that in some cases misinformation can affect memory reports without necessarily destroying original memory traces.

Bekerian and Bowers (1983) hypothesized that reinstating the context associated with the original information may allow subjects to recall that original information more accurately. In fact, they found that presenting questions about the details from the originally witnessed event in the same order as the details were originally encountered allowed misled subjects to perform equally as well as controls. In contrast, presenting subjects with the same questions in random order produced a misinformation effect. Thus, reinstating the original context alleviated the effect of misleading post-event information. Note, however, that the conditions under which recovery is obtained are very specific; a persisting misinformation effect is the more common result (Bowers & Bekerian, 1984).

Another method that is sometimes successful at recovering original information is the use of a warning (Christiaansen & Ochalek, 1983). As mentioned earlier, warning subjects about the presence of misleading suggestions resulted in equal performance between misled and control groups, as a result of increased scrutiny of incoming information. This method, like reinstatement of context, demonstrates that, in some cases, it is possible to recover information that would otherwise be lost due to exposure to misleading suggestions. These results suggest coexistence of two memories.

Morton, Hammersley, and Bekerian (1985) proposed a coexistence account of the misinformation effect. In this memory model, information is represented in individual memory units called Records. Each of these memory units is headed by an access key which enables the retrieval of that record. This access key, called a Heading, contains coded information about the contents of the Record. Thus, the theory is referred to as the Headed Records theory. According to this theory, the search process is initiated by the formation of a Description, or the gathering of the relevant information available. One must also consider the goals of the search, or the Task Specification. The search involves finding a match between a Heading and the Description. Once a match is located in memory, the information in the Record is accessed. Upon favorable examination of the contents of the record according to Task Specification, the search is terminated.

Searching one's memory for lost car keys provides a good example of this model at work. The searcher feels it necessary to find the keys. This is Task Specification. She thinks to herself, "Where did I put them—on the kitchen table, in the living room, or in the bedroom?" The places she thinks about are the Descriptions that she will use when scanning her memory. If she formulates the correct Description, it will match the Header to the particular Record which contains the information about her keys. With successful access to that Record, she will remember where she laid the keys.

According to Morton, et al., the misinformation effect results when the Headed Record for the originally witnessed information is not accessible relative to the Headed Record for the misleading post-event information. For example, suppose a person witnessed an accident involving a stop sign, was later misinformed that the traffic sign was a yield sign, and was subsequently asked to recall the type of sign. To retrieve the memory of the original information, the Headed Record for the original information, the stop sign, must be discriminable from the Headed Record for the misleading information, the yield sign. Morton, et al. claim that the information in the Headed Records for the original and misleading information is not distinguishable. In this case, the Headed Record to be matched would be the more recent in memory, that of the yield sign, resulting in the inaccurate reporting of the misinformation.

A more recent notion that embodies the idea that two memories can coexist is the notion of "source misattribution.." The idea here is that inaccurate reports of witnessed events are due to confusion between the source of the original information and the source of subsequently received misleading information (Johnson & Lindsay, 1986). Traces for the original and misleading post-event information might both be stored, but the misinformation is mistakenly attributed to the original event. Perhaps because the misinformation is more recent and therefore more salient in memory, it is incorrectly assessed to be what was witnessed originally.

Until recently, the misinformation effect was thought to arise from either an alteration of traces or an interference with traces previously stored. Doubt was cast upon this assumption when McCloskey and Zaragoza (1985) modified the standard testing procedure used previously, and gathered evidence in favor of their view that misleading post-event information neither alters the original information in memory nor renders it inaccessible. In fact, they claimed that the misinformation effect has little to do with memory impairment. Rather it is the result of a bias inherent in the standard testing procedure (used in nearly all the aforementioned studies). McCloskey and Zaragoza criticized the standard testing procedure on the grounds that it created a response bias and that subjects could be responding based on demand characteristics.

To appreciate their views, consider once again subjects who view a slide presentation of an accident involving a stop sign. Later, subjects in the misled group receive misinformation that the sign was a yield sign. Control subjects receive no misleading information. A response bias could be created due to the differential guessing rates of misled and control subjects who, say, never stored the original information in the first place. In the case of control subjects, on a standard test where they must choose between two alternative responses, the stop sign or the yield sign, performance would not be biased. On the other hand, subjects in the misled group who never stored the original information but do remember the misleading suggestion would be biased toward choosing the misleading option, the yield sign, on the test. This bias is not the result of memory impairment, because the original information was never stored in the first place. Rather, reporting the misinformation when the original information was never stored is termed misinformation acceptance.

The second criticism of the standard testing procedure is that it allows for demand characteristics to influence reports. For example, suppose a subject remembers the original information as well as the misleading information. At test, he or she may opt to give the misinformation response either because he or she assumes that the misinformation must be right since the experimenter provided it and must know, or because he or she simply wants to do well on the test. In either case, the response does not accurately reflect a change in memory. Thus, according to McCloskey and Zaragoza's view, the presentation of the yield sign neither alters nor renders inaccessible the memory for the stop sign.

In order to correct for these drawbacks, McCloskey and Zaragoza (1985) excluded the misinformation item from the test options. Cleverly, they paired the original, correct item with a novel item, one that had not been encountered by the subjects before. (They called this the modified test.) In doing so they eliminated the possibility of response bias. The logic behind this test format was straightforward. If memory were impaired by misinformation, then subjects who had received misleading information would perform less well than control subjects on this modified test because their memory for the original item would be weakened. Using the modified procedure, McCloskey and Zaragoza (1985), in a series of six experiments, found no difference between misled and control subject performance. From these results they concluded that the misinformation had no effect on event memory.

Several researchers reacted to conclusions by McCloskey and Zaragoza, arguing them to be too strong. Although McCloskey and Zaragoza did demonstrate that the idea that misinformation completely erases original memories is implausible, their results by no means rule out the possibility of other, more subtle forms of impairment. Put another way, the modified test has been criticized as being insensitive for detecting impairment of an original event-memory. Researchers have long observed that subjects are reasonably good at distinguishing between familiar and totally novel stimuli (Hintzman, 1969, reviewed by Johnson & Lindsay, 1986). Recall that in the modified recognition test, subjects make a forced choice between the item originally seen and a novel item. If the misleading suggestion slightly impairs the strength of the originally seen item, this test would not detect this impairment. For as long as one item is more familiar than the other on the recognition test, subjects will likely succeed in making a familiarity judgment and will choose the correct response.

Another criticism levelled against the modified testing procedure is its insensitivity to indirect impairment of original information. For instance, suppose the original information and misinformation coexist in memory, but due to recency or saliency the misinformation is more readily accessible. Because the modified procedure does not allow subjects to give the misinformation response, this sort of impaired accessibility would not be detected on the modified test. When they do not find the shiny yield sign as a response option, they dust off the old stop sign and correctly choose it.

One popular trend in misinformation research is to design experiments which avoid the potential pitfalls of the standard test procedure, and which are also sensitive to possible memory impairment. For example, Tversky and Tuchin (1989) used a "yes/no" test rather than the standard or modified test. Subjects followed the same procedure of viewing a slide presentation, and then read a narrative account of the event that contained misleading suggestions in the misled condition. Finally they took a yes/no test designed to assess their memory for the original event. For example, subjects would see a slide depicting an event that included a man holding a hammer. Later, they would be misinformed that the tool was a screwdriver. Then during the test period, they received yes/no questions concerning three tools—hammer, screwdriver, and wrench—scattered throughout the test series.

Results showed misled subjects were less accurate than controls at recognizing the original event item, thus demonstrating a typical misinformation effect. Results also showed that whereas misled and control subjects were equally adept at correctly rejecting the novel test item, misled subjects incorrectly rejected the original item and accepted the misinformation item more than controls. In addition, some subjects responded "yes" to more than one alternative for a critical item (i.e., to both the hammer and then later the screwdriver), and this occurred twice as often among misled subjects. The fact that subjects demonstrated memory for both the original information and the misinformation could mean that both items coexist in memory (at least for some subjects). Apparently subjects were unable to distinguish between what they saw in the slide presentation and what they read in the narrative, although both items were familiar at test.

Tversky and Tuchin concluded that misleading post-event suggestions do interfere with ability to remember information originally witnessed accurately. In addition, they concluded that the differing results from studies utilizing the standard versus modified procedures occurred because subjects used different judgment methods. There are two ways to succeed on a forced-choice recognition test. One can accept a familiar item, or one can reject an unfamiliar item. In the case of the standard testing procedure, when faced with the original item and the misinformation item, if the subject remembers the item in the slides, he or she will correctly select the original item at test. However, if that subject does not remember, the misinformation item may seem more familiar and, as a result, will be selected at test. When the modified test is employed, subjects in either condition simply make a novelty judgment resulting in the rejection of the novel item.

For that reason, one would expect equal performance for misled and control subjects.

Belli (1989) utilized a similar yes/no test in order to differentiate between memory impairment and misinformation acceptance. Belli agreed with McCloskey and Zaragoza that some subjects might accept misinformation at test not because their original memory was impaired, but because the original item was never encoded in the first place. But Belli also hypothesized that some portion of the misinformation effect is actually due to memory impairment, either source misattribution or impaired accessibility of the original item. Using a yes/no test with questions about the original and novel items, Belli devised a clever means of separating out the effects of demand characteristics, misinformation acceptance, and memory impairment.

For example, suppose again that subjects were shown the slide depicting a man holding a hammer. Later the tool was incorrectly described as a screwdriver. By definition, misinformation accepters are subjects who did not see the hammer for some reason, but processed and stored the erroneous post-event information (screwdriver). Misinformation acceptance would result in subjects responding "no" when questioned about the original item (hammer) as well as when asked about the novel item (wrench). For both types of questions, misinformation accepters would be more likely to respond "no" than control subjects. Saying "no" to wrench is the correct response. The reason subjects are able to respond correctly is because they mistakenly think that they saw the post-event item, the screwdriver. In response to the original event-item question, "no" would be an incorrect response, since the hammer had actually been present in the slides. Can the entire misinformation effect be explained as the decrement in performance due to misinformation acceptance, or is memory impairment also implicated? To answer that crucial question, Belli used the following logic. If misinformation acceptance is all that is going on, then depressed original item performance will be countered by an equal and opposite enhanced effect on novel item performance. On the other hand, if the reduction in performance on the original item exceeds the benefits in performance on the novel item, this would constitute evidence for genuine memory impairment. This is exactly what Belli found—original item impairment that exceeded the enhancement on the novel item.

Experiments such as Belli's, which eliminate the influence of demand characteristics, and allow the misinformation effect to be decomposed into misinformation acceptance and memory impairment may well lead to a better understanding of what underlies post-event distortion of recollection.

Do subjects really believe in their memories?

Postevent suggestions clearly alter people's reports of events they have witnessed. Whether these altered reports reflect memory interference or not, a question has arisen about whether subjects who claim to have a particular (false) memory truly believe they experienced the false items. Zaragoza and Koshmidir (1989) explored whether subjects really do believe in the misinformation items that they selected on a test. These investigators argued that just because subjects report a misinformation item (or select it on a test) does not mean that they believe they saw it. Subjects might report the misinformation item because they believe it is an accurate depiction of what happened, not because they really remember seeing it. To drive this point home, they consider a hypothetical situation in which a witness does not remember a stop sign that was part of a witnessed event, but does remember reading a report that refers to a yield sign. That witness might testify in court about seeing a yield sign simply because the witness believes the yield sign was there and wants to appear credible.

To determine whether subjects in typical misinformation studies do believe that they saw the misinformation items, or whether they can distinguish between what they think might be true and what they actually remember seeing, Zaragoza and Koshmidir performed several experiments. Subjects saw an event, got misinformation or neutral information, and were tested on slides of individual items (some of which depicted the original information and some of which depicted misinformation). At the time of the test, subjects were forced to distinguish between 1) what they were sure they SAW, 2) what they READ in a post-event narrative, 3) what was CONSISTENT with their memory but for which they did not remember the source, and 4) what was INCONSISTENT with their memory. Prior to taking the test, these options were thoroughly explained with examples. The aim here was to force subjects to distinguish between items that they originally perceived, items suggested in a post-event narrative, and items which were consistent with their memory for the event but for which they did not remember the source. Evidence that subjects believe that they saw the misinformation would be obtained if misled condition subjects were more likely than control condition subjects to claim they "SAW" the misinformation.

Consider a subject who saw a sequence involving a critical object such as a hammer, and was later tested on a slide containing a screwdriver. Misled subjects who got "screwdriver" on a post-event narrative were not more likely than controls to say later that they were sure that they SAW the screwdriver.

What about performance when tested on the original slide containing the "hammer?" Were misled subjects less likely to claim that they saw "hammer?" No, they did not use the SAW response less often than control subjects. These results were taken by Zaragoza and Koshmidir to support the contention that misled subjects report misinformation items (on the standard test), but they do not believe that they saw them.

The Zaragoza and Koshmidir research is a commendable first step towards more directly determining whether subjects truly believe that they saw the misinformation. However, the Zaragoza and Koshmidir conclusion rests squarely on the finding that misinformation did not influence the extent to which subjects used the SAW response. There are many reasons why, however, given the details of their procedure, subjects might not have been prone to use the SAW response (Foster, 1988). An honors thesis conducted in the Loftus laboratory took these problems into consideration, and altered the Zaragoza and Koshmidir procedure in an effort to eliminate potential biasing aspects.

First, in the Zaragoza and Koshmidir studies, subjects were tested by viewing a slide containing the misleading item (e.g., screwdriver). It is possible that subjects who got misinformation did believe that they saw the misleading item, but they rejected the test slide depicting the misinformation as the one they had seen because it did not match the mental picture of the misinformation that the subject had in mind (The screwdriver in the slides did not match the screwdriver in the mind's eye). Zaragoza and Koshmidir claim that this is an unlikely reason for their results because they used some critical items that had only one mental image (e.g., a 7-up can), but in fact these critical items do not have this characteristic. In any event, the problem was eliminated by testing subjects on the "name" of the item (e.g., "Did you see a screwdriver?") instead of a visual scene containing that item.

Another biasing aspect of the Zaragoza and Koshmidir design is the fact that subjects may choose either SAW or READ, but not both. It is easy to imagine a situation where a subject distinctly remembers reading about a critical item, and also thinks he or she saw it in the slides. In this case, if the memory for reading was even slightly stronger, the response selected would be READ. This could occur even if the subject truly believes he or she saw the item in the slide presentation. By including the option SAW and READ, Foster's study avoided this possible bias.

In attempting to replicate the Zaragoza and Koshmidir experiment, the option INCONSISTENT was found to be ambiguous to subjects. For example, subjects could think that this meant remembering seeing one thing and reading another. Alternatively, it could be interpreted as meaning that the item being tested was neither seen nor read. The solution adopted was to use the terms FAMILIAR and UNFAMILIAR rather than CONSISTENT and INCONSISTENT.

Perhaps the most important problem with the Zaragoza and Koshmidir method is that they gave highly explicit instructions warning subjects not to say they saw something if they only remembered reading about it. The "warning" implores subjects not to claim seeing something falsely when they did not. As Zaragoza and Koshmidir have acknowledged, this warning could cause subjects to scrutinize their memories more than they normally would. Foster eliminated this suspicion-arousing element in order to see if subjects spontaneously discriminate sources of information in memory.

After this strong warning, subjects were tested: they looked at a test slide and indicated the one response alternative (SAW, READ, etc.) that best described their memory for the critical item depicted in the slide. They were instructed to select SAW "only if they were sure they remembered seeing that particular item in the original slide sequence." So as not to scare people away from the SAW response, Foster instructed subjects to choose the SAW response if they think they saw the item.

The same predictions regarding true belief were made in this study as were made in the Zaragoza and Koshmidir study. In this case, the results support the contention that subjects truly believe misinformation. When tested on their memory for the misleading item (the screwdriver), misled subjects were significantly more likely than controls to select the SAW response. When tested on the original item (the hammer), misled subjects were significantly less likely than controls to choose the SAW response.

In sum, these results provide evidence for the claim that misled subjects do believe they saw the misleading information. Because several aspects of Zaragoza and Koshmidir's procedure were altered, it is impossible to tell which of them were responsible for the different results obtained. Further research must tease apart the influences of the various procedural manipulations made in this study.

A more recent study by Loftus and Toland (1989) addresses the issue of true belief from a new angle. The research began with the hypothesis that if subjects truly believe in the misinformation, they ought to be willing to bet money on their memories. Subjects in this experiment witnessed an event in a slide presentation, received misleading post-event information in the form of a narrative, and then took a yes/no recognition test. For each of the test questions, subjects were required to place a hypothetical bet of between one and ten dollars on the accuracy of their answer. "True belief" in a given memory would be demonstrated by a bet of ten dollars, the maximum possible amount.

Results showed that while people were more often willing to place a maximum bet of ten dollars on their real memories, 40% of the time they were willing to place the maximum bet on suggested memories. In contrast, subjects very rarely placed high bets on completely false memories, ones which they had never seen or about which they had been given misleading information. These results suggest that in many cases, about 40% of the time, subjects believe their suggested memories as much as they do their real memories. Moreover, some subjects agreed that they saw an item at test, but were not willing to place a high bet on the accuracy of their answer.

If we can generalize these results to the Chinese citizens' "memories" for the massacre in Tiananmen Square, we can speculate that when people's reports of the event comply with the information put forth by the government, some of them may reflect true belief, but some may not. Needless to say, the conditions surrounding the people of China cannot be simulated in any laboratory, and other factors are no doubt at work not only influencing people's willingness to report inaccurate information, but possibly even impairing the memories they once held.

Analogous to the idea of subjects complying with experimental demands is the overwhelmingly more forceful pressure on Chinese citizens to succumb to the government's demand to profess belief in the altered version of the Tiananmen Square massacre. Given the strength of so many citizen's memories for that shocking event, we cannot dismiss the contention that many people would report memories that they do not truly believe, but that they are forced to report. People holding weaker or second-hand memories for the massacre, on the other hand, would be much more likely actually to incorporate the false information regarding the instigation of, as well as the magnitude of, the massacre. Those with no memory at all would accept the misleading information because no conflict of information would arise. But someone with a weak memory for the event might be susceptible to suggestion, given circumstances that enhance susceptibility. We can speculate that a weak initial memory could be impaired or interfered with by misinformation, resulting in true belief in a false memory. Perhaps those whose memories are suggestible are better off. After all, those whose memories cannot be modified by misinformation that the Chinese government has put forth may have no choice but to live in silence . . . or not at all.

The underlying research fundamental to the arguments made here was supported by a grant from the National Institute of Mental Health.

References

Bekerian, D.A., & Bowers, J.M. (1983). Eyewitness testimony: Were we misled? *Journal of Experimental Psychology: Learning, Memory, and Cognition, 9*(1), 139–45.

Belli, R.F. (1989). Influences of misleading postevent information: Misinformation interference and acceptance. *Journal of Experimental Psychology: General, 118*, 72–85.

Bowers, J.M., & Bekerian, D.A. (1984). When will postevent information distort eyewitness testimony? *Journal of Applied Psychology, 69*, 466–72.

Ceci, S.J., Ross, D.F., & Toglia, M.P. (1987). Suggestibility of children's memory: Psycholegal implications. *Journal of Experimental Psychology: General, 116*, 38–49.

Christiaansen, R.E., & Ochalek, K. (1983). Editing misleading information from memory: Evidence for the coexistence of original and postevent information. *Memory and Cognition, 11*(5), 467–75.

Foster, C. (1988). Unpublished honors thesis. University of Washington.

Greene, E., Flynn, M., & Loftus, E.F. (1982). Inducing resistance to misleading information. *Journal of Verbal Learning and Verbal Behavior, 21*, 209–19.

Johnson, M.K., & Lindsay, D.S. (1986). Despite McCloskey and Zaragoza, suggestibility effects may reflect memory impairment. Unpublished manuscript, Department of Psychology, Princeton University.

Loftus, E.F. (1979a). *Eyewitness Testimony*. Cambridge, MA: Harvard University Press.

Loftus, E.F. (1979b). Reactions to blatantly contradictory information. *Memory and Cognition, 7*, 368–74.

Loftus, E.F., Miller, D.G., & Burns, H.J. (1978). Semantic integration of verbal information into a visual memory. *Journal of Experimental Psychology: Human Learning and Memory, 4*(1), 19–31.

Loftus, E.F., & Toland, K. (1989). Manuscript in preparation. University of Washington.

McCloskey, M., & Zaragoza M. (1985). Misleading postevent information and memory for events: Arguments and evidence against memory impairment hypotheses. *Journal of Experimental Psychology: General, 114*(1), 1–16.

Morton, J., Hammersley, R.H., & Bekerian, D.A. (1985). Headed records: A model for memory and its failures. *Cognition, 20*, 1–23.

Schooler, J.W., Foster, R., & Loftus, E.F. (1988). Some deleterious consequences of the act of recollection. *Memory and Cognition, 16*(3), 243–51.

Shaughnessy, J.J., & Mand, J.L. (1982). How permanent are memories for real life events? *American Journal of Psychology, 95*(1), 51–65.

Sheehan, P.W. (1989). Response to suggestions of memory distortions in hypnosis: Sampling cognitive and social factors. In V.A. Gheorghiu, P. Netter, H.J. Eysenck, & R. Rosenthal (eds.), *Suggestion and Suggestibility: Theory and Research* pp. 295–303. Berlin: Springer Verlag.

Smith, V.L., & Ellsworth, P.C. (1987). The social psychology of eyewitness accuracy: Misleading questions and communicator expertise. *Journal of Applied Psychology, 72*, 294–300.

Tousignant, J.P., Hall, D., & Loftus, E.F. (1986). Discrepancy detection and vulnerability to misleading postevent information. *Memory and Cognition, 14*, 329–38.

Tversky, B., & Tuchin, M. (1989). A reconciliation of the evidence on eyewitness testimony: Comments on McCloskey and Zaragoza. *Journal of Experimental Psychology: General, 118*, 86–91.

Zaragoza, M.S., & Koshmidir, J.W. (1989). Misled subjects may know more than their performance implies. *Journal of Experimental Psychology: Learning, Memory, and Cognition, 15*, 246–55.

13

SUGGESTION, PLACEBO, AND EXPECTATION: Immune Effects and Other Bodily Change

John D. Shea

This paper will deal with ideas about the role of suggestion, in interaction with individual characteristics, in helping to shape immune responses, and in other aspects of health experience. Since the capacity for bodily self-change seems to be considerable (e.g., Barber, 1978, 1984), it would be useful to have a better understanding of the minimum requirements and the optimal conditions for achieving change, and of those individuals who may demonstrate such change more easily. This discussion will consider three areas of relevance to these issues: firstly the nature of the placebo effect, its relationship to suggestion, and the extent to which it might be invoked; secondly, some external and internal conditions which facilitate self-change and healing through suggestion; and thirdly the individual qualities, or personality characteristics that might be associated with initial health and body status, and with the capacity for change through suggestion.

Placebo, suggestion, and expectation

Placebo

There has always been a recognition, extending as far back as Hippocrates and Galen (Shapiro, 1960), that "faith," "the imagination," or "the placebo effect" has an influence on somatic events. Every double-blind clinical trial of new drugs stands as testimony to the fact that the imagination affects bodily health. Only recently has it been recognized as more than just a contaminating influence in scientific studies. The placebo effect is an example of the inherent capacity of the individual to achieve self-healing.

Shapiro offered a popular definition of placebo (1971), stating that placebo is "any therapy, or that component of therapy, that is deliberately used for its non-specific, psychologic, or psychophysiologic effect, or that is used for its presumed specific effect on a patient, symptom, or illness, but which is without specific activity for the condition being treated." Peek (1977) examined the implications of the defining statement and, concluding that some terms were ambiguous and restrictive, suggested an alternate definition: "A placebo is some treatment or procedure (or component of a treatment or procedure) that has an effect on the phenomena under study and is not explained in the theoretical domain in which the phenomena are described" (p. 331). Peek goes on to argue that psychology, not biology, is the explanatory domain for placebo effects.

Frank (1961) has argued that faith, or lack of doubt in the efficacy of the placebo agent, can explain the placebo effect. Evans (1974) also speaks of the idea of "plausibility and expectation that it will work." Peek (1977) sees the concept of faith as crucial to the occurrence of placebo effects and also the way that psychotherapeutic effects might come about. Peek notes that "not lacking faith frees a person to do as well as he can. Further, such a person who does not lack faith is less likely to count anything as final failure" (p. 333).

The domain of suggestion

Despite recent efforts to delineate the field of suggestion (Edmonston, 1989; Eysenck, 1989; Gheorghiu, 1989a, 1989b; Kruse, 1989) the area is still a very difficult one, with frequent confusion of terms, and problems of overlap with hypnosis. Gheorghiu (1989a) proposes that suggestion involves a stimulus situation with a certain demand character or "guiding idea," which leads to "a determining tendency" to behave in certain ways. Such guiding ideas may be expressed in a social context through nonverbal stimuli, through moods that are demonstrated, or through words. They may occur in unstructured ambiguous situations upon which the individual imposes some meaning or organization.

Some writers have acknowledged substantial overlap in the notions of suggestibility and placebo (e.g., Eysenck, 1989). Evans (1985) explained placebo effects as involving primary suggestibility, anxiety reduction, and the marshalling of "powerful cultural expectations and beliefs." However, laboratory tests of hypnotic susceptibility have shown an unreliable relationship, or no relationship, to placebo responding (Evans, 1977, 1981; McGlashan, Evans, & Orne, 1969; Evans, Gustafson, O'Connell, Orne, & Shor, 1969; Orne, 1974, Shapiro, 1971). For instance, the McGlashan, et al. study indicated that virtually all subjects were capable of achieving modest, limited pain relief from verbal suggestions given during "hypnosis," but that subjects high in hypnotic talent achieved a much greater control over pain.

Wickramasekera (1976) expressed doubts that this study was a fair test of placebo versus hypnosis. There are other problems as well. For instance, the parameters of experimental and clinical pain do not overlap in several areas (Melzack, 1973). Not surprisingly, there are reports, including some described by Evans (1974) himself, indicating that analgesic placebos are about twice as effective in clinical trials as in experimental trials. Netter (1989) has described data showing that in pathological pain (as opposed to experimental pain) a positive correlation existed between suggestibility and decrease of headaches after sufferers were given drugs or placebos. Thus it is not at all clear that placebo responses are always distinct from other classes of suggestibility behavior.

The lack of relationship between suggestibility dimensions is not new, of course. Thorn (1962) has noted that suggestibility measures are hardly ever correlated. Placebo effects offer even more interesting difficulties, since subjects do not necessarily respond reliably to placebos (Shapiro, 1971).

The factor-analytic path of investigation that has often been used in the search for dimensions of suggestibility (Eysenck, 1947; Evans, 1974) can lead to the deliberate selection of factors that are orthogonal (i.e., uncorrelated by definition). Furthermore, factor solutions that are achieved depend entirely on the items that are used in the analysis. Only if those items adequately represent the domain under investigation can the factors derived be treated with some confidence. A satisfactory taxonomy of the domain of suggestion is so far lacking, thus our test item sets have been limited. Sample sizes have usually been small and culturally biased. Despite efforts to discover a unitary dimension of suggestibility, none has yet been established (Evans, 1989), nor do we have a generally agreed set of suggestibility dimensions.

The power of placebo effects

Beecher's (1959) analysis of double-blind studies of drug treatments for clinical pain indicated that 35% of the patients with a wide variety of post-operative pain found significant relief with inert medication. Evans (1985) confirmed these observations and noted that the responsive patients received about 56% of pain relief from placebos regardless of the potency of the drug studied. This seems to imply that the organism has an almost unlimited capacity to respond with intentionality to provide pain relief, and that there are qualities of the "suggestion" situation which determine ceiling effects.

The placebo effect may be evident in a wide range of illnesses, varying treatment modalities, and even in the mere expectation of getting help. For instance, Klopfer (1957) described an extraordinary case of a cancer patient whose condition waxed and waned according to the level of his faith in a placebo treatment. Evans (1985) notes that double-blind studies of nonpharmacological insomnia treatment techniques show about a 58% effectiveness ratio, and studies of psychotropic drugs for the treatment of depression (such as tricyclics) indicate a 59% to 62% placebo component. Thus Evans concludes that placebo is about 55–60% as effective as active medications, irrespective of the potency, or the target area, of these active medications.

Reviewers of placebo research commonly conclude that the placebo response must be a real general component of all clinical interactions (White, Tursky, & Schwartz, 1985; Wickramasekera, 1980). Ashton (1990) observes that an awareness of such effects should lead us to a healthy scepticism about the unique value of specific, competing psychotherapeutic approaches.

People who are responsive to placebo effects are also capable of responding negatively to other suggestions, and it may be such effects which create illness in the first place. Harding and Maher (1982) have demonstrated such effects with asthmatics, and more dramatic evidence of such effects is found in analyses of "voodoo" death, or pointing the bone (Cannon, 1963).

Mechanisms

How do thoughts about healing become translated into an organic effect? Evans (1974) and Jospe (1978) suggest a role for trait anxiety in such effects, finding increased pain tolerance associated with anxiety reduction in trait-anxious people receiving treatment. But some issues remain unexplained. For instance, placebo response with analgesic drugs varies in proportion to the efficacy of the drug itself, an effect which implies something more than simply a blanket anxiety reduction. Also, placebo analgesia often mimics precisely other "pharmacological properties of the active agent with which it is being compared," such as dose response, time-effect curves, and side-effects (Evans, 1974). Placebos may even reverse the action of powerful drugs (Shapiro, 1971), and people can become addicted to placebos, showing many of the formal traits of drug dependence (dosage increases over time, withdrawal effects, etc.). These effects seem much too specific for a unidimensional explanation. If primary suggestibility and anxiety do not account for the major part of the placebo response, following Evans's (1985) categorization, we are left with expectancy aroused by cultural or medical belief systems.

Wickramasekera (1980) offered a new model of the placebo response. His analysis claims the potential for classical conditioning in all effective therapeutic interventions, whether chemical, surgical, or psychological. It is suggested that vicarious or actual respondent and operant conditioning can, through association with effective experiences (the unconditioned stimuli), establish neutral places, things, procedures, and people as conditioned stimuli for the relief of pain (Wickramasekera, 1977). The conditioned placebo response may comprise a complex patterned psychophysiological response that is perceived subjectively as an emotion like hope. Components of this psychophysiological response may be able to dissipate pain and disinhibit adaptive behavioral and biological resources (Wickramasekera, 1980). It is suggested that the placebo response is well established through repeated associations with active experiences (the unconditioned stimuli). It then becomes increasingly abbreviated, involves minimal or no awareness, becomes very rapid or automatic, and involves a bypass of the verbal or dominant hemisphere, like hypnosis. Therefore, the placebo response can be potentiated or attenuated by the same variables that determine suggestibility or hypnosis.

Such a model seems plausible in the area of analgesia, given that we all experience pain and pain relief in our lives. It also offers an explanation for the relationship between placebo effect and potency of the drugs used in analgesia studies. However, since the model relies on the prior association of neutral stimuli with powerful, effective interventions (e.g., drugs), it seems inadequate to explain physiological outcomes which are entirely novel, such as the effective use of hypnosis with cases of fishskin disease (e.g., Mason, 1952).

Immune research

Our own research into the effects of hypno-relaxation training on immune responses, and on relationships between immune responses and psychosocial variables, suggests that subjects' expectations about positive experiences profoundly determine results. The first study relevant to this issue (further described in Shea, Girgis, Husband, Burton, & Clover, 1989) involved the random allocation of subjects to relaxation or control groups. Blood was sampled and antigens applied to the skin to test for cell-mediated immunity. After this, the hypno-relaxation interventions began and ran for a four-week period, after which immune measures were taken again.

There were unexpected results. The most striking finding was an initial difference between the relaxation and control groups. The control subjects scored significantly lower than the relaxation group on a variety of immune measures, before any intervention. Differences between the groups was reduced over the following weeks. This reduction was related to an increase in immune responses from the controls rather than from the relaxation group. Ruling out the possibility of some unexplained difference between the randomly chosen groups, it appeared that subjects brought different expectations to the first blood-sampling session. In this way, the immune responses of the controls, but not the relaxation group, were negatively affected.

It appears that the control group alone suffered severe anticipatory stress related to the venipuncture. Many subjects came near to collapse, or actually fainted before venipuncture. This effect, well-known to medical practitioners, suggests a profound level of distress. It would be difficult to think of another commonly occurring experience which could produce an equivalent response. Yet there is a curious lack of reference to the issue in the psychological literature dealing with measures of immunity.

Another similar study was designed to test the matter further (also described in Shea, et al., 1989). Eighty-eight subjects were allocated to the relaxation and control groups before blood sampling occurred. An additional baseline measure was taken one week after the first. Measures of state stress were also taken on each blood sampling occasion to discover whether there actually was a difference between the experimental groups, and to see whether state stress changed over time.

Results confirmed the unexpected earlier findings. State stress was higher and immune responses were "lower" for the first sampling occasion compared with the second. But this effect occurred predominantly in the control subjects. There was no difference in state stress, and little change in the immune measures, between the second sampling occasion and the third. This was despite the greater intervening period and the presentation of the relaxation-training program. Furthermore, the initial immune depression observed in control subjects was greater at times of greater academic stress (being almost nonexistent at the beginning of the university year), and greater for subjects reporting more life-change stress.

The findings from both studies indicate that the venipuncture experience is stressful, and emphasize the need to control for such effects when blood is sampled. Probably the most widely cited study in support of the supposed effects of hypnosis on immune responses is that of Hall, Longo, and Dixon (1981). The authors describe an intervention using hypnosis with imagery which was associated with apparently increased immune responding at the second test occasion, though only for a younger group and only for those who were highly hypnotizable. Taking into account the venipuncture stress, noted in our studies, and other research indicating that fear of "needles" is strongly age-related (Agras, Sylvester, & Oliveau, 1969), the "improvement" in the younger group between the first and second session may simply be the effect of younger subjects recovering from an initial stress response, rather than the effects of hypnosis. The greater change in the high hypnotizables may be explained by a correlation between "absorption," an important predictor of hypnotizability, as well as trait stress. Since there was no control for trait stress in the Hall, et al. study, there is no way of estimating its effects. The same kind of analysis might be applied to many other studies of immunity which have failed to take into account the initial stressful effects of venipuncture.

While the effect that is most apparent in our two studies is the greater immune depression and the greater state stress of control subjects, the equanimity of the relaxation subjects is just as interesting. This might have occurred through some different assessment of the venipuncture situation itself, or through re-evaluation of other stressful experiences such as the academic stress and life change stress, or some combination of the two. In any case, simply expecting to be in a relaxation group led to a relatively enhanced immune response in the face of an acute environmental stressor. This effect far outweighed any effect of the four-week relaxation intervention.

Hypnosis, relaxation, imagery, and suggestion

The hypnotic induction offers a formal situation for the presentation of suggestions for healing. But there are questions about whether hypnosis offers anything different from other psychological strategies that create similar physiological effects, and allow for similar mentation. Frankel (1976) notes that many forms of hypnosis are behaviorally indistinguishable from progressive relaxation, yoga, Zen, and transcendental meditation. However, hypnotic states can be induced in subjects who are both mentally alert and physically active, suggesting a distinction between states of deep relaxation and the hypnotic "trance." Other writers find no distinction between hypnosis and relaxation (e.g., Edmonston, 1989) but see that both may facilitate the deliberate or incidental response to suggestion.

Barber (1978, 1984) and Rossi (1988) have provided extensive and fascinating descriptions of recorded instances of the use of suggestion with and without hypnosis for bodily change and healing. There seemed no special advantage for hypnosis over other forms of suggestion. The overwhelming conclusion from these descriptions is that there is an extraordinary capacity to use suggestions to achieve profound organic changes. While the authors mentioned concur that manipulation of blood flow may facilitate the developments that are described, clearly the changes described require very specific responses, which have yet to be explained.

Right hemisphere activation

A connection has been proposed between specific brain wave patterns and subjective experiences, including imagery enhancement and deep physical relaxation, that often accompany relaxation, meditation, and hypnotic states. Kamiya (1968, 1969) observed that subjects could learn to switch off alpha brain rhythms at will, and that visual imagery facilitated such control. Subjects reported that they preferred to turn alpha brain waves on, rather than off, since the subjective experience was interesting and surprisingly pleasant. It was a relaxing, noncritical, and nonanalytical experience.

Green and Green (1977) noted an "unusually high percentage of theta rhythms (4–8 Hz) in the EEG of trained meditators during periods of deep reverie." (p. 127), during which they reported dreamlike hypnagogic imagery. With feedback, most subjects could increase their production of theta, and this was associated with a dramatic increase of hypnagogic imagery. Theta was associated with "a deeply internalised state and with a quieting of the body, emotions, and thoughts, thus allowing unheard or unseen things to come to the consciousness in the form of hypnagogic imagery" (p. 143). Some subjects reported an increase in dream recall and the vivid recall of childhood experiences during the theta practice sessions. Lehmann, Koukkom, and Andrege (1980) used a paradigm similar to that found in sleep studies of brain waves. They correlated reports of mentation types with recorded brain rhythms and found much greater visual imagery, less associative thinking, and less rational problem-solving in theta than in alpha states.

More recently, research has focused on arousal patterns in the different hemispheres (Robbins & McAdam, 1974). The left hemisphere was the more activated during a verbal task, both hemispheres were more equally involved during a mixed auditory and visual imagery task, and the right hemisphere was the more activated during the visual imagery task. Right hemispheric activation has been found when listening to stories (Ornstein, Herron, Johnstone, & Swencionis, 1979), and with experiences rated high on "imagery" and "affect" (Ehrlichman & Wiener, 1980). Within hemispheres, regions of activation might vary too, sometimes apparently according to the sensory processes involved in experimental tasks (Davidson & Schwartz, 1977), or depending on whether imagery involved positive or negative affect

(Davidson, Schwartz, Saron, Bennett, & Goleman, 1979; De Pascalis, 1989).

Bakan (1978) noted that the left dominant hemisphere is typically involved with language, logic, propositional thought, and analytic functions. Its mode of functioning has been described as abstract, lineal, rational, focal, conceptual, reality-oriented, propositional, and secondary process. The right "non-dominant" hemisphere is associated with perceptual-spatial and nonverbal functions, visual and body imagery, music, and nonanalytic functions. Its mode of functioning has been described as concrete, nonlineal, pictorial, diffuse, metaphoric, affective, archaic, appositional, integrative, and primary process. Thus the right hemisphere is involved in the exercise and strengthening of psychological functions such as divergent thinking, creativity, stereopsis, ego integration, and problem solving.

The transition from a normal to an altered state of awareness may be characterized by an increased involvement of the right cerebral hemisphere in cognitive processing during the administration of a hallucinogen (Goldstein & Stolzfus, 1973) and sexual orgasm (Cohen, Rosen, & Goldstein, 1976). Other research has indicated such reversal in EEG amplitude asymmetries with the switch from verbal to visual and music processing tasks (Galin & Ornstein, 1972). Right hemispheric functioning may be enhanced during transcendental meditation and hypnosis (Morgan, MacDonald, & Hilgard, 1974; Pagano & Frumkin, 1977). Mészáros, Crawford, Szabó, Nagy-Kovács, and Révész (1989) found support for the idea that there is differential EEG hemispheric involvement in the waking state and hypnosis that is moderated by hypnotic level. They also reported different asymmetry between the anterior and posterior regions for high versus low hypnotizables.

This research may partially account for several well-known hypnotic effects, including inducing emotional states (e.g., Galin, 1974), memory phenomena (especially involuntary memories), and the dichotomy of awareness indicated by the "hidden observer effect." The latter suggests a split in consciousness that may be related to hemispheric asymmetries (Rossi, 1988).

In the hypnotic context, Rossi (1988) proposes that suggestions about getting more and more comfortable may initiate a shift in autonomic system balance from sympathetic toward parasympathetic dominance. This is facilitated by stillness of the musculature and the consequent reduction in proprioceptive and kinesthetic sensation. Closing the eyes further enhances this change, often leading to alpha wave production and eventually theta wave formation in the brain.

While many of these studies seem to implicate hypnosis in the kinds of changes that go along with right hemisphere activation, they do not exclude the possibility that the same thing happens with relaxation and meditation. Indeed, Benson (1983) speaks explicitly of the sympathetic to parasympathetic switch that characterizes the "relaxation response." Meares (1983) insists that meditative states involve "atavistic regression," which seems to encompass the right hemisphere phenomena described above.

Hypnotic responsiveness and right hemisphere functioning

Kamiya's studies (e.g., 1968, 1969) indicated that individuals who were good at producing alpha brain waves were more introspective, more likely to have practiced some form of meditation, and more likely to use words such as "images," "dreams," and "feelings." This raises the question about a possible relationship between hypnotizability and the capacity to initiate shifts in brain functioning. Using lateral eye movements as an indicator of cerebral dominance, greater hypnotizability has been related to right hemispheric dominance (Bakan, 1978; Gur & Gur, 1974).

Chromatic binocular rivalry research (Ruggieri, Capozzi, & Clavenzani, 1989) also supports the idea that hypnosis involves a relative inhibition of the left hemisphere and enhanced activity of the right hemisphere, and also that this "central inhibitory balance" (indicated by the disappearance of right ocular dominance) occurs more readily in high hypnotizables. De Pascalis (1989) reports greater amplitude-integrated alpha in the EEGs of high hypnotisables, and task-related asymmetries, but no clear relationship between waking state EEG asymmetry and hypnotic susceptibility.

Spiegel (1989) describes research using cortical event-related potentials (ERPs) to study the neurophysiological effects of hypnotically produced halluncination. High hypnotizables showed a greater decrease in ERPs in generating a hallucinated image, and in reducing perception of the visual stimulus, implying a greater involvement of the right hemisphere. Marucci, De Pascalis, Penna, and Pessa (1989) found that high hypnotizables showed lower 40Hz EEG activity than lows. Furthermore, they showed greater right hemisphere activation during rest and visual perception conditions.

Crawford (1989) proposed that people high in hypnotizability have greater cognitive and physiological flexibility, as instanced by greater shifts in activation between the two hemispheres on waking tasks, and the capacity for hypnosis itself. Thus they have a greater capacity to control the focus of attention. For instance, they showed a dramatic increase in cerebral blood flow, especially in the temporal region, implying an increase in cerebral metabolism, and a greater integrated EEG amplitude ("more power") during hypnosis. High hypnotizables were more right hemisphere dominant in the posterior region, and more left hemisphere dominant in the anterior region, while the lows showed opposite effects.

Mészáros, Crawford, Szabó, Nagy-Kovács, and Révész (1989) indicated that high hypnotizables showed different EEG asymmetry between anterior and posterior regions than lows. The highs were more right hemisphere dominant in the posterior parieto-occipital region than lows, and this did not change with hypnosis. The highs were less right hemisphere dominant in the anterior fronto-central region than lows during hypnosis, but not waking.

Imagery

Sheikh and Kunzendorf (1984) provide strong evidence that imagery is causally linked with physiological effects. This is based on individual differences in the area of heart rate control, electro-dermal control, vasomotor control, salivary control, pain tolerance, and clinical effects. In an interesting variation of this work, Ahsen (1984) showed that merely imaging an increase in heartbeat resulted in improved imagery responses in low imagers. Thus individual differences in imagery capacity depend, to some extent, on how imagery is being used.

Images offer a way of developing symbolic suggestions that may be particularly effective in creating psychological or physiological change under conditions of right hemisphere dominance. The role of the right hemisphere in imagery production suggests the importance of processes which facilitate right hemisphere dominance. In a review of research studies in the area, Bakan (1980) concluded that the right hemisphere does have a primary role in the production of "raw imagery." This is facilitated during sleep, dreaming, muscular relaxation, free association, mind wandering, and under the effects of some drugs that block interhemispheric communication. When the cerebral hemispheres are in good communication, the raw imagery of the right hemisphere is transformed or transduced by the left hemisphere.

Achterberg (1985) and Achterberg and Lawlis (1980, 1984) have presented evidence for the view that mind-body communication and healing are mediated by "the body image." This is an organization of visual imagery that is apparently constructed in the fronto-limbic system, particularly with the help of the right cerebral hemisphere. They have tested and extended their theories about bodily healing in treatments offered for cancer patients (referred to below) with apparent success.

Ultradian rhythms

Bakan (1978) hypothesizes a relationship between dreaming, REM sleep, and relative dominance of the right hemisphere system. He points to evidence concerning a basic duality in the sleep process, changes from NREM to REM sleep, and a related duality in hemispheric functioning. Bakan also presents evidence linking REM/dream sleep to the functional activation of the right hemisphere, noting in particular that the mentation of dreaming and of the waking right hemisphere is characterized by a reliance on imagery, affect, and primary process thought. He concludes that there is a cyclic ascendance in the functioning of the right hemisphere system during sleep, and perhaps in wakefulness, which is manifested by changes at the physiological (EEG) and psychological levels (dreams, fantasies).

Bakan further argues that dreaming is a right hemispheric function, and that it is largely dependent on imagery. Loss of dreams is associated with right hemisphere injury. He suggests that a functional disconnection of hemispheres occurs during sleep. Also, there is a striking decrease in sympathetic tone, motor function, and motor tone during REM sleep. But the fantasy of body movement and body imagery is greatest during REM sleep. Right hemispheric functions are related to parasympathetic activity.

Reviewing earlier research, Rossi (1988) proposes that there are cycles of parasympathetic and right hemisphere activity which replace patterns of sympathetic and left hemisphere activity. They occur on about a 90-minute cycle throughout the 24-hour day. Rossi suggests that psychosomatic stress may be understood in terms of distortions of these rhythms, and that hypnotherapy may facilitate healing by permitting these rhythms to return to normal. Rossi proposes that simply experiencing a comfortable therapeutic trance can normalize our ultradian rhythms, and influence the regulation of many endocrinal and autonomic system processes that control our basic metabolism. He states that "this normalization process . . . may be the most practical, effective, psychobiological means we have at present for accessing and potentiating healing and rejuvenation of mind-body processes" (Rossi, 1988, p. 148).

Imagery, relaxation, and cancer

The work of LeShan (1977) and Achterberg (1985) points to the role of belief, specific aspects of mentation, and the experience of physiological and psychological calmness in achieving bodily healing effects. The use of imagery shows us that the development and understanding of a personal symbolic system could have therapeutic potential. Green and Green (1977) examined 400 documented cases of "spontaneous remission" from cancer. They concluded that the only common features were a change in attitude, the development of hope for the future, and an increase in positiveness in patients' approach to the disease. The recent approaches to therapeutic hypnosis that have been effective in enhancing immunocompetence with cancer patients reveal at least five basic applications: relaxation, imagery, reframing, meditation, and reinforcing coping skills (Rossi, 1988).

Achterberg, Lawlis, Simonton, and Matthews-Simonton (1977), Simonton, Matthews-Simonton, and Sparks (1980), and Achterberg (1985) used imagery, or visualization, with "incurable" cancer patients. They found that the extent of recovery was significant for patients who imaged their immunological systems attacking tumors. This was statistically related to the patient's "judged ability to form visual images." This, in turn, was partly influenced by their understanding of their immune systems. The above visualization/relaxation procedure involves a "cognitive reframing approach" in which the cancer cells are described as "weak," and "confused," while the immune system's white blood cells are "strong" and "powerful." Thus the intervention involves characteristics of symbolic and literal suggestion, imagery, and verbal reframing which are enhanced through the use of a hypnosis-like relaxation procedure.

A very different approach was used by Ainslie Meares (1983) which he called "mental ataraxis," a form of intensive meditation aimed at producing an "inner stillness." He claimed that this approach involves the "absence of striving, of trying, and of using one's willpower." He believed that it is the stillness which allows the organism to achieve a balance and to overcome the effects of stress. Meares advocated an entirely passive state of mind during this kind of meditation, without the use of images. He seemed to have developed a scepticism about visualization because of the failure of one of his cancer patients, who apparently used the process and failed to thrive.

Ian Gawler (1984) was one of Ainslie Meares's most spectacular "cures." Suffering from bone cancer which had reached his lungs, he had a prognosis of two weeks to live when he began meditating for four to five hours a day under Meares's guidance. The advance of the cancer stopped at this point. But according to Gawler's analysis, the cancer did not regress until he developed a genuine belief in the possibility of self-healing. Eight years later Gawler remains healthy, and runs a foundation that assists cancer patients to heal themselves.

Gawler does not use the lengthy meditation that Meares advocated. Instead, he prefers a hypnotic-like relaxation situation, and the use of healing images or visualizations of a specific or purely symbolic nature.

Newton (1983) offered a strategy for cancer patients taking elements from both the Achterberg-Simonton visualization approach, and the Meares's stillness approach. Poor visualisers could make good clinical progress, and thus he tended to downplay the significance of the visualisation procedure with these people, always giving emphasis to calmness of mind in his patients. This condition, achieved by a variety of procedures, allowed for the full implementation of healing suggestions that were explicit and implicit in the treatment situation. Other therapeutic approaches for cancer have been offered by Margolis (1983) and Finkelstein and Greenleaf (1983).

There is wide agreement that the kind of body-mind change that is associated with hypnotic relaxation, meditation, and other forms of relaxation facilitates the healing process with cancer patients. The use of suggestion through images that symbolize the organism's fight plays an important role in many of these interventions. Recent intervention studies in Europe (Grossarth-Maticek, Kanazir, Schmidt, & Vetter, 1985) have successfully used a combination of approaches, including cognitive reframing, and training in the expression of repressed emotions. This indicates that suggestions for healing purposes may sometimes be effective without formal relaxation, meditation, or hypnosis experiences.

Hypnosis, suggestion, and immune responses

Recent research demonstrates that hypnosis, or hypnosis-like relaxation (e.g., Kiecolt-Glaser, Glaser, Strain, Stout, Tarr, Holliday, & Speicher, 1986) and biofeedback-assisted relaxation (Peavey, Lawlis, & Goven, 1985) can have measurable effects on aspects of immune functioning. Again the predominant impression from this work is that forms of relaxation, with or without a formal hypnotic induction, achieve similar effects.

Peavey (1983) investigated the effect of a training program designed to enhance relaxation by biofeedback. She found that while the number of neutrophils remained the same, they were found to function better with successful relaxation training. Schneider, Smith, and Witcher (1984) combined belief with imagery training to explore the relationship between imagination and the immune system. Subjects were able to increase greatly or decrease the number of circulating neutrophils in their bloodstream.

Various studies have indicated enhanced or reduced skin responses to allergens or other antigens through suggestion. Ikemi and Nakagawa (1962) manipulated expectations in both hypnosis and nonhypnosis groups and found similar effects, using plants that produced allergic reactions with sensitive subjects. Black (1963) found that hypnotized subjects could suppress the skin response to the application of tuberculin antigen. Smith and McDaniel (1983) used a behavioral conditioning paradigm to demonstrate the role of expectation in modulating this response. Associating one color with the antigen and one with saline solution, and giving repeated applications of these materials, they found a suppression of the response on one arm when the colors were switched.

Smith, McKenzie, Marmer, and Steele (1985) examined the effect of meditation in a single subject on the application of the varicella zoster antigen to the skin. The subject received the skin test weekly for nine weeks, being asked to react normally during the first three, to inhibit the response during the next three, and again to react normally in the last three. Results indicated that this subject did indeed reduce her immune response on both the skin response, and the measure of lymphocyte proliferation. Smith, et al. suggest that their work establishes the "intentional direct psychological modulation of the human immune system."

Our own research (Shea, et al., 1989) suggests that mere allocation to a relaxation group had a profound effect on immune responses, even before any intervention began. It also showed that, within a group of relaxation subjects, positive changes in immune responding were more highly related to the number of relaxation practice sessions at home than to the subjective depth of relaxation achieved.

This research confirms the value of hypnosis and other relaxation procedures for enhancing immune responses. As with the treatment of cancer, important factors include the suggested relaxation, the implicit meaning of this relaxation for the organism's well-being, explicit suggestions about cognitive change, and the use of symbolic suggestions via imagery. Spanos (1989) suggests that encouraging an active interpretational set in hypnosis may improve the capacity for responding to novel suggestions. Perhaps that is another way of speaking about positive thinking.

Personality, immunity, and illness

Epidemiological studies point to the importance of psychological factors in illness, predicting vulnerability to disease and resistance to illness for coronary heart disease (e.g., Friedmann & Rosenmann, 1974; Kobasa, 1979; Vaillant, 1977) and cancer (Levy, 1984; Greer & Watson, 1985; Thomas, Duszynski, & Shaffer, 1979). A persistent theme in the literature has been the linking of the repression of emotions, especially anger and anxiety, with the later appearance of cancer (e.g., Grossarth-Maticek, et al., 1985; Temoshok, 1985; Eysenck, 1987). However, the personality pattern so often associated with cancer includes the lack of capacity for self focus, and the low use of fantasy (e.g., Biondi & Pancheri, 1985). This brings suggestion into the discussion, since imagery and fantasy often seem to involve symbolic self-suggestions. When this idea is considered alongside the wide use of hypnosis, relaxation, and imagery in the psychological treatments of cancer patients, a search for a suggestion-related personality characteristic related to immunity, cancer incidence, and potential recovery from cancer seems appropriate.

Shapiro (1971) has drawn attention to the particular qualities of placebo responders which may allow them to be more successful in manipulating their own health status. He describes placebo nonresponders as "rigid and stereotypic, and ... not psychologically minded" (p. 445). Wickramasekera (1980) argued that placebo responders resemble good hypnotic responders since both use their rich subjective repertoires to elaborate on the stimulus properties of a drug potentiating it. Or, they may utilize negative attributions to negate the effects of a drug. Some of these qualities seem like those which define absorption.

Absorption, the capacity for focused attention (Tellegen & Atkinson, 1974), seems to be the best predictor of hypnotic ability (Nadon, Laurence, & Perry, 1987). Also, high absorbers are very good at manipulating autonomic functions (e.g., Qualls & Sheehan, 1979; Shea, Anseline, & Campbell, 1985), and tend to use imagery spontaneously in order to achieve such control. Thus it seems appropriate to explore the role of absorption in health status.

Personality and immunity

Some years ago my colleagues and I began research into the effects of personality, and short-and long-term stress on immune responses. In a pilot investigation, measures of state and trait stress were unexpectedly positively related to immune status. These findings were curious since the direction of effect is opposite to that reported in other studies (e.g., Dorian, Keystone, Garfinkel, & Brown, 1982; Kiecolt-Glaser, et al., 1986), although they fit in with some of the thinking about vulnerability to cancer (e.g., Eysenck, 1987). In a second experiment (described in Shea, et al., 1989), the Willoughby Neuroticism scale was used as the sole stress measure, together with the Tellegen-Atkinson Absorption scale (Tellegen & Atkinson, 1974). Absorption was used for reasons suggested above.

Thirty-six subjects, who were extreme scorers on the Willoughby scale and the Absorption scale, gave blood by venipuncture, and delayed hypersensitivity skin tests were applied. Both neuroticism and absorption affected immune responding. High neuroticism was associated with higher T lymphocyte cell numbers, and greater redness and swelling responses to a number of antigens. High absorbers showed lower responses on some of the delayed hypersensitivity measures. However, the most pervasive personality effects in these analyses were interactions between absorption and neuroticism. For example, higher T lymphocyte numbers (various measures) occurred in the low absorption/high neuroticism group, and the lowest cell numbers were in the low absorption/low neuroticism group or the high absorption/high neuroticism group. With regard to delayed skin hypersensitivity, the low absorption/high neuroticism group showed the largest scores for skin redness and swelling.

The findings of the first experiment were supported in this second study. Again, the high neuroticism subjects, or one subgroup of these, the low absorption/high neuroticism group, showed larger numbers of T lymphocytes, and greater skin responses to antigens applied to the skin. These responses imply superior immune responding. Furthermore, there was consistency between the in vitro measures of cell number, percentages, and ratio, on the one hand, and delayed hypersensitivity skin responses on the other. Thus there are good indications within the study, as well as by comparison with the pilot study, that suggest the reliability of the phenomena observed.

A further experiment was conducted to examine systematically relationships between neuroticism and absorption and immune responses, taking into account other factors including acute and chronic stressors. This time eighty-eight subjects who were extreme scorers on neuroticism and absorption were selected from a larger group of students, and a greater range of immune cells and functions was examined. Again there were a number of effects related to the personality variables. High neurotics had a higher number of monocytes. High absorbers had higher numbers of basophils and neutrophils. There were also interaction effects between the two personality variables. It is noteworthy that the high absorbers/high neurotics were either the highest or lowest scorers in 11 of the 15 variables examined. This suggests a systematic relationship with immune responses in general, which was confirmed in multivariate analyses. These analyses emphasized the relatively poor natural killer-cell activity of the high absorbers/high neurotics group, and their relatively high macrophage responses.

Differences with the preceding experiment can probably be partly accounted for by the powerful effects of academic stress, as reflected in the month of testing, and experimental group (hypno-relaxation or control). When groups from the same experimental condition and similar month of testing were compared, greater similarities were found.

This research has identified a sub-group of highly stressed individuals, those high neurotics who are also high absorbers, who have characteristically low measures on a number of immune variables (e.g., natural killer-cell activity, T4 cell numbers, T8 cell numbers and percentages, cortisol), and high measures on other immune variables (e.g., basophils, monocytes, neutrophils, eosinophils). While some aspects of this immune response pattern are characteristic of relatively depleted immune responding, the pattern is complex and requires further study before its health significance is established. Also worthy of attention is the point that for some of the immune responses, the subjects who scored at the opposite extreme to the high absorbers/high neurotics were the low absorbers/high neurotics. Thus relationships between trait stress (as measured by the Willoughby scale) and immune responding were moderated by absorption.

Conclusion

This discussion has considered questions about the power and distribution of self-healing abilities that follow suggestion, and some of the personal strategies and personal qualities that might be useful in potentiating self-change and self-healing. It seems a reasonable conclusion that placebo effects pervade all forms of health interventions, and that these effects are often extraordinary. Greater changes in immune responses were described in this paper resulting from expectation of relaxation training than from the relaxation training itself. A fascinating body of research suggests that psychological strategies such as hypnosis, relaxation training, and meditation may facilitate the development of changes in the system's readiness to focus on, and utilize imagery for self-change and healing. Some of these changes are seen at the level of asymmetries in the functioning of the brain hemispheres. It seems that particular individual qualities may be advantageous in the use of suggestion for healing, as well as affecting initial predispositions to illness. Nonetheless, my own experience of training people in self-hynosis or deep relaxation suggests that most people can acquire these skills sufficiently to make a significant impact on their well-being. Thus, every person may be susceptible to suggestive modes of influence. It might also be remembered that hypnosis, and other forms of altered attention, may be induced without going through a relaxation ritual. We might speculate that, in such cases, there is an immediate switch to the cerebral conditions that facilitate suggestion. When it comes to harnessing self-healing effects, we have a long way to go before we can prescribe courses of therapeutic action that have predictable consequences for any given individual. But published studies suggest an enormous potential for self-change that is usually untapped. It is worth noting too that since placebo effects fall within the domain of psychology, systematic research offers potential benefits to the profession as well as to the patient.

References

Achterberg, J. (1985). *Imagery and Healing*. Boston: Shambala.

Achterberg, J., & Lawlis, G. (1980). *Bridges of the mind/body*. Champaign, IL: Institute for Personality and Ability Testing.

Achterberg, J., & Lawlis, G. (1984). *Imagery and Disease*. Champaign, IL: Institute for Personality and Ability Testing.

Achterberg, J., Lawlis, G., Simonton, O., & Matthews-Simonton, S. (December, 1977). Psychological factors and blood chemistries as disease outcome predictors for cancer patients. *Multivariate Clinical Experimental Research*.

Agras, W.S., Sylvester, D., & Oliveau, D. (1969). The epidemiology of common fears and phobia. *Comprehensive Psychiatry, 10*, 151–56.

Ahsen, A. (1984). Heartbeat as stimulus for vivid imagery: A report on individual differences and imagery function. *Journal of Mental Imagery, 1984, 8*(2), 105–10.

Ashton, R. (1990). The mighty placebo. *Mind*, 6, 6.

Bakan, P. (1978). Dreaming, REM sleep and the right hemisphere: A theoretical integration. *Journal of Altered States of Consciousness, 3*(4), 285–307.

Bakan, P. (1980). Imagery, raw and cooked: A hemispheric recipe. In J. Shorr, G. Sobel, P. Robin, & J. Connella (eds.), *Imagery* (pp. 35–53). New York: Plenum Press.

Barber, T.X. (1978). Hypnosis, suggestions, and psychosomatic phenomena: A new look from the standpoint of recent experimental studies. *American Journal of Clinical Hypnosis, 21*(1), 13–27.

Barber, T.X. (1984). Changing unchangeable bodily processes by (hypnotic) suggestions: A new look at hypnosis, cognitions, imaging, and the mind-body problem. *Advances, 1*(2), 7–40.

Beecher, H. (1959). *Measurement of subjective responses: Quantitative effect of drugs.* New York: Oxford University Press.

Benson, H. (1983). The relaxation response: Its subjective and objective historical precedents and physiology. *Trends in Neuroscience,* July, 281–84.

Biondi, M., & Pancheri, P. (1985). Stress, personality, immunity, and cancer: A challenge for psychosomatic medicine. In R.M. Kaplan & M.H. Criqui (eds.), *Behavioural epidemiology and disease prevention.* New York: Plenum Press.

Black, S. (1963). Inhibition of immediate-type hypersensitivity response by direct suggestion under hypnosis. *British Medical Journal,* April 6, 925–29.

Cannon, W. (1963). *The wisdom of the body.* New York: W.W. Norton and Co.

Cohen, H.D., Rosen, R.C., & Goldstein, L. (1976). Electroencephalographic laterality changes during human sexual orgasm. *Archives of Sexual Behaviour, 5,* 189.

Crawford, H.J. (1989). Cognitive and physiological flexibility: Multiple pathways to hypnotic responsiveness. In V.A. Gheorghiu, P. Netter, H.J. Eysenck, & R. Rosenthal (eds.), *Suggestion and suggestibility: Theory and research* (pp. 155–68). Berlin: Springer-Verlag.

Davidson, R., & Schwartz, G. (1977). Brain mechanisms subserving self-generated imagery: Electrophysiological specificity and patterning. *Psychophysiology, 14,* 598–602.

Davidson, R., Schwartz, G., Saron, C., Bennett, J., & Goleman, D. (1979). Frontal versus parietal EEG asymmetry during positive and negative affect. *Psychophysiology, 16,* 202–03.

De Pascalis, V. (1989). Hypnotic susceptibility, alpha waves, and 40-Hz EEG rhythm, and personality. In V.A. Gheorghiu, P. Netter, H.J. Eysenck, & R. Rosenthal (eds.), *Suggestion and suggestibility: Theory and research* (pp. 221–40). Berlin: Springer-Verlag.

Dorian, B.J., Keystone, E., Garfinkel, P., & Brown, G.M. (1982). Aberrations in lymphocyte subpopulations and functions during psychological stress. *Clinical and Experimental Immunology, 50,* 132–38.

Edmonston, W.E. (1989). Conceptual clarification of hypnosis and its relationship to suggestibility. In V.A. Gheorghiu, P. Netter, H.J. Eysenck, & R. Rosenthal (eds.), *Suggestion and suggestibility: Theory and research* (pp. 69–78). Berlin: Springer-Verlag.

Ehrlichman, H., & Wiener, M. (1980). EEG asymmetry during covert mental activity. *Psychophysiology, 17,* 228–35.

Evans, F.J. (1974). The placebo response in pain reduction. In J.J. Bonica (ed.), *Advances in neurology: Vol. 4, Pain* (pp. 289–96). New York: Raven.

Evans, F.J. (1977). The placebo control of pain: A paradigm for investigating non-specific factors in psychotherapy. In J.D. Brady, J. Mendels, W.R. Reyer, & M. T. Orne (eds.), *The future of psychiatry* (pp. 129–36). New York: Spectrum.

Evans, F.J. (1981). The placebo response in pain control. *Psychopharmacological Bulletin, 17,* 72–76.

Evans, F.J. (1985). Expectancy, therapeutic instructions and the placebo response. In L. White, B. Tursky, & G.E. Schwartz (eds.), *Placebo: Theory, research and mechanisms* (pp. 215–28). New York: Guilford.

Evans, F.J. (1989). The independence of suggestibility, placebo response, and hypnotisability. In V.A. Gheorghiu, P. Netter, H.J. Eysenck, & R. Rosenthal (eds.), *Suggestion and suggestibility: Theory and research* (pp. 145–54). Berlin: Springer-Verlag.

Evans, F.J., Gustafson, L.A., O'Connell, D.N., Orne, M.T., & Shor, R.E. (1969). Sleep-induced behavioral response: Relationship to susceptibility to hypnosis and laboratory sleep patterns. *Journal of Nervous and Mental Disease, 148*, 467–76.

Eysenck, H.J. (1947). *Dimensions of personality.* London: Routledge and Kegan Paul.

Eysenck, H.J. (1987). Anxiety, learned helplessness, and cancer: A causal theory. *Journal of Anxiety Disorders, 1*, 87–104.

Eysenck, H.J. (1989). Personality, primary and secondary suggestibility, and hypnosis. In V.A. Gheorghiu, P. Netter, H.J. Eysenck, & R. Rosenthal (eds.), *Suggestion and suggestibility: Theory and research* (pp. 57–68). Berlin: Springer-Verlag.

Finkelstein, S., & Greenleaf, H. (1983). Cancer prevention: A three year pilot study. *The American Journal of Clinical Hypnosis, 25*(2–3), 177–87.

Frank, J.D. (1961). *Persuasion and healing.* Baltimore: Johns Hopkins Press.

Frankel, F. (1976). *Hypnosis: Trance as a coping mechanism.* Plenum Medical Book Company.

Friedmann, S., & Rosenmann, R.H. (1974). *Type A behavior and your heart.* New York: Knopf.

Galin, D. (1974). Implications for psychiatry of left and right cerebral specialization: A neurophysiological context for unconscious processes. *Archives of General Psychiatry, 31*, 572–83.

Galin, D., & Ornstein, R. (1972). Lateral specialization of cognitive mode: An EEG study. *Psychophysiology, 9*, 412.

Gawler, I. (1984). *You can conquer cancer.* Melbourne: Hill of Conquest Publishing Company.

Gheorghiu, V.A. (1989a). The development of research on suggestibility: Critical considerations. In V.A. Gheorghiu, P. Netter, H.J. Eysenck, & R. Rosenthal (eds.), *Suggestion and suggestibility: Theory and research* (pp. 3–56). Berlin: Springer-Verlag.

Gheorghiu, V.A. (1989b). The difficulty in explaining suggestion: Some conceivable solutions. In V.A. Gheorghiu, P. Netter, H.J. Eysenck, & R. Rosenthal (eds.), *Suggestion and suggestibility: Theory and research* (pp. 99–112). Berlin: Springer-Verlag.

Goldstein, L., & Stolzfus, N.W. (1973). Psychoactive drug-induced changes of interhemispheric EEG amplitude relationships. *Agents Actions, 3/2*, 124–32.

Green, E., & Green, A. (1977). *Beyond biofeedback.* New York: Delta.

Greer, S., & Watson, M. (1985). Towards a psychobiological model of cancer: Psychological considerations. *Social Science in Medicine, 20*, 773–77.

Grossarth-Maticek, R., Kanazir, D.T., Schmidt, P., & Vetter, H. (1985). Psychosocial and organic variables as predictors of lung cancer, cardiac infarct and apoplexy: Some differential predictors. *Personality and Individual Differences, 6*, 313–21.

Gur, R.C., & Gur, R.E. (1974). Handedness, sex, and eyedness as moderating variables in the relationship between hypnotic susceptibility and functional brain asymmetry. *Journal of Abnormal Psychology, 83*, 635–43.

Hall, H.R., Longo, S., & Dixon, R. (1981, October). *Hypnosis and the immune system: The effect of hypnosis on T and B cell function.* Paper presented at the 33rd Annual

Workshop and Scientific meeting of the Society for Clinical and Experimental Hypnosis, Portland, Oregon.

Harding, A., & Maher, K. (1982). Biofeedback training of cardiac acceleration: Effects on airways resistance in bronchial asthma. *Journal of Psychosomatic Research, 26*(4), 447–54.

Ikemi, Y., & Nakagawa, S. (1962). A psychosomatic study of contagious dermatitis. *Kyushu Journal of Medical Science, 13*, 335–50.

Jospe, M. (1978). *The placebo effect in healing.* Toronto: Methuen.

Kamiya, J. (1968). Conscious control of brain waves. *Psychology Today, 1*(3), 57–60.

Kamiya, J. (1969). Operant control of the EEG alpha rhythm and some of its reported effects on consciousness. In C. Tart (ed.), *Altered states of consciounsess* (pp. 507–17). New York: Wiley.

Kiecolt-Glaser, J.K., Glaser, R., Strain, E.C., Stout, J.C., Tarr, K.L., Holliday, J.E., & Speicher, C.E. (1986). Modulation of cellular immunity in medical students. *Journal of Behavioral Medicine, 9*(1), 5–21.

Klopfer, B. (1957). Psychological variables in human cancer. *Journal of Projective Techniques, 21*, 331–40.

Kobasa, S.C. (1979). Stressful life events, personality and health: An inquiry into hardiness. *Journal of Personality and Social Psychology, 37*, 1–11.

Kruse, P. (1989). Some suggestions about suggestion and hypnosis: A radical constructivist view. In V.A. Gheorghiu, P. Netter, H.J. Eysenck, & R. Rosenthal (eds.), *Suggestion and suggestibility: Theory and research* (pp. 91–98). Berlin: Springer-Verlag.

Le Shan, L. (1977). *You can fight for your life.* New York: Evans and Co.

Lehmann, D., Koukkom, M., & Andrege, A. (1980). EEG patterns and daydreaming mentation. Proceedings of the German EEG society (1979). *EEG and Clinical Neurophysiology, 50*, 134.

Levy, S. (1984). Emotions and the progression of cancer. *Advances, 1*, 10–15.

Margolis, C. (1983). Hypnotic imagery with cancer patients. *The American Journal of Clinical Hypnosis, 25*(2–3), 128–34.

Marruci, F.S., De Pascalis, V., Penna, M.P., & Pessa, E. (1989). 40-Hz EEG and hypnotisability during mental activity. In V.A. Gheorghiu, P. Netter, H.J. Eysenck, & R. Rosenthal (eds.), *Suggestion and suggestibility: Theory and research* (pp. 205–20). Berlin: Springer-Verlag.

Mason, A. (1952). A case of congenital ichthyosiform erythrodermia of Brocq treated by hypnosis. *British Medical Journal, 2*, 422–23.

Meares, A. (1983). A form of intensive meditation associated with the regression of cancer. *The American Journal of Hypnosis, 25*(2–3), 114–21.

Mészáros, I., Crawford, H.J., Szabó, C., Nagy-Kovács, A., & Révész, Z. (1989). Hypnotic susceptibility and cerebral hemisphere preponderance: Verbal-imaginal discrimination task. In V.A. Gheorghiu, P. Netter, H.J. Eysenck, & R. Rosenthal (eds.), *Suggestion and suggestibility: Theory and research* (pp. 191–204). Berlin: Springer-Verlag.

McGlashan, T.H., Evans, F.J., & Orne, M.T. (1969). The nature of hypnotic analgesia and placebo response to experimental pain. *Psychosomatic Medicine, 31*, 227–46.

Melzack, R. (1973). *The puzzle of pain.* New York: Basic Books.

Morgan, A.H., MacDonald, H., & Hilgard, E.R. (1974). EEG alpha: Lateral asymmetry related to task and hypnotisability. *Psychophysiology, 11*, 275.

Nadon, R., Laurence, J., & Perry, C. (1987). Multiple predictors of hypnotic susceptibility. *Journal of Personality and Social Psychology, 53*(5), 948–60.

Netter, P. (1989). Sensory suggestibility: Measurement, individual differences, and relation to placebo and drug effects. In V.A. Gheorghiu, P. Netter, H.J. Eysenck, & R. Rosenthal (eds.), *Suggestion and suggestibility: Theory and research* (pp. 123–34). Berlin: Springer-Verlag.

Newton, B. (1983). Introduction: Hypnosis and cancer. *The American Journal of Clinical Hypnosis, 25*(2–3), 89–91.

Orne, M.T. (1974). Pain suppression by hypnosis and related phenomena. In J.J. Bonica (ed.), *Pain.* New York: Raven.

Ornstein, R., Herron, J., Johnstone, J., & Swencionis, C. (1979). Differential right hemisphere involvement in two reading tasks. *Psychophysiology, 16*, 398–401.

Pagano, R., & Frumkin, L. (1977). The effect of transcendental meditation on right hemispheric functioning. *Biofeedback and Self-Regulation, 2*, 407–09.

Peek, C.J. (1977). A critical look at the theory of placebo. *Biofeedback and Self-Regulation, 2*, 327–35.

Peavey, B.S. (1983). Biofeedback-assisted relaxation: Effects on phagocytic immune functioning. *Dissertation Abstracts International, 43*(11–B), 3769–70.

Peavey, B.S., Lawlis, G.F., & Goven, A. (1985). Biofeedback assisted relaxation: Effects on phagocytic capacity. *Biofeedback and Self-Regulation, 10*, 33–47.

Qualls, P.J., & Sheehan, P.W. (1979). Capacity for absorption and relaxation during electromyograph biofeedback and no-feedback conditions. *Journal of Abnormal Psychology, 88*, 651–62.

Robbins, K., & McAdam, D. (1974). Interhemispheric alpha asymmetry and imagery mode. *Brain and Language, 1*, 189–93.

Rossi, E.L. (1988). *The psychobiology of mind-body healing.* New York: W.W. Norton and Co.

Ruggieri, V., Capozzi, R., & Clavenzani, G. (1989). Perceptual styles in chromatic binocular rivalry, hypnotic susceptibility, and cerebral dominance. In V.A. Gheorghiu, P. Netter, H.J. Eysenck, & R. Rosenthal (eds.), *Suggestion and suggestibility: Theory and research* (pp. 241–48). Berlin: Springer-Verlag.

Schneider, J., Smith, W., & Witcher, S. (1984, October). *The relationship of mental imagery to white blood cell (neutrophil) function in normal subjects.* Paper presented at the 36th Annual Scientific Meeting of the International Society for Clinical and Experimental Hypnosis, San Antonio, Texas.

Shapiro, A.K. (1960). A contribution to the history of placebo effect. *Behavioral Science, 5*(2), 109–35.

Shapiro, A.K. (1971). Placebo effects in medicine, psychotherapy and psychoanalysis. In A. Bergin & S. Garfield (eds.), *Handbook of psychotherapy and behaviour change.* New York: Wiley.

Shea, J.D.C., Anseline, W., & Campbell, E. (1985). Imagery, the capacity for imaginative involvement, and voluntary control of heart rate. In D.F. Marks & D.G. Russell (eds.), *Imagery 1: Proceedings of the First International Imagery Conference.* Dunedin, New Zealand: Human Performance Associates.

Shea, J.D.C., Girgis, A., Husband, A., Burton, R., & Clover, K. (1989, August). *Mental health, relaxation training, and immune responses.* Paper presented to the World Federation for Mental Health, World Congress, Auckland, New Zealand.

Sheikh, A., & Kunzendorf, R. (1984). Imagery, physiology, and psychosomatic illness. In A.A. Sheikh (ed.)., *International review of mental imagery.* New York: Human Sciences Press.

Simonton, O.C., Matthews-Simonton, S., & Sparks, T.F. (1980). Psychological intervention in the treatment of cancer. *Psychosomatics, 21*(3), 226–33.

Smith, G., & McDaniel, S. (1983). Psychologically mediated effect on the delayed hypersensitivity reaction to tuberculin in humans. *Psychosomatic Medicine, 46,* 65–73.

Smith, G., McKenzie, J., Marmer, D., & Steele, R. (1985). Psychological modulation of the human immune response to varicella Zoster. *Archives of International Medicine, 145,* 2110–12.

Spanos, N.P. (1989). Interpretational sets, hypnotic responding, and the modification of hypnotisability. In V.A. Gheorghiu, P. Netter, H.J. Eysenck, & R. Rosenthal (eds.), *Suggestion and suggestibility: Theory and research* (pp. 169–76). Berlin: Springer-Verlag.

Spiegel, D. (1989). Cortical event related potential correlates of hypnotic hallucination. In V.A. Gheorghiu, P. Netter, H.J. Eysenck, & R. Rosenthal (eds.), *Suggestion and suggestibility: Theory and research* (pp. 183–90). Berlin: Springer-Verlag.

Tellegen, A., & Atkinson, G. (1974). Openness to absorbing and self-altering experiences ("absorption"), a trait related to hypnotic susceptibility. *Journal of Abnormal Psychology, 83,* 268–77.

Temoshok, L. (1985). Biopsychosocial studies on cutaneous malignant melanoma: Psychosocial factors associated with prognostic indicators, progression, psychophysiology, and tumour-host response. *Social Science in Medicine, 20*(8), 833–40.

Thomas, C.B., Duszynski, K.R., & Schaffer, J.W. (1979). Family attitudes reported in youth as potential predictors of cancer. *Psychosomatic Medicine, 41,* 287–302.

Thorn, W.A.F. (1962). The placebo reactor. *Australasian Journal of Pharmacy, 43,* 1035–37.

Vaillant, G.E. (1977). *Adaptation to life.* Boston: Little, Brown and Co.

White, L., Tursky, B., & Schwartz, G.E. (eds.). (1985). *Placebo: Theory, research and mechanisms.* New York: Guilford.

Wickramasekera, I. (ed.). (1976). *Biofeedback, behavior therapy, and hypnosis.* Chicago: Nelson-Hall.

Wickramasekera, I. (1977). On attempts to modify hypnotic susceptibility: Some psychophysiological procedures and promising directions. *Annals of the New York Academy of Sciences,* 143–53.

Wickramasekera, I. (1980). A conditioned response model of the placebo effect: Predictions from the model. *Biofeedback and Self-Regulation, 5*(1), 5–18.

PART FOUR

APPLICATIONS AND IMPLICATIONS

14

THE APPLICATION OF INTERROGATIVE SUGGESTIBILITY TO POLICE INTERVIEWING

Gisli H. Gudjonsson

There are two main theoretical approaches to interrogative suggestibility. Schooler and Loftus (1986) refer to these as the "individual differences approach" and the "experimental approach." The former approach is best illustrated by the work of Gudjonsson (1983, 1984a) which was integrated into a detailed theoretical model by Gudjonsson and Clark (1986). The model has specific applicability to police interrogation and views suggestibility as being dependent upon the coping strategies that people can generate and implement when confronted with the *uncertainty* and *expectations* of the interrogative situation. The model tries to explain individual differences in suggestibility. The main premise behind the model is that people vary considerably in their reactions to police interrogation, even when the conditions of the situation are similar.

The experimental approach can be well illustrated by the work of Loftus and her colleagues (Loftus, Miller, & Burns, 1978; Schooler & Loftus, 1986). Here the emphasis is on understanding the conditions under which leading questions are likely to affect the verbal accounts of witnesses. Individual differences in cognitive and personality functioning do not feature significantly in this approach. Interrogative suggestibility is viewed as being mediated by a central cognitive mechanism, referred to as "discrepancy detection." The implication is that people are suggestible when the conditions are such that they are unable to discriminate satisfactorily between what they observed and what is suggested to them.

The two theoretical approaches mentioned above are clearly complementary to each other. Schooler and Loftus (1986) argue that the experimental approach could benefit from considering how differences in personality and cognitive abilities influence the impact of leading questions. Conversely, it is argued that the individual differences approach might enrich their model by more explicitly taking into account the importance of information-processing mechanisms, such as discrepancy detection.

The present paper does not discuss in any detail the experimental approach to interrogative suggestibility. This does not imply that the model has no important application to police interviewing. It clearly does, particularly in relation to the conditions and types of questioning that are most likely to distort memory. The advantage of the individual differences approach in forensic practice is that it focuses on procedures and techniques that are directly applicable to the assessment of the individual case.

The Gudjonsson and Clark model of interrogative suggestibility provides a framework for understanding the process and outcome of police interviewing. This framework helps to provide testable hypotheses for research, in addition to general principles that can be applied to the individual case. The Gudjonsson Suggestibility Scales (Gudjonsson, 1984a, 1987), which have been extensively used to test the hypotheses derived from the Gudjonsson and Clark model, are the only reliable tests currently available for assessing quantitatively individual differences in interrogative suggestibility (Irving, 1990).

In this paper I will discuss the implications and applications of the Gudjonsson and Clark theoretical model in relation to the empirical and experimental evidence currently available. With regard to application, discussion is mainly focused on the assessment of cases where a confession is subsequently retracted or disputed.

The Gudjonsson and Clark model

Gudjonsson and Clark (1986) define interrogative suggestibility as "the extent to which, within a closed social interaction, people come to accept messages communicated during formal questioning, as the result of which their subsequent behavioural response is affected." This definition implies that the interrogative suggestibility consists of five interrelated components, as follows: (1) a closed social interaction between the interrogator and the interviewee; (2) a questioning procedure which involves two or more participants; (3) a suggestive stimulus; (4) acceptance of the suggestive stimulus; and (5) a behavioral response to indicate whether or not the suggestion is accepted.

The above definition indicates that interrogative suggestibility has certain characteristics which differentiate it from other types of suggestibility. Indeed, Gudjonsson (1986) argues that interrogative suggestibility differs from other types of suggestibility in three important ways.

1. It involves a questioning procedure within a closed social interaction.

2. The questions asked deal mainly with past experiences and

events, recollections, and knowledge states. This makes it very different from traditional types of suggestibility, which are primarily concerned with motor and sensory experiences of the immediate situation.

3. Interrogative suggestibility has a component of uncertainty which is related to the cognitive processing capacity of the individual.

Gudjonsson (1989) has added a fourth component. That is, an important feature of interrogative suggestibility is that it typically involves a stressful situation with important consequences for the person being interviewed, whether a witness, a victim, or a suspect.

The Gudjonsson and Clark model is essentially a social-psychological model, where interrogative suggestibility is construed as arising through a particular relationship between the person, the environment, and significant others within that environment. The model integrates the "leading questions" and "negative feedback aspects" of suggestibility described by Gudjonsson (1984a). The potentially damaging effect of leading questions is well recognized in the literature and has been extensively researched (e.g., Loftus, 1979). The role and importance of negative feedback was not fully recognized or systematically researched until the work of Gudjonsson (1983). Within the Gudjonsson and Clark model, negative feedback is conceptualized as "a signal communicated by an interrogator to a witness, after he/she has responded to a question or a series of questions, intended to *strengthen* or *modify* subsequent responses of the witness" (Gudjonsson & Clark, 1986, pp. 93–94). Feedback may be positive (i.e., reinforcing the previous response) or negative (i.e., tending to modify an unwanted answer).

The model states that interrogative suggestibility is dependent upon the coping strategies that subjects can generate and implement when dealing with the *uncertainty* and *expectations* of the interrogation. The three necessary prerequisites for the process of suggestibility are: (1) *uncertainty,* which means that witnesses do not know definitely or surely the right answer to a question and are therefore potentially open to suggestion; (2) *interpersonal trust:* the person must believe that the interrogator's intentions are genuine and that there is no trickery involved (people who are suspicious of the interviewer are reluctant to yield to suggestions); and (3) *expectation of success:* uncertainty and interpersonal trust are necessary but not sufficient for the person to yield to suggestions; this is because if a person is uncertain about an answer he or she can give a reply of "don't know" or "not sure." Many people are reluctant to declare their uncertainty because they believe that they should be able to provide a definite answer and feel they are expected to do so.

The model predicts that most people are open to suggestions when the necessary conditions of uncertainty, interpersonal trust, and heightened expectations are present. The extent to which the person gives in to suggestions is a function of his cognitive appraisal of the situation and the coping strategies adopted.

Implications of the model

A number of hypotheses can be generated from the model. Some of these are as follows.

1. The main premise of the model is that interrogative suggestibility is distinct from other types of suggestibility, particularly that found in a hypnotic context.

2. The three components, *uncertainty, interpersonal trust,* and *expectation* can be manipulated by an interrogator to alter the person's susceptibility to suggestions.

3. People who enter the interrogation with a suspicious cognitive set (e.g., those who do not trust the police and are suspicious of them) are less suggestible than those with a trusting cognitive set.

4. The type of coping strategies people are able to use during the interview affects their level of suggestibility. For example, avoidance coping is likely to facilitate a suggestible response whereby people give answers that to them seem plausible and consistent with the external clues provided, rather than only giving definite answers to questions they clearly remember. In contrast, a nonsuggestible coping strategy involves a critical analysis of the situation and a facilitative problem-solving action.

5. People with poor memory recollection and low intelligence are generally more suggestible than those with higher cognitive abilities.

6. Suggestibility is related to such variables as low self-esteem, lack of assertiveness, and anxiety.

7. The model views suggestibility during interviewing as a dynamic process. This implies that suggestibility is potentially *situation-bound.* This is particularly true in relation to negative feedback, whose impact will vary according to intensity, quality, and nature of the feedback in addition to the person's past experiences. According to the model, the person's response to feedback, particularly negative feedback, is more affected by situational and mood variables than responses to leading questions. However, the model does recognize that suggestibility can be reasonably stable over time because of the cognitive and personality factors that mediate suggestibility. Therefore, stable individual differences in suggestibility can be measured reli-

ably and would predict *how* people are likely to respond during real-life interrogation.

8. The model allows predictions to be made about when people are likely to give distorted or false testimony during questioning. For example, people are likely to become more suggestible during interviewing if they are placed under pressure by the interviewer and when they are in an anxious mental state.

Testing aspects of the model

After laying the foundations for the theoretical work on interrogative suggestibility (Gudjonsson & Gunn, 1982; Gudjonsson, 1983), Gudjonsson (1984a) presented the construction and early validation of a suggestibility scale that could be used to assess the individual's responses to "leading questions" and "negative feedback" instructions when being asked to report a factual event from recall. The scale, referred to as the Gudjonsson Suggestibility Scale (GSS 1), is particularly applicable to legal contexts, such as police officers' questioning of witnesses to crime and interrogation of criminal suspects. It employs a narrative paragraph describing a fictitious mugging, which is read out to the subjects. They are then asked to report all they can recall about the story. After the person has given free immediate and delayed recall to the story (the delay generally amounts to about 50 minutes), he/she is asked 20 specific questions, 15 of which are subtly misleading. After answering the 20 questions the person is told that he/she has made a number of errors (even if no errors have been made), and it is therefore necessary to ask all the questions once more. The person is asked to be more accurate than before. Any change in the person's answers from the previous trial is noted as "shift." The extent to which people give in to the misleading questions is scored as "yield." "Yield" and "shift" are typically added together to make up "total suggestibility," although it is worth noting that the "yield" and "shift" scores are poorly correlated and load factorially on different factors (Gudjonsson, 1984a). Indeed, there are good arguments for keeping "yield" and "shift" separate for clinical interpretation as the latter gives a better indication of how well the person copes with interrogative pressure.

Following the early development of the suggestibility scale, Gudjonsson constructed a parallel form, labelled GSS 2 (Gudjonsson, 1987). The two scales are identical except for the content of the narrative paragraph and interrogative questions (Gudjonsson, 1989). The correlation between the two scales within the same session was 0.90

and 0.92 ("total suggestibility") for normal and forensic subjects respectively (Gudjonsson, 1987). For a group of forensic patients tested on two separate occasions the correlation was 0.81. The correlations were consistently slightly lower for "shift" than for "yield," which is consistent with the prediction from the Gudjonsson and Clark model. The findings give strong support for the test-retest reliability of interrogative suggestibility, even when people are tested many months apart. Therefore, interrogative suggestibility, as measured by the Gudjonsson Suggestibility Scales, appears highly stable over time when the experimental conditions are similar.

Much of the early work on the GSS 1 was concerned with validating the scale and developing the theoretical basis for the Gudjonsson and Clark model. More recently, various experiments have been carried out to test the various hypotheses derived from the model. Many of the hypotheses listed above have been tested and supported experimentally.

Evidence that interrogative suggestibility differs from the susceptibility to hypnosis comes from two recent empirical studies. In the first study, Hardarson (1985) found no significant correlation between scores on the Harvard Group Scale of Hypnotic Susceptibility and interrogative suggestibility as measured by the GSS 1. In a more recent study, Register and Kihlstrom (1988) used a variant of the GSS 1 during an experiment into hypnosis. No significant difference in interrogative suggestibility was found between hypnotizable and nonhypnotizable subjects, supporting the hypothesis of Gudjonsson (1986) that interrogative suggestibility is independent of hypnotizability.

Two studies have shown that it is possible to manipulate the "expectations" of the subjects prior to interrogation in order to reduce or enhance suggestibility as measured by the GSS 1. Gudjonsson and Hilton (1989) investigated the "expectation" component of the Gudjonsson and Clark model by giving three groups of subjects different instructions about their expected performance. One group ("High expectation group") were told that they should be able to remember most of the GSS 1 story and give a definite answer to all the questions. Group 2 were given no explicit instructions about their expected performance. Group 3 ("Low expectation group") were told that they were not expected to be able to find a definite answer to all the questions. A significant difference was found in suggestibility between the three groups as predicted. Similar instrumental manipulation was used in a recent study by Hansdottir, Thorsteinsson, Kristinsdottir, & Ragnarsson (1990). The two studies give strong support for the hypothesis that immediately prior to "interrogation" subjects' cognitive set can be manipulated to increase or reduce subsequent suggestibility. The Gudjonsson and Hilton findings tentatively suggest that it may be easier to lower than heighten suggestibility by instructions, but both types of instructions are probably important.

What is the main implication of these findings for police interviewing? The most important implication is that police interviewers should be aware that certain expectations communicated to subjects prior to or during the interview can markedly affect the accuracy of the information obtained.

Gudjonsson (1988a) recently showed that interrogative suggestibility is significantly related to the coping strategies that subjects report using during the test. Those subjects who proved to be most suggestible tended to use "avoidance" coping during the interrogation. This means that they failed to be able to evaluate each question critically and gave answers that to them seemed plausible and consistent with the external cues provided. Nonsuggestible subjects, on the other hand, were able to adopt a critical analysis of the situation which facilitated the accuracy of their answers.

Gudjonsson (1988a) also provides strong support for the hypothesis that interrogative suggestibility is partly mediated by anxiety. Employing the Spielberger "State-Trait Anxiety Inventory," it was found that state anxiety correlated highly significantly with interrogative suggestibility. The strongest correlations were with regard to how subjects responded to negative feedback. That is, the subjects who gave in most to the interrogative pressures were those who rated themselves as being most anxious at the time.

Gudjonsson (1989) has studied the "trust" aspect of the Gudjonsson and Clark (1986) model among criminal suspects. His findings indicate that there is a negative relationship between interrogative suggestibility and behavioral indicators of suspiciousness or anger. A possible explanation is that when people are highly suspicious of the interrogator, or when they are in an angry state of mind, their critical faculties are heightened and their cognitive focus is more narrow. This makes them less trusting and accepting of suggestions. Similarly, a suspicious or an angry interrogator may be unreceptive to information from a suspect who contradicts his/her own hypotheses, irrespective of whether or not the information is sound and reliable.

Forensic application

The Gudjonsson Suggestibility Scales were specifically developed for forensic application. They measure objectively how witnesses and criminal suspects are likely to cope with the various demand characteristics of the police interrogation. Of particular interest are individuals who have made a serious self-incriminating confession to the police during interrogation, which they subsequently retract. Gudjonsson and MacKeith (1988) have recently discussed the legal, psychological, and psychiatric aspects of retracted confessions. They consider that the two basic enduring psychological characteristics relevant to erroneous testimony, including cases of false confession, are *interrogative suggestibility* and *compliance*. These two personality or behavioral characteristics are considered by Gudjonsson (1988b) to overlap to a certain extent.

In order to study the validity of interrogative suggestibility in predicting actual behavior within a police interrogation, a comparison can be made between two groups of criminal suspects; those who are able to resist police interrogation pressures in spite of some salient evidence against them (e.g., forensic evidence) and those who make a self-incriminating confession which they subsequently retract. Two studies have shown the difference in suggestibility between "resisters" and "alleged false confessors" in criminal trials.

In an early study, Gudjonsson (1984b) compared the suggestibility scores of 12 alleged false confessors and 8 resisters. The resisters consisted of defendants who had all persistently denied any involvement in the crime they had been charged with in spite of forensic evidence against them. The resisters were found to be significantly more intelligent and less suggestible than the alleged false confessors. A particularly striking finding was the difference between the two groups in the type of suggestibility which related to their ability to cope with interrogative pressure (Yield 2 and Shift on the GSS 1).

In a more recent study Gudjonsson (1991) compared the suggestibility scores of 20 resisters and 20 alleged false confessors who were "matched" for age, sex, intelligence, memory recall capacity, and the seriousness of the offence. Highly significant differences in suggestibility emerged between the two groups, with the pattern of results being very similar to that found by Gudjonsson (1984b). That is, the ability of the suspect to cope with interrogative pressure is more important than his/her tendency to give in to leading questions per se. A separate analysis of 14 resisters and 72 alleged false confessors, where I.Q. and memory were used as covariates rather than "matching" the two groups on the relevant variables, gave almost identical results. The most important implication of these findings is that it is erroneous to assume that differences in suggestibility between resisters and alleged false confessors are largely or necessarily mediated by differences in intelligence.

Conclusions

In this brief paper I have discussed some of my theoretical and empirical work on interrogative suggestibility. The focus of the paper has been on the application of theory and research findings in relation to police interviewing. It has been emphasized that interrogative suggestibility is a special type of suggestibility, which bears little resemblance to the concept of suggestibility as traditionally defined. This special type of suggestibility can be reliably measured and has important implications for the process and outcome of police interviewing.

References

Gudjonsson, G.H. (1983). Suggestibility, intelligence, memory recall and personality: An experimental study. *British Journal of Psychiatry, 141*, 35–37.

Gudjonsson, G.H. (1984a). A new scale of interrogative suggestibility. *Personality and Individual Differences, 5*, 303–14.

Gudjonsson, G.H. (1984b). Interrogative suggestibility comparison between "false confessors" and "deniers" in criminal trials. *Medicine, Science and the Law, 24*, 56–60.

Gudjonsson, G.H. (1986). Historical background to suggestibility: How interrogative suggestibility differs from other types of suggestibility. *Personality and Individual Differences, 8*, 347–55.

Gudjonsson, G.H. (1987). A parallel form of the Gudjonsson Suggestibility Scale. *British Journal of Clinical Psychology, 26*, 215–21.

Gudjonsson, G.H. (1988a). Interrogative suggestibility: Its relationship with assertiveness, social-evaluative anxiety, state anxiety and method of coping. *British Journal of Clinical Psychology, 27*, 159–66.

Gudjonsson, G.H. (1988b). Compliance in an interrogative situation: A new scale. *Personality and Individual Differences, 10*, 535–40.

Gudjonsson, G.H. (1989). Theoretical and empirical aspects of interrogative suggestibility. In V.A. Gheorghiu, P. Netter, H.J. Eysenck, & R. Rosenthal (eds.), *Suggestion and suggestibility: Theory and research* (pp. 135–43). London: Springer-Verlag.

Gudjonsson, G.H. (1991). Suggestibility and compliance among alleged false confessors and resisters in criminal trials. *Medicine, Science and the Law*, in press.

Gudjonsson, G.H., & Clark, N. (1986). Suggestibility in police interrogation: A social psychological model. *Social Behaviour, 1*, 83–104.

Gudjonsson, G.H., & Gunn, J. (1982). The competence and reliability of a witness in a criminal court: A case study. *British Journal of Psychiatry, 141*, 624–27.

Gudjonsson, G.H., & Hilton, M. (1989). The effects of instructional manipulation on interrogative suggestibility. *Social Behaviour, 4*, 189–93.

Gudjonsson, G.H., & MacKeith, J.A.C. (1988). Retracted confessions: Legal, psychological and psychiatric aspects. *Medicine, Science and the Law, 28*, 187–94.

Hansdottir, I., Thorsteinsson, H.S., Kristinsdottir, H., & Ragnarsson, R.S. (1990). The effects of instructions and anxiety on interrogative suggestibility. *Personality and Individual Differences, 11*, 85–87.

Hardarson, R. (1985). Samband daleidslu-og yfirheyrslu maemis vid personuleika og namsarangur. B.A. Thesis, University of Reykjavik.

Irving, B. (1990). The codes of practice under the Police and Criminal Evidence Act 1984. In R. Bluglass & P. Bowden (eds), *In principles and practice of forensic psychiatry* (pp. 152–59). New York: Churchill Livingstone.

Loftus, E. F. (1979). Eyewitness Testimony. Cambridge, MA: Harvard University Press.

Loftus, E.F., Miller, D.G., & Burns, H.J. (1978). Semantic integration of verbal information into visual memory. *Journal of Experimental Psychology: Human Learning and Memory, 4*, 19–31.

Register, P.A., & Kihlstrom, J.F. (1988). Hypnosis and interrogative suggestibility. *Personality and Individual Differences, 9*, 549–58.

Schooler, J.W., & Loftus, E.F. (1986). Individual differences and experimentation: Complementary approaches to interrogative suggestibility. *Social Behaviour, 1*, 105–12.

15

MONOIDEISTIC DISORDERS AND THE PROCESS OF SUGGESTION: Anorexia Nervosa as a Paradigm

Mordecai Kaffman

Summary

In a number of psychiatric disorders, one finds at the core of the clinical syndrome a constricted cognitive construct, functioning as a closed circuit around a rigid idea. Despite its illogical nature, it is accepted unconditionally, while infiltrating every aspect of the individual's life with considerable expenditure of physical and psychic energy. For more than fifteen years I have been investigating the clinical sources and the mechanism of these "monoideistic" disorders. Among these syndromes are paranoid disorders, some types of depression and obsessive states, anorexia nervosa, dysmorphophobia, and monosymptomatic hypochondrial psychosis. In all of these disturbances, the monoideistic nucleus seems fixated to a closed pattern of communication between the afflicted person and significant others. This monothematic communication keeps repeating itself in all the person's intrafamily and interpersonal relationships, eventually attaining the characteristics of hypnotic-like commands. In this article, anorexia nervosa is presented as a typical example of a monoideistic disturbance.

Monoideism and constructed reality

It was James Braid (1795–1860), a Scottish surgeon, who, in the middle of the last century, was the first to argue that hypnosis was the result of prolonged fixation of attention on an idea or subject of limited scope. Braid hypothesized that the concentration of attention on well-focused hypnotic suggestions leads, aided by suggestibility and imagination, to a changed conception of reality. This is the case whether its source is external or intrapsychic, verbal or extraverbal. Braid gave this altered state of consciousness the name "monoideism."

That term stressed the decisive role of suggestion, based on well-focused and dominant ideas and images, in the creation of the changed consciousness. For many years Braid tried unsuccessfully to replace the term "hypnosis," in use to this day, with "monoideism." He was convinced that total concentration on any single idea, to the exclusion of competing processes, served as a central mechanism in hypnosis (Kravis, 1988). Today there are tens, perhaps even hundreds, of theories that try to provide an answer to basic questions about the nature and essence of hypnosis. Braid's hypothesis on the important role played by monoideism still stands. Even techniques of inducing hypnosis by way of roundabout messages, alternately hidden or implanted, are based on turning the person's attention to some well-concentrated and well-emphasized ideas, clearly different from the other irrelevant material. An example is the interspersal and confusion approaches of Erickson (1979). The seemingly casual confusion is, in fact, very carefully directed, pushing the person to search for light and for supportive anchors. It is a kind of confusion that obligates the person to center attention on some specific clear and reasonable material; in other words, it is an indirect invitation to focus on the direct suggestive instructions that are buried in the hypnotic message.

Today it is generally accepted that sharpened concentration of mental activity around a single repetitive idea strengthens the influence of that idea on one's mental and physical state. Sometimes this leads to the building up of a system of beliefs that is grasped by the person as objective reality, whereas in fact it is based on constant repetition, suggestibility, and imagination. In this connection let us not forget that we, human mortals, from prehistoric times to modern *homo sapiens*, are affected by, and make constant use of, systems of beliefs that guide our lives. In most cases we are convinced that this infrastructure of beliefs faithfully reflects the knowledge that comes to us through objective perception of reality and investigation. If it is not accepted by others as universal truth, we feel it is only because of blindness, stupidity, or malice. The self-induced belief in the truth of our convictions and the need to fight against all heretics sometimes reaches extreme and powerful expression: witness the recent, passionate war of millions of fanatic "true believers" against Salman Rushdie, although it is quite clear that most of them never even laid eyes on *The Satanic Verses*, the proscribed volume.

The British biologist Young (1978) has prophesied that some day scientists will locate an anatomic central locus in the brain and some biochemical substance that will explain the basic human capacity to believe and create new sets of beliefs. This presumed brain center will in all likelihood function in a way similar to other recognized biological mechanisms that influence hunger, pain, sex, mood, and so forth. Whether there is a "belief center" in our brain or not, we already know that the potential of converting thoughts and ideas, even in the absence of objective grounds, into an imagined reality is something immanent in all of us. Two well-known examples will suffice. There is ample evidence in dispersed primitive tribes (Africa, New Zealand, Australia, Haiti) of cases of deep depression and self-induced starvation—leading even to the deaths of healthy individuals—which are the result of the absolute belief in a *voodoo* curse. This curse is the result of someone inadvertently breaking some taboos of the particular tribe (Wolberg, 1959). In a parallel manner, in certain districts of China there is a belief named *Koro,* described in medical scripts over three thousand years old. It is still adhered to by certain sections of Chinese peasantry. According to this belief, under great stress, whether communal or individual, a very dramatic phenomenon may sometimes be observed among men. They suddenly begin to feel that their sex organs are dwindling, gradually moving into the abdomen. The victim, frightened to death, is totally convinced that his life is in danger. Koro may appear in isolated individuals, or it may take the form of an epidemic involving hundreds of people. In the latter case, reciprocal suggestive contagion in the closely knit community spreads the superstitious belief and transforms it into an undisputed reality. It is a fearsome scene. In a state of Koro, the panic-stricken man is convinced that he is about to lose his sex organs. He will try with all his strength—sometimes assisted by others—to hold onto his penis in order to prevent its disappearance (Tseng, et al., 1988). Orthodox medicine is not equipped to deal with such fanciful phenomena. A "witch doctor" may do better.

There is no end to examples of the power of belief. Furthermore, it is not limited to primitive people or simple-minded and uneducated sectors of the population. In fact, fundamentalist believers of late come more and more from the well-educated strata. Fortune-tellers of all sorts are not unemployed. Recently it was reported that the Israel Defense Army (ZAHAL) turned to a fortune teller for help in the search of missing soldiers. To this very day, hundreds of thousands of people, among them some heads of government, conduct their affairs and reach decisions according to the prophecies of astrologists.

Aided by the normal trait of suggestibility, significant changes in the consciousness and convictions of individuals and groups can be obtained by concentration on repetitious stimuli or ideas. A monotonous, repetitive stimulus can penetrate and modify our consciousness through one or more of our senses. It may be a visual stimulus, such as prolonged continuous looking at a fixed or oscillating object, or a person, or an empty roadway. It might be an auditory stimulus, such as listening for a long time to a monotonous melody, or to the continuous beating of a drum. It could also be a repeated prayer or a mantra. It might involve the turning of our attention to the regular rhythm of our breathing, the execution of recurrent ceremonial body movements, monotonous dancing, and so on. This is only a partial list of the means to achieve altered states of consciousness, such as can be found in mystical ecstasy, prolonged meditation, the hypnotic trance, or the "trance" of acupuncture. Indeed, monoideistic thinking and repetitive circular stimuli are powerful agents in many areas of life. This is true in religion, politics, art, and certainly in bringing around psychotherapists of different schools of thought to accept their respective psychological theories.

In the present article I propose to concentrate on the influence of monoideistic thinking on a person's mental health. Specifically it will deal with the function performed by monoideistic thinking in creating psychopathological states, with accompanying characteristics and symptoms reminiscent of hypnotic suggestion.

Characteristics of monoideistic disorders

To the best of our knowledge, Robert White (1941) was the first to point out that there is no scientific confirmation of the hypothesis that it is possible to improve the physical and psychological state of a person by hypnosis, *beyond* that person's potential in the waking state. Conversely, White drew our attention to the fact that the quality and productivity of the person's performance in the hypnotic state may become impaired, even *below* the normal level in the waking state. He noted that, in the hypnotic state, the person does not possess clarity of thought. Instead, he or she can be seen to lack alertness, a sense of humor, and the capacity to make a decision in a complex situation. Indeed, all these handicapping manifestations turn out to be characteristically present in the disorders with which I intend to deal in the present chapter. In my view, hypnosis plays a very important role in these disorders.

About fifteen years ago I used the term "monoideism," introduced by Braid, but in a different context (Kaffman, 1981a). I wanted to unite under the common heading of "psychiatric monoideistic illnesses" mental states with a wide variety of symptoms, but with the shared characteristic of circular engrossment around a rigid idea. Among these were paranoid disorders, obsessive psychosis, some types of reactive depression, monosymptomatic hypochondrial psychosis, dysmorphophobia, and anorexia nervosa. Obviously, these are diverse nosological entities. Nevertheless, they have a common denominator. In all these disturbances, the victim is slavishly committed to a restricted ideational content that keeps repeating itself like a broken record. It does so without any opportunity for questioning or distancing oneself from it. I have hypothesized that the pathological cognitive message, which appears in each of the above illnesses—unbending and unchangeable over a long period of time—in all probability functions in a manner similar to a monotonous hypnotic stimulus. The following are some of the common distinguishing marks of all the monoideistic psychiatric syndromes whose cognitive structure is maintained and reinforced by a process of self-hypnosis.

1. A circular inner dialogue develops between the individual and an internalized fixed set of ideas. It is *extremely* limited in scope, content, and meaning. It is a monotonous dialogue that keeps repeating itself day and night and gets stronger with time. The person becomes fused with the monoideistic message. He or she is held as if by a magnetic force from which there is no release.

2. The hypnotic quality of the preoccupation with the dominant idea leads to a deep inner conviction that the monoideistic thoughts and arguments are rational, logical, and true. Objective counter-arguments that point to the distortions of reality in the individual's arguments meet with an impenetrable wall of refusal to change the monoideistic idea even by one iota.

3. The monoideistic conviction exerts a tremendous influence on the world outlook as well as the feelings and behavior of the individual. This is so whether the conviction appears as megalomanic or persecutory delusions of a paranoid person, or as the drive of a young anorectic person to persevere in uncompromising self-starvation. In most cases the monoideistic preoccupation becomes the chief motivating force in the person's life. Extreme changes are another consequence of this all-consuming monoideism. Relations with family and friends are altered radically. It affects the quality of one's work and study, as well as the ability to enjoy leisure-time occupations. Accompanying phenomena include a striking egocentricity and the marked inability to maintain interpersonal relations based on empathy and mutuality. A person with a monoideistic disorder loses much of his or her capacity for spontaneous reactions. Humor disappears. It becomes more difficult to concentrate, read, or write. Areas of interest and enjoyment become increasingly restricted. Over a period of time, a depressed state of mind prevails. Apparently, this is caused by the significant decrease in the mental and physical energy available to the person, due to the constant preoccupation with negative and un-

constructive thoughts and behavior. The secondary depression, usually present in all monoideistic disturbances, becomes intensified as the sources of satisfaction and joy dwindle. It is clear that many of the affective disorders are nosogenetically connected to biological and interpersonal factors. However, one should never forget the existence of specific depressive reactions characteristic of all monoideistic ailments. A good example is the secondary depression that often appears in anorexia nervosa. It is so apparent that some researchers—still a minority—propose that some of the cases of anorexia nervosa, especially cases of bulimia nervosa, be included in the broad category of primary affective disorders (Pope & Hudson, 1988).

In the present chapter we are concerned only with monoideistic global and ego-syntonic psychiatric entities. In these cases, the person displays complete cognitive submission and identification with the content of the central idea. We are not concerned here with psychopathological disorders with an alien and ego-dystonic ideational content (e.g., disturbing phobias or ritualistic compulsions) toward which the victim assumes an avoidant and negative stance. In fears, phobias, and rituals, as distinct from monoideistic mental disorders, people are usually highly motivated to get well. They will readily admit that the cognitive content of their phobias or obsessions are undesirable, unreal, and illogical. In contrast to this, there is a congenial well-focused thought nucleus at the center of the psychiatric monoideistic syndrome proper. The victim becomes totally absorbed in a fixed monothematic pathogenic belief. In turn this dictates the behavioral and emotional reactions that fit the individual's monoideistic conviction. This constant focus on the hardened message transforms itself into the dominant ego-syntonic content of the person's life. No clinician will have difficulty in bringing up examples of such cases. It may be a paranoid individual who lives according to the delusional dictates that he or she is under great threat from dangerous foes from outer space. Or it may be someone with dysmorphophobia who experiences vexing delusions about becoming or appearing physically deformed. Here, the person—in most instances a woman—repeatedly seeks plastic surgery to correct a nonexistent physical defect. It may be a case of monosymptomatic hypochondria, wherein the person continuously complains of some unbearable well-focused physical ailment or disability. Such people do this with total disregard of all the negative tests and the prolonged, fruitless treatment by medical specialists. Or maybe we are dealing with an anorectic girl, starved, perhaps on the verge of death, demanding with uncompromising obstinacy respect for her right to continue starving herself to the bitter end.

Roots of monoideistic disorders

There are three central questions pertaining to the totality of the psychiatric syndromes of the type we have been discussing: 1) how does monoideistic thinking arise and how does it develop and grow steadily stronger? 2) what is the mechanism which transforms the preoccupation with a restricted set of ideas or beliefs into a chronic disturbance which shackles the person with chains that are so difficult to remove? 3) how does the self-persuasion become so deep as to leave no opening for any rational discourse? That is, why is it of no avail to reveal to the afflicted persons that there is no basis for the delusions that are driving them to perdition?

Over the past twenty years at the Kibbutz Clinic, we have handled the cases of over 250 people with monoideistic disorders. These include cases of anorexia nervosa, paranoia, dysthimia, and monosymptomatic hypochondria. As a result, it has become clear to us that, in every case of a monoideistic syndrome, a two-step process may be discerned.

During the first stage the dominant idea slowly penetrates the person's consciousness, initially with no striking signs of pathology. It is like water which, dripping slowly but persistently, finds its way right through a rock. In the vast majority of the monoideistic disorders we have found an intra-family message which repeats itself endlessly in the family interaction. Of course, prevalent environmental social and cultural influences may play a primary or auxiliary role in infusing the dominant idea into the family belief system, as well as the consciousness of the individual. But it is the family which represents the primary vehicle for the transfer, delivery, and maintenance of the monoideistic belief. The family message is injected systematically and uninterruptedly from pre-school days by central figures in the individual's life. Small wonder that it penetrates consciousness as reliable and ego-syntonic. This process is enhanced by the fact that even in a paranoid delusional message, however imaginary and illogical, one may always find a kernel of truth (Kaffman, 1981b). Take, for example, the paranoid family message that one must be suspicious of all persons around; or that the whole world is wicked, filled with injustice, discrimination, and existential dangers. All these are paranoid messages, but they are also partly true, as is clear from the headlines of the daily newspaper. Or, to take another example, the underlying idea of ego-syntonic self-starvation in anorexia nervosa. This reflects quite accurately a family and social dictate that, to be happy, a girl must preserve her girlish figure and scrupulously avoid any food that is "fattening." Thus the monoideistic message, whether paranoid, hypochondriac, obsessive, or anorectic, is generally planted in the first years of the child's life. These are especially problematic in enmeshed families, ones that foster mutual dependence with faulty individuation. The implanted message remains carefully guarded whenever it is perceived as a central existential subject, for reasons unique to the given family.

The acceptance of the family message as objective truth, or at least as a reasonable representation of reality, involves overriding one's critical thinking capacity. This is influenced by a variety of factors. One central factor is the systematic repetition of a monoideistic message in an enmeshed family, trapped on a one-way street with a "No Exit" sign. Parenthetically, the association of intra-family overdependent entanglement and a recurrent, rigid family message (present in all monoideistic syndromes) can be clearly recognized in the clinical condition of *folie à deux*. This refers to a communicated psychosis in which two or more intimately related persons share identical delusions.

Another factor contributing to the hypnotic-like process of turning a suggestive idea into seemingly objective truth is the degree of prestige, authority, or superiority attached to the person (or the group) from whom the suggestion emanates. We do not tend to accept suggestions from persons whom we consider to be of lower standing and inferior power. At the root of all religions are lofty messages, emanations, and miracles by "representatives" of supernatural powers. Within a family the parents constitute the source and the model for the family's principles, myths, and beliefs. It is from them that a constant stream of suggestive messages keeps flowing. These involve interactions that are repeated an infinite number of times between the authoritative parental figures and the child who cannot in practice escape their impact. And so the family message passes from generation to generation. There is good reason to expect that this circular mechanism of repeated communication between parents and children constitutes the basis of an intergenerational chain of belief constructs whose influence is no less than that of the genetic code. From our clinical experience we have learned to identify suggestive pathogenic messages that pass from one generation to the next generation, perhaps with variable intensity, but with no change in content. Thus the transgenerational message may appear as a specific phobia characteristic of a particular family, or a paranoid *folie à famille* including parents and children, or a sequential family drive for perfectionist achievement, or a two-generational anorectic syndrome, etc. From many cases of hypochondriasis at the Kibbutz Clinic, I can point to numerous instances where we found a characteristic hypochondriacal syndrome in three, even four, generations. The familial scenario of somatization and excessive concern over questions of health passed with only minor changes from grandparents to their children, grandchildren, and even great-grandchildren.

To explain this type of familial transmission one may make use of the Ferenczi (1965) hypothesis which states that all children go through a stage in life when they have absolute faith in their parents. According to Ferenczi, hypnotic belief-construction is in fact a state, where the hypnotist brings the subject back to a stage of childhood when the parents enjoyed the unbounded confidence of their offspring. There is, however, room for some legitimate doubt regarding the trustworthiness of these basic hypotheses. The question is: is there not an exaggerated use of speculation and sophistry in our tying a repeated family message, affecting the individual's set of beliefs, with hypnotic processes? The implication that hypnotic processes are present in all cases of parent-child dependence, with repetitious monothematic communication, may turn hypnosis into a banal concept, a catch-all devoid of specific meaning. On the other hand, there is no doubt that hypnotic experiences do occur in daily life. In fact, no clear demarcation line exists between a hypnotic trance proper and a certain change in consciousness as a result of influences of a hypnotic character. Let us imagine a guru of a sect who has a simple, repetitious, and barren message about ways of reaching the only and absolute truth via supernatural self-realization powers. It might involve a mystical atmosphere of group euphoria and social isolation, accompanied by guided imagery exercises or a prolonged state of meditation. Now, does this guru make use of hypnotic instruments to create a change in the state of consciousness of the believers? Our answer is clear: yes. Yet we cannot ignore the fact that the guru works under propitious conditions and circumstances which enhance the chances for arousing an altered state of consciousness.

Under "normal" conditions of open two-way communication between parent and child, between a man and his wife, or between teacher and student, the chances of monoideistic hypnotic induction are considerably reduced. In fact, it is necessary to distinguish between two distinct types of communication. One is the closed monoideistic communication system, where the interpersonal tie is based on one-way communication, with a dominant partner holding an absolute monopoly of the truth. But there also exists an open system of communication based on compromise and mutual understanding. The open system also entails listening to one another, the belief in relative truths, and the acceptance of doubt as a legitimate element in all scientific and other cognitive inquiries. This fosters independent thought. The chances for the appearance of a monoideistic hypnotic system of communication increase whenever the interpersonal message is repeatedly transmitted, with no possibility of challenging its truth. The risk is also greater in the context of rigid and dependent relationships in a closed family and social circle, in the presence of an authoritative figure broadcasting an absolute set of beliefs cast all of one piece, in black and white, not open to question or compromise.

In 60 cases of paranoid disturbances treated at the Kibbutz Clinic over the past twenty years we have been able to assess the characteristic features of communication within the nuclear family of the identified patient. We found that, from childhood on, the paranoid person was under the influence of a one-sided communication. At least one of the parents (or a parental figure) transmitted rigid messages expressing feelings about discrimination, suspicion, and hostile scheming in the environment. These families lacked such properties as flexibility, common sense, a healthy capacity for doubt and, above all, humor (Kaffman, 1983). These are all factors that neutralize the suggestive influence of the strong message. The above type of interaction, with its clearly paranoid coloration, acting over a long period, no doubt enhances the emergence of a system of unchangeable beliefs. It is a belief system portraying the outside world as untrustworthy, unjust, and filled with enemies with hostile intentions. It is particularly difficult to escape from such a system of beliefs in the framework of a closed and socially isolated family.

Freud described the case of Judge Schreber as a typical paradigm of a paranoid disturbance, expressed by delusional thoughts about cruel supernatural powers that take control of Schreber's body. Schreber's case is, in fact, a classic example of the intergenerational transfer of a paranoid message. The delusional thoughts of Judge Schreber are a faithful transcript of the paranoid principles of his father, Dr. Daniel Schreber. The father was well-known in his day for the way he recommended and applied all his life "special" rigid methods of raising obedient children, totally submissive to the will of their parents. The methods were based on severe physical punishment with all types of mechanical devices that limited the child's freedom of movement. Other inhuman ways of subjugating the child's body and soul were used with the aim of developing a new healthy race of children, both in his family and in Germany as a whole. Doubtless there is complete correspondence between the persecutory delusions of the son and the paranoia of his famous father (Kaffman, 1983).

Up until now we have been speaking of the monoideistic disorders in their first stage, marked by a process of slow penetration of the dominant idea over an extended period. The second stage, that of the monoideistic disorder proper, begins when the central idea turns into an obsessive *dybbuk*. This is generally in the wake of high psychological stress, and in circumstances viewed by the person as an existential threat. At this point in life, an attempt is made to prevent, or to defend against, anxiety-evoking stressors or a fear of possible failure and disappointment in the face of a threatening challenge. The person selects the option of escape by way of surrender to and "marriage" with the latent monoideistic message. Clinical experience has taught us that the disorder arises mostly as an escape from life's developmental tasks and challenges. These assume, in the eyes of the victim, extremely dangerous, even catastrophic proportions.

In the early stages of the disturbance, the central idea in the family message is still under the partial control of the patient's will. Take, for example, anorexia nervosa. The syndrome generally begins with a diet, often no different from many of the diets taken up by nearly all adolescent girls at one time or another. At this early point, the anorectic girl often belongs to a group of girls who all have a common goal of reducing their weight before summer swimming season. However, the anorectic girl slowly begins to lose all sense of proportion as the compulsive idea to reduce weight takes control of her entire personality. But what differentiates the anorectic girl from the others who continue with their "normal" moderate diet? Our thesis is that, with regard to girls who are caught in the net of anorexia nervosa, one can recognize four distinctive features: a) a pre-existent fertile soil of family preoccupation with food and body weight; b) an entangled, closed, overdependent relationship with one or both of her parents; c) a perceived stressful and threatening life situation, met with self-defeating responses of avoidance and flight; and d) continued reinforcement of the anorectic escape by monoideistic intra-family transactions which assume hypnotic-like characteristics. The anorectic person and the people around that person find themselves in a closed circle of interaction about food. Dieting becomes the central issue in family life and is discussed boringly and at great length several times daily. The anorectic girl and her parents, especially the mother, get tied up in endless angry arguments around the topics of food, meal, and diet. With time the anorectic symptoms may develop a functional autonomy. At this point, the parents and all the people involved may have decided in desperation to end the unsuccessful battle. Even so, the individual may continue the compulsive preoccupation, sometimes for years, even for the rest of that individual's life. The monoideistic idea then continues to broadcast intra-psychic suggestive instructions, probably through a process of auto-hypnosis.

In our view there is a strong similarity between a monoideistic disorder and a cult which has succeeded in controlling the total environment of its followers. In both cases, it is impossible to question the all-embracing "truth" which dictates to the individual a set of rigid rules of behavior in every area. The individual succumbs to the herd quality of the cult, with no scope for individual choices. The members of most of these totalist-monolithic cults resemble those people affected by monoideistic disorders. They think, speak, and function as if they were programmed and turned into robots. They display absolute devotion and conformity toward a system of beliefs which allows no room for doubts or independent critical judgment. Most of their mental energy and sense of humor is taken up by their monothematic preoccupation, with ever-decreasing interest in an outside world to which they find it hard to relate with warmth, empathy, and spontaneity.

An etiopathogenic model of monoideistic disorders

One might describe schematically a developmental model of the psychiatric monoideistic disorders. It would include generic etiopathogenic factors that are identical with those of other psychiatric disorders, in conjunction with specific factors based on hypnotic suggestion. As we see it, hypnotic influences begin to play a part in the early stage of the family transmission of a dominant set of ideas and beliefs. They come into full play in the second stage of the disorder. That is when the affected person, and the surrounding significant people, react rigidly to the initial symptoms, thus strengthening the monoideistic message by complementary stereotyped transactions.

Monoideistic disorders may be related to biological as well as constitutional factors, both preparing the ground for the development of a particular clinical picture. There is no reason to negate the supposition that the monoideistic message, purveyed mainly by the subject's parents, has been received and incorporated in the context of a suitable biological background. But, clearly, the biological factors can only provide the foundation upon which the monoideistic belief develops as the result of rigid transactions of a suggestive-hypnotic nature. These implant and reinforce in the individual, slowly but continuously, the nucleus of the dominant idea. Thereafter, the fully developed monoideistic disorder may evolve under suitable conditions.

Recently, we published a study of 66 people with anorexia nervosa (60 female, 6 male). They were treated at the Kibbutz Clinic, with a follow-up of at least four years on each person (Kaffman & Sadeh,

1989). All these people fulfilled the DSM-3-R diagnostic criteria for anorexia nervosa. All presented the typical monoideistic picture of relentless pursuit of a thin body size by ego-syntonic self-starvation. They also exhibited the typical and constant rigid preoccupation with food and the shape of one's body, with the aim of weight reduction beyond any reasonable limit. We examined when and how these people (mostly kibbutz-born adolescent girls) internalized the message that assigns such central importance to body shape and weight, and hence to dieting. Clearly, not only the girls we examined, but nearly all of us are strongly influenced by social pressure in Western culture in the direction of "obesity-phobia." But the question is: why is it that only a small minority abandon reason and critical judgment to the extent that weight loss becomes an irrational compulsion? Our clinical findings suggest at least a partial answer to this intriguing question. We have found a significant difference in the family data of our sample of anorectics compared to a control group of women who adhered to a diet that may be considered "normal." For the vast majority of people with anorexia nervosa, the subjects of food, diet, and body weight were central in the daily life of the family. Repeated messages about these themes characterized the communications between the parents and was also seen in the interactions between the parents and their children. This family preoccupation is based on various rationalizations, including health, aesthetics, the preservation of youth, and the view that slenderness is essential for love, acceptance, and success (see innumerable Hollywood films).

Our study examined all cases of restrictive anorexia nervosa that were treated in the Kibbutz Clinic in the last fifteen years. We found that in 83% of cases, at least one parent, usually the mother, was for years strongly involved in issues of diet and prevention of weight gain (Kaffman & Sadeh, 1989). The daughters of these mothers (and to a significant minor extent also the sons) received the repetitive message that obesity is a threat and a matter for great concern. The message, conveyed either directly or indirectly, has the effect of turning the spontaneous process of eating in response to hunger into an artificially nurtured process. The family-focused message, combined with cultural and environmental pressures in the form of a war against overweight, filters its way into the consciousness of the young person throughout childhood and puberty. It usually reaches its maximum intensity toward the middle and late stages of adolescence.

Our study contains an additional finding which helps us to understand the intra-family transmission of the dominant idea of an exaggerated dread of weight gain. This is the existence of a *premorbid* family structure with excessively dependent and suffocating ties between the daughter and her parents, particularly between mother and daughter. Through a combined use of anamnestic family data and family interviews, we found that 94% of restrictive anorectics were involved in a very closed and enmeshed system of family relations. This blocks, or at least interferes with, the normative developmental process of individuation and intergenerational independence. The anorectic syndrome serves as a very strong cement that keeps mother and daughter connected together in a continued state of dependency, frequently with symbiotic characteristics. By means of the monoideistic disorder, the anorectic girl remains closely bound to her parents. The disorder offers special dispensation from coping with developmental challenges that call for a degree of personal autonomy and emotional maturity which the anorectic girl lacks.

All the anorectic people who were referred to the Kibbutz Clinic in the past twenty-five years (124 people) showed the first signs of the disorder in adolescence, with an average age of 14–15. In modern society this is an age filled with pressures and anxieties, as the adolescent tries to achieve personal identity and independence. At the same time, he or she faces major changes in intellectual development, social roles, body image, sexual interest, emotional ties, and peer relationships. The process of distancing from one's parents in the course of developing this personal autonomy should normally be expected. Anorexia nervosa represents one of the pathological options that provides an escape from the tasks imposed by the process of growing up. Instead, the adolescent and the parents get stuck in a closed circuit over the young person's self-imposed starvation diet.

Energy sources of the anorectic syndrome

In the families described above, the first instances of food reduction evoke the immediate attention of the parents. Frequently this involves the mother encouraging her daughter to stick to her diet, until one day the girl's compulsive perseverance in her starvation diet lights up a red warning light. Gradually a set of stereotyped family interactions and reactions develop in the form of pleas, and angry demands and threats. Most of these take place inside a symmetrical closed circle, providing strong secondary gains for the anorectic person in terms of attention, sympathy, escape from responsibility, control of important persons, and gratification of dependency needs. Passionate arguments usually take place within the family, with strong repetitious verbal and extraverbal exchanges. People in the vicinity also get involved in efforts to find logical counter-arguments and effective measures to convince the anorectic person to desist from the proclaimed goal to continue starving. As the person shows clear signs of malnutrition, the topic of diet becomes more and more urgent, focused, and dominant. It has high *hypnotic* potential. This is especially the case since the process usually takes place in circumstances of social isolation and weakened physical and mental defenses, resulting from the energy-reducing diet. The family's persevering preoccupation, with so limited a behavioral focus and so small an ideational content, creates the foundation for a vicious circle. Add to this the fact that the anorectic person is clearly motivated to persevere in a behavior that allows successful escape from anxieties over tasks calling for independence, ones which are considered dangerous and threatening. Hence, the continued preoccupation with the diet reflects the influence of the hypnotic components in the monothematic system of communication. It also indicates that an escape from frightening age-appropriate life challenges provides a strong foundation for an ego-syntonic deviant engagement. So anorexia nervosa transforms itself into one of the most rigid monoideistic ailments, with the victim ruled mentally, physically, and behaviorally by a bizarre central idea of limited content and scope.

The starvation theme is perceived as an order by some superior force, to be obeyed without questioning. In the fascinating Kafka story, *The Hunger Artist* (1948), the hero is asked why he does not stop fasting after long years dedicated to the cult of starvation. His answer is: "Because I have to fast, I can't help it." This, in fact, is the answer of every anorectic person we have treated: "I can't do it any other way." The central pathognomonic phenomenon in anorexia nervosa is a total surrender to the idea of the danger of gaining weight. A normative social phenomenon in Western society (i.e., dieting as a way of achieving a slender figure) has turned into a monoideistic situation with marked characteristics of a hypnotic process. This process is further aggravated by the biological complications induced by starvation, such as the distortion in the person's awareness of taste, hunger, and satiation. Thus, at the second stage of the disorder, the person feels totally unable to adjust the diet so as to stick to a reasonable weight. Progressive weight loss turns into the central aim in life and, like a cult dogma, demands one's unconditional and absolute devotion.

Indeed, the constant musings on the subject of food and the danger of gaining weight, and the interactions that accompany these musings, operate in a closed feedback circuit. There exists a concentrated focus of attention that heightens the possibility of hypnotic responses. Obvious changes take place in the individual's belief system, in his or her interpretation of reality, and in self-control. In the analysis of clinical cases of anorexia nervosa, one cannot help discerning elements of self-hypnosis. Take, for example, the classic case of Ellen West, who was treated by Binswanger (1958). A typical chronic anorectic patient, Ellen West committed suicide at the age of 33, after thirteen years of her torturing illness. In her diary she described her monoideistic enslavement in great detail. "It is a fixed idea, a compulsion to think all the time about food. It is a curse that pursues one in the waking state and in sleep, a curse accompanying anything one may be occupied with, that does not leave you alone, never and at no place." One person treated at our clinic put it this way: "I started dieting at 13. After several months I lost all contact with my feelings. Eating and not eating were the only two 'feelings' I was left with, and the scales were the only standard. . . . It became the center of my life and its main content. . . . I was ready to pay any price—I preferred to die lean rather that to live fat."

Over a hundred years ago Lasègue (1873) wrote in convincing and earthy language, though without using the term "hypnosis," how the monoideistic situation crystallizes in compulsive anorexia nervosa:

> The diet gradually becomes the sole subject of pre-occupation and conversation. The patient gets surrounded by a kind of atmosphere, from which there is no escape during the entire day. The anorectic is subject to the influence and responses of the surrounding medium, and the disease becomes developed and condensed so much the more as the circle, within which revolve the ideas and feelings of the patient, become gradually more narrowed. . . . The anorectics find themselves unable to resist the pressing entanglement . . . and at the end of a variable time of this mischievous concentration. . . . The patient no longer troubles herself in search of logical arguments (p. 150).

Therapeutic considerations

As the hypnotic monoideistic process gains in strength, the anorectic people tend to show ever greater denial of their thinness. This indicates a distortion in the body image that often assumes delusional dimensions. The anorectic person will deny or disregard an emaciated appearance, despite the clear image reflected in the mirror or the rational proofs offered by other people. As is well known, it is not enough to refute a delusional conviction with its irrational components by reasoned argumentation. There is as little sense in trying to conduct a logical discussion in the case of anorexia nervosa as in the case of a paranoid disturbance, or with adherents of cults like Hare

Krishna, the Moonies, or Scientology. Cognitive rational treatment cannot penetrate the thick armor around the dominant cognitive nucleus that perpetuates itself in a closed circle of monoideistic commands of suggestive-hypnotic force. Hence, in the advanced stage of the monoideistic disorder one must consider as legitimate, even vital, any therapeutic method that helps break the connection with the fuelling sources of the dominant idea. Therefore, it is not surprising that some of the techniques in the treatment of psychiatric monoideistic ailments, especially anorexia nervosa, are reminiscent of the strategy of cult "de-programming." This is an intervention meant to free blind adherents of a cult from its fetters by forced physical detachment. This is intended to prevent contact with the source of the cult's messages, until such a time that the person is again able to think in an independent, critical manner.

This concurs with the main recommendation of Braid (Kravis, 1988) in treating what he called "monomania" and what we now prefer to call "monoideistic" disorder. That is, one must find ways of diverting the dominant thought into a channel of alternate occupations, so that healthy thought will replace the morbid burrowing. While the logic of this tautological recommendation is unquestionable, the question remains: how do we bring about the desired change of converting the dogmatic obsession and the monoideistic preoccupation into open and pluralistic cognitive consciousness? How do we free the person from a blind enslavement to a closed thought-circuit? Generally speaking, there are two main components in our method of therapy, both aimed at breaking the closed thought circle of the patient. The first consists of locating and neutralizing the sources of reinforcement of the monoideistic message. This is done mainly by means of family therapy, since the family constitutes the prime context in which the repetitive message is cultivated and maintained. The second strategic component includes the transmission of an alternate message, which is also marked by some monoideistic characteristics. Thus, the therapy, like the disorder itself, is strongly focused on a central, well-defined, dominant idea. But this time, the message is new and constructive, inviting the individual to reach an understanding with the existential anxieties that led to an avoidance of life's challenges. The new message urges these people to leave the cage in which they have locked themselves. They are encouraged to perform specific tasks and activities with the help of positive ecosystemic influences and resources. It is an invitation and a *repetitive* challenge to grow and fill life with variegated, constructive content. This is done in spite of the person's existential fears. The therapist maintains an empathic attitude, based on respect for, and positive ties with the afflicted person. How to compose and present this menu is, of course, the central subject of therapy, specific for every person. That canvas is too broad for this chapter.

Quite often with anorexia nervosa, the monoideistic syndrome is severe, and cooperation from the person is not forthcoming. In such instances, we generally recommend home-hospitalization within the confines of the kibbutz, with the parents denied contact with the patient. This temporary separation from the parents causes, in most cases, a decline in the amount of cognitive "fuel" available for maintaining the compulsive preoccupation with food and body weight. Incidentally, the recommendation of temporary parent-child separation is an old one. About a hundred years ago, Charcot (1889) took a clear stand in favor of isolating the anorectic person and removing that individual from contact with the parents. "The results of parent-child separation are rapid and marvelous," Charcot wrote, "so it is necessary to separate both anorectic children and adults from their parents, whose influence, as experience teaches, is primarily pernicious. . . ." (pp. 162–3).

Those who suffer from anorexia nervosa are captured in a monoideistic fortress. They use every means at their disposal to stop outside interference—tears, screams, pleas, threats, vain promises that they will put an end to dieting. Sometimes the parents will join the plea. This is especially common when the therapist recommends rest, far from familial or social stimuli that may again activate thoughts about food and dieting. At the first stage of therapy, the therapist must appear unequivocal and firm, in full control of the situation. The main aim of the therapist is to break the closed thought-circuit and the repetitive preoccupation with food by disconnecting the person from the sources of monoideistic "fuel." Other subjects will constitute the focus of the family therapy in the next stage of treatment after the immediate danger of starvation has been overcome. These might include matters related to the anorectic syndrome such as anxiety-filled avoidance of threatening stress situations and the struggle for individuation and separation from the parents. It should be noted that, when separating anorectic persons from their parents, we avoid any hint of blame for their responsibility or guilt for the development of the anorexia. The temporary separation, which we recommend in severe cases, is presented to the parents in positive terms: "As a sacrifice by good and loving parents, who understand that they are helping to reduce the negative impact of a stream of associations about food, ones that parents naturally arouse in their children." The brief separation (usually 2–4 weeks) is also explained as a necessary cease-fire and a mental rest period for all concerned. At all stages of the therapy we do our best to work *with* the parents, never against them.

To conclude, we have shown that a common denominator exists in all clinical entities that we call psychiatric monoideistic disorders. As we have outlined, they share similar etio-pathogenic factors. We have indicated that there exists a strong parallel between the processes and mechanisms that are responsible for the ordinary hypnotic process and the influences that are at work in the development and maintenance of these pathological monoideistic syndromes. Finally we have pointed to some therapeutic assumptions in attempting to counter such disturbances, using anorexia nervosa as a paradigm.

References

Binswanger, L. (1958). The case of Ellen West: An anthropological-clinical study. In R. May, E. Angel, & H. Ellenberger (eds.), *Existence: A new dimension in psychiatry and psychology* (pp. 237–364). New York: Basic Books.

Charcot, J.M. (1889). Disease of the nervous system. In R. Kaufman & M. Heiman (eds.), *Evolution of psychosomatic concepts—anorexia nervosa: A paradigm* (pp. 162–63). New York: International Universities Press, 1964.

Erickson, M., & Rossi, E. (1979). *Hypnotherapy: An exploratory casebook.* New York: Irvington Publishers.

Ferenczi, S. (1965). Comments in hypnosis. In R. Shor & M. Orne (eds.), *The nature of hypnosis* (pp. 77–88). New York: Holt, Rinehart and Winston.

Kaffman, M. (1981a). Monoideism in psychiatry: Theoretical and clinical implications. *American Journal of Psychotherapy, 35,* 235–43.

Kaffman, M. (1981b). Paranoid disorders: The core of truth behind the delusional system. *International Journal of Family Therapy, 3,* 29–41.

Kaffman, M. (1983). Paranoid disorders: Family sources of the delusional system. *Journal of Family Therapy, 5,* 107–16.

Kaffman, M., & Sadeh, T. (1989). Anorexia nervosa in the kibbutz: Factors influencing the development of a monoideistic fixation. *International Journal of Eating Disorders, 8,* 33–54.

Kafka, F. (1948). The artist's fast. In *Kafka's stories* (Hebrew) Tel Aviv: Schoken.

Kravis, N. (1988). James Braid's psychophysiology: A turning point in the history of dynamic psychiatry. *American Journal of Psychiatry, 145,* 1191–1206.

Lasègue, C. (1873). On hysterical anorexia. In R. Kaufman & M. Heiman (eds.), *Evaluation of psychosomatic concepts—anorexia nervosa: A paradigm* (p. 150). New York: International Universities Press, 1964.

Pope, H., & Hudson, J. (1988). Is bulimia nervosa a heterogeneous disorder? Lessons from the history of medicine. *International Journal of Eating Disorders, 7,* 155–66.

Tseng, W., Kan-Ming, M., Su, J., Li-Shuen, L., Li-Wah, O., Guo-Qian, C., & Da-Wei, J. (1988). A sociocultural study of koro epidemics in Guangdong China. *American Journal of Psychiatry, 145,* 1538–43.

White, R. (1941). A preface to the theory of hypnotism. *Journal of Abnormal and Social Psychology, 36,* 477–505.

Wolberg, L. (1959). Hypnotherapy. In S. Arieti (ed.), *American Handbook of Psychiatry* (Vol. 2, p. 1469). New York: Basic Books.

Young, J. (1978). *Programs of the brain.* (pp. 251–52). New York: Oxford University Press.

16

SUGGESTIBILITY, IRRATIONAL BELIEFS, AND EMOTIONAL DISTURBANCE

Albert Ellis

Suggestibility or gullibility to externally based teachings is obviously one of the main human characteristics—as much of the other material in this book attests. Because I am a therapist and the founder of one of the most popular forms of psychological treatment—rational-emotive therapy (RET) and its close sibling, cognitive-behavioral therapy (CBT)—I am naturally interested in the relationship of suggestibility to emotional and behavioral disturbance. On the basis of almost a half century of clinical practice and research, as well as wide reading in the psychological, sociological, and anthropological literature, let me present my latest theories and findings in this respect.

Definition of distubance

It may be almost impossible to give a general, noncultural definition of emotional and behavioral disturbance because of widespread cultural differences. Thus, in the United States a man may be deemed to be "neurotic" or "maladjusted" because he has little "self-respect" and direly needs others' approval, while the same man may be considered "normal" or "healthy" in many Asian communities. So I will not insist, in this chapter, on any global definition of disturbance but will largely stick to people in Western civilization and define them as "neurotic" when they hold beliefs which, in their own culture, are self-defeating. Usually, this means that they have extreme negative feelings, such as anxiety, depression, and self-hatred, and that they behave self-destructively and/or antisocially, and are often afflicted with compulsions, addictions, and phobias.

Like most other therapists, I assume that emotional disturbances result from both inherited and learned dispositions (Ellis, 1962, 1976, 1988a; Epstein, 1989; Eysenck, 1967; Franklin, 1987; Freud, 1965; Rosenthal, 1971; Skinner, 1971). But I also assume that both externally and internally based suggestibility plays a prime role in virtually all neurosis and self-defeating behavior. Let me explain.

Externally based suggestion leading to disturbance

Almost all psychoanalysts, and most other therapists, believe that parental behavior (e.g., neglect) and influence (e.g., negative suggestions) significantly contribute to, and even directly cause, children to become emotionally disturbed and to continue to be neurotic (and even psychotic) for the rest of their lives. Well, they are probably wrong for several reasons: (1) millions of children who were treated abominably by their parents *do not* become neurotic, while millions who were very well treated do; (2) many children gullibly agree that their parents are right about denigrating them as incompetent and vulnerable, but many do not; (3) children raised in radically different ways and in amazingly different cultures often become neurotic and often develop remarkably similar symptoms of disturbance.

The trouble with the psychoanalytic and behaviorist theories that parental influence causes childhood (and later adulthood) disturbance is that they tend to confuse the acquiring of human values, goals, rules, and standards with the acquiring of irrational beliefs and actions *about* such values. Because children and adolescents are usually quite gullible and easily influenced, they *normally* follow the rules and mores of their parents, peers, and cultures. But obviously when five children are reared by the same mother and father, grow up in the same neighborhood, and go to the same schools, one or two frequently become neurotic and three or four do not. How come?

Because, among other reasons, they are biologically different and therefore *apply* their externally imbibed standards in different ways. Thus, although all five children in a family may consider themselves Protestants, one may choose to be a devout Fundamentalist, one may be reasonably religious, two may attend church irregularly, and one may become a fervent atheist.

Similarly, rational-emotive theory holds that people are also suggestible and thus inclined to adopt similar values and rules. Rigid demands and allied emotional disturbances are then created *about* these rules. All five children in the same family, once again, may agree with their parents' and culture's value that it is good to love a member of the other sex and to marry that person. But child No.1 may have a desperate *need* for marriage and may neurotically mate with an impossible partner and never allow herself even to think about a divorce. Child No. 2 may hate himself so much for being rejected by a loved partner that he may thereafter addict himself to lifelong bachelorhood. And children Nos. 3, 4, and 5 may arrange to have fairly successful, unneurotic marriages. Following the same marriage-favoring goals, the first two of these five children may make themselves neurotic and the other three may not.

According to RET, emotional disturbance does not usually stem from externally inculcated family and cultural rules, but largely from the dogmatic, absolutist "shoulds" and "musts" people idiosyncratically construct *about* these rules (Ellis, 1962, 1988a; Ellis & Dryden, 1987; Ellis & Grieger, 1977, 1986; Ellis & Harper, 1975). Thus, in the above example, all five children may believe, "I'd like to have a good marriage, so I'll try to arrange to wed and stay happily wedded." But child No. 1 may add to this rational *preference,* "I *absolutely must* marry and stay married at all costs, no matter how badly my partner treats me!" And child No. 2 may add to his sensible *desire,* "I *must* never be rejected when I pick a suitable partner to marry; and since I actually was rejected as I *should not* have been, I am clearly an *unlovable person* who will *never* win a good mate, so I must never again risk marrying at all!"

Now of course, child No. 1 and child No. 2 may have learned their absolutist "musts" and "shoulds" from their parents and then carried these insistences into adult life. If so, we had better ask ourselves, "Why didn't children Nos. 3, 4, and 5 *also* learn the same neurosis-creating "musts"? And if they did learn them, why did they *not* carry them on into adulthood?" The RET answer is that, quite *probably* but not *necessarily,* children Nos. 3, 4, and 5 are naturally or biologically *not* prone to carry on irrational, self-defeating parental commands, while children Nos. 1 and 2 are naturally *prone* to do so.

So RET theory holds that while most children are quite suggestible to parental (and cultural) goals and standards, a distinctly smaller number are highly susceptible to dogmatic "musts" and "shoulds" *about* these goals. Moreover, a good many of these highly-suggestible-to dogma people, even if their family and culture rarely give them "musts" *about* their standards, will tend easily to *invent* or *construct* these "musts" themselves—for that, as I will show below, is their temperament or nature. Many of them seem to be *born* "musturbators" and have great difficulty *not* transmuting their strong preferences (e.g., "I *really* would like to do well") into imperatives (e.g., "Therefore, I *have* to!").

Let me make one other important point. When parents actually do suggest to children Nos. 1, 2, 3, 4, and 5, "You *have to* behave well, especially to us, and you're no damned good and we hate you if you behave badly!", what do they actually *do* when their five children distinctly act abominably—as even "normal" children often will? Answer: they usually scream at them for five or ten minutes, punish them rather mildly, and shortly after act kindly and lovingly to them again. They thereby give the children a great deal of empirical experience that they merely hate their rotten *behavior* and not their total *selves,* and they show these children that they are not *shits* or *rotten people* but that they only sometimes *act shittily* or *behave rottenly.* When children Nos. 1 and 2, unlike children Nos. 3, 4, and 5, therefore conclude that *they* are hateful and unlovable when they are scolded, they are going well beyond their empirical experience and making vast, invalid overgeneralizations. That, I again hypothesize, is largely their defective philosophical *nature*—which significantly differs from that of children Nos. 3, 4, and 5.

To conclude this section: most humans take the suggestions of their family, peers, and culture quite seriously and adopt goals and rules that others feed them during their childhood and adolescence (not to mention during their adult years). Fewer of them take the *partial* "musts" of their parents (e.g., "You must follow our rules or we won't like your *behavior* but will not totally damn *you*") and change them into *absolute* "musts" (e.g., "If I don't follow my parents' musts, they really will hate *me,* and they are right in doing so because unless I do what I *must* I am a thoroughly hateful, rotten *person!*"). So almost all humans, particularly when young, are very suggestible to family and cultural goals, values, and standards. However, many of these people are significantly less susceptible to suggested dogmas and imperatives *about* these standards.

Internally based suggestion leading to disturbance

If humans frequently do not follow the "musturbatory" imprecations of their family, peers, teachers, and other associates, why do they often construct or invent them for themselves and then habitually perpetuate them? The answer to this question was given during the early part of this century by Emile Coué (1923). Following Bernheim (1947/1886), who realized that hypnosis mainly works through suggestion, Coué said that it really works through autosuggestion. Hypnotized people take the suggestions of the hypnotist and keep vigorously telling *themselves* to follow these suggestions; so it is really their *self*-suggestion (or, if you will, *self*-hypnosis) that induces them to react.

Moreover, Coué (1923) firmly hypothesized, if people want to change their feelings, behaviors, and physiology, they can do so more effectively without using a hypnotist but instead strongly giving themselves positive thoughts and directions, such as, "Day by day in every way I'm getting better and better," and, "If I keep visualizing myself succeeding in business (or sports, or love, or sex, or almost anything else) I can, I can, I can succeed!"

Following Coué, a host of other writers, such as Peale (1952) and Maltz (1960), have strongly espoused positive thinking and positive visualization; and many, such as Simonton and Mathews-Simonton (1978) have claimed virtual miracles for it. More realistic and better-validated claims have been made by cognitive-behavioral therapists, such as Lazarus (Lazarus & Folkman, 1984) and Meichenbaum (1977).

Coué and his followers failed to see *why* positive suggestion often works well until, in an early paper on rational-emotive therapy (RET) presented at the American Psychological Association convention in Chicago in 1956 (Ellis, 1958, 1962) and in other RET writings (Ellis, 1957a, 1957b), I pointed out that neurotic disturbances largely stem from people's *negative* autosuggestions. They suggest to themselves *rational* or *preferential* cognitions, such as, "I'd like to do well and be approved by significant others, but if I don't *too bad,* I can still be pretty happy," and they then strongly and persistently add *irrational* or *dogmatic* and *absolutist* self-suggestions, especially, "I *must* do well and *have to* be approved by significant others!" Once they devoutly convince themselves of these imperatives, they then easily and often conclude, "Because I am not doing as well as I *must,* (1) It's *awful* and *terrible!* (2) I *can't stand* it! (3) I'm a *worthless, undeserving person!* and (4) I'll *always* fail and *never* get the approval I need!"

People are capable of making and convincing themselves of a wide range of negative self-suggestions, without starting with grandiose "musts." However, they seem to derive them very easily from their "musturbatory" demands on themselves, on others, and on environmental conditions; and RET hypothesizes that most of the unrealistic and illogical inferences that lead them to be disturbed are derived from, or "logically" flow from tacit, underlying unconditional "shoulds."

Thus, if a person *only* has flexible preferences (flexible because they include *alternate* possibilities of enjoyment), she will tend to suggest to herself—and truly believe—"I want love, sex, a career, or good health very much, *but* I don't *have* to have it and definitely can find other enjoyable (though perhaps not *as* enjoyable) pursuits and thus lead a pretty happy life." Strongly and steadily believing this, why would she tend to add, "And if I don't get the love, sex, career, or good health I want but definitely do *not* need, it's awful, I can't stand it, I'm no good, and will always fail and be completely deprived?" I think that she rarely would (Ellis, 1987, 1988a; Ellis & Dryden, 1987, 1989).

I am hypothesizing, then, that virtually all humans easily adopt or create strong preferences for accomplishment, approval, comfort, and satisfaction, and that they quite often add tacit and overt "musturbatory" commands that these preferences be met. Once they learn to use language, they tend to speak to themselves (as well as to others), make their implicit demands explicit, and often keep telling themselves—yes, *suggesting* to themselves—"I *must* do well," "I *have* to be loved," "I *must* eat food I really like," etc.; and their explicit self-suggestions make their tacit insistences even stronger and reinforce their tendencies to disturb themselves when it looks like they will not be fulfilled. If I am correct in my assumptions, external suggestions profoundly affect people's goals, standards, values, rules, preferences, and desires because people are normally born highly teachable and gullible. These suggestions also sometimes distinctly affect the dogmatic, disturbance-creating imperatives that their goals and preferences *must* be achieved and that their strong displeasure *must* not exist. But I also hypothesize that people often take their strong desires and tacitly and explicitly construct—yes, mainly construct—autosuggestions that transmute them into neurotic, self-defeating insistences. Their explicit autosuggestions then reinforce, solidify, and help rigidify their tacit irrational demandingness.

Therapeutic uses of suggestion

Suggestibility has, of course, distinct advantages and therefore, probably, is biologically built into the human race. If children and adolescents, for example, were not highly suggestible, they would tend to be extremely rebellious and would have a difficult time learning family, peer group, school, and communal rules. So although suggestibility has its real drawbacks, it is hardly all bad.

The therapeutic use of suggestion goes back many centuries, probably to the time when human language first appeared. It is likely that mothers and fathers have always suggested to overly fearful children that there was really nothing much to be afraid of; that teachers and lecturers early in human history suggested what they thought was sage advice to anxious and depressed members of the audiences; that writers on tablets and scrolls—e.g., Biblical writers—have always suggested self-help materials; and that priests, rabbis, witch doctors, and shamans have from time immemorial suggested all kinds of remedies for the physical and emotional afflictions of their devotees.

More formally, suggestion combined with hypnosis began to be used for psychotherapy fairly widely in the middle of the nineteenth century, though Bernheim (1947/1886), as noted above, seems to have been the first therapist to call a spade a spade and say that therapeutic hypnosis really *is* largely suggestion. Then, around 1895, a French dentist, Coué (1923), began to insist that autosuggestion is just as effective, if not more so, than hypnotic or external suggestion and, as again noted above, he led the way to the current great popularity of positive thinking and visualization.

That positive self-suggestion often works has now been attested to by thousands of case histories and a good many controlled studies (Maltz, 1960; Lazarus & Folkman, 1984; Meichenbaum, 1977; Peale, 1952). However, although I have at times used it effectively as part of RET (Ellis, 1957a, 1962, 1971, 1973, 1988a; Ellis & Becker, 1982; Ellis & Harper, 1975), I have also pointed out the limitations of using positive autosuggestions or rational self-statements to reduce emotional and behavioral disturbance (Ellis, 1979).

1. Positive suggestions often cover up, but do not really eliminate, negative tacit philosophies and overt self-statements. Thus, if I suggest to myself, "Failing in love is inconvenient but doesn't make me an unlovable person," I can easily still believe underlyingly, "But it really *does* make me unlovable!" Furthermore, I can believe the latter philosophy very strongly, while lightly (and ineffectually) continuing to parrot the former.

2. Many of the positive autosuggestions invented by people and taught by therapists are realistic and true, but not sufficiently general or elegant. For example, if I am afraid to fail at writing a story because I believe I will then be a rotten writer and an inadequate person, I can positively suggest to myself, "I think I will write a good story," or, "Even if I write this story badly, I'll learn by doing so and write better ones later." These may be true statements and may help me start writing. But they will still leave me with the basic philosophy that if I never write a good story (which, of course, I never may), I will then be an inadequate person.

3. Much positive thinking and positive visualization helps people perform better but helps to escalate, instead of to reduce their "musturbatory" outlook. Thus, if I visualize myself as playing tennis very well, I may actually (because of my behavior rehearsal and cognitive practice) improve my game. But I may easily reinforce my neurotic philosophy that if I *don't* play well, I am a crummy individual.

4. Like Coué's famous autosuggestion, "Day by day in every way I'm getting better and better," many autosuggestive "therapeutic" statements are pollyannaish and misleading. I can strongly suggest to myself, "I am one of the greatest painters who has ever lived!" and thereby get myself to paint and paint. But how soon will it then take

me to become disillusioned and to give up painting? Not, probably, too long!

5. Positive autosuggestion, whether accepted from others or created for oneself, may have the great disadvantage of helping to make many of its devotees more gullible and less prone to original and independent thinking. Let us remember that gullibility leads to ultraconformity, "suckerism," and lack of individuality. If I gullibly accept the "facts" that I absolutely need others' approval in order to accept myself, that if I do your bidding you will certainly treat me equally well, and that the Lord will provide (if my fairy godmother fails me), will I really be an emotionally healthy, self-caring citizen? I doubt it!

For reasons like those just listed, positive thinking and visualization may often be used to good avail in striving for emotional health and behavioral effectiveness but they often give limited and dubious results. What, then, can be more elegantly used to minimize and at times almost eliminate profound negative suggestion and autosuggestion, which leads to so much neurosis? According to RET, as noted above, humans are both biologically and environmentally prone to take others' and their own self-defeating suggestions, including absolutist "shoulds," "oughts," and "musts." They then foolishly double- and triple-bind themselves so that they make themselves inappropriately anxious, depressed, and enraged instead of appropriately disappointed, sad, and frustrated when things go wrong for them.

RET, however, takes the optimistic view that humans have several health-oriented predispositions, which, augmented by their social learning, can enable them to stop the dragon of negative suggestion in its tracks, largely (though not completely) overcome it, and work their way (yes, *work* their way) into a state of reasonably good (though still imperfect) mental and emotional health. Let me now list some of these biologically and sociologically based self-correcting and self-actualizing tendencies and the ways in which RET shows people how to overcome their innate tendencies to give cavalierly too much credence to others' and to their own negative, destructive suggestions.

Therapeutic counter-suggestion

Scientific thinking

Humans are born suggestible and gullible but are also, as Kelly (1955) pointed out, natural-born scientists. They easily tend to observe, theorize, experiment, check their findings, reason, think about their thinking, and even think about thinking about their thinking.

Because of their gullibility, dogmatism, absolutism, and "musturbation," all of which are antiscientific, they easily imbibe and create irrational beliefs that neuroticize them. But with considerable effort and persistence (which seem to be indigenous to many scientists), they can undo their cognitive-emotive disturbances.

Science has three main tests of its theories: empiricism, logic, and flexibility. If a scientific hypothesis is to be considered "valid" or "probably true," it has to be (1) potentially falsifiable but so far backed by empirical data; and (2) logically consistent; and (3) nonrigid and susceptible to future revisions. By the same token, I discovered that emotional health seems to exist when people are (1) realistic and empirically oriented; (2) logically consistent; and (3) nonrigid and willing to seek alternative solutions to their life problems when their current solutions do not seem to work very well (Ellis, 1988a, 1989; Ellis & Dryden, 1987; Ellis & Yeager, 1989).

In using RET to uproot absolutist "musts" and their destructive derivatives, three forms of disputing people's irrational Beliefs (iBs) are regularly employed. These are all derived from scientific thinking. Each of these will be illustrated with an example.

1. Empirical Disputing

Irrational Belief: "Because I failed many times, I have to *keep* failing." *Disputing:* "Prove that because I failed many times I have to *keep* failing." *Answer:* "No matter how many times I fail, this never proves that I *can't* succeed now and in the future.

2. Logical Disputing

Irrational Belief: "Because I very much want a person to love me, he or she *has* to do so." *Disputing:* "How does it follow that because I very much want a person to love me, he or she *has* to do so?" *Answer:* "It doesn't follow. This is complete non sequitur."

3. Alternative-Seeking Disputing

Irrational Belief: "I *can't stand* your rejection and can't be happy *at all* without your loving me." *Disputing:* "Why *can't* I *stand* your rejection or be happy *at all* without your loving me?" *Answer:* "I obviously *can* stand it, though I'll never like it, because I *am* standing it right now and am *not* dying of it. And, of course, I can find several *other* ways to be happy even if you always reject me."

In addition to the above methods, RET shows people how to dispute and to give up their strong self-suggestions that it is *awful* and *catastrophic* to fail, to be rejected, to be treated unfairly, and to suffer pain and discomfort. Instead, they are made to realize that they can see those happenings as very unfortunate and inconvenient but *not* totally bad, *not* more than bad, and *not* worse than they absolutely *should* be (Ellis, 1962, 1971, 1973, 1988a; Ellis & Becker, 1982; Ellis & Harper, 1975). RET teaches disturbed individuals that self-defeating suggestions usually include surplus, out-of-reality meanings that make unpleasant events much worse than they actually are and thereby foment exaggerated, neurotic reactions to life's hassles and often *make* them into "catastrophies" and "horrors."

It is also often desirable to counter the self-suggestion that I have labeled "*I-Can't-Stand-It-itis.*" Sometimes people insist that they utterly *must* have what they want and *must* never have what they don't want. When these "musts" are not gratified, they tend to conclude, and to *suggest* strongly to themselves, "I *can't* stand it! I can't bear it!" RET shows them how to *examine* their "I can't-stand-it-itis" repetitively and scientifically by asking themselves, "*Why* can't I *stand* frustration? *Prove* that I can't *bear* it!" By doing so, they can determinedly answer, "Of course I *can* stand it—that is, live and still be reasonably happy in spite of this frustration—though I rarely if ever will like it!" (Ellis, 1972a, 1978).

RET is also useful in countering *self-denigrating* self-suggestions. When people neurotically demand that they absolutely *have* to do well and be approved by significant others and they fail to meet these "necessities," they very often conclude, and again keep powerfully suggesting to themselves, "I'm an *incompetent, rotten person,* who is so basically inept that I don't *deserve* success or happiness and am *unable* to achieve it!" RET, using scientific questioning of these devout self-suggestions, encourages them to ask, "How does my unsuccessful *behavior* make *me,* a *whole person,* incompetent, rotten, and undeserving of enjoyment?" Answer: "It never does! I *perform* my unsuccessful behavior, but I *am* not my particular acts. All of my *deeds* may be measurable (by how well they achieve my chosen goals). But *I,* my *personhood,* is too complex and ongoing to be given any global, final rating. And I *deserve* to live and enjoy myself because I *choose* to try to do so, because I am human, and not because I perform well or win certain people's approval."

Other people are inclined to auto-suggest in such a way that they become convinced of false *overgeneralizations.* Such people dogmatically insist, for example, that they *must* succeed or they *have to* be loved. When they then fall short of these goals, they frequently overgeneralize and foolishly suggest to themselves, "I'll *never* be able to succeed and get what I want! I'll *always* fail. My chances of having any kind of good life at all are *hopeless!*" This type of overgeneralizing, as Alfred Korzybski (1933) stated, renders them not insane but unsane. To help them stop destructive autosuggestion like this, RET teaches them how to dispute their irrationality scientifically. They are instructed to ask themselves, "Where is the evidence that I'll *never* be able to succeed and will *always* fail and lead a hopelessly miserable existence?" The fairly obvious answer is: "The notions of '*Never' and 'Always'* exist only in my head, not in reality. I *can* most likely succeed at many of the things I want and, when I don't, I can *still* considerably enjoy life."

RET practitioners also teach clients and other people how to construct or adopt *rational coping self-statements.* These are to be used instead of their destructive autosuggestions. These can be blithe, empirical self-suggestions or positive thoughts, such as, "I can hit the tennis ball better and better," or "I don't have to be afraid of riding in elevators." Much better, they can be positive philosophies, such as, "If I never am good at tennis, I can still enjoy the game and accept myself as a deserving person," and, "Even if I panic in an elevator, it's only inconvenient and not the end of the world!"

RET has for many years pointed out that humans so naturally and easily disturb themselves that they very frequently create *secondary disturbances.* They strongly suggest to themselves, "I must not be anxious or depressed!" In so doing, they make themselves anxious about their anxiety and depressed about their depression (Ellis, 1962, 1979, 1988a; Ellis & Dryden, 1987; Walen, DiGiuseppe & Wessler, 1980; Wessler & Wessler, 1980). They often create both ego disturbance (self-downing) and discomfort disturbance (low frustration tolerance) about their primary disturbances. Using RET, we actively look for secondary as well as primary neuroses. We also look for ego as well as discomfort disorders, and find the absolutist "musts" by which our clients create those self-destructive feelings and behaviors. People are then shown that they can question and challenge their self-sabotaging suggestions about their disturbances and that they can logically and empirically convince themselves that there is no reason that they *must* not be disturbed; that it is not *awful* (but only inconvenient) when they are; that they definitely *can* stand (but not like) being disturbed; that they are never *rotten people* for being emotionally dysfunctional; and that they do not have to continue *always* to be disturbed.

Other cognitive methods of counter-suggestion

As just shown, RET relies heavily on scientific, hard-headed thinking and disputing to help people counterattack their insistent irrational autosuggestions and to help replace them with empirical, logical, alternative-seeking philosophies. It also uses several other effective cognitive methods of undermining cavalier gullibility and suggestibility.

Psychoeducational techniques

RET encourages victims of their own and of other's destructive suggestions to read rational-emotive self-help books (e.g., Ellis, 1988a; Ellis & Becker, 1982; Ellis & Harper, 1975), to listen to cassettes (e.g., Ellis, 1972b, 1988b), and to attend lectures, workshops, courses, and intensives given at the Institute for Rational-Emotive Therapy in New York and its other worldwide affiliations.(1)

Referenting

Clients and other people frequently indulge in immediate gratification—such as smoking, overeating, and alcohol and substance abuse—that lead to long-range self-defeatism, because they wrongly keep suggesting to themselves that they can indulge in it with impunity. To help combat this kind of addiction, RET teaches them *referenting*. They make a list of several disadvantages of their addiction and a list of the advantages of stopping their indulgence in it. They then give serious thought to these disadvantages ten or twenty times a day until they sink into their heads, and people begin to act upon the good reasons for overcoming their addiction (Danysh, 1974; Ellis, 1985, 1988a; Ellis & Abrahms, 1978; Ellis & Becker, 1982; Ellis, McInerny, DiGiuseppe, & Yeager, 1988).

Imaging and visualization

Following Coué (1923) and Lazarus (1984), RET often shows people how to visualize that they *can* do a difficult task (such as asserting themselves with certain people) instead of continuing to suggest and convince themselves that they *can't*. And when they keep suggesting to themselves that they will do poorly at a task (such as public speaking, writing, or doing their therapy homework), it encourages them to imagine that they can do it quite well, thereby helping them to do behavior rehearsal and bring about a beneficial self-fulfilling prophecy (Ellis, 1988b; Maultsby, 1971; Maultsby & Ellis, 1974).

Teaching and proselytizing

Suggestion very often works through vigorous teaching and proselytizing. For example, members of religious and political groups actively indoctrinate outsiders in their doctrines, and not only convert many of them but simultaneously reindoctrinate themselves. Although RET eschews dogma and devoutness, it often encourages clients and supporters to teach RET principles and practices to their friends, relatives, and associates, so that they can more successfully absorb and use them to overcome their own self-defeating suggestions (Ellis, 1985, 1988a; Ellis & Whiteley, 1979).

Recordings of therapy sessions

Ever since cassette recording became popular in the early 1970s I have encouraged my clients to record their therapy sessions and to listen to them several times in-between sessions. They often then discover that they hear my therapeutic suggestions more effectively while playing them back than they did during the live sessions. They also report that during the playback they are able to think more clearly about their own foolish, negative self-suggestions and to counterattack them effectively (Ellis & Abrahms, 1978; Ellis & Whiteley, 1979).

Semantic precision

Korzybski (1933) showed that dysfunctional thinking affects people's language; in turn, their language helps them think even more dysfunctionally. In RET, therefore, we show people how to change their language and thus overcome their negative self-suggestions. If they say, "I *must* perform well to be a *worthwhile person,*" they are shown how to suggest to themselves correctly, "I *had better* perform well, *not* to be worthwhile, but to get more enjoyable results." Instead of suggesting, "People make me enraged by acting unfairly to me," they are encouraged to tell themselves, "I choose to enrage myself about the unfair things that people do" (Ellis, 1985; Ellis & Whiteley, 1979).

Modeling

Bandura (1969, 1986) has shown that children and adults imbibe suggestions from others by modeling themselves after the verbal and nonverbal behaviors of others and that they can change themselves by again modeling therapeutic behaviors. Consequently, RET therapists model sensible actions and appropriate feelings in order to counter clients' negative self-suggestions, and particularly to model unconditional acceptance of clients who stubbornly refuse to accept themselves (Ellis, 1985; Ellis and Abrahms, 1978). I also model RET for the public by giving live weekly demonstrations with volunteer clients at the Institute for Rational-Emotive Therapy in New York. Members of the audience frequently use the RET methods that I show the demonstrators in order to work on their own disturbances, and thereby appreciably help themselves (Dryden, Backx, & Ellis, 1987).

Reframing

When people use others' and their own suggestions to frame their life situations very negatively, RET often uses the technique of reframing to show them that bad things usually have a good side as well. Thus, people are shown that being rejected by someone results in their getting rid of that nonaccepting person *fast*. If, for example, they get fired from a good job they may learn a valuable lesson about how to behave on subsequent jobs. RET also teaches people to take the challenge—and adventure!—of stubbornly refusing to make themselves depressed and panicked, but only appropriately sorry and disappointed, when bad events occur (Ellis, 1985, 1988a; Ellis & Abrahms, 1978).

Problem-solving

RET teaches people to give up their powerful, dogmatic self-suggestions that a single great solution to a life problem must be achieved and that it is terrible if it is not. Moreover, it includes effective problem-solving whereby therapists show their clients how to figure out and arrive at alternative viable options and solutions to their difficulties. RET helps people make and widen their *choices* of where they want to be (and not to be) and to choose alternate thoughts, feelings, and actions instead of one-sidedly following the limited, rigid suggestions they often give themselves (Ellis, 1985, 1988a; Ellis & Whiteley, 1979).

The scope of this chapter does not allow for a discussion of the many other RET strategies used to help people surrender their disturbing self-suggestions. Some of these techniques can be classified as "emotive" and include shame-attacking exercises, forceful coping statements, and forceful self-disputing methods. In addition, RET achieves counter-negative self-suggestions via a variety of behavioral or, more accurately, cognitive-behavioral techniques. Parenthetically, it should be noted that RET theory and practice has always been cognitive-behavioral in nature. Those wishing to explore its emotive and behavioral interventions in more detail are referred to the wide range of sources cited in this chapter.

Conclusion

Rational-emotive therapy (RET) theorizes that much human disturbance is importantly connected with, and largely stems from, externally accepted and internally constructed suggestion. This is especially the case with neurotic states of anxiety, depression, self-damnation, and addiction. Humans are biologically and socially prone to gullibility and easily accept goals, standards, and values of their family and culture. But their main neuroses seem to stem only partly from imbibed irrational standards. To a considerable extent, they also originate in the dogmatic, absolutist, rigid "*musts*" and *commands* that they often idiosyncratically construct and invent—yes, invent—about their (rational and irrational) standards. Humans are, very importantly, self-suggesters. They add their own autosuggestions to externally imbibed teachings. They have strong innate tendencies to observe and think about their thoughts, feelings, and behaviors and to use the scientific methods of empiricism, logic, and flexible thinking to change and actualize themselves. But they also have innate tendencies to make false inferences, to think illogically, and to be dogmatic, devout, and anti-scientific. Rational-emotive therapy (RET) hypothesizes that if they were scientific, flexible, and undogmatic, they would be much less neurotic; and it has devised many cognitive, emotive, and behavioral methods of helping them reach these goals. As the founder of RET, I have no illusions that humans will fully surmount their suggestibility to social standards (which might alleviate some of their irrationality), or that they will completely conquer the "musturbatory" autosuggestibility that gets them into most of their neurotic difficulties. But I believe that if they use rational-emotive therapy (RET) and its therapeutic cousin, cognitive-behavior therapy (CBT), they will make themselves less gullible, more adept at critical thinking, and a hell of a lot less emotionally self-defeating.

Note

1. The headquarters for the Institute for Rational-Emotive Therapy is located at 45 East 65th St., New York, New York 10021.

References

Bandura, A. (1969). *Principles of behavior modification.* New York: Holt, Rinehart & Winston.

Bandura, A. (1986). *Social foundations of thought and action: A social cognitive theory.* Englewood Cliffs, NJ: Prentice-Hall.

Bernheim, H. (1947). *Suggestive therapeutics.* New York: London Book Company. (Original publication, 1886.)

Coué, E. (1923). *My method.* New York: Doubleday, Page.

Danysh, J. (1974). *Stop without quitting.* San Francisco: International Society for General Semantics.

Dryden, W., Backx, W., & Ellis, A. (1987). Problems in living: The Friday night workshop. In W. Dryden (ed.), *Current issues in rational-emotive therapy* (pp. 154–70). London and New York: Croom Helm.

Ellis, A. (1957a). *How to live with a neurotic: At home and at work.* New York: Crown. Rev. ed., Hollywood, CA: Wilshire Books, 1975.

Ellis, A. (1957b). Outcome of employing three techniques of psychotherapy. *Journal of Clinical Psychology, 13,* 344–50.

Ellis, A. (1958). Rational psychotherapy. *Journal of General Psychology, 59,* 35–49. Reprinted: New York: Institute for Rational-Emotive Therapy.

Ellis, A. (1962). *Reason and emotion in psychotherapy.* Secaucus, NJ: Citadel.

Ellis, A. (1971). *Growth through reason.* North Hollywood, CA: Wilshire Books.

Ellis, A. (1972a). *Conquering low frustration tolerance.* Cassette recording. New York: Institute for Rational-Emotive Therapy.

Ellis, A. (1972b). *Psychotherapy and the value of a human being.* New York: Institute for Rational-Emotive Therapy.

Ellis, A. (1973). *Humanistic psychotherapy: The rational-emotive approach.* New York: McGraw-Hill.

Ellis, A. (1976). The biological basis of human irrationality. *Journal of Individual Psychology, 32,* 146–68. Reprinted: New York: Institute for Rational-Emotive Therapy.

Ellis, A. (1978). *I'd like to stop but—dealing with addictions.* Cassette recording. New York: Institute for Rational-Emotive Therapy.

Ellis, A. (1979). *The intelligent woman's guide to dating and mating.* Secaucus, NJ: Lyle Stuart.

Ellis, A. (1985). *Overcoming resistance: Rational-emotive therapy with difficult clients.* New York: Springer.

Ellis, A. (1987). The impossibility of achieving consistently good mental health. *American Psychologist, 42,* 364–75.

Ellis, A. (1988a). *How to stubbornly refuse to make yourself miserable about anything—yes, anything!* Secaucus, NJ: Lyle Stuart.

Ellis, A. (1988b). *Unconditionally accepting yourself and others.* Cassette recording. New York: Institute for Rational-Emotive Therapy.

Ellis, A. (1989). Rational-emotive therapy. In R. J. Corsini & D. Wedding (eds.), *Current psychotherapies,* 4th ed. (pp. 197–202). Itasca, IL: Peacock.

Ellis, A., & Abrahms, E. (1978). *Brief psychotherapy in medical and health practice.* New York: Springer.

Ellis, A., & Becker, I. (1982). *A guide to personal happiness.* North Hollywood, CA: Wilshire Books.

Ellis, A., & Dryden, W. (1987). *The practice of rational-emotive therapy.* New York: Springer.

Ellis, A., & Dryden, W. (1989). *The essential Albert Ellis.* New York: Springer.

Ellis, A., & Grieger, R. (eds.). (1977). *Handbook of rational-emotive therapy.* Vol. 1. New York: Springer. Ellis, A., & Grieger, R. (eds.), (1986). *Handbook of rational-emotive therapy.* Vol. 2. New York: Springer.

Ellis, A., & Harper, R.A. (1975). *A new guide to rational living.* North Hollywood, CA: Wilshire Books.

Ellis, A., McInerny, J.F., DiGiuseppe, R., & Yeager, R.J. (1988). *Rational-emotive therapy with alcoholics and substance abusers.* New York: Pergamon.

Ellis, A., & Whiteley, J.M. (1979). *Theoretical and empirical foundations of rational-emotive therapy.* Monterey, CA: Brooks/Cole.

Ellis, A., & Yeager, R. (1989). *Why some therapies don't work: The dangers of transpersonal psychology.* Buffalo, NY: Prometheus.

Epstein, S. (1989). Cognitive experiential theory. In L. Pervin (ed.), *Handbook of personality theory and research* New York: Guilford.

Eysenck, H.J. (1967). *The biological basis of personality.* Springfield, IL: Thomas.

Franklin, J. (1987). *Molecules of the mind.* New York: Delta.

Freud, S. (1965). *Standard edition of the complete psychological works of Sigmund Freud.* 24 Vols. London: Hogarth.

Kelly, G. (1955). *The psychology of personal constructs.* 2 Vols. New York: Norton.

Korzybski, A. (1933). *Science and sanity.* San Francisco: International Society of General Semantics.

Lazarus, A.A. (1984). *In the mind's eye.* New York: Guilford.

Lazarus, R.S., & Folkman, S. (1984). *Stress, appraisal, and coping.* New York: Springer.

Maltz, M. (1960). *Psycho-cybernetics.* Englewood Cliffs, NJ: Prentice-Hall.

Maultsby, M.C., Jr. (1971). Rational-emotive imagery. *Rational Living, 6*(1), 24–27.

Maultsby, M.C., Jr., & Ellis, A. (1974). *Technique for using rational-emotive imagery.* New York: Institute for Rational-Emotive Therapy.

Meichenbaum, D. (1977). *Cognitive-behavior modification.* New York: Plenum.

Peale, N.V. (1952). *The power of positive thinking.* New York: Fawcett.

Rosenthal, D. (1971). *Genetics of psychopathology.* New York: McGraw-Hill.

Simonton, O., & Mathews-Simonton, S. (1978). *Getting well again.* Los Angeles: Tarcher.

Skinner, B.F. (1971). *Beyond freedom and dignity.* New York: Knopf.

Walen, S.R., DiGiuseppe, R., & Wessler, R. L. (1980). *A practitioner's guide to rational-emotive therapy.* New York: Oxford.

Wessler, R.A., & Wessler, R.L.(1980). *The principles and practice of rational-emotive therapy.* San Francisco: Jossey-Bass.

17

SUGGESTION IN EDUCATION

Annette Shuck

Suggestion, while not referred to by that name, is advocated by the authors of a myriad of self-help books and articles, as well as by most professional therapists regardless of theoretical orientation. The suggestive power of religion and religious leaders has been demonstrated throughout history. Positive suggestion in the area of athletics has been used by coaches of all sports. Suggestion is an indispensable aspect of most forms of media advertising. Parents guard impressionable children from the suggestive dangers of certain types of television programs, and some modern music. Suggestion is an integral part of medicine in Soviet-Bloc countries, with its use tried sporadically in the West.

This chapter looks specifically at the process of suggestion in relation to education. In this regard, I will attempt to answer several important questions. For instance, what part has suggestion played in educational methodology, and what part can it play in the future? What has been the historical emphasis of suggestion and education? Is suggestion a manipulative technique or a humanistic approach to learning, or both? Is it ethical to use suggestion on unsuspecting students, or is this what teachers have already done? Also, do educators know the difference between negative and positive suggestions to students? For example, some teachers say to certain pupils when handing out an assignment, "This is going to be an easy task"—patting them on the back with a smile. On the other hand, a teacher might say to another student, "You'll probably fool around the entire class period and won't finish today's assignment—just like your performance on all the other days!"

Suggestions can have a potentially significant impact on student performance. They can also make a great deal of difference in the way that students come to perceive themselves and others. Before we proceed, however, we must specify what is meant by the term "suggestion," with special reference to its use in the area of education.

Definitions

In his classic work, *The Psychology of Suggestion,* Boris Sidis (1973/1898) states that "the fact of suggestibility existing in the normal individual is that of the highest importance in the theoretical field of knowledge, in psychology, in sociology, ethics, history, as well as in practical life, in education, politics and economics . . ." (p. 17). So we might consider suggestion as it is associated with other persuasive mind techniques utilized in education. In addition to "suggestibility," I will also refer to the approaches known as suggestopedia, hypermnesia, and suggestology.

It is difficult to isolate characteristics of the constructs of "suggestion" and "suggestibility," since they are so universally used and in so many different ways. Sidis, at the turn of the century, gave the following definitions: "By suggestion is meant the intrusion into the mind of an idea; met with more or less opposition by the person; accepted uncritically at last; and realized reflectively, almost automatically. By suggestibility is meant that peculiar state of mind which is favorable to suggestion" (Sidis, 1973/1898, p. 15). While referring specifically to an educational definition of the suggestibility process, Bancroft (1976) speaks of a suggestion in terms of its ability to "activate the reserve capacities of the mind and memory."

The "scientific" study of suggestion has been applied to the educational arena by the Lozanov method of suggestology and suggestopedia (Bulgaria), and also the Tomatis method of suggestopedia (France). The two methods utilize additional definitions in the educational environment. Suggestopedia refers to the application of suggestion for pedagogical purposes. Psychological experiments in this area are often aimed at increasing memorization capacities. Suggestology is primarily aimed at the investigation of subsensory signals or subliminal stimuli which come from the physical or social environment, and which are absorbed into the unconscious mind before receiving a conscious expression. Hypermnesia is facilitated by relaxation techniques (derived from Savasana yoga and autogenic therapy) which increase the subject's suggestibility to spoken suggestions or unconscious stimuli (Bancroft, 1976).

Historical overview of suggestion in education

Suggestion has been largely neglected, at least officially, in historical Western pedagogy. This may reflect the longstanding presence of rigid and inflexible educational trends. However, suggestion has always been a part of education, as it has with all forms of human interaction. Suggestion sometimes goes unnoticed in educational settings, and we often fail to recognize its importance in the classroom.

As Lindeman (1979) notes, the eighteenth century brought with it an increased interest in suggestibility, especially in the field of medicine. In the later 1800s Freud looked at suggestibility and hypnosis and rejected the concepts. However, at this time Sidis and Emile Coué recognized suggestibility as an important technique for influencing people. In France, an owner of a drug store, promoted positive suggestions in children while they slept. He claimed, "A suggestion a day—just like milk or Cocoa for breakfast" (Lindeman, 1979).

In 1920, Charles Baudouin (a close follower of Coué) wrote *Suggestion and Autosuggestion,* which proposed that suggestion was a vital part of rearing children. Autosuggestion was seen to be a crucial part of early childhood training, since it appears that children are readily suggestible in the waking state. He added that suggestion is not a violation of the child's individuality, arguing that it is a means of training or enhancing the child's autosuggestive skills. Baudouin's theory also considered spontaneous suggestion, as well as the relationship between emotion and suggestibility.

In an early study of suggestibility in children, Aveling and Hargreaves (1921) administered seven separate tests of suggestibility while looking specifically at the effects of prestige of the suggester on the acceptance of suggestions. Their overall results indicated considerable variance in children's responses to suggestion. Estabrooks (1929) used a complex battery of tests to measure suggestion, suggestibility, psychogalvanic reflex, and intelligence in boys at an elementary school in Oxford. He found that there was little intercorrelation among the tests which were employed to measure suggestibility. However, Estabrooks did report that emotional factors played a role in the suggestibility process, a view that was consistent with Baudouin's theory.

Otis (1924) used a suggestibility pre-test on 1,045 children and gave a revised form of the pre-test to 377 children as a post-test. He concluded that: a) children have the ability to resist suggestion; b) response to suggestion varies with chronological age; c) mental age is most important in resisting suggestion; and d) girls have a slight advantage over boys in resisting suggestion. Experiments in the 1930s continued to measure suggestibility, but the emphasis on research shifted to the practical realm, with consideration given to the actual use of suggestion in the classroom. The concept of hypermnesia in the learning of academic subjects began to be investigated. Hurlock (1930) found that some popular beliefs about suggestibility could not be substantiated by quantitative research. She found, for example, that children were not as suggestible as commonly believed, and also that the differences between race and sexes were negligible. Hurlock found that differences in suggestibility were partially a function of the personality of the individual child.

Huse (1930) had subjects memorize paired-associate symbols, with only some receiving the suggestion that they would have no difficulty with the task. Those not receiving suggestions showed a significant disadvantage in recall. However, Mitchell (1932) found that hypnotic suggestion was not helpful in the memorization of nonsense syllables. Gray (1934) tried to determine whether hypnosis aided students in learning to spell. He found that hypnotic suggestion only resulted in an improvement of about two percent.

The research of White, Fox, and Harris (1940), and their survey of previous research, indicates that hypnosis is sometimes an aid to memory, while at other times it has no appreciable effect. These researchers asked the question, "Could the *type* of material to memorize be the key variable?" In order to determine the answer, they used three different types of material: (1) paired-associate nonsense words, (2) poetry, and (3) nonvérbal movie scenes. The results indicated that hypnotic suggestion did not aid the recall of nonsense material, but did give a 53% advantage for learning meaningful material like poetry. Hypnotic suggestion yielded an 83% advantage in recall of the movie scenes. The authors felt that the paired-associate words were strictly cue-response material which did not favor creative reconstruction, whereas the poetry or movie scenes did. These authors proposed other ways to produce hypermnesia other than hypnosis, including relaxation twilight sleep and free association. Relaxation is the one characteristic that they all appear to have in common. It may be that a sustained state of alert attention would be the best mental state for learning; "the mind sometimes works better when left a little to itself" (White, Fox and Harris, 1940).

Intelligence has been investigated as a factor influencing the suggestion process. Reymert and Kohn (1940) found no relation between degree of suggestibility and I.Q. But they did find that suggestibility decreases with a person's mental age and general state of development. They also reported that older persons are less susceptible to suggestive factors in their environment. In contrast, Simmons (1940) found that persons with a high I.Q. yield to fewer suggestions than those with a low I.Q.

Leuba (1941) hypothesized a distinction between suggestion and the hypnotic state. He said that the fundamental characteristic of the hypnotic state was not suggestibility, but rather the fixation of attention onto one specific set of stimuli. His view of suggestibility and hypnotic state may explain some of the discrepancies in late educational research, in which the hypnotic effects of the experiments are suspected to be the result of the experimenter's exhortations. Teachers began to report the use of suggestions in their classrooms during the 1940s. For example, Franklin Taylor (1941) taught his students the power of suggestion by demonstrating a unique card trick. There was actually no card trick other than what Franklin told his students and what they believed. The explanation of the "trick" was used to teach the value of suggestion in the learning process.

Weitzenhoffer (1953) summarized research dealing with hypnotic suggestion as it influences memory. While some researchers found that hypnosis was an aid to recall, others found the opposite. The type of material memorized, and whether it is meaningful or not, again seemed to be an important factor. Like White, Fox, and Harris (1940), Weitzenhoffer also points out that other similar techniques can improve recall and learning. Among these are relaxation, abstraction, and free association. He too indicates that relaxation is the common denominator in many mental functions, especially those involving creative thinking and reconstruction. Weitzenhoffer summarizes his research as follows: 1) suggestibility is highest at the ages 7 to 8; 2) women and girls are more suggestible than men and boys; 3) suggestibility is greater for individuals of higher than lower intelligence (as measured by the Stanford-Binet Intelligence Test). Weitzenhoffer made no definitive conclusions regarding personality traits, but he did state that attitudes and motivation appear to have influence on suggestibility.

Zuckerman and Gross (1956) conducted a correlational study of dependency and suggestibility. It was found that people with strong dependency needs were more likely to respond to suggestion than people with a strong need for autonomy. If this hypothesis is accepted, then the successful use of suggestion as an educational tool would certainly depend on certain needs and personality traits of the student. During the 1960s, more practical applications of suggestion were designed for use in the classroom. Also, the issue of hypnotic versus nonhypnotic suggestibility was made with regard to memory and learning. London and Fuhrer (1961) performed a hand dynamometer weight-holding and tremor test on hypnotized and nonhypnotized subjects. After the first test, subjects were directed to perform at maximum capacity, and then retested. The results indicated that "hypnosis," as such, adds nothing magical to performance. The authors concluded that motivational instructions are clearly more important than the hypnotic "trance."

During this period, advocates of hypnotic suggestion for learning purposes drew attention to different types of trance states, both active and passive. They discussed the difference here as a reflection on various states of suggestibility or hypersuggestibility. They found that students who were given suggestions in the waking state of hypnosis did significantly better than subjects who were hypnotized with traditional procedures. London and Cooper (1968) also concluded that hypnosis *per se* does not help learning or recall. Rather, it was simply the suggestions themselves concerning memory and motivation to learn that were seen to result in the better performance observed in some experiments. The positive use of suggestions on learning included studies to improve reading performance of slow learning students (McCord, 1963).

In the 1970s, suggestion and hypnosis continued to be utilized as a pedagogical tool. Stanley Krippner (1970) summarized this trend. He indicated that, because suggestion is a frequent concomitant of the teaching process, it is likely that many educators have unwittingly used some form of it in many of their most successful pedagogical efforts. Sometimes, teachers employ suggestive procedures when they attempt to relax their pupils before starting a difficult assignment. In addition to possible improvements in the area of memory and learning, potential benefits from the use of suggestion in the classroom include the reinforcement of good learning habits, improving concentration, increased motivation, and greater self-discipline and self-control.

A study using perceptual suggestibility was conducted by Trippi (1973). In this study, Trippi projected eight 35mm. slides of two odd-shaped, but identically sized, figures upon a screen. Degree of suggestibility was determined by the number of times a subject indicated that one of the figures was larger than the other as suggested by the examiner. In this study, Trippi found that educationally handicapped students (enrolled in a special class) were less suggestible than those who were enrolled in the regular class.

Recent research of the 1980s has tried to apply more statistically sophisticated methodologies in examining the effects of suggestibility on learning in educational settings. Many of these studies have stemmed from research in the area of suggestopedia (see Lozanov, 1979). This particular teaching technique is receiving an increasing amount of attention in the United States. Also known as "superlearning" and "accelerated learning," suggestopedia employs suggestion in an attempt to train students to learn large amounts of material in much less time than conventional teaching practices. The results of studies using the American adaptation of suggestopedia (called Suggestive-Accelerative Learning and Teaching, or SALT) have been quite remarkable. For instance, Thomas (1983) maintains that the SALT method is now allowing a great many students throughout the United States to learn with more speed and pleasure, and with less conscious effort.

Shuck and Ludlow (1984) carried out a study of suggestibility in which mildly mentally retarded students were compared to nonretarded students, aged 10 to 16 years. Subjects were grouped according to low or high suggestibility and were exposed to positive, negative, or neutral suggestions concerning their performance on a paired-associate learning task. A split-plot design assessed interactions between variables of subjects' category and suggestibility, as well as treatment conditions, such as suggestion provided and trials. Results showed that retarded students improved more than their nonretarded counterparts in terms of the number of trials taken to learn the paired-associate learning task. This study also found that subjects performed somewhat better on their learning tasks when they were given positive suggestions about their performance. It was concluded that the suggestibility of many retarded students (who may come to learning situations with the expectancy to fail) could be used by trainers to facilitate faster learning of simple tasks, especially if positive performance suggestions are employed.

Review of the literature presents somewhat conflicting research in the areas of suggestion and suggestibility. This could be due in part to the interpretation of the concepts of hypnosis and suggestion. Barber (1962) indicates that suggestion and hypnosis may be one and the same—only differing in degree. Research also indicates that no test has been able to demonstrate the existence of the hypnotic state (Barber & Calverley, 1966). Barber and Calverley (1966) point out that there is no evidence of any physiological difference between a normal waking state using suggestion and a supposed hypnotic state. He indicates that individuals can overcome fatigue and pain, do well or poorly on a learning task, not through hypnosis, but through mere suggestion procedures. Barber's evidence leads to the conclusion that hypnosis may be no more than a technical name for human suggestibility. Suggestibility, in turn, may be almost the same as motivation or a change in expectancy. The same preconditions are required in all cases: (a) a willingness to do what the suggester asks; (b) a belief in one's ability to do it; and (c) the ability to do it.

Social Learning Theory (Rotter, 1966) is also useful in the examination of students who demonstrate learning deficits. Specifically, the generalized concept of "expectancy" lends itself nicely to the question of suggestibility—that is, how much past failure experience is generalized to the present situation (Rotter, 1954; Shuck 1976). Research on this subject found that mentally handicapped subjects have a lower general expectancy for success, and a higher tendency toward avoidant behavior than the normal student (Heber, 1957; Shuck, 1976). If, in fact, the retarded student has more failure experience than the normal child, it would follow that the retarded student has a low general expectancy for success. Ellis (1962) has indicated that the failure for the retarded student has a cyclic effect which increases the probability of failure in any particular situation. Prehm and Mayfield (1970) found that retarded students required a significantly greater number of trials to complete each stage of the learning process than did normal subjects. However, it appears that most of the difference between groups for each trial series was evident at the first series or the response learning stage. Shuck (1976) found that the difference in learning performance between first trial and second trial was greater for high suggestible retarded subjects than high suggestible normal subjects. This shows that high suggestible retarded subjects, although needing a large number of initial trials, learned at a fast rate. They also took fewer trials than the low suggestible retarded subjects on the second trial. In other words, it appears that suggestibility and the use of suggestions may play an even greater role in learning with students classified as being slow learners, or those having learning disabilities or emotional problems.

Overall, the high suggestible group (normal and retarded) learned more during the paired-associate task than did the low suggestible group in all treatment conditions (positive, negative, and neutral). High suggestibility might therefore be used as an indicator for predicting learning performance. When considering the practical application of these data, one might propose that suggestibility level could be used as a control variable in the decision making on classroom placement. One could match teacher style and student learning style relative to the effect suggestions have on a student's learning.

Research has also looked at factors, other than mental age or intellectual level, that affect degree of suggestibility. For example, personality or emotional state has been viewed as leading contributors to the person's level of suggestibility (Otis, 1924; Reymert & Kohn, 1940; Simmons, 1940). Most likely, both of these characteristics greatly influence a student's suggestibility and should be considered in teaching and conducting future research.

White, Fox, and Harris (1940) pose the question, "Why is hypnosis sometimes an aid to memory while other times it has no appreciable effect?" It seems to make an important difference if the material to be learned is non-meaningful (e.g., paired-associate tasks) or meaningful (e.g., learning material that evolves out of personal experiences). Knowledge which is personalized and integrated into a student's repertoire of experiences is easier to learn. Also, it only makes sense that a state of relaxation would aid students in the application of basic knowledge and problem solving.

Finally, as is still evident today, suggestion and suggestibility are human behaviors that researchers find difficult to target and measure quantitatively. However, they are critical in considering the best learning approaches and environments for students. Consequently, research in the area of suggestion and education should be highly prioritized to perhaps find the missing link in the many failures of our educational system.

The following section focuses on a holistic approach to learning, while emphasizing a positive environment and positive suggestions in order to enhance learning. Suggestology and suggestopedia present a style of teaching that compliments today's fast-moving "subliminal" suggestive environment in the fields of advertising, business, sales, and sometimes everyday communication.

Suggestology and suggestopedia

One can define suggestology as the scientific study of suggestion and suggestopedia. One primary goal of this area is the application of suggestion to educational pedagogy. An important underlying assumption of suggestopedia is that people use only a small portion of their potentially available brain capacity. Additionally, it is assumed that a variety of environmental, social, and psychological variables may prevent people from making effective use of their capacity for learning. Lozanov believed that traditional classrooms typically have tense and inflexible environments as well as depersonalized lessons. Furthermore, he felt that these classrooms are usually characterized by low expectations, which lead to a fear of learning, lack of self-confidence, and a general stifling of the student's potential for learning (Thomas, 1983).

The effective use of suggestion is the key component of the suggestopedia technique. Lozanov and his followers believe that, through conscious and unconscious suggestion, students can come to view learning as a positive, pleasurable, and relaxing experience. It is also thought that, when students enjoy learning, they are much more likely to realize their full intellectual capabilities. In order to do this, however, the "anti-suggestive" barriers to learning (defined by Lozanov as the factors that inhibit learning: boredom, lack of self-confidence, and other negative variables) must be countered (Bancroft, 1976). Suggestopedia employs suggestion in an effort to break down these barriers to learning. Below are some of the ways that this is done.

(1) One primary goal of suggestopedia is a dynamic and enthusiastic classroom. The traditional arrangement of desks in rows is aban-

doned. Instead, students are seated in comfortable armchairs (usually in a semi-circle) which are located in a simulated living room setting. The social and physical environment of this type of classroom is an essential pedagogical factor, and this is referred to as "double planeness" (Bancroft, 1976). The families of students enrolled in suggestopedia programs are also encouraged to become involved.

(2) Music, (usually of the Baroque period) is often played in the classroom in order to create a relaxed atmosphere. Lyrics of specially written songs may even contain elements of a particular lesson. Thomas (1983) gives the example of an algebraic concept that may be incorporated into the plotline of an opera which is being listened to by mathematics students.

(3) The classroom environment includes simulated "real life" events. This enhances the learning process by reducing the artificial classroom environment that characterizes traditional learning scenarios. It also affords the opportunity for spontaneous emotional reactions to familiar everyday situations. The movements and gestures of the teacher are accompanied by concrete language and communicational activities. Belanger (1985) describes how students are sometimes allowed to mime typical meetings in the street, to improvise car or airplane travel, to discuss the dangers of smoking, and so forth.

(4) Learning is based on a holistic, or Gestalt, model of the human personality, one which emphasizes relationships rather than isolated elements. Suggestopedia involves an interplay of emotion and intellect aimed at tapping the student's full potential. A suggestopedia classroom often displays posters or other materials which are intended to reinforce lessons on a nonverbal, unconscious level (Bancroft, 1976; Thomas, 1983). An example might be students in a Spanish class who speak dialogues while surrounded by travel posters of Spain, and songs of that country are played in the background.

(5) Lozanov's suggestopedia uses positive verbal and/or nonverbal suggestion in trying to draw on the student's functional, intellectual, and emotional "reserve potentials." Ideally, the teacher should have a positive attitude which conveys his/her confidence in the students. According to this theory, the teacher then becomes an authority figure with "prestige and respect," which is seen as necessary if suggestopedia is to work (Belanger, 1985).

(6) Students who are shy and unsure of themselves are given additional encouragement. Selected individuals may even be given new identities which are practiced with role-playing. In that same Spanish class mentioned above, for example, insecure students might gain confidence by pretending that they are Spanish citizens talking about their imaginary lives (Thomas, 1983).

(7) Belanger (1985) and Bancroft (1976) outline a "cognitive syn-

thetic" teaching method which combines the best elements of already existing material. In the initial (active) phase of this approach, the student models (imitates) the intonation, gestures, and linguistic behavior of the teacher. At this stage, a literal knowledge level is acquired by the learner. Later, these repetitive exercises are replaced by the second phase which entails a deeply relaxed condition of "concert-pseudo-passiveness" (Bancroft, 1982). As the individual becomes more relaxed, he/she becomes more open to suggestions of various kinds—especially if the general atmosphere is relaxed and pleasant. Students might receive the suggestion that they will feel less fatigue and stress, that they will have renewed energy, or that they will feel greater motivation and ability to work. Relaxation is accomplished by an appropriate choice of background music. It is during this state of relaxation that "supermemory" is achieved (Thomas, 1983). Also, higher levels of learning, synthesis, interpretation, and problem solving are encouraged. At this point in the learning process, suggestions are positive and stimulating. Negative suggestions are avoided at all times with this method.

(8) Bancroft (1976) points out that voice intonation is critical to the suggestopedia method. The words themselves have a strong suggestive effect, especially when they are communicated with a soft but commanding tone. No objections are usually forthcoming from these "self-confident" tones. A low rhythmical voice carrying a subtle suggestion can have an especially strong influence. It is believed, in Lozanov's approach, that an authoritative tone of voice can add to the suggestive effect of speech, thus enhancing motivation on the part of the student. Maximum effectiveness is achieved when the material to be learned, or memorized, is presented, not only rhythmically, but with measured pauses between words and phrases. Bancroft (1976) gives the example of a monotonous, rhythmic presentation which can engage the "nonspecific," or unconscious, mental process. It is thought that this can again help to overcome antisuggestive barriers.

(9) Lozanov (1979) also developed the pedagogical concept of "infantilism." Student infantilism is thought to increase in proportion to teacher authority. It is the job of the suggestopedic teacher to suggest to students that they have confidence in their ability, that they will have no problems with memorization and other forms of learning, and that they will experience a child-like curiosity for new information (Bancroft, 1982). Infantilization is considered easier to achieve in group settings since the group lends itself to feelings of spontaneity. However, according to Lozanov's theory, infantilism does not decrease adult intellectual abilities. Instead, certain beneficial characteristics of the "infant" are drawn upon in the service of learning.

The future of suggestion in education

In examining the historical trends and looking at the future of the role of suggestion in education, I will reflect on the questions posed at the beginning of the chapter. First, it appears that, historically, suggestion has been employed only sporadically in educational pedagogy. This could be due in part to the confusion of the terms suggestion and hypnosis. However, as was presented earlier, it appears that hypnosis is merely a form of suggestibility. In addition, some students may not be initially motivated by positive suggestions because of past failure experiences from home, peers, school, and so on. Curiously, these students sometimes respond better to negative suggestions which require that they learn other ways of reacting and thinking in a positive environment. Suggestibility and learning are situationally related. Both will vary in terms of the educational environment. It is known, for instance, that some individuals can be more easily influenced by particular personalities. Combinations of environments and personalities could also be investigated to determine their influence on suggestibility, and therefore learning. For example, suggestibility might be enhanced by a relaxed environment with music playing in the background. Such a setting would lend itself to the use of subtle suggestion.

Teachers need to look at the suggestibility concept in relation to its influence on children in social, as well as learning situations. Teachers provide various forms of suggestions in a normal classroom situation. Suggestions can be used by teachers as verbal expressions to indicate how the student is expected to perform a certain task. Such suggestions can also be present in the facial expressions of the teacher when he/she is presenting directions or informally communicating with a student. Body language can be another subtle form of suggestion. Suggestions communicated to the student, either positive or negative, can be an influencing factor on behavior and academic performance. Whether or not suggestions can be a manipulative or humanistic technique in education depends on how they were used in the students' past reinforcement repertoire (Shuck, 1976).

Teachers, administrators, and school staff must receive training on the positive use of suggestion. This could serve to relax students, increase learning potential, and expand minds. This approach, being holistic, will help students to improve self-concepts and to have a more positive attitude toward learning and education. Teachers therefore need to be evaluated on their use of positive suggestion in the classroom to assure a "humanistic," rather than a manipulative or negative approach to learning. Students and parents should be apprised of the program utilizing a positive suggestive approach to learning so that no one will be an unsuspecting "victim." In addition, the students' understanding of the method would facilitate the application of the same techniques of positive suggestion and problem solving to everyday life situations.

Western European and North American critiques of suggestology are often negative, with reference made to a lack of scientific data. Even so, there have been some impressive results, and the utilization of suggestopedia's underlying principles constitute a most original contribution to education. Despite the criticisms of specific suggestopedic educational approaches, there does appear to be a historical trend, and a recent renewal of interest in suggestive educational techniques. A growing number of educators feel that, with the proper controls (e.g., evaluating teachers' verbal, nonverbal, and written suggestions to students), these could represent valuable educational tools.

Suggestopedia is notable for its attempt to fuse the relaxed "suggestion state" (based on Eastern philosophies such as Yoga) with the basic principle that all education, to one extent or another, utilizes suggestion. Many educators now maintain that suggestion can be used in a humanistic way to create successful learning experiences for students of all abilities.

Education needs to re-evaluate its effectiveness on student learning, especially in light of the low national group achievement scores in this country. It appears that the use of suggestion techniques in the classroom can benefit students on both an academic and personal level. These methods should therefore be given serious consideration by any open-minded educational community.

References

Aveling, F., & Hargreaves, H.C. (1921). Suggestibility in children. *British Journal of Psychology, 12,* 53–75.

Bancroft, W.J. (1976). Suggestology and suggestopedia: The theory of the Lozanov method. ERIC Document. ED132857.

Bancroft, W.J. (1982, April-May). The Tomatis method and suggestopedia: A comparative study. Revised version of a paper presented at the VIIth International Conference of the Society for Accelerative Learning and Teaching, Colorado.

Barber, T.X. (1962). Hypnotic age regression: A critical review. *Psychosomatic Medicine, 24,* 286–99.

Barber, T.X., & Calverley, D.S. (1966). *Fact, fiction, and the topic hypnosis: Multidimensional analysis of hypnotic behavior.* Harding, MA: Medfield Foundation.

Baudouin, C. (1920). *Suggestion and autosuggestion.* London: George and Allen Unwin, Ltd.

Belanger, B. (1985). Suggestopedia and teacher training. Presented at a Symposium for International Association for Accelerative Learning, Rio de Janeiro.

Ellis, N.R. (1962). Amount of reward and operant behavior in mental defectives. *American Journal of Mental Deficiency, 66*, 613–17.

Estabrooks, G.H. (1929). Experimental studies in suggestion. *The Pedagogical Seminary and Journal of Genetic Psychology, 36*, 120–39.

Gray, W.H. (1934). The effect of hypnosis on learning to spell. *The Journal of Educational Psychology, 25*, 473.

Heber, R.F. (1957). *Expectancy and expectancy changes in normal and mentally retarded boys.* Ann Arbor, Mich: University Microfilms.

Hurlock, E.B. (1930). The suggestibility of children. *The Pedagogical Seminary and Journal of Genetic Psychology, 38*, 59–73.

Huse, B. (1930). Does the hypnotic trance favor the recall of faint memories? *Journal of Experimental Psychology, 13*, 519–29.

Krippner, S. (1970). The use of hypnosis and the improvement of academic achievement. *The Journal of Special Education, 4*, 451–59.

Leuba, C. (1941). The use of hypnosis for controlling variables in psychological experiments. *Journal of Abnormal and Social Psychology, 36*, 271–74.

Lindeman, M.L. (1979). Suggestion in education: The historical path of suggestopedia. Presented at the IVth Conference of Texas Teachers of English to Speakers of Other Languages, Clear Lake City, Texas.

London, P., & Cooper, L.M. (1968, October). Reactivation of memory of hypnosis and suggestions. ERIC Microform ED037796.

London, P., & Fuhrer, M. (1961). Hypnosis, motivation, and performance. *Journal of Personality, 29*, 321–33.

Lozanov, G. (1979). Accelerated learning and individual potential. *Prospects: Quarterly Review of Education, 9*, 414–25.

McCord, H. (1963). Improving reading ability through combined tutoring and hypnotherapy. *Journal of Developmental Reading, 7*, 142–43.

Mitchell, M.B. (1932). Retroactive inhibition and hypnosis. *Journal of Genetic Psychology, 7*, 343–59.

Otis, M. (1924). A study of suggestibiity of children. *Archives in Psychology*, 70.

Prehm, H.J., & Mayfield, S. (1970). Paired-associate learning and retention in retarded and non-retarded children. *American Journal of Mental Deficiency, 74*, 622–26.

Reymert, M.L., & Kohn, H.A. (1940). An objective investigation of suggestibility. *Character and Personality, 9*, 44–48.

Rotter, J.B. (1954). *Social Learning and Clinical Psychology.* New York: Prentice-Hall.

Rotter, J.B. (1966). Generalized expectancies for internal versus external control of reinforcement. *Psychological Monographs: General and Applied, 80*(1), 1–28.

Shuck, A. (1976). *Effect of positive, negative and neutral suggestions on paired-associate learning in low and high suggestible mentally retarded and normal children.* Unpublished doctoral dissertation, West Virginia University, Morgantown.

Shuck, A., & Ludlow, B. (1984). Effects of suggestibility on learning by retarded and nonretarded students. *Psychological Reports, 54*, 663–66.

Sidis, B. (1973). *The psychology of suggestion.* New York: Arno Press. (Originally published in 1898.)

Simmons, R.M. (1940). A study of a group of children of exceptionally high intelligence quotient in situations partaking of the nature of suggestion. *Teacher College Record, 42,* 78–80.

Taylor, F.V. (1941). A novel classroom demonstration of suggestion. *Journal of Abnormal and Social Psychology, 39,* 279–82.

Thomas, E. (1983). Suggestopedia: A new way to learn. ERIC document ED235063. SMERC Information Center, San Mateo County Office of Education, Redwood City, CA.

Trippi, J.A. (1973). Special-class placement and suggestibility of mentally retarded children. *American Journal of Mental Deficiency, 78,* 220–22.

Weitzenhoffer, A.M. (1953). *Hypnotism: An objective study in suggestibility.* New York: John Wiley and Sons.

White, R.W., Fox, G.F., & Harris, W.W. (1940). Hypnotic hypermnesia for recently learned material. *Journal of Abnormal and Social Psychology, 35,* 88–103.

Zuckerman, M., & Gross, J. (1956). Suggestibility and dependency. *Journal of Consulting Psychology, 22,* 328.

18

ADVERTISING AND HYPNOTIC SUGGESTION: The Construct of Advertising Suggestion

Stephen J. Gould

The processing of advertising by consumers involves varying degrees of attention and concentration. Advertisers seek to focus attention on their ads in order to persuade consumers to buy products. In this respect, the advertising process is like hypnosis in that a hypnotist seeks to concentrate and focus an individual's attention in order to induce him or her to follow a persuasive suggestion. Packard (1957) noted the suggestive power of advertising, and Fromm (1976, p. 110) compared advertising to an "opiate" or outright hypnosis. In a similar vein, Pollay (1986) stated one consumerist argument critical of advertising: "The repetitive, fantastic, one-sided, and often exhortative rhetorical styles of advertising combine, it is felt, to blur the distinction between reality and fantasy, producing hypnoid states of uncritical consciousness wherein the subject is reduced to passivity and a relative sense of powerlessness" (p. 26).

Many have argued from a related perspective that advertisers should not use persuasion or emotion in advertising at all, but instead, should only provide information to consumers concerning price, availability, and other product attribute information. Further, advertising is thought to have a macro-programming effect on consumers in making them more materialistic and in defining their very outlook. These effects occur because advertising is pervasive, it repetitively reinforces the same values, it is professional and sophisticated in the process of persuasion, and it reaches an audience detached from its traditional cultural roots (Pollay, 1986).

But is the view that advertising is hypnoid-like true? And even if it is true, is this altogether a negative thing? Some, like Matson (1967), find the effects of the mass media to be overblown and note that the individual is fully capable of resistance to persuasion. Others in the advertising and marketing field (a pervasive number) make the argument that advertising transforms needs into wants for specific products and/or brands but does not create these needs (Alderson Associates, Inc., 1964). According to this view, the individual manifests and perceives his or her own needs; the advertiser merely addresses those already existing needs. To consider these issues further, the following topics will be discussed: (1) the basis for comparing advertising and hypnosis effects, (2) the construct of advertising suggestion, (3) a model of the advertising suggestion process, and (4) conclusions.

The basis for the comparison of advertising and hypnotic effects

Shor (1960, p. 151) described hypnosis as a cognition which consists of two processes: (1) a "special, temporary orientation to a small range of preoccupations" involving goal-directed striving and role-taking, and (2) "the fading of the usual everyday cognitive orientation to generalized reality into relatively nonfunctional unawareness." He supposed that hypnotic-like states involving these two processes would occur for individuals highly susceptible to hypnosis. Hilgard (1965) found that hypnotic-like states may involve the elements of conformity, trance-like experiences, role-playing, concentration, absorption, and impulsivity as opposed to rationality. Advertising may also be said to be hypnotic-like in that it results in absorbing states or heightened suggestibility which involve these elements (Hilgard, 1965; Hirschman, 1985; Shor, 1960). In general, advertising, marketing, and consumer behavior involve conformity (Venkatesan, 1966), hypnoid states (Pollay, 1986), role-playing and attentive focus (MacInnis & Jaworski, 1989), and impulsive buying behavior (Stern, 1964).

In the development of hypnosis theory, an important issue concerns the view of hypnosis as a distinctive state versus the view of hypnosis as a social psychological phenomenon (Tellegen, 1979). One hypothesis is that some people respond to hypnosis as active participants while others respond to hypnosis more passively and have things happen to them (Coe, 1978; Edmonston, 1981). I will provisionally adopt such a view here in comparing advertising response and hypnotic states. In other words, it is most likely that hypnotic states are not exactly reproduced in the advertising response state, which is one of many waking states, but instead that there is perhaps some sort of hierarchy of states into which both fit (Sarbin & Coe, 1972). In fact, Sarbin and Coe found that the customer in a supermarket would be at very low levels of involvement relative to hypnosis, as well as to other phenomena. In addition, various types of responses within each setting, considered separately, may comprise their own distinct hierarchies of states. Thus, such an intermediate approach fits with various existing, hierarchical consumer behavior/advertising constructs and paradigms, including: hyperarousal/hypoarousal, high/low involvement, extensive/limited/routine problem solving, brain laterality effects, central/peripheral processing, and active/passive processing (Hirschman, 1985; Howard, 1989; Krugman, 1965, Olson & Ray 1989; Petty, Cacioppo, & Schumann, 1983).

Another way of relating advertising to the hypnosis process is to consider hypnosis experiments which have aimed at persuasion as a goal. Advertising effects might be seen as comparable, in one sense, to waking state conditions in such experiments. However, it can be argued that while the processing of advertising by an individual is indeed done in a waking state, it also involves hypnotic-like absorption. One study which can serve as a bridge between the two settings is that of Malott, Bourg, and Crawford (1989). These researchers used cognitive responses (thought given in response to the presentation of a message) and various attitude measures, as is commonly done in advertising and consumer research (e.g., MacKenzie & Lutz, 1989). Malott, et al. found differences between the waking and hypnotic state, and particularly that hypnotized subjects generated fewer counterarguments to the message. They also found significant differences between high and low hypnotizable subjects, both in the hypnosis and waking state conditions. High hypnotizable subjects tended to generate more favorable thoughts and agree more with the message than low hypnotizable subjects. Malott, et al. concluded that these differences in response to persuasive communications could be seen in terms of "context (i.e., induction) and trait (i.e., hypnotizability level). . ." (p. 37).

Based on their perspective, it can be hypothesized that the persuasibility of advertising messages, which often can be easily counterargued, should be subject to individual differences based on hypnotizability, i.e., high hypnotizability should be positively related to advertising response. It is also likely that there is an intermediate variable, which can be considered, that is an analogue to hypnotizability, but which is more specific to the advertising domain, i.e., susceptibility to advertising absorption. This susceptibility reflects one's general likelihood of becoming absorbed in advertising. Furthermore, it is likely that hypnotizability is positively related to it and that it in turn is associated with favorable advertising response. However, because of the diverse nature of advertising (i.e., copy, media, products, and consumer lifestyle factors), it is likely that there exist specific susceptibilities as well (e.g., susceptibility to advertising with sexy models or to television commercials).

Further, the effects demonstrated in the Malott, et al. (1989) study might be extended with consideration of the Elaboration Likelihood Model (ELM) (Petty, Cacioppo, & Schumann, 1983). The ELM predicts that central modes of persuasion (i.e., those which emphasize issues and a message) will be more effective when individuals are likely to elaborate a message. On the other hand, the peripheral route to persuasion (i.e., cues other than the central message of the advertising copy, such as the attractiveness of product endorsers, music, beautiful visuals, etc.) will be more effective when the likelihood of elaboration is low. When consumers are highly involved with a product, Petty, Cacioppo, and Schumann (1983) find that central cues will serve as a more important route to persuasion, while for low involvement, peripheral cues will be more effective.

Since Malott, et al. only considered weak arguments, we can theorize what their findings might mean when strong arguments, which increase the likelihood of elaboration, are included. When presented with strong arguments, highly hypnotizable subjects should still counterargue less than those who are not hypnotizable. However, this difference should be less important when translated into brand attitudes, since the strong argument probably makes counterargumentation and elaboration salient for all, whether they are very hypnotizable or not. In other words, strong arguments are more likely to serve as a cue for cognitive activity than are weak arguments. Involvement with the product will serve as a moderator of the relationships. Highly involved individuals will be more prone to counterargument as they elaborate more on various arguments, whether weak or strong. Therefore high involvement in a particular situation, such as being in the market for a product, may displace hypnotizability and advertising susceptibility as factors in determining the degree of counterargument. On the other hand, under conditions of low involvement, highly hypnotizable individuals will still tend to counterargue less than those who are less hypnotizable, although both will be more responsive to peripheral cues. However, hypnotizable individuals should be even more responsive to peripheral cues and thus less likely to engage in counterargumentation.

Advertising suggestion

Since advertising is not in fact inducing a state of hypnosis as the term is commonly employed, though the state is perhaps hypnosis-like and absorbing, the possibility of its providing a form of waking state suggestion is probably the most important issue to consider when comparing the two phenomena. Weitzenhoffer (1989, p. 28) defines a suggestion in the following terms:

> What is called a *suggestion* will be a communication or sequence of communications to the subject primarily intended to bring about some

> observable, overt action or actions. . . . These communications are called suggestions *on the assumption* that the resulting effects will *not* be voluntary acts. More correctly, we refer to these as *intended* suggestions in contrast to *effective* suggestions because it is not known at the time they are given whether such communications will actually function as suggestions.

Weitzenhoffer (1989) also indicates that there are waking state suggestions, or what he prefers to call nonhypnotic suggestions, in which there is no formal hypnotic process. Following his reasoning, I will define a new construct: advertising suggestion. Advertising suggestion is a communication delivered to a waking state individual in order to produce a belief or attitude change, a sale, or other behavioral response, such as the use of a seat belt. As with other suggestions, it is an intended suggestion at the time it is delivered, although there may be previous experience and/or marketing research concerning the efficacy of a particular ad, campaign theme, or copy execution, which indicates the likelihood of it becoming, or continuing to be, an effective suggestion.

A key aspect of parallelism between hypnotic and advertising suggestion is the degree of involuntariness that is present in each domain. While there has been a great deal of conceptual confusion concerning the term "suggestion," it would seem that persuasive phenomena must be involuntary for them to be categorized as suggestions (Weitzenhoffer, 1980). However, according to Weitzenhoffer, some individuals will see their responses to suggestions as having been made voluntarily, while others will see them as having been made involuntarily. A further complication involves the idea that conscious voluntary elaboration will be built up around hypnotically induced automatic responses. While it is likely that much response to advertising is involuntary, I would expect that if we asked people whether they responded involuntarily, they would likely deny it. Instead, it is more likely that they would probably be more willing to ascribe this phenomenon to others, and that they would be held back by social desirability and also perhaps an inability to recognize or acknowledge it within themselves. On the other hand, with hypnosis there is some expectation and probably a greater acceptance of one's own involuntary response.

In consonance with Weitzenhoffer (1980), there are a number of involuntary responses that advertising induces around which conscious voluntary elaboration may occur. For example, consider a person who has come to buy a product because s/he responded to an ad that was favorably placed on one side of a magazine as opposed to another (Janiszewski, 1988), a form of advertising suggestion in that it involuntarily induces response. Such an individual will, if asked, likely say that s/he likes or prefers the product rather than being able to surmise that there is more to it than that, i.e., the influence or effect of the ad's placement. Thus, a further element in the involuntary element of response is the unconscious processing of information in such areas as automatic behavior (Cialdini, 1984), classical conditioning and mere exposure effects (Allen & Madden, 1985), and subliminal stimulation (Moore, 1988). While such research is indicative of relatively unconscious processing, theoretical understanding lags behind (Pratkanis & Greenwald, 1988). As an involuntary persuasive phenomenon, unconscious processing underlies advertising suggestion, as will be discussed concerning (1) automatic behavior and (2) subliminal stimulation.

Automatic behavior

With regard to nonconscious procedural knowledge, researchers have looked at such phenomena as automatic behavior, scripts, and schemata (Cialdini, 1984; Smith & Houston, 1985). Cialdini (1984) details many of the automatic rules of behavior that people follow and that can be manipulated by others who come to understand these rules. These rules can also be seen as the scripted ways in which the individual responds with very little thinking. Cialdini notes that there are fixed-action, mechanistic, ritualistic patterns which can be triggered by a "trigger feature." Indeed Gheorghiu (1989) defines suggestion as "the potential trigger of responses." Thus, trigger features may be viewed as a form of suggestion—the individual processes them and acts upon their directions. For example, Cialdini reported a study in which men rated a car better on a number of characteristics if there was a seductive young woman (the trigger feature) in an ad, than in the condition where there was no such female model. Moreover, the men exposed to the female model did not believe that the presence of the woman had influenced their choice when later asked about their responses. It is these trigger features, as well as scripted thoughtless responses which ads stimulate, that provide an avenue for advertising suggestibility. These triggers are peripheral cues (e.g., music, attractive models) used by advertisers to enhance the delivery of their message. Thus, advertising suggestion involves the triggering of automatic feelings and responses which are transferred to the product.

It should be noted that while the trigger has been identified with peripheral cues, even the central message of an ad may elicit automatic responses. This is the case, even though the process involves active, cognitive processing. It can be argued, for instance, that even rational or cognitive processing of information really has emotional content. Additionally, getting a "rational, informational" argument accepted by the consumer can lead to simultaneous or subsequent persuasive effects through the processing of peripheral characteristics. For example, music in an ad (where the consumer accepts its main premise) may, through mood enhancement, help push the consumer toward a positive buying decision. The importance of this point is to hypothesize that advertising suggestion may be very widespread and that even cognitive processing of central messages invokes involuntary processes.

Subliminal stimulation

The process of subliminal stimulation should be relevant to advertising suggestion because it is said to involve the unconscious processing of stimuli (Moore, 1988), much as the hypnotist's suggestion is processed and then repressed or forgotten. It represents one of the most persistent and largely unsupported ideas of advertising, i.e., the alleged existence and effectiveness of subliminal stimulation, which is said to involve covert visual or auditory cues that generate unconscious processing (Moore, 1988). It is a phenomenon which the public in particular has embraced and which induces fear of being manipulated (Moore, 1988), in much the same way that many people fear hypnotic manipulation. One man who has brought subliminal advertising to the attention of the public is Key (1980), who finds that embedded sexual organs in ads can seduce consumers into buying products. But his work has not been very persuasive for the mainstream of advertising researchers (Moore, 1988). However, even if subliminal phenomena are not very operative, peripheral cues, which involve varying degrees of (un)conscious processing and attending, do appear to be operative. Indeed, advertisers have so many other suggestibility tools to work with that the use of subliminal stimulation may really be a moot point for their bottom line.

A model of advertising suggestibility

The advertising process may be considered as analogous to the process of hypnotic suggestibility, a term that refers to the mechanisms responsible for the "formation of suggestive directedness and its transformation into suggestible responses" (Gheorghiu, 1989, p. 104). In terms of the actors and states involved, both processes may also be seen as representing variations of the traditional communications model (Runyon, 1984). In this model, a source encodes a message to be delivered through some medium to a receiver who decodes and often acts upon the message delivered, a form of feedback to the source. In the case of hypnosis, the hypnotist communicates a message through the medium of the hypnotic trance-inducement process. In turn, the hypnotized person receives and decodes this message. Response to suggestion, either during the trance or post-hypnotically, constitutes feedback as to whether the hypnotist has effectively communicated with the subject. Likewise, the advertising process is traditionally viewed as a communications process in which a source (the advertiser) communicates a message through some medium (e.g., television, magazines) to the consumer. The consumer then provides feedback to the advertiser in the form of attitude change and product purchase. In considering the advertising-communications process in relation to the hypnotic process, we can identify three key elements that are involved in advertising suggestibility (shown in Figure 18.1): (1) the advertising stimulus (source and medium) as the intended suggestion, (2) the consumer state, produced during and immediately after seeing and/or hearing the ad (receiving and decoding the ad), equivalent to the hypnotic trance state, and (3) consumer response to the ad's suggestion after s/he has passed from its immediacy, equivalent to post-hypnotic response (e.g., purchase as a result of effective advertising suggestion).

Advertising stimulus

The advertising stimulus is analogous to the hypnotist in that both constitute the source and medium of communication. There are two major types of source effects considered in the advertising/consumer behavior context: (1) source credibility and (2) source attractiveness. Source effects may be seen to operate as triggers of past associations (Kamen, Azhari, & Kragh, 1975) and positive effects are thought to be effective persuaders (McGuire, 1985). Actually, the source and medium are often considered separately. But for our purpose of analogizing the advertising stimulus to the hypnotist as a total stimulus, the source and medium may be considered as jointly constituting the stimulus or inducing effect. From another perspective, the hypnotist may be viewed as the source. The hypnotist's voice, as well as the instruments of hypnosis, may be considered the medium (Chertok, 1986). The main point is to reflect upon the total effect a stimulus has in persuading the consumer or hypnotized subject. This total effect

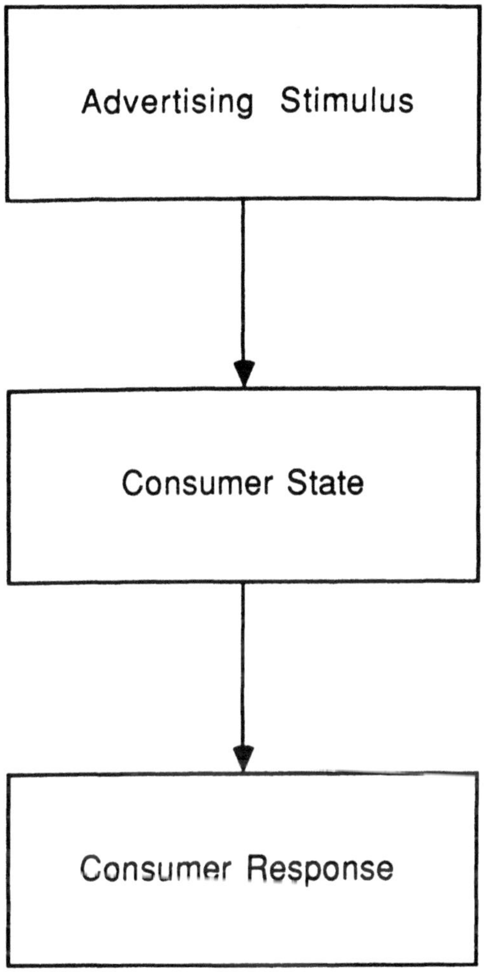

Figure 18.1. The process of advertising suggestion.

reflects the synergy of a number of source and media effects. For example, the stimulus of television commercials reflects a whole host of executional factors, such as new or improved product information, tone, comparisons with other brands, length of time the product is on the screen, and many others (Stewart & Koslow, 1989). Stewart and Koslow report that advertising effectiveness is enhanced when the main focus of the commercial is on the product and its benefits. However, they also find that no one factor explains much of the total variance and that, from a creative point of view, all elements must be considered. With regard to advertising suggestibility, the need to look at many factors implies not only complexity, but also that each ad is its own creative gestalt.

The overall situation involved in the delivery of commercials or other forms of advertising to consumers is analogous to the context of the hypnosis induction. Various studies have shown that by merely defining a situation as involving hypnosis (or changing expectancies regarding the situation) hypnotizability and the response to suggestions can be influenced (Spanos, Gabora, Jarrett, & Gwynn, 1989). For example, Spanos, et al. note that defining a situation as hypnosis may cause some individuals to have suppressed, as opposed to facilitated, responses to suggestions. In this vein, it could be argued that advertising always carries with it a popular definition of being "propaganda which is trying to sell me something," i.e., by its very nature, it carries with it an automatic rule which says "be on guard." This natural context is similar to defining a situation as hypnosis. However, in contrast to the hypnotist's ability to define a hypnotic situation as being one of imagination rather than hypnosis (Spanos, et al., 1989), advertising generally cannot escape its overt commercial context. As one strategy to get around this problem, some print ads, for instance, have been designed to imitate editorial matter. It is hoped that people will not easily differentiate the two, and that they will let down their guard when choosing to attend to such an ad. Moreover, in spite of its negative perceptions, advertising can still be persuasive because people are probably open to it more than they either care to admit or are able to recognize.

Consumer state

In hypnosis, the subject's state reflects such things as the voice of the hypnotist, muscular relaxation, and the attenuation of external stimuli, to create a total psychic-somatic effect (Chertok, 1986). Likewise, the consumer state with respect to an advertisement will reflect a similar total effect. This is created in part by the advertising copy's central and peripheral cues, but also reflects the individual's needs and characteristics. In this section, we will focus more closely on: (1) consumer needs, (2) personality traits, (3) mood, and (4) psychophysiological correlates.

Consumer needs or motives

Consumers have been seen as having two basic needs or motives: utilitarian and expressive (MacInnis & Jaworski, 1989). Utilitarian needs concern the use of products to solve problems. Expressive needs concern the use of products either for socially expressive reasons, such as the expression of one's self-image, or for experiential reasons, such as sensory stimulation. These perspectives influence what types of cues an individual will attend to. Utilitarian needs will focus attention on product attribute information, while expressive needs will focus attention on symbolic or experiential aspects of a product. Thus for advertising suggestibility to occur, there should be congruence between the need that the ad is expressing and the consumer's need. In addition, the more motivation (involvement) to process brand information that there is on the part of the consumer, the more s/he will focus on the ad as opposed to some other activity (MacInnis & Jaworski, 1989). Just as a hypnotist commands attention, an ad may command attention. At the same time, both the hypnotist and ad face distracting noise which interferes with communication. The hypnotist especially faces the problem of distractions with less hypnotizable subjects who either will not, or cannot, focus enough on the induction cues of the hypnotist. The ad also faces a myriad of distractions from everyday life, such as one's ability to turn to another channel.

Personality traits

In assessing suggestibility, McGuire (1989) discussed net influence as the compensatory combination of two mediators in relation to personality traits: (1) the agreement mediator (motivation and gullibility), and (2) the comprehension mediator (a cognitive facilitator of understanding). The former mediator tends in general to reduce net influence, i.e., the more one possesses a positive personality trait, such as self-esteem or intelligence, the less agreeable one will be to a message. The latter mediator tends in general to increase net influence in relation to a positive trait, i.e., the more intelligent one is, the more one will be able to comprehend and favor a message. Both mediators, taken together, tend to counteract one another as comprehension overtakes and crosses agreement. The overall effect results in a non-monotonic inverse-U curve that characterizes net influenceability and indicates that people who are intermediate on various traits will be the most suggestible. McGuire also notes that situational influences can alter these relationships. One situation, which he calls the suggestion situation, involves messages which are easily comprehended. This situation corresponds to many, if not most, advertising situations, especially television commercials which seem to be addressed to an audience's lowest common denominator (high mass appeal). Using intelligence as the trait in his example, McGuire suggests that comprehension will vary directly with intelligence, and agreement inversely as in his more general case. Also, since the message is so simple, agreement will always be lower than comprehension. In this case, net influence will also steadily decline as intelligence rises.

Further, McGuire (1989) depicts another situation which involves the use of a tax accountant in a tax advice situation. Here, the message is complex, resulting in exactly the opposite relationship between influenceability and intelligence—they are positively related. Such a situation may correspond to targeted advertising (e.g., certain print and direct mail ads) where the message may be complex and designed for specific audiences who possess higher intelligence, or else, a particular and well-developed interest in the advertised product (e.g., computer ads addressed to computer hackers). However, in spite of not being targeted, people of lower intelligence or less developed interests nonetheless may have enough curiosity to look at a computer ad. This is because advertisers must sometimes use more general media to reach a more specialized audience (e.g., a high-tech ad in a general interest newspaper). Such individuals may express somewhat higher degrees of agreement, but dramatically lower degrees of comprehension relative to more interested or intelligent individuals, thus reducing their degree of net influence. Finally, there are other advertising situations that fall in between those with high degrees of mass appeal or specialized appeal. These also probably correspond to McGuire's general U-shaped situation discussed above.

A number of psychological traits, other than intelligence or self-esteem, are likely to influence an individual's susceptibility to advertising. As previously hypothesized, it is likely that hypnotizability is positively related to an individual's likelihood of being persuaded by an ad. In addition, some traits which should be associated with one's persuasibility include self-monitoring and control orientation (Zuckerman, Gioioso, & Tellini, 1988), and public self-consciousness (Gould 1987).

Mood

An important situational variable, and one which is likely to influence advertising suggestibility, is that of mood. Mood states often may bias evaluations in conjunction with stimuli congruent with the individual's mood (Gardner, 1985). In particular, positive mood may be a factor in the positive response to persuasive messages. In general, the pleasantries surrounding a persuasive message make it more persuasive (e.g., Dribben & Brabender, 1979). Goldberg and Gorn (1987) found that happy television programs induced more positive response to commercials than did sad ones. This research indicates that advertising suggestibility and attitude toward the ad would be enhanced by positive moods, and that ads which enhance mood are likely to increase suggestibility.

Psychophysiological response and hemispheric laterality

Researchers in both the advertising and hypnosis domains have investigated psychophysiological response and also hemispheric laterality (e.g., Carter, Elkins, & Kraft, 1982; Olson & Ray, 1989). However, to my knowledge, no one has compared the psychophysiological effects of watching a commercial to the effects of being hypnotized. Such a comparison between these states, done on a longitudinal basis with measurements at various intervals of the exposures to hypnosis and advertising, might help to mark and identify these phenomena. An intriguing recent study of brain wave response to television commercials found that alpha waves and higher frequency beta waves are positively correlated (Olson & Ray, 1989). Such a finding is contrary to the previous belief that they have a reciprocal relationship. This also signifies that overall brain activation may be more important than the activity of any particular type of wave. Also, it may be that attending or focusing on something may evoke both lower frequency, relaxed waves as well as more active, higher frequency waves, supporting the idea that the suggestion process involves a combination of attentional activity and relaxation (Edmonston, 1981).

Consumer response to the ad

Positive response to an ad in behavioral terms (i.e., purchasing a product) may be seen in two broad contexts when related to the time in which the individual actually sees the influencing ad: (1) the individual sees an ad (consumer state), and then later purchases the advertised brand (consumer response), and (2) the individual encounters an ad and, while under its immediate influence, acts upon its message (a virtually simultaneous consumer state and response). The former case is analogous to a post-hypnotic response to a suggestion. The latter case occurs in such situations as in-store, point-of-purchase advertising, or direct marketing advertising (e.g., a television commercial proclaiming that there are open telephone lines at that very moment to call for product purchase) in which the consumer can immediately act in response to the ad. This is analogous to the individual acting while still under hypnotic trance. It is also similar to the effects described under the consumer state above, except that now the consumer may make an immediate behavioral response. Presumably in both instances of responses, as well as for both advertising and hypnotic settings, the effect has been to induce the individual to engage in behavior which s/he might not have otherwise.

However, the process of response to advertising should also be viewed as one which occurs over time as a continuous, multivariate process. The reason is that an individual is often exposed to multiple showings of the same ad, competing ads, product experience, other people's opinions, and the like. All of these factors can affect response to any single advertisement or advertising campaign. Thus, advertising tends to occur in naturalistic, uncontrolled environments while hypnotic suggestion tends to be more controlled, and response to it more proximate in time. To the degree that a hypnotic suggestion is given for a distal period (post-hypnotic), the response will be more like that of the advertising setting, i.e., a consumer may purchase a product in response to an ad s/he saw at an earlier point in time (sometimes weeks, months, or years prior to the purchase).

Traditional advertising effects or response models, particularly for high involvement products, have considered consumers' viewing of advertising as a learning process in which they first form beliefs, then attitudes (brand preferences), then intentions to purchase, and finally make purchases (e.g., Runyon, 1984). Each one of these elements represents a communications goal of the advertiser (and also feedback to him or her) and may be subject to advertising suggestibility. Following the hierarchy up the ladder, it then is not too difficult to suggest that "if you believe this is true, then you must form a preference for this product and try it." The very fact that the consumer is involved and cognitively active does not take away from the ability of an advertising suggestion to work. Gheorghiu (1989) likens the dynamics of the suggestion process in a sales situation to the effects of asking leading questions (similar to the hierarchy of effects) that provide the answers and eliminate the need to look for rival answers—a situation that would be highly involving and otherwise likely to produce counterarguments, as in advertising for a high involvement product. Under conditions of low involvement, there is a variety of hierarchy-of-effects models which differ from the traditional model. An example would be a situation in which awareness leads to purchase behavior without any intervening attitude at all, or when attitudes are formed after purchase rather than before it (DeBruicker, 1979). Low-involvement advertising usually involves repeated exposure to the same ad and/or to different ads for the same brand. Thus, the process of advertising suggestion actually occurs over and over again, since its staying power is usually not that strong. It does, however, follow a general pattern. Burke and Edell (1986) find that, over time, an ad's effectiveness, after initial increases, will level off and then decline.

Conclusion

The hypnotic and advertising processes are related in that both involve communications which seek to persuade individuals to take behavioral action, often behavior in which they might not otherwise engage. They also both involve absorbing states which attempt to focus the individual and make him or her open to suggestion. However, while hypnosis consciously tries to make suggestions to the individual, no one in advertising speaks of making suggestions. The thought of advertising as being suggestive is likely to be controversial, and only a few critics have even suggested that it is "hypnotic." But whatever friends or foes of advertising might think, it does possess suggestive qualities which must be accounted for and investigated. Future research should include an assessment of advertising suggestibility in relation to the stimulus, state, and response variables discussed above. This would involve creating a measure of advertising suggestibility and then investigating it in terms of advertising stimulus, psychophysiological, personality, and advertising response correlates. In addition, researchers should assess advertising suggestibility in relation to hypnotic parallels of susceptibility and suggestion, absorption, psychophysiology, and personality traits. Thus, future research should see the emergence of the study of hypnotic-like states and related forms of suggestibility as either a major subfield within the hypnosis community, or else as a full-fledged psychological subfield in its own right.

References

Alderson Associates, Inc. (1964). Needs, wants, and creative marketing. In J.H. Westing & G. Albaum (eds.), *Modern Marketing Thought* (pp. 18–20). New York: Macmillan.

Allen, C.T., & Madden, T.J. (1985). A closer look at classical conditioning. *Journal of Consumer Research, 12,* 301–15.

Burke, M.C., & Edell, J.A. (1986). Ad reactions over time: Capturing changes in the real world. *Journal of Consumer Research, 13,* 114–18.

Carter, B.D., Elkins, G.R., & Kraft, S.P. (1982). Hemispheric asymmetry as a model for hypnotic phenomena: A review and analysis. *The American Journal of Clinical Hypnosis, 24,* 204–10.

Chertok, L. (1986). Relation and influence. *American Journal of Clinical Hypnosis, 29,* 13–22.

Cialdini, R.B. (1984). *Influence.* New York: William Morrow.

Coe, W.C. (1978). The credibility of posthypnotic amnesia: A contextualist's view. *International Journal of Clinical and Experimental Hypnosis, 26,* 218–45.

DeBruicker, F.S. (1979). An appraisal of low-involvement consumer information processing. In J.C. Maloney & B. Silverman (eds.), *Attitude research plays for high stakes* (pp. 112–30). Chicago: American Marketing Association.

Dribben, E., & Brabender, V. (1979). The effect of mood inducement upon audience receptiveness. *The Journal of Social Psychology, 107,* 135–36.

Edmonston, Jr., W.E. (1981). *Hypnosis and relaxation: Modern verification of an old equation.* New York: John Wiley.

Fromm, E. (1975). *To have or to be?* New York: Harper.

Gardner, M.P. (1985). Mood states and consumer behavior: A critical review. *Journal of Consumer Research, 12,* 281–300.

Gheorghiu, V.A. (1989). The difficulty in explaining suggestion: Some conceivable solutions. In V. A. Gheroghiu, P. Netter, H.J. Eysenck, & R. Rosenthal (eds.), *Suggestion and suggestibility: Theory and research,* (pp. 99–112). Berlin: Springer-Verlag.

Goldberg, M.E., & Gorn, G.J. (1987). Happy and sad TV programs: How they affect reactions to commercials. *Journal of Consumer Research, 14,* 387–403.

Gould, S. (1987). Gender differences in advertising response and self-consciousness variables. *Sex Roles, 16,* 215–25.

Hilgard, E.R. (1965). *Hypnotic susceptibility.* New York: Harcourt, Brace and World.

Hirschman, E.C. (1985). Dual consciousness and altered states: Implications for consumer research. *Journal of Business Research, 13,* 223–34.

Howard, J.A. (1989). *Consumer behavior in marketing stategy.* Englewood Cliffs, NJ: Prentice-Hall.

Janiszewski, C. (1988). Preconscious processing effects: The independence of attitude formation and conscious thought. *Journal of Consumer Research, 15,* 199–209.

Kamen, J.M., Azhari, A.C., & Kragh, J.R. (1975). What a spokesman does for a sponsor. *Journal of Advertising Research, 15,* 17–24.

Key, W.B. (1980). *The clamplate orgy.* Englewood Cliffs, NJ: Prentice-Hall.

Krugman, H.E. (1965). The impact of television advertising: Learning without involvement. *Public Opinion Quarterly, 29,* 349–56.

MacInnis, D.J., & Jaworski, B.J. (1989). Information processing from advertisements: Toward an integrative framework. *Journal of Marketing, 53,* 1–23.

MacKenzie, S.B., & Lutz, R.J. (1989). An empirical examination of the structural antecedents of attitude toward the ad in an advertising pretesting context. *Journal of Marketing, 53,* 48–65.

Malott, J.M., Bourg, A.L., & Crawford, H.J. (1989). The effects of hypnosis upon cognitive response to persuasive communication. *The International Journal of Clinical and Experimental Hypnosis, 37,* 31–40.

Matson, F.W. (1967). The folklore of mass persuasion. In F.W. Matson & A. Montagu (eds.), *The human dialogue: Perspectives on communication* (pp. 371–79). New York: The Free Press.

McGuire, W.J. (1985). Attitudes and attitude change. In G. Lindzey & E. Aronson (eds.), *Handbook of social psychology* (pp. 233–346). New York: Random House.

McGuire, W.J. (1989). A mediational theory of susceptibility to social influence. In V.A. Gheorghiu, P. Netter, H.J. Eysenck, & R. Rosenthal (eds.), *Suggestion and suggestibility: Theory and research* (pp. 305–21). Berlin: Springer-Verlag.

Moore, T.E. (1988). The case against subliminal manipulation. *Psychology and Marketing, 5,* 297–316.

Olson, J., & Ray, W. (1989). Exploring the usefulness of brain waves as measures of advertising response. Report No. 89-116, Cambridge, MA: Marketing Science Institute.

Packard, V. (1957). *The hidden persuaders.* New York: D. McKay.

Petty, R.E., & Cacioppo, J.T., & Schumann, D. (1983). Central and peripheral routes to advertising effectiveness: The moderating role of involvement. *Journal of Consumer Research, 10,* 18–37.

Pollay, R.W. (1986). The distorted mirror: Reflections on the unintended consequences of advertising. *Journal of Marketing, 50,* 18–36.

Pratkanis, A.R., & Greenwald, A.G. (1988). Recent perspectives on unconscious processing: Still no marketing applications. *Psychology and Marketing, 5,* 337–53.

Runyon, K.E. (1984). *Advertising: Second edition.* Columbus: Charles E. Merill.

Sarbin, T.R., & Coe, W.C. (1972). *Hypnosis: A social psychological analysis of influence communication.* New York: Holt, Rinehart and Winston.

Shor, R.E. (1960). The frequency of naturally occurring "hypnotic-like" experiences in the normal college population. *International Journal of Clinical and Experimental Hypnosis, 8,* 151–63.

Smith, R.A. & Houston, M.J. (1985). A psychometric assessment of measures of scripts in consumer memory. *Journal of Consumer Research, 12,* 214–24.

Spanos, N.P., Gabora, N.J., Jarrett, L.E., & Gwynn, M.I. (1989). Contextual determinants of hypnotizability and of relationships between hypnotizability scales. *Journal of Personality and Social Psychology, 57,* 271–78.

Stern, H. (1964). The significance of impulse buying today. In J.H. Westing & G. Albaum (eds.), *Modern Marketing Thought* (pp. 21–23). New York: Macmillan.

Stewart, D.W., & Koslow, S. (1989). Executional factors and advertising effectiveness: A replication. *Journal of Advertising, 18,* 21–32.

Tellegen, A. (1979). On measures and conceptions of hypnosis. *The American Journal of Clinical Hypnosis, 21,* 219–37.

Venkatesan, M. (1966). Experimental study of consumer behavior conformity and independence. *Journal of Marketing Research, 3,* 384–87.

Weitzenhoffer, A.M. (1980). Hypnotic suggestibility revisited. *The American Journal of Clinical Hypnosis, 22,* 130–46.

Weitzenhoffer, A.M. (1989). *The practice of hypnotism: Vols. 1 & 2.* New York: John Wiley & Sons.

Zuckerman, M., Gioioso, C., & Tellini, S. (1988). Control orientation, self-monitoring, and preference for image versus quality approach to advertising. *Journal of Research in Personality, 22,* 89–100.

INDEX

ABOUT THE CONTRIBUTORS

Michael J. Apter is currently Visiting Professor at Purdue University in Indiana. Previously he was Reader in Psychology at the University of Wales.

Etzel Cardeña currently holds a position in the Department of Psychiatry and Behavioral Sciences at the Stanford University School of Medicine.

Albert Ellis is President of the Institute for Rational-Emotive Therapy in New York City.

Hans J. Eysenck is currently Professor Emeritus of Psychology at the University of London's Institute of Psychiatry.

Vladimir A. Gheorghiu is Professor of Psychology at the University of Giessen.

Frederick X. Gibbons is Professor of Psychology and Director of the Graduate Program in Social Psychology at Iowa State University.

Stephen J. Gould is currently an Assistant Professor in the Department of Marketing, Rutgers State University of New Jersey.

Gary Groth-Marnat is a Lecturer in Psychology at Curtin University, Australia.

Gisli H. Gudjonsson is a Senior Lecturer and Head of Forensic Psychology Services, Institute of Psychiatry, University of London. He is also a Top Grade Clinical Psychologist to the Bethlem Royal and Maudsley Hospitals.

Ernest R. Hilgard is currently Professor Emeritus of Psychology at Stanford University.

Hunter Hoffman is a graduate student in Cognitive Psychology at the University of Washington.

Mordecai Kaffman is Medical Director and Chief Psychiatrist of the Kibbutz Child and Family Clinic in Derech Namir 147, Tel-Aviv, Israel.

Simon Kemp is a Senior Lecturer in the Department of Psychology, University of Canterbury, Christchurch, New Zealand.

Peter Kruse is Assistant Professor of Psychology at the University of Bremen.

Elizabeth Loftus is Professor of Psychology and Adjunct Professor of Law at the University of Washington.

Steven Jay Lynn is a Professor of Psychology at Ohio University. He is the

President of the American Psychological Association, Division of Psychological Hypnosis (1990) and is a Fellow of the American Psychological Association.

Sue Boney McCoy is a doctoral student in the Graduate Social Psychology Program at Iowa State University.

Judith W. Rhue is an Associate Professor in the Department of Family Medicine of the Ohio University College of Osteopathic Medicine.

John F. Schumaker is a Lecturer in Psychology at the University of Newcastle, Australia.

John D. Shea is a Senior Lecturer in the Department of Psychology at the University of Newcastle, Australia.

Annette Shuck is a Professor of Special Education and Counselling Psychology in the Division of Education at the University of the Virgin Islands.

David Spiegel currently heads the Psychiatry Clinic at Stanford University.

Kelly Toland is doing graduate work in Cognitive Psychology at the University of Washington.

Graham F. Wagstaff is a Senior Lecturer in Psychology at the University of Liverpool, England.

Colleen Ward is a Senior Lecturer in the Department of Psychology, University of Canterbury, Christchurch, New Zealand.

For Product Safety Concerns and Information please contact our EU representative GPSR@taylorandfrancis.com
Taylor & Francis Verlag GmbH, Kaufingerstraße 24, 80331 München, Germany

www.ingramcontent.com/pod-product-compliance
Ingram Content Group UK Ltd.
Pitfield, Milton Keynes, MK11 3LW, UK
UKHW022214190926
475702UK00003B/350
* 9 7 8 1 0 4 1 2 7 1 8 0 2 *